The Political Discourse of the Polish-Lithuanian Commonwealth

This book contributes to ongoing European research into the political discourse of the early modern era, analyzing the political discourse of the Polish-Lithuanian Commonwealth (1569–1795). The primary source material comprises the broadly understood political literature from the end of the sixteenth century until the end of the eighteenth century. The author selects and analyses concepts and ideas that are particularly important for the noble political discourse, with the aim of understanding what these concepts meant for the participants in public debate, who used them, how they explained and described the world, how they allowed for the formulation of political postulates and ideals, whether their meaning changed over time, and if so, then to what extent and under what influences. The research focuses not only on the understanding of the concepts that functioned in the period under study but also on their use as instruments in the political struggle. The book is addressed to readers from the academic milieu – students and researchers – but is likewise accessible to more general readers interested in the history of political language and concepts as well as the history of political thought.

Anna Grześkowiak-Krwawicz is Professor and Head of the Enlightenment Literature Department at the Institute for Literary Research, Polish Academy of Sciences, and President of the Polish Society for Eighteenth Century Studies.

Routledge Research in Early Modern History

Making the Union Work
Scotland, 1651–1763
Alexander Murdoch

Major-General Hezekiah Haynes and the Failure of Oliver Cromwell's Godly Revolution, 1594–1704
David Farr

John Stearne's Confirmation and Discovery of Witchcraft
Text, Context and Afterlife
Scott Eaton

From Classical to Modern Republicanism
Reflections on England, Scotland, America, and France
Mark Hulliung

The Renaissance of Plotinus
The Soul and Human Nature in Marsilio Ficino's
Commentary on the *Enneads*
Anna Corrias

Voices in the Legal Archives in the French Colonial World
"The King is Listening"
Edited by Nancy Christie, Michael Gauvreau, and Matthew Gerber

The Political Discourse of the Polish-Lithuanian Commonwealth
Concepts and Ideas
Anna Grześkowiak-Krwawicz

For more information about this series, please visit: https://www.routledge.com

The Political Discourse of the Polish-Lithuanian Commonwealth

Concepts and Ideas

Anna Grześkowiak-Krwawicz

TRANSLATED BY
DANIEL J. SAX

NEW YORK AND LONDON

First published in English 2021
by Routledge
52 Vanderbilt Avenue, New York, NY 10017

and by Routledge
2 Park Square, Milton Park, Abingdon, Oxon, OX14 4RN

Routledge is an imprint of the Taylor & Francis Group, an informa business

© 2021 Taylor & Francis

Published in Polish as *Dyskurs Polityczny Rzeczypospolitej Obojga Narodów. Pojęcia i idee*. Torun, Wydawnictwo Naukowe Uniwersytetu Mikolaja Kopernika, 2018.

This translation has been funded by the Foundation for Polish Science.

Library of Congress Cataloging-in-Publication Data
Names: Grześkowiak-Krwawicz, Anna, author.
Title: The political discourse of the Polish-Lithuanian Commonwealth : concepts and ideas / Anna Grześkowiak-Krwawicz ; translated by Daniel Sax.
Other titles: Dyskurs polityczny Rzeczypospolitej Obojga Narodów. English Description: New York, NY : Routledge, 2021. | Series: Routledge research in early modern history | Includes bibliographical references and index.
Identifiers: LCCN 2020020468 (print) | LCCN 2020020469 (ebook) | ISBN 9780367423247 (hardback) | ISBN 9780367823535 (ebook) | ISBN 9781000197006 (adobe pdf) | ISBN 9781000197044 (mobi) | ISBN 9781000197082 (epub)
Subjects: LCSH: Political culture—Poland—History. | Political culture—Lithuania—History. | Poland—Politics and government—1572–1763. | Poland—Politics and government—1763–1796. | Lithuania—Politics and government—17th century. | Lithuania—Politics and government—18th century.
Classification: LCC JN6766 .G7913 2021 (print) | LCC JN6766 (ebook) | DDC 320.943809/03—dc23
LC record available at https://lccn.loc.gov/2020020468
LC ebook record available at https://lccn.loc.gov/2020020469

ISBN: 978-0-367-42324-7 (hbk)
ISBN: 978-0-367-82353-5 (ebk)

Typeset in Sabon
by codeMantra

Contents

Introduction   1

Remarks from the Translator   13
DANIEL J. SAX

1   *Rzeczpospolita* – The Commonwealth   19

2   *Prawo* – The Law   39

3   *Wolność* – Freedom   70

4   From *Forma Mixta* to the Separation of Powers   93

5   *Zgoda* – Concord   117

6   *Cnota* – Virtue as Advice for the Commonwealth   139

7   *Amor Patriae* – Patriotism   169

8   The Perceived Superiority of the "Old Ways":
Dawny – Age-Old   195

9   In Conclusion, What Concepts
Were Absent? Property   221

Bibliography   239
Index   263

Introduction

Whoever undertakes to study matters of morality and politics should first establish the exact meanings of words.[1]

"The meaning of words, the meaning of expressions, maxims, propositions, means and aims, cannot be agreed upon singularly by everyone. Moreover, [the notions of] interest, virtue, reason, common good, truth, wealth, freedom, honor, glory are subject to either a thousand doubts or to excessively contradictory explanations and understandings in political materials."[2]

These are the thoughts with which a certain eighteenth-century author of political treatises (Leonard Wołczkiewicz Olizar, mostly forgotten today, perhaps rightfully so) chose to begin a political disquisition in 1790. Although he was not a preeminent thinker, there is no denying that here he very aptly put his finger on a very important issue that somewhat escapes the attention of historians – namely, the issue of the political language used by participants in political discussions of previous times, above all the precise meanings carried by the words they used.

Certainly, no historical period can be properly made sense of without first getting to understand its political language. However, this is not always an easy task, and it is certainly a difficult one in the case of the political language of the Polish-Lithuanian Commonwealth (1569–1795). The way we discuss politics today is far removed from the discourse of political debates in those times. Three or four centuries on, Polish words like *prawo* (law), *wolność* (freedom) or *Rzeczpospolita* (Commonwealth) remain outwardly unchanged, but their meanings have shifted from how they were understood in previous centuries, often considerably so. To borrow a phrase from C.S. Lewis, modern readers may get tripped up by the "dangerous meanings"[3] of such familiar but misleading words.

This book sets out to explore in detail some of the terms and concepts used in the political discourse in the Polish-Lithuanian Commonwealth, and to scrutinize the underlying ideas in depth. This is an important problem, if only because the political language of any historical period lays out certain frames of reference for people who engage in discussions on matters of state importance, whether as theorists or as active participants.[4] Even more significantly, there is a strong link between political language and political reality – so much so that one can hardly be understood without the other. Political language and political reality are profoundly intertwined, mutually influencing one another: the outside world shapes the discourse, but the words used to describe political institutions, solutions, values and ideals similarly color people's reactions and interpretations. Sometimes it is not until certain processes or phenomena are named that they end up being perceived, and conversely, the absence of certain concepts or ideas from the political lexicon may cause them to go unnoticed in reality as well. With regard to Polish political writings, this has been noted by Hans-Jürgen Bömelburg.[5] Getting to understand the political language of a period is therefore the starting point for understanding what participants in those discussions and debates were able to describe, realize or understand. Often it also helps to explain why political commenters felt a certain way about this or that specific political decision.

The political discourse of the Polish-Lithuanian Commonwealth has, to date, attracted little interest from historians. What scholarly efforts do exist in this regard were mainly made as part of broader studies on social consciousness in past periods[6] or on the political culture of the Polish nobility, the *szlachta*.[7] The political discourse as such, including its key political terms and concepts, has only been studied by a handful of researchers in small-scale, nonsystematic projects.[8] Even those modest studies, though isolated, demonstrate the vast potential of this subject. But even so, the political discourse of the Polish-Lithuanian Commonwealth seems to have essentially escaped the attention of historians, who have largely ceded the subject to linguists and philologists, presumably because they felt those disciplines to be better suited in terms of research methods.[9]

This gap in our scholarly knowledge seems particularly glaring in the broader context of European research, where analyses of political discourse and political concepts have attracted considerable interest from historians since the 1970s. Examples include research by French scholars on the political language of the French Revolution,[10] or the two mighty schools of historical research, German and Anglo-Saxon, which for several decades all but dominated research on discourse in Europe.[11] In both schools, the founders strove to develop methodologies for studying political language that were firmly guided by the needs of historical research, but also drew upon the language sciences, perhaps not so much linguistics as the philosophy of language.[12] Incidentally, the actual findings in those cases, as they relate to specific issues, tend to be more interesting than the methodologies themselves, which are often quite vague or even downright inconsistent.

One thing that should be pointed out straightaway about this book is that it is not modeled on any specific school of historical research. Every effort has been made to apply an independent methodology best suited to the subject matter and the goals at hand. The aim is to try to glean a better understanding of the political discourse in the Polish-Lithuanian Commonwealth, as viewed and described through the lens of its key terms and concepts. Unlike in the *Begriffsgeschichte* tradition, my intention is not to identify conceptual innovations reflecting fundamental shifts in society. Instead, I seek to identify which of those terms and concepts served as building blocks of political discourse in the Commonwealth, and how they worked. In other words, terminological and semantic change, though important to my analysis, are not treated as indicators of social and political change, but rather as reflections of changes in the way the state was discussed.

Moreover, we should note that the choice of the book's subtitle – "concepts and ideas" – is meant to reflect the fact that the book sets out to present not just words but also the underlying ideas. This is particularly relevant given that no comprehensive scholarly treatment is currently available on the political thought of the Polish-Lithuanian Commonwealth.[13] My goal is not to come up with abstract definitions of concepts, but to place them in the broader context, and to identify the network of their mutual interconnections.[14] It is a cliché to say that the meaning of a word depends on who says it and in what context – the word *commonwealth* or *republic* did not mean the same thing to Jean Bodin as to Stanisław Orzechowski (or, we might add, to Cicero); Thomas Hobbes had a different understanding of the word *citizen* than his contemporaries who were opposed to Charles I; the word *nation* meant different things to Jean-Jacques Rousseau and to Michał Wielhorski. On top of that, the meanings and connotations of words also depend in subtler ways on the broader context of the utterance. For instance, *freedom* might mean one thing when contrasted with *despotism*, but quite another when contrasted with *anarchy*. English-speaking researchers who put an emphasis on the diversity of political language note that seemingly identical concepts can take on different meanings in different linguistic settings; a word like *law* does not mean the same thing when it appears as part of the "language of jurisprudence" vs. in a republican narrative.[15] It is ultimately the broader context that throws light on how different concepts add up to form a specific political vision, and it helps to pinpoint the exact role and place of such terms and concepts within the general vision.

Accordingly, although each chapter herein is headed by a leading keyword, each of those terms is analyzed within the framework of a broader network of concepts. The chapters devoted to "the Commonwealth" (*Rzeczpospolita*) or to "virtue" (*cnota*) will also contain discussions of terms such as *citizen* and *citizenship*. The concept of "public good" (*dobro publiczne*), an important idea in the political discourse and in the system of values of the Polish nobility, is examined in the chapter devoted more broadly to the "homeland" (*ojczyzna*) and patriotism. Similarly, "anarchy" (*anarchia*) obviously belongs in the chapter on "freedom" (*wolność*).

One further explanation is in order. The term *political discourse* features prominently in the title of the book and in this introduction. The concept of discourse, including political discourse, has gained a certain popularity in the humanities and in social sciences. It has been used and abused so much in various contexts to a point where it provokes an understandable wariness, but the decision to use it in the title here was not guided by intellectual fashion. Rather, I believe this is the best label to describe the book's scope of interest. It is superior to the traditional formulations (history of political thought, history of ideas) because the focus of analysis is not just on political ideas or visions of the state, but also on the words used to describe them; not only on how the concepts were understood historically, but on how those were used in political conflicts or for purposes of persuasion in topical debates. This book is not a piece of research on political culture (even though political language is obviously part of it and offers illuminating insights into the subject). My basic goal is to understand and describe the political discourse of the First Commonwealth, understood broadly to mean the way (or ways) in which matters relating to the political community were discussed in the public forum.[16]

The book is mostly structured around specific concepts or, in some cases (like *virtue* or *mixed government*), around clusters of concepts grouped around a single idea and its associated political vocabulary. The general objective is seeking to understand what a given term or concept might have meant to people who used it in political debates: how did it color people's perceptions or interpretations of the world? What kinds of political goals and ideals did it help to formulate? Did its meaning change over time? And if so, to what extent, and under what influence? The book also tries to reveal how such terms or concepts (along with the related political constructs) would have fit within the broader system of political values – and, conversely, how they in turn influenced that system. How one chooses to define terms like *freedom*, *commonwealth* or *citizen* has a strong influence on one's view of the world, and on one's opinions on various political actions and solutions.

Another important problem examined at length here touches on what we might call the rhetorical function of those concepts, though the word *rhetorical* is perhaps too narrow to reflect the full range of their uses as arguments in political debate, political weapons, means of persuasion, or even tools of verbal and emotional manipulation.[17] We might say that my subject is not just the meaning of the terms and concepts, but also their historical usage. The question is not only what people took them to mean, but also what they wanted to achieve by using them. In this respect my approach is obviously more closely aligned with the English-speaking tradition, where those questions were always treated as important.[18] However, our ways part at the conceptual crossroads marked "political languages."[19] The idea of "political languages" is certainly interesting, but the distinctions in the English literature appear too arbitrary, and the assumption that markedly different "languages" might have co-existed side by side appears to present some thorny methodological problems (those shared by any *a priori* assumption). The book aims to paint a general picture and involves a fair amount of exploration in under-researched areas. As such, the goal is to look for commonalities in the political discourse of the period, even at the cost of some oversimplification.

This brings us to a rather fundamental question: what was this thing that we have been rather vaguely calling "the political discourse of the Polish-Lithuanian Commonwealth"? What source materials can we use to study it? The unending political debates in that country generated an enormous amount of source materials of varying quality, on a range of topics and in a number of genres. They include formal speeches delivered in parliamentary sessions, local assemblies (*sejmiks*) or courts (recorded for posterity and for personal glory, such speeches were occasionally distributed for propaganda purposes), but also printed theoretical treatises and lengthy disquisitions on matters of state, political works in prose and verse, and topical ephemera produced to influence current events. Over the two centuries of its existence, the Polish-Lithuanian Commonwealth produced not hundreds but thousands of political texts. Any attempt to paint an overall picture must therefore be necessarily selective. In this book, the main source material for analyzing political discourse and its concepts is what we might broadly refer to as political literature, ranging from entire treatises of varying levels of theoretical sophistication, all the way down to small topical pamphlets. Both original source texts (printed and manuscripts) and their published twentieth- and twenty-first-century editions were utilized.[20] The material is rich and also relatively homogeneous. It allows us to study not only the way individual concepts were used in specific discussions and debates but also how those same concepts were defined and explained at more length, including in extended theoretical constructs. Such theoretical constructs are particularly important because by looking at those explanations (which again varied in terms of theoretical sophistication) we can form some idea of what we might call the conceptual framework within which the participants in the debate operated, and to note indications of change, which can usually be first identified in more detailed theoretical disquisitions. On the other hand, topical texts (somewhat akin to what we might call opinion journalism) provide examples of how those terms and concepts were used in political debates and conflicts.

I hasten to add that unlike some researchers[21] I assume that both the theorists and the political players were using the same political language. Despite their differences in intellectual prowess, political intent and, in some cases, their respective visions of the state, both groups used the same set of concepts and political values and understood those concepts and values in similar ways. Within the general context of reflection on matters of state in Poland-Lithuania, the line separating theory and partisan debate was very fluid. Given the political situation in the Commonwealth, not many theoretical treatises were pure abstractions divorced from the political context. Participants in the debates had freedom of expression and a sense of agency, meaning that even general musings on society were swiftly applied with regard to the country and its improvement. In many cases the reverse was also true – authors of partisan and evidently topical writings set within the context of actual events often pivoted to general commentary on the country's political system and fundamental political values. In particular, this applies to texts written at the turn of the sixteenth and seventeenth centuries (a period of debate on the Commonwealth's emerging political system), or in the late eighteenth century (when debate on state reform was reignited after a period of political stagnation).

To round off the picture, the book also contains a very small selection of parliamentary speeches (*mowy sejmowe*), sermons and political verse. This self-imposed constraint on the source material was deliberate. The experience of the German school seems to suggest that being too inclusive with one's sources poses the risk of ending up with a patchy and haphazard selection of data. This means that the emerging picture is hazy, and the scholarly constructs are far removed from actual discourse. General studies must steer clear of the trap of "everythingism." As I set out to identify the functioning and evolution of political terms and concepts over the two centuries of the Polish-Lithuanian Commonwealth I was keenly aware of how incomplete and scattershot my sources could be. Even given the rigorous constraints that limited my material to political writings, the resulting picture is still based on a fraction of the totality of available material relating to the country's political discourse. Accordingly, every effort was made to keep the selection criteria consistent.

Another fundamental caveat is in order here: the book focuses on discourse produced by members of the noble class for their fellow noblemen. This is not to imply that bourgeois voices were silent in the political debates on matters of state in the period between the Union of Lublin (1569) and the Third Partition (1795) (we cannot talk about peasant voices in that period in any meaningful sense). A small number of sixteenth- and seventeenth-century theorists were either members of the bourgeoisie or noblemen with bourgeois backgrounds (Sebastian Petrycy, Łukasz Górnicki, Jan Januszowski, Szymon Starowolski). A sizeable body of political writings, including some interesting treatises, was also produced in the cities of Royal Prussia in the seventeenth and eighteenth centuries by the likes of Christoph Hartknoch, Bartholomaeus Keckerman or Gottfried Lengnich. Finally, during the Four-Year Sejm in the late eighteenth century the bourgeoisie not only began to fight for their rights but also, in some cases, joined the broader national debate on political reform (Józef Pawlikowski, Stanisław Staszic). However, even though their works influenced political opinion (as was the case with Staszic), they did not influence the actual shape of the discourse. A sizeable proportion remained marginal and exerted no influence even on the public debate (particularly writings from Prussia and the learned disquisitions of Petrycy). Those works that did enter the mainstream of the debate used the same political language as those of the nobility, whether to express their views or, less often, to register dissent (Staszic). Then as now, the most prominent voices in political matters unsurprisingly came from people who had (or believed they had, or wished to have) an impact on the political decisions.[22] In the case of the Polish-Lithuanian Commonwealth, that meant its nobleman citizens who shaped the country's political discourse for more than two hundred years.

I keep referring to discourse in the singular, but the question certainly arises as to whether we can actually talk about a single discourse. Perhaps we should distinguish between distinct political languages, though in a different sense than that suggested by the Anglo-Saxon researchers. Researchers who study the discourse of the Noble Commonwealth face the problem of differences in the languages of the Polish and Lithuanian nobility. Regretfully, this book has no answers on that score. To restate, this is an early foray into a new field, the main goal being to capture the commonalities in the discourse of the Polish-Lithuanian nobility that stemmed from a shared class identity and a shared role in creating the Commonwealth. At this level of analysis, the key concepts appear to have more similarities than differences. I hope that my findings can provide a starting point for future in-depth analyses, some of which could also focus on the differences in the discourse, whether between Poland and Lithuania or among the small groups and communities within the noble class and outside of it. This book, however, focuses primarily on change over time, and therefore tackles the question whether, and to what extent, the political discourse of the nobility changed over the 200 years of the Polish-Lithuanian Commonwealth.

Linguistic diversity in the strict philological sense was also a problem. At least two languages, Polish and Latin, were used in political debates in the Polish-Lithuanian Commonwealth, and that is even before consideration is given to Ruthenian (which played a major role in Lithuania and in the eastern territories) and German (used in Royal Prussia).

For a very long time, Latin was equal to Polish in political discourse. Until the mid-eighteenth century Latin was used in serious treatises and, less frequently, for topical political pamphleteering, as well as for delivering learned orations. In some periods, particularly in the seventeenth and early eighteenth centuries, Latin was incorporated more or less whole-sale into Polish texts (which often are more precisely described as Polish-Latin texts).[23] Still, it can be argued that a uniform body of political discourse was being created in the two languages, modeled predominantly along classical lines.[24] It has been noted that the Polish nobility had adopted a unique form of *latinitas* as one aspect of its internalized tradition of classical antiquity[25]; the same applies to political language. The classical influence was particularly important in the sixteenth century as the language was still in its formative stages. Participants in the debate on the state and statehood were aware of the changes to the country's political system. At the same time, the nobles were looking for ways to describe the surrounding political reality and their own ideals, as they sought to increase their political clout. This is particularly apparent in political treatises of the 1560s and 1570s, where writers were coming up with complete visions of the ideal state that they felt would (or should) take shape in the Polish-Lithuanian Commonwealth. Even more interesting material for analysis can be found in texts written during topical political debates in the period between the first free election (1573) and the *rokosz* of Sandomierz (1606–1607). The authors of those texts were trying to define the basic concepts in that discourse, such as "the state," "political power," "freedom" or "the law" (sometimes as a kind of side-note to topical discussions of current events). They were looking for a new vocabulary capable of describing the changing political realities, for that purpose they modified the meanings of familiar terms or tried to place those terms in new contexts. The classical tradition, as filtered through the Church Fathers and the Renaissance humanists, was their chief tool and resource. The texts of classical antiquity (mostly Roman, though the Greek tradition, particularly Aristotle, was also known and accepted) were a source of political terminology, but also provided conceptualizations of the state and the individual's place within it, and the ways in which politics was discussed.[26] This was a crucial period in terms of the emergence of political discourse, so much so that it could be described as a *Sattelzeit*, a time of transition, though it was more short-lived and less fundamental than the transition that led to the emergence of modernity, as discussed in conceptual history, or *Begriffsgeschichte*.[27] The political language developed at the time proved exceptionally enduring: it would take a century and a half before a comparable transition occurred again. One might say that at the turn of the sixteenth and seventeenth centuries participants in political discussions had successfully developed a language that was ideally suited to the needs of people participating in public life in the Polish-Lithuanian Commonwealth. At any rate, no need for change seemed to be felt for a long time.

Over time, that political language became ossified. New terms or concepts were no longer being added, and the existing ones were increasingly turning into mindless clichés.[28] It might be argued that at some point in the first half of the eighteenth century the political language lost its capacity to describe, or even to take notice of, the threats faced by the Commonwealth. It was no longer able to reflect the altered social and political structures, let alone to formulate the much-needed changes of course which were already in progress at the time. Unlike their Renaissance predecessors, participants in political discussions during the reign of King Stanisław August (1764–1795) were not looking for words to describe new political and legal structures; instead, they sought to develop a new language capable of discussing the crisis of the state. They began to expand the political language with new concepts borrowed from Enlightenment philosophers, first by using calques, then by deriving a new discourse on that basis. This way they were able to name developments and problems that had previously gone overlooked, to achieve a greater precision in formulating political ideas, and to clear up misunderstandings caused by conceptual conflation or confusion. Particularly during the Four-Year Sejm (1788–1792), a heated nationwide political debate ignited both in and out of the Sejm in a process not unlike the early stages of the Noble Commonwealth, with hundreds of participants forging (wittingly or not) a new language to describe the changed situation of Poland and Europe.

This brief, broad-brush characterization of the complicated phenomenon that was the political discourse of the Polish-Lithuanian Commonwealth seems like a necessary backdrop to research into the key terms and concepts of that discourse, with all their meanings, functions and changes. The selection comprises terms and concepts of fundamental importance to capturing the political discourse of the noble class. The chapters are headed with terms such as *Rzeczpospolita* (the Commonwealth), the law, freedom, *monarchia mixta*, concord, virtue, *amor patriae*, tradition (*dawny* or "age-old" ways) and property (a concept conspicuous by its absence from the political discourse). The terms so selected are by no means exhaustive, and should each be treated as catchphrases, each with a nested network of coexisting and interrelated concepts that cumulatively formed the full picture of the political world. As such, there are no separate chapters on terms such as *citizen*, *public good*, *anarchy*, *corruption* or *equality*; however, each of these terms is examined under the rubric of its overarching concept.

Like any timeframe, the start and end dates in this study are largely a matter of convention. Still, the selected dates seem to frame the subject matter accurately. The end point is quite uncontroversial: the year 1795 marks the formal collapse of the Polish-Lithuanian Commonwealth (which had *de facto* ceased to exist as an independent state in 1792 following the defeat in a war with Russia). This makes it a good threshold date as the change in the geopolitical situation profoundly influenced the political language and terminology, and effectively put an end to the old discourse.[29] The opening date is less obvious. It was chosen to coincide with the Union of Lublin (1569), but we could just as well move the starting point back to the political debates in the reign of King Sigismund August, the last of Poland's Jagiellonian kings. Ultimately, 1569 was chosen not for formal reasons (as marking the official birth of the Polish-Lithuanian Commonwealth), but rather to recognize the importance of the first free election of a king of Poland several years later (1573). The participants in that political event were aware of its status as a watershed moment and tried to adapt their language to the new situation. This means that the period under analysis is dictated by events in the real world, and not in the discourse as such. The book may not contain many references to specific political events, but the analysis of the terms and ideas present in the political discourse was motivated throughout by a reflection on the circumstances in which that discourse took shape and operated.

In closing this introduction, let me reiterate that I am acutely aware that this is no more than an early foray, a preliminary outline of an important research problem. Each of the terms and concepts examined herein could easily merit a book in its own right, and my analyses will inevitably contain some of the oversimplifications that haunt general studies. By way of recompense, this attempt to paint a comprehensive picture of the political discourse of the Polish-Lithuanian Commonwealth over the 200 years of its existence promises to reveal the rich and fascinating nature of that phenomenon, and to identify its enduring elements and evolutionary changes. Inasmuch as possible, I present my subject within the broader European context, of which the political discourse of the Polish-Lithuanian nobility was very much part, rooted as it was in a shared classical tradition first filtered through Christian thought, then through Italian humanism. Even as that culture became ossified and disconnected from new European trends at the turn of the seventeenth and eighteenth centuries, the discourse still retained political concepts and political language known in other countries, particularly in the so-called free states. Interestingly, as Europe was reembracing classical antiquity and, to an extent, republican ideals in the second half of the eighteenth century, that language in a way converged again with the language of at least some Enlightenment philosophers, just as it underwent serious changes in its own right.

Notes

1 Bogusławski (1786, 44).
2 [Olizar] (1790, III).

3 "Dangerous senses" or "dangerous meanings," cited after Condren (1994, 52).

4 "[A] political theorist, like any other user of language who wishes to be understood, is limited by the vocabulary available to the public being addressed" (Richter 1989, 71; see also: Richter 1995, 133).

5 Bömelburg (2011, 251–252).

6 Augustyniak (1989, 2004)

7 Opaliński (1995) remains one of the most important works on the subject.

8 Rosner(1986);Butterwick(2005);Butterwick(2012);Butterwick-Pawlikowski (2017b); Brzeziński (2008); Janicki (2004); Grześkowiak-Krwawicz (2012b).

9 Pepłowski (1961); Bem-Wiśniewska (1998); Szczepankowska (2004) – who devotes considerable attention to the language of legislation and to debates on the rule of law; Legomska (2010); Janowska, Pastuchowa, and Pawelec (2011); Dawidziak-Kładoczna (2012).

10 The general direction of French research was set by Regine Robin in *Histoire et linguistique* (1973) and in the joint publication Guilhaumou et al. (1974), see also: Guilhaumou (1989; 1998; 2006). The findings of a team at L'Institut National de la Langue Française were published in *Dictionnaire des usages socio-politiques de la langue Française (1770–1815)* appearing in a series of volumes since 1985.

11 On a technical point, we should note that the term "discourse" was used only by researchers from the Cambridge school. Each of the schools generated a large literature; a summary of their findings and a discussion of the underlying theoretical assumptions can be found in Hampsher-Monk, Tilmans, and van Vree (1998); as well as in Richter (1995); Trencsenyi (2004).

12 For a relatively long time the two schools consistently ignored each other's research. Since the latter half of the 1990s, however, a new generation of researchers has begun to look for commonalities. Among other things this has yielded the joint publication Hampsher-Monk, Tilmans, and van Vree (1998), and more recently the collection of articles by Palonen (2014) – the latter being probably the most thorough outline of the two research methods available at this time.

13 Probably the most successful attempt is Jarra (1968). Regrettably, Jarra was writing in London in the 1960s, and was therefore cut off from new findings in ongoing Polish research and also from some of the source material. Wyrwa (1978) is an important book, though it is not really a history of political thought in the strict sense. Instead, it is more akin to a general study of Poland's political history in the Renaissance, with detailed references to the political ideas of the better-known writers. In terms of more recent scholarship, the only researcher to come up with a general study on the subject was Dorota Pietrzyk-Reeves in her *Ład Rzeczypospolitej* (Pietrzyk-Reeves 2012). Similarly, most of the available studies on specific historical periods are considerably dated, some very much so: Tarnowski (1886, 2nd edition: 2000); Czapliński (1966); Konopczyński (1966; written before 1952 and published posthumously); Olszewski (1961).

14 Whereas R. Koselleck tried to focus on individual concepts, one of the assumptions in his continuator R. Reichardt's *Handbuch politisch-sozialer Grundbegriffe in Frankreich* was that "the concepts don't exist in a disparate way, but in networks of meanings, in 'magnetic fields' of overlapping semantic circles, and they change their meaning due exactly to this interaction," cf. Trencsenyi (2004, 149), also: Koselleck (1998); Olsen (2012); Reichardt (1998); Brunner, Conze, and Koselleck (1972–1997); Reichardt, Schmitt, and Lüsebrink (1985-).

15 Pocock (1987, 34)

16 Modern political discourse has been variously defined, using relatively complicated terminology, for instance as:

> a sequence of speech acts performed by agents within a context furnished
> ultimately by social practices and historical situations, but also – and also
> in some ways more immediately – by the political languages by means of
> which the acts are to be performed;
>
> Pocock (2009, 67)

> Political discourse is, or at any rate purports to be a bridging language,
> a supra-discourse spanning and connecting the several sub-languages,
> it is the language that we supposedly share in our common capacity as
> citizens...
>
> Ball (1998, 79)

   I am deliberately using a much simpler definition in this book.
17 "Political concepts are weapons of war, tools of persuasion and legitimation,
   badges of identity and solidarity" Ball (1998, 82).
18 Richter (1995, 133).
19 Pocock (2009, 75–77 *passim*) for a definition of political language; see also
   Pocock (1987, 20–32); Hampsher-Monk, Tilmans, and van Vree (1998),
   particularly the *Epilogue* by Van Gelderen (1998).
20 Particularly useful in this regard are the collections of political writings
   edited by Jan Czubek (1906; 1918) and Stefania Ochmann-Staniszewska
   (1989/1990/1991) and also, though to a lesser degree given the quite narrow
   focus on the Four-Year Sejm, the six-volume *Materiały do dziejów Sejmu
   Czteroletniego* (Michalski, Rostworowski, Woliński 1955–1964, vols 1–5;
   Eisenbach, Michalski, Rostworowski, Woliński 1969, vol 6), as well as Augustyniak (2013).
21 Pietrzyk-Reeves (2012, 203).
22 "The study of political language takes its departure from the languages of
   ruling groups, which articulate their concerns," Pocock (1987, 24).
23 Axerowa (2004, 157–160); Axer (2004a, 151–156).
24 Cf.: Augustyniak (2004)
25 Axer (2010, 15–81).
26 Sinko (1939); Kot (1911); Backvis (1975, 467–511, 515 *passim*); Opaliński
   (2002, 160–166 *passim*); Pietrzyk-Reeves (2012).
27 The founders of conceptual history (*Begriffsgeschichte*) identified the threshold between early modernity and modernity in German-speaking countries
   as 1750–1850, and in France as 1680–1820. Earlier periods were not of interest to that research tradition.
28 Frost (1990, 54); Augustyniak (1999, 36).
29 Janowski (2009).

Remarks from the Translator

Daniel J. Sax

When a book is devoted to examining the history of words and concepts in one language, translating it into another is surely never an easy task. This has of course been recognized by many historians and translators before, sharing what has been called "one fundamental experience: the extraordinary difficulty of translating the meaning of terms and concepts from one language into another, from one cultural tradition into another, and from one intellectual climate into another."[1]

There are a number of reasons, however, why the task was particularly challenging in this case. The overarching purpose of this book is to preliminarily examine some of the core concepts prominent in the political discourse of the Polish-Lithuanian Commonwealth in the sixteenth through eighteenth centuries, and to do so by examining abundant quotations drawn from prominent political speeches and writings dating from those times, thus giving readers a chance to engage directly with the language used by the orators and writers. As such, it operates on two levels, one involving the author's conceptual analysis, the other involving numerous samples from primary sources. In these remarks regarding the English translation, I would like to briefly describe three particular issues that the translation of such a book poses – problems of Polish-English equivalence, the problem of Latin and its role in the political discourse of the centuries in question, and the conundrum of translating historical language – as well as the approaches the author and I adopted to resolving them.

I

On the first point, let us note that while Polish and English speakers do share, to a considerable degree, the common European cultural heritage, not surprisingly the two languages quite often fail to offer straightforward equivalents, even for core concepts. Although the English "freedom" quite adequately conveys Polish *wolność*, and Polish *cnota* is quite straightforwardly renderable as "virtue" in English (the Polish terms are examined in Chapters 3 and 6 herein), things are not so easy for some of the other concepts examined in this book.

In relatively simple cases, terms might have broader or narrower ranges in the two languages. For instance, take Polish *prawo* and *zgoda* (the two concepts are considered in Chapters 2 and 5 herein): *prawo* can mean "a law" or "the law" or "right," while *zgoda* can mean both "consensus" and "concord," in addition to other senses. This requires not only cautious attention to selecting one or the other equivalent, when this is possible, but also sometimes recognizing the limits of such an approach when it is not and, for instance, falling back instead on the Polish terms themselves. In other words, it demands less of what has come to be known in the field of translation theory as a "domesticating" approach to translation, and more of a "foreignizing" approach instead.[2] The result is a book with a decidedly metatextual slant, a book written in English that is nevertheless *about* concepts and words in Polish.

The problem of equivalence is also sometimes further complicated by certain historical, cultural and linguistic subtleties. This is true, for instance, for the concept that is perhaps the most important in the Polish political discourse of the sixteenth through eighteenth centuries: that of the *Rzeczpospolita* (the subject of Chapter 1). Although the Latin term *respublica* was borrowed into Polish just as it was into English (as *republika* and "republic," respectively), in Polish it was also recast as a calque translation: with Latin *res-publica* giving rise to Polish *rzecz-pospolita*, quite transparently reflecting the underlying meaning of "public/common thing." The closest equivalent in English is undoubtedly "commonwealth," used sometimes herein (as is reflected for instance in the common usage of the name "Polish-Lithuanian Commonwealth"), but it nevertheless often fails to convey the full depth of the Polish term. Mindful of this, we have largely opted to use the term *Rzeczpospolita* in English throughout the book.

Another challenging case-in-point, this time involving a clash of cultural and grammatical connotations, is the Polish term *ojczyzna* (discussed in Chapter 7). Given its etymological derivation from *ojciec* "father," at first blush the closest equivalent might seem to be "fatherland," with connotations such as military strength, valiant sons and the heritage of forefathers. However, Polish *ojczyzna*, like Latin *patria* and its descendants in many modern European languages (e.g., French *la patrie*), is a noun of feminine gender, whereas English "fatherland" wears a decidedly masculine guise. As examples cited in the book show, the Polish *ojczyzna* often appears metaphorically in the political discourse as a mother figure, giving birth to her citizen-sons, indeed even suckling them – things not a "fatherland" but rather "motherland" might attempt in English. We opt to resolve this clash by prioritizing the gender-neutral "homeland" in English.

Yet another example of a lack of straightforward equivalence, this one more of a purely linguistic nature, is afforded by the Polish adjective *dawny* (the focus of Chapter 8). *Dawny* can most often be conveyed in English as "former," but there is a subtle yet sometimes crucial difference in the meaning of the two terms: *dawny* qualifies something as having existed in the possibly distant past, while making no judgement about its current status, whereas "former" adds to this a strong implication that the state of affairs being described no longer obtains. When time-worn customs are praised on the grounds of their being old, considerable caution has been taken in translating uses of Polish *dawny*, predominantly not as "former" but rather most often as "old," "age-old," or even "ancient."

II

A second challenging aspect of translating the kind of political discourse discussed in this book lies in the fundamentally polylingual nature of that discourse, above all the fact that political writings and speeches were very often produced in a mixture of Polish and Latin. As many examples cited in this book serve to illustrate, authors and orators often switched back and forth between Polish and Latin – sometimes several times during the course of a single sentence![3] The result is a very characteristic style of language that is quite challenging to read and even more to translate, and might best be described as "Polish/Latin" political discourse.

In an essay on translation, after considering a somewhat similar issue, Jacques Derrida once posed the question:

> [L]et us note one of the limits of theories of translation: all too often they treat the passing from one language to another and do not sufficiently consider the possibility for languages to be implicated *more than two* in a text. How is a text written in several languages at a time to be translated? How is the effect of plurality to be "rendered"?[4]

Our answer, for the purposes of this book, is to again take a foreignizing approach. Except in extreme cases of tangled interweavings of the two languages (verging on unintelligibility), we often leave the Latin intact, and so Polish-Latin mixtures are typically "rendered" into English-Latin mixtures. While admittedly demanding, this is in keeping with our overarching objective to give the reader a glimpse not only of the content, but also the stylistic flavor of the many quotations from sixteenth- to eighteenth-century literature cited herein.

III

A third important issue is that, apart from conceptual mismatches and apart from sometimes quite heavy Latin admixtures, the very fabric of the somewhat archaic Polish used in the statements quoted herein is quite challenging to translate. How should once best render in English now archaic Polish words (e.g., *azaż, zelować, sprzyjaźliwość*) and word-forms (e.g., *inaksze, do obywatelów*), now-lost senses of modern Polish words (e.g., *wysadzić, irritować, schodzić*)? Even more importantly, how should one best convey in English the effect of the complex, interlaced word order commonly found in Polish texts from the sixteenth through eighteenth centuries?

We are certainly not the first confront such conundrums, of course. Translation scholar George Steiner writes:

> Translators may opt for forms of expression centuries older than current speech. They may choose an idiom prevalent only a generation back. Most frequently, the bias to the archaic produces a hybrid: the translator combines, more or less knowingly, turns taken from the past history of the language, from the repertoire of its own masters, from preceding translators or from antique conventions which modem parlance inherits and uses still for ceremony.[5]

In our case, on the whole, we felt that three broad approaches were possible to the historical primary-source quotations cited herein. One is the option taken in, for instance, the English translations of major Polish historical texts published in Biskupski and Pula (1990). There, texts from across these same three centuries – from *Nihil Novi* (1505) to the *Połaniec Manifesto* (1794) – are all translated into uniform modern-day English. This is, of course, not without certain merits: it prioritizes fluidity of reception, allowing readers to concentrate on content rather than on form. However, as we have noted, part of the objective of the book in Polish is to familiarize readers directly with the distinctive language used in the Polish political discourse, as well as with its evolution over the centuries considered. Choosing this option would have meant abandoning any similar objective for the English version (we decided not to give up so easily).

Another approach would involve, wherever possible, citing actual past translations of the texts into English of an approximately similar era. This would also have its merits, mainly giving the archaic language a certain stamp of authenticity (albeit probably at a certain cost in terms of of readability). Regrettably, this is only possible in a few cases, as precious few of the primary-source texts cited herein exist in contemporary English versions.[6] Moreover, translations produced in the past eras also have their own shortcomings, for example, not always adhering to modern expectations of faithfulness.

We, in turn, have opted for a third approach: we introduced a certain moderate archaization into our translations of Polish authors, using a certain set of features of Early Modern English we expect to be readily recognizable to modern readers. These archaisms are carefully gradated from the 1500s to the 1700s, and as such are meant to serve as recognizable "timestamps," as well as a way for us to attempt to convey something of the archaic flavor of the original writings/speeches.[7] Care was taken to ensure that these archaisms are attested in English texts of approximately similar age.

On the other hand, with the sole exception of these consciously chosen archaized forms, for the sake of improved readability we have decided to retain modern English spelling throughout the translations of primary sources. The result is inevitably "a hybrid" (quoting Steiner above), to be sure, but one born out of consistent decisions dictated by an overarching goal: to convey to the reader not only the content, but also the form and flavor of the passages, as well as some sense of the passage of time between them (through whole centuries).

* * *

The three translation-related strategies described in the above remarks – a generally foreignizing approach to conceptual equivalence throughout the book, and a generally Latin-preserving and archaizing approach to the historical quotations – are in fact interrelated in certain complex ways. For instance, the decision to transplant Latin material grafted into the Polish texts directly into the English texts themselves certainly further augments both the foreignization and archaization strategies. Latin also bears upon the complex issues of conceptual equivalence; for instance, the two senses of *zgoda* were sometimes differentiated by the Old-Polish authors themselves via the Latin terms *consensus* vs. *concordia* (a distinction mirrored in our English translations here).

In all of this, we have done our best to provide the reader with a relevant, readable and reliable translation. At times, the challenge has been akin to tightrope-walking, maintaining a sensible balance on several fronts at once. We have often relied on a foreignizing strategy in the conceptual analysis, but at the same time have tried hard not to overwhelm the English reader and to ensure that each Polish or Latin term inserted in the English text is worth the reader's effort. We have significantly archaized our translations of the historical passages, whilst at the same time endeavoring to maximize their relevance. The resulting book admittedly makes certain demands of readers, but (hopefully) also rewards their efforts with a wealth of insights.

Notes

1 Junker (1996, 6); also echoed in Richter (2011, 2).
2 Venuti (1995), with the distinction going back to Schleiermacher (1813).
3 To take just one example from among the many to be found in this book: "nie trzeba nam tego wywodzić, jako jest potrzebna *reunio disunitorum animorum*; bo *mala*, które z tego *emanarunt* rozróżnienia, nie tylko widzimy, ale *sentimus*" from: *Krótko zebrane praeiudicia Reipublicae universae* [1672], in Kluczycki (1880–1881, vol. 2., 1210).

4 Derrida (1985), word order and emphasis as in Graham's translation.
5 Steiner (1975: 342). Of course, this choice between *"modernizing* the text and *keeping it archaic* is not the same as the one between *foreignizing* or *domesticating* it." Umberto Eco (2001: 22, his emphasis). In the context of English translations of older Polish texts, interesting discussions have been offered by Bałuk-Ulewiczowa (2000) and Wilczek (2005). A certain broader theoretical framework is given to the question by Jones and Turner (2004).
6 For example, the 1589 translation of Goślicki (1568), or Franciszek Bukaty's 1791 translation of the *Constitution of the Third of May* (1791).
7 That is to say, these archaisms are consciously introduced with a specific "deictic" purpose, in the sense of Richardson (1998), as "linguistic and contextual signals which encourage the reader to interpret the time relationship between source and target text in different ways" (Jones and Turner 2004).

1 *Rzeczpospolita* – The Commonwealth

The Polish term *Rzeczpospolita*, derived from the Latin *res publica* meaning "public thing" or "common thing," was the most characteristic word of the noble political discourse in the Polish-Lithuanian Commonwealth. It was invoked in virtually every public statement, whether delivered verbally as addresses to the Sejm (the national assembly), before regional gatherings of nobles called *sejmiks* ("little Sejms"), or in courts, or written as polemical letters or serious political treatises. Statistical research confirms that it was used more frequently than any other political term throughout the whole of the Polish-Lithuanian Commonwealth's existence from the sixteenth to the eighteenth centuries.[1] For quite some time, researchers have accentuated its popularity and the crucial role that it plays in understanding the Old-Polish political language.[2] At the same time, they stress that the word had multiple meanings, noting the difficulties that lie in attempting to define it in unambiguous terms. This problem was most aptly summed by Tomasz W. Gromelski when he wrote that "the word had a great number of meanings or indeed none at all."[3] Despite that rather pessimistic observation, he nevertheless attempted to systematize the different meanings ascribed to it. He was not the first to do so – various authors have devoted many monographs to systematizing and explaining those meanings, but the interpretations that they proposed have been fairly divergent.[4] Nevertheless, no one has yet attempted to look at this problem in a more synthetic manner by shedding light not only on the elements that comprise the picture, namely the idea of the Commonwealth/republic in the political discourse from the sixteenth to the eighteenth centuries, but also on its origins and the changes that it underwent over time as well as on the consequences that the adoption of specific concepts entailed for views about the political world. This is particularly relevant given that this was perhaps the most important key term, serving as a focal point for many of the political ideals espoused by the nobles.

From today's perspective, the term *Rzeczpospolita* seems to have had multiple referents: one and the same word essentially expressed a concept of the state, a notion of citizens' place in it and also a vision of its government. As previous scholars have pointed out, the word was, at least sometimes, not only synonymous with the state in general or a state characterized by a specific system of government (though not necessarily a republic in today's sense of the word), and not merely the official name of the union between Poland and Lithuania as a specific political entity with a specific territory, but also an expression used to refer to all those who lived in that state (though this use was quite rare) and (more frequently) to all the citizens, which meant all members of the noble class, as well as the structure that formed its system of government – the set of three estates comprising the Sejm, or sometimes only the chamber of deputies (*izba poselska*). Finally, in normative terms, the word denoted the supreme political value, the ideal of political order, and a common good that required constant care.[5] Nevertheless, we must bear in mind that this division reflects an attempt to systematize the problem from the standpoint of today's criteria and today's views on the state. For those participating in political debates from the end of the sixteenth century at least to the middle of the eighteenth century, such a breakdown would have been artificial, needless and perhaps not entirely comprehensible. In their eyes, the word *Rzeczpospolita* comprised all those things at the same time. Depending on the context or the purpose of their statements, they nonetheless placed emphasis on different aspects of the term, and one and the same spoken or written statement could include the word in several meanings. Such fluidity is best visible when we try to separate the situations in which this word refers to a certain political construct or a specific territory, from those in which it denotes the community of people who form this construct or live in that territory. For quite some time, researchers of the First Polish Republic have described and analyzed "the citizens' full identification with the state,"[6] noting "the disappearance of the separate nature of the state and society and their interpenetration"[7] in the Polish statements. In fact, it is difficult to call this a "disappearance" – rather, a vision of the state was invoked that simply took no account of any such separation.

It has long been argued that the Polish political thought and the Polish political discourse were deeply rooted in the antique tradition, mostly the Roman tradition.[8] In particular, this holds true for the sixteenth century, when the groundwork was being laid for how the nobles thought and talked about the Commonwealth. It was the ancient concept of *rei-publicae* that served as the point of departure, as evidenced by the republican vision put forward by such prominent Renaissance theoreticians as Andrzej Frycz Modrzewski, Wawrzyniec Goślicki, Andrzej Wolan, Sebastian Petrycy as well as Stanisław Orzechowski and Krzysztof Warszewicki, which means authors whose views were indeed very different.[9] Although they often differed diametrically in how they viewed the surrounding political reality and proposed different measures to make it more ideal, they all concurred with their classical masters in understanding their republic as a commonwealth of people united by a single right to achieve a good life, an "association bound by utility," as Orzechowski wrote, echoing Cicero.[10] What exactly was meant by "utility," that is, what benefits it entailed, will be discussed below. Here, it is important that, in such a construal of the state/republic, the society and the state formed a single "political community," indivisible and in a sense organically bound.[11] The latter characteristic, derived both from Aristotle's theories and from the medieval concepts of the state, was reflected in very popular allegories in which the Commonwealth was likened to a human body. Such comparisons serve as excellent illustrations of different aspects of the understanding of that concept – the component parts of the body of the Commonwealth could include both its provinces and the different "nations" that inhabited them, in addition to members of the different estates, as well as the elements that comprised and upheld its system of government – the latter role was typically attributed to the law, which was regarded as the spirit of the Commonwealth in line with the views of Demosthenes.[12] Importantly, in such a construal the Commonwealth was something more than a political construct that comprised specific elements – it was an organism, a certain organic whole whose composite parts fit together well. Appeals to such an organicist vision of the state in Polish political discussions are a very interesting issue that merits more in-depth analysis. Here, it is necessary to stress the popularity and durability of that vision, which was reflected in all types of statements, including artistic ones,[13] and survived until the beginning of the eighteenth century, although at that time it was a rather clichéd embellishment of oratory performances deprived of any deeper theoretical underpinnings. At the turn of the seventeenth century, however, the picture of *corpus reipublicae* was part of a consistent vision of the state deeply rooted in the Mediterranean tradition. Such an interpretation was by no means a Polish peculiarity – similar visions of the state as a body were sketched out in all of Europe. Likewise, there was nothing peculiar in the antique concept of the *republica* as a society governed by laws for the sake of the common good. The distinctiveness of the Polish discourse lay in the transfer of this concept from the level of theoretical deliberation to the level of political discussions and debates, in its being applied directly to the deliberators' own state. A telling example of this can be found in the invocations of the classical definition of the republic – in the theoretical writings of Modrzewski, Wolan, and Petrycy, it is treated as a general definition of the state, whereas Orzechowski already used it as a direct description of the Polish political reality.[14] It also appears in this concretized sense in the political writings of the first interregnum (1573): "The *Rzeczpospolita* is nothing other than the thing of the people, and the people is a society united and joined by a common law for the common good and utility," wrote one of the sixteenth-century authors,[15] taking his cue from "the wise Cicero" and using the definition as an argument in political discussions to refer to his own *Rzeczpospolita*. Although such theoretical citations were relatively rare in political commentary of the time and were eventually replaced entirely by more specific references, the vision of the Commonwealth as being at once both a political construct and the society forming it remained the foundation of Polish political discourse. We can say that a certain usurpation of the classical theoretical concept occurred here, that Cicero's or Modrzewski's *respublica* first became the Republic of the Kingdom of Poland, and then the Polish-Lithuanian Commonwealth. There was a certain mechanism of mutual influence and reinforcement here: the classical tradition influenced the Polish understanding of the concept, but at the same time a certain "internalization" of that tradition led to a Polish interpretation thereof that differed somewhat from the interpretation generally proposed in the European discourse. That also gave rise to what would become an amazing durability of certain elements of this Polish image of the Commonwealth, specifically those drawn from ancient models, above all the identification of the state and the (differently understood) community that formed it. The Polish theory of the state remained faithful to the vision of the state as *civitas* for much longer than Western European theories, and that vision was encapsulated in the notion of the *Rzeczpospolita*.

When we analyze statements from the early period of the Polish-Lithuanian Commonwealth's existence, especially those that contributed to ongoing political discussions, it appears especially striking that their authors identified strongly with the Commonwealth and often added the pronoun "our(s)": such statements as *"respublica nostra libera"* (our free republic) and *"wszystkiej Rzeczypospolitej naszej"* (our whole Commonwealth) often appeared in the political writings of the first interregnum (1573) and the *rokosz* (rebellion) of Zebrzydowski (1606–1607). Over time, similar statements became increasingly less frequent, which at first appears surprising, but they never disappeared from the discourse entirely. Indeed, there were very few of them in the writings from the period of the reign of John II Casimir (1648–1668). However, that did not mean that their authors distanced themselves from the Commonwealth – rather, we may get the impression that they found this relationship so obvious that they no longer needed to stress it, unlike the participants in the pre-election debates who posited a new order for the Commonwealth or those who fought in the *rokosz* in 1606 for their vision (and their authority). The exclamation uttered by an anonymous author[16] in 1573 – *"Tota respublica* – us, us alone!"* – would be repeated until the end of the Polish-Lithuanian Commonwealth's existence. It is echoed faithfully in the rhetorical question asked by Andrzej Zamoyski in 1764: "Of what does the republic consist, if not of us ourselves?"[17] Even at the end of the eighteenth century, when Polish political writers, influenced by Western theorists, also slowly began to employ a terminology distinguishing the state itself from the community inhabiting that state and from the form of government, the old tradition remained very strong. Even authors who were familiar with foreign theories and used the related terminology still held dear the concept that the "republic is formed by each and every citizen."[18] In his most famous work, Hugo Kołłątaj, who was well-versed in the most recent concepts of governance and proposed his own concept of the state and the nation, used the term "*Nieprzestanna Rzeczpospolita*" (the Perpetual Commonwealth) to refer to the community of citizens that "interminably" held sovereign power in the state.[19]

One important element of this picture of the Commonwealth as a nearly organic community was the conviction, derived from the classical concepts, that any harm done to the republic was automatically done to its members. One *rokosz* pamphlet[20] depicted the spirit of Hetman Jan Zamoyski as asking about the future of his own son: "If ill should befall the Commonwealth, can any good truly come unto him?" There could be only one answer to that wholly rhetorical question: "no." As Jan Leszczyński wrote in 1665: "just as we belong to the Commonwealth on equal terms with the other estates, so too do these misfortunes affect us, and any cruelties that befall the Commonwealth threaten the sons of the homeland just the same."[21] That aspect was fairly frequently invoked by critics of the Polish reality, for example Łukasz Opaliński, who warned: "Ye are destroying the Commonwealth, in other words yourselves."[22] This argument proved very long-lived; indeed, it was even invoked in the eighteenth century by Stanisław Leszczyński, Stanisław Konarski, and Andrzej Zamoyski. Such an understanding of the Commonwealth and complete identification with it could, moreover, lead to the conclusion that the reverse was equally true – any harm done to an individual was also done unto the Commonwealth. It is difficult to say when similar thinking appeared for the first time. It was formulated in a way that raised no doubt by defenders of Marshal Jerzy Lubomirski during his conflict with King John II Casimir (1665–1666), who explained that "*in uno corpore Reipublicae idem omnibus membris mali sensus est,*"[23] which led them to conclude "that the lord marshal is aggrieved, and that the whole of the Commonwealth perishes in him."[24] Similar interpretations were not very frequently found in the discourse, although they were presumably close to the heart of many noble citizens.

Here, it is worth stressing the integrative role of the concept of the state as a community, at least for those who considered themselves members of the common *Rzeczpospolita*. That role was particularly evident in the sixteenth century. It would be banal to stress that at the time of the Union of Lublin the society of the Polish-Lithuanian Commonwealth was highly diverse. Indeed, the writers of the time realized that diversity. As one anonymous author wrote in 1573, "in a single Commonwealth and common kingdom resides the Pole, Lithuanian, Prussian, Ruthenian, Masurian, Samogitian, Courlander, Podlesian, Volhynian and Kievian."[25] In the late sixteenth and early seventeenth centuries, neither language nor faith could act as the integrating element, nor could territory fully play such a role. Instead, at least for the nobles, this integrating element was meant to be the Commonwealth itself.[26] It was something more than the union of two states – as the Act of the Union of Lublin (1569) itself expressed it, this was to be something qualitatively new, giving rise "not to different ones, but to a single common *Rzeczpospolita*, which brought two states and nations together and fused them into a single people."[27] In this depiction, one can not only see a broad understanding of the word "republic," but also hear echoes of organic theories, with the *Rzeczpospolita* "bringing together and fusing" two parts into a single body. The question of attitudes to the union and the integration of Poland and Lithuania's political systems are complex, and they concern social, political and economic issues. However, it was also reflected in the political language. It would be an overstatement to say that the fact of the emergence of the common *Rzeczpospolita* was clearly reflected in the political discourse immediately after 1569. Even in the debates held during the first interregnums, it was often difficult to say whether authors who wrote about "*nasza Rzeczpospolita*" (our Commonwealth) or even "*wszystka Rzeczpospolita*" (the whole Commonwealth) were referring to the entire Commonwealth, or only traditionally to the Polish Crown.[28] However, even then there were unambiguous mentions of "the miscellany of nations belonging to the single Commonwealth."[29] Assertions that the Lithuanians and Poles had found themselves "in a single republic" could be found in texts by authors from both the Crown and from Lithuania.[30] An analysis of the writings of Zebrzydowski's *rokosz* leave practically no doubt that the authors were concerned for the whole of the republic, although they did not place any special emphasis on this fact. It appears that by that time, the term was obviously linked to the entire Polish-Lithuanian state and the community that inhabited it. As shown by Edward Opaliński's research, the need for greater specificity or the placement of greater emphasis on this fact only became visible in moments of tension or threat, when they were "manifestations of solidarity or calls for it."[31] This is excellently illustrated by a statement made by the author of a pamphlet written in 1653, when the community faced the danger of a breakup: "yet the sons of the Crown and of the Duchy of Lithuania I consider to form a single body republic."[32] Some scholars point out that the term *Rzeczpospolita* used in reference to both the whole of the Polish-Lithuanian state did not lose importance until the latter half of the eighteenth century, a time of extensive unification, when it began to be supplanted in the discourse by the concepts of "homeland" (*ojczyzna*) and simply "Poland," but the issue nonetheless requires more detailed analysis.[33]

As stated above, the *Rzeczpospolita* was an integrative idea for those who belonged to it, but at the same time this concept quickly began to play an "excluding" role, so to speak – shutting out those who were outside the community of people it referred to. Definitions of the republic drawn from classical ones were essentially neutral and could be interpreted as embracing all the inhabitants of a state. Likewise, organic visions of the *Rzeczpospolita* allowed it to comprise all the estates.[34] That is indeed how the concept had been treated by such writers as Modrzewski, Wolan, Petrycy and Górnicki,[35] including in specific reference to their own state. It was later treated in a similar way by authors of more theoretical deliberations. However, they did so in isolation from the reality of the Polish-Lithuanian state. With reference to the authors' own community, a narrower understanding of the republic very quickly began to dominate in the political discourse. It was suggested by Orzechowski, who was not prevented by Cicero's definition, which he cited very eagerly, from answering the question "What is it that ye call 'the republic'?" with words spoken by the protestant character Ewangelik in his *Quincunx*: "the Polish Chivalry together with the Crown Council."[36] In Orzechowski's case, the matter was not fully clear, because he was not consistent in this respect, in addition to having his own, fairly original vision of the *Rzeczpospolita*. A more telling example is offered by discussions held during the first interregnum, which included statements identifying the Commonwealth with all noble citizens, for example in the statement of one author who warned that "nothing else can be decided, apart from what the Commonwealth has empowered the envoys to decide"[37] in the coronation Sejm and the already mentioned exclamation "*Tota respublica* – us, us alone!" The identification of the *Rzeczpospolita* with "us nobles" is a lot more frequently confirmed not so much openly as indirectly, through the context of statements. The same holds true also for later writings, but in moments of tension it was also asserted openly, and without any hesitation:

> 'Tis in the hands of the noble, knightly estate, which when it comes together from all the Crown lands and the Grand Duchy for a great gathering in a certain place, not only for a Sejm [...] but also for negotiations with the rulers, that is then the Commonwealth.[38]

It is possible to doubt whether everyone would agree that the *Rzeczpospolita* was identified with a *rokosz*, but linking it to the noble community caused no objections even on the part of the royalists.[39] The statement "We are the *corpus Reipublicae*, the circle of the noble estate, through which this homeland arose"[40] was repeated with pride in the following centuries. The Commonwealth elected its king and entered into a contractual agreement with him (*pacta conventa*), forged confederations and finally showed concern for the situation of those inhabitants who did not comprise it. The (rare) statements in which authors called for the situation of the peasants to be improved often highlighted the degree of the latter's exclusion from the community. "The need is great for the republic to ensure, by the example of other nations, that the lords should not harass their subjects according to their will," cautioned Szymon Starowolski, concluding "that this was a duty of the republic."[41] We should note an important caveat here, namely that this usurpation of the *Rzeczpospolita* by the nobles was essentially never total, the "entire republic" could sometimes – not only in the sixteenth century and not only in theoretical writings – also refer to all the inhabitants of the Polish-Lithuanian state, with space found within the concept likewise for the burghers, the Cossacks,[42] or even the peasants, because this was a possible interpretation of the priest Jan Chądzyński's words: "this hell of the Polish lords should be done away with, and a Polish republic establish'd in a humane way, so that the peasants, too, are not under oppression, not only imposed by foreigners but by their own lords."[43] But such assertions were merely marginal throughout the seventeenth century and a significant portion of the eighteenth; the peasant and burgher were almost entirely absent from the political discourse of these times, and they were in any case clearly seen as situated outside the Commonwealth and by the same token somewhat outside the perceptual horizon of those involved in political life. And hence the above-cited sixteenth-century author's "us, us alone!" remained audible almost to the end of the Polish-Lithuanian Commonwealth's existence. The program of political reforms presented to the Sejm in 1789 (*Zasady do formy rządu*) still left no doubt that it was speaking of the *Rzeczpospolita* as a noble republic.[44]

This understanding of the word *Rzeczpospolita* was definitively influenced by the socio-political reality of the Polish-Lithuanian state, yet the choice of tradition in speaking about that state was not without a certain importance here. The nobles were indeed the strongest political and economic force within the state, but it was the very adoption of a terminology drawn from the classical age that enabled the noble society itself to be called a "republic." We can say that this specific situation informed the political discourse, but at the same time its adoption in a certain distinct form itself began to shape the view of reality slightly, allowing certain elements to be perceived, others not. This narrowing in the scope of how the term *Rzeczpospolita* was understood was not at odds with the previously cited classical tradition, and in fact it was not even a narrowing *per se*, but more of selective choice of aspects to be brought forward. The classical *res-publica* in the interpretation of Cicero and the Roman republican authors was, after all, a common thing of all citizens, their common interest and common good,[45] and we should hasten to add: only theirs. Western European authors like Jean Bodin and his successors (all the way down to Thomas Hobbes), identifying the republic with any "lawful" state,[46] held that every participant/member of the society of a state was its citizen, a man who was bound by the laws of that country, and further the subject of the monarch that ruled that country.[47] That view was shared by certain Polish theorists of the Renaissance – Modrzewski,

Petrycy, and to some extent also Wolan.[48] However, political discourse ended up following a different route, namely one followed by Italian humanists, and identified citizens as those individuals who participated in political life[49] yet agreed, in accordance with not just Roman thought but also the Ancient Greek concept of participation, that members of a commonwealth had the right to make decisions about it, and only those who did so were its rightful members.[50] It was argued, echoing Aristotle's views, that "the state is a body of citizens."[51] It is suggestive how quickly and decisively the word *civis/cives* (citizen/citizens) was incorporated into the Polish political discourse, not only as a Latin term but also as the Polish equivalent (*obywatel/obywatele*). It had started to appear (in both versions) back in Jagiellonian times, such as in Orzechowski's definition, and was already used frequently in the political discussion of the first interregnum. There is also generally no doubt that it referred there only to the participants in the debate of those times, to the people who took an active role in making political decisions. It was argued that "citizens should deliberate what they should take to the election, or with what to send those going" and that they should discuss public matters, because "*in libera patria omnium civium liberae voces sunt et esse debent.*"[52] A concept drawn from the classical tradition was thus fluidly incorporated into the contemporary Polish discourse, and used no less fluidly to refer to the noble community or its individual members. The issue of who was a citizen was made crystal clear by the author of a conversation in verse between the characters Lech and Piast (mythical rulers of Poland), in which Piast addresses the listeners/readers with such words: "But be ye citizens wary [...] this means you, the chivalry..."[53] Interestingly, it would appear (although this would require further verification) that the term *obywatel/civis* lost popularity somewhat over time, occurring more rarely starting in the mid-seventeenth century, although it does not disappear from the discourse entirely. It regained its former popularity in the 1760s, brought back somewhat by the philosophy of the Enlightenment, especially Jean-Jacques Rousseau. For our purposes here, it is important that the political discourse of the Polish-Lithuanian Commonwealth adopted from classical sources the vision of a republic more as an association of active citizens than as a category embracing all of a state's inhabitants – "*civis qui sunt verum rei publicae corpus*"[54] – and applied it to the community of nobles.

However, the nobility constituted the *Rzeczpospolita* not just through their "civic stance"; it was no less important, or perhaps even more so, that the nobility formed an essential element (although in this case not necessarily the only one) of the Commonwealth not as a state or as an association, but as a political construct. Classical political thought at least since Aristotle had held that for a republic to be able to achieve the objective set for it, in other words to guarantee the good of its members, it had to take a specific form, ensuring that the interests of all individuals were protected without violating the interests of the community as a whole. In the modern era, following Polybius and Cicero, the principle was adopted that this ideal would be fulfilled by a mixed form of governance, the *monarchia mixta* or *mixtum imperium*. This concept was adopted without reservation also by Polish theoreticians of the state in the sixteenth century, and from them also by participants in the political debate.[55] Importantly, they all (with Modrzewski as the sole exception, it seems) treated it not as a theoretical proposal, but as a description of the existing reality. In the sixteenth and seventeenth centuries, that construct was invoked in statements about "reforming the Commonwealth," "shaking the Commonwealth" or – God forbid – "replacing the Commonwealth." At the same time, specific institutions were subordinated to this theoretical model. In 1615, Wacław Kunicki put this succinctly yet firmly: "Commonwealth, we say to name the king, senators, nobility."[56] Such a construal of the word *Rzeczpospolita* by the nobles was noticed as early as in the sixteenth century by the contemporary foreign observers,[57] and it has also been described by modern scholars, who point out the identification of the republic with the Sejm.[58] The latter view appears to be confirmed by statements about "deliberations of the whole Commonwealth"[59] that appeared from the end of the sixteenth century at least to the mid-eighteenth century and the famous words from Stanisław Leszczyński's *Głos wolny wolność ubezpieczający* [Free Voice Safeguarding Freedom]: "And where is the Commonwealth? At the Sejm, every two years."[60] However, such comments must be treated with caution. It appears that the Sejm was not so much identified with the republic as regarded as its embodiment, just like in a monarchy the king embodied the state. The Sejm was a place in which "the power and majesty of the whole Commonwealth"[61] were manifest, rather than constituting the republic *per se*.

It is worth pointing out how the role of the king changed depending on how exactly the Commonwealth was understood. The king had his place within the concept of the state understood as a community yet was by no means necessary. In the Commonwealth understood as a political construct, however, the king was essential: "It compriseth the king, the senate, the knightly estate, but these three estates make up the single body of the Commonwealth,"[62] one *rokosz* participant otherwise averse to the monarch wrote in 1606. One of the last to reiterate this view was Stanisław Leszczyński, who argued in the middle of the eighteenth century that the king as the first estate "comprises, together with the two others, one inseparable whole of the Commonwealth, which is a symbol of the Most Holy Trinity: three estates, but one Commonwealth."[63] These quotes invoke the characteristic organicist imagery, in which all component parts were naturally essential in comprising the overall body of the state. This was an engrossing issue for participants in political discussions starting from the period of the first free election, when the question was first asked whether a "headless" Commonwealth was still a republic.[64] The answers to that question varied not only depending on the political goals of their authors but also depending on those who referred to this aspect of the concept of the Commonwealth in their speeches or writings. That caused a certain inconsistency in the discourse and, in a sense, also in the vision of the state, wherein the king on one occasion appeared as an element, perhaps crucial element of the Commonwealth, while on another (sometimes in one and the same statement) as an external or even downright dangerous factor. The first to capture this inconsistency in full and describe it in the form of conclusions at the beginning of the eighteenth century was Stanisław Karwicki, who broke with the antique tradition (though it is difficult to say to what extent he did so consciously) and concluded that the concept of mixed government was a misunderstanding, reserving the concept of the *Rzeczpospolita* for the noble community and its representatives in the Sejm, and presenting it in clear opposition to the king.[65] The problem was not ultimately resolved until the second half of the eighteenth century, when the concept of the Commonwealth ceased to be linked with the construct of *monarchia mixta*. At that time, the word *Rzeczpospolita* was used to refer to a country with a specific form of government, sometimes referred to as free or republican government, but no longer to the distinctive triple construct, consisting of the three specific estates.

The *Rzeczpospolita*, as the name of a political community with certain characteristics that distinguished it from other countries, is yet another important aspect of the functioning of this concept in the political discourse from the sixteenth to eighteenth centuries. As stated above, the concept of *respublica* was commonly used to denote any state in the sixteenth century. However, Polish statements, at least from Orzechowski onwards, were characterized by a clear tendency to narrow down the meaning of this concept. It appears that this was influenced by a certain usurpation of the classical concept of *respublica* as a mixed monarchy and the treatment of the Polish-Lithuanian Commonwealth as one, combined with the growing conviction that the Commonwealth was special, different from most European monarchies. "And so do not call it our kingdom, but rather our homeland, or *Rzeczpospolita*" – an anonymous author[66] cautioned in 1573. At that time, such a clear distinction between a republic and a monarchy was not yet obvious, and many statements from that period could be summed up by what one scholar had asserted with respect to the sixteenth-century Englishmen: namely that they saw a commonwealth as the antithesis not of monarchy, but of tyranny.[67] Even then, statements made by participants in the political debate were clearly characterized by a sense that their country was a republic unlike any other. To stress this fact, they sometimes added the adjective "free" – "*respublica nostra libera.*"[68] "*Libera respublica quae sit?*" asked the author of perhaps the most famous pamphlet published during Zebrzydowski's *rokosz*, answering:

> We call it *rempublicam liberam* when not one but three estates govern there and rule *simul et semper* [...] and they govern through a common law, so called since everyone voluntarily ordains that law upon themselves, *ratione* the law be not burdensome upon him who ordains it upon himself.[69]

Importantly, this was not simply a description of the Polish reality, but rather a more general definition formulated under the influence of classical theories, and it was only later in his deliberations that the author sought to adapt it to the Polish reality. That was the clear opposition of a republic and monarchy, or as the author of the pamphlet quoted above put it, *reipublicae – absolutii dominii*. Such an interpretation on the one hand stressed the originality of the Polish-Lithuanian Commonwealth and on the other one treated it as part of a certain tradition of states with a specific model of government. That was noticed already in the sixteenth century – the author of a pre-election pamphlet from 1573 entitled *Naprawa Rzeczypospolitej* [Repairing the Republic] referred to that specific tradition, when he named the three "republic-establishers" Lycurgus, Solon, and Romulus, thus referring to the old republics of Sparta, Athens, and Rome, which Poland was believed to surpass in terms of the excellence of solutions in the field of governance.[70] The author of the *rokosz* pamphlet cited above explicitly included his country in that tradition:

> And here be the form of Republics which we call free [...] and which have numbered but three in the world: that of the Romans, [...] then it went to the Venetians, where it remains to this day. Our forebears formed this third of their own, *ad normam* the Venetian one...[71]

Also, throughout the whole seventeenth century and a large portion of the eighteenth, citizens of the Commonwealth considered themselves heirs to "the old republics." From the sixteenth to the end of the eighteenth century, however, they also included their country in the fairly elitist group of European republics, which comprised Italian republics, especially Venice,[72] in the sixteenth century, was expanded to include Holland and the Helvetic states in the seventeenth century, in the eighteenth century also Sweden of the freedom era and with a certain reluctance England: "And so do help me, my companions, the English, Dutch, Swedish, Venetian republics," the voice of freedom personified appealed in a pamphlet dating from 1733.[73] From the sixteenth century onwards, those countries were invoked whenever authors wanted to propose certain changes in the organization of their community in line with the principle formulated by Karwicki in the eighteenth century: "but that we should improve the government, following the examples of those re-publics, which were also or are now famed for liberty – that no sensible politician can deny."[74] At the end of the eighteenth century, there was also space there for the newly formed republic of the American colonies, and finally revolutionary France.[75] That was when a somewhat different terminology started to be used, in addition to the traditional term *wolne rzeczypospolite* (free commonwealths), to speak instead about *republiki* (republics) and *wolne państwa* (free states), and such use was most likely influenced to some extent by the terminology derived from the works of French philosophers. On the other hand, those terms were not really anything new – the phrase "free states" had been in use at least since the beginning of the seventeenth century, albeit not very frequently.[76]

Interestingly, the classical concept of mixed government as a basis for the Commonwealth started to be slowly abandoned in the 1770s, but the Polish discourse did not narrow this concept to countries without kings, as in the construal of the word "republic" that dominated the Western European discourse. Such narrow definitions sometimes appeared in textbooks that were adaptations of foreign writings, and on several oc-casions in the fervor of violent political disputes of the Four-Year Sejm, when opponents of hereditary monarchy proposed the Commonwealth without a king and adjusted their definitions accordingly.[77] Even then, however, such statements were merely marginal. That was partially due to the fact that their own Commonwealth had a crowned ruler but also due to the adopted vision of the republic, distinguished from other coun-tries not only by its system of government but above all by freedom. Freedom was perceived as an immanent trait of a republic and at the same time as its hallmark. It had been mentioned among the benefits that came with living in the Polish-Lithuanian Commonwealth already back in the sixteenth century, to some extent influenced by the classical definitions (in this case Cicero and Sallust).[78] As Andrzej Maksymilian Fredro wrote in mid-seventeenth century: "It is safer in every regard to live in the full freedom of a republic than under a monarchy."[79] The view had theoretical underpinnings as well. Like the Roman authors before them and like later advocates of republican forms of government in early modern-age Europe, the participants in the political debate felt that free-dom was possible only when citizens decided about their own affairs and those of the state by participating in political life.[80] Freedom of this sort was only rendered possible by republics, "be they under kings or not under kings."[81] This proved to be an exceptionally durable conviction – it is excellently illustrated by the above-cited definition of *liberae rei-publicae* dating from 1606, whose author stressed that the Polish-Lithuanian Commonwealth was governed by a law that "everyone ordains upon themselves."[82] Konarski's definition from more than

150 years later has a similar ring to it: "Republics are free when not governed by one but self-governed by more, chosen from among the people, or by the whole people itself, according to laws and all justice."[83] In 1788, Hugo Kołłątaj, already making use of the modern categories of civil and political freedom, stated resolutely that "an important need of every free nation is civil freedom, which is what republics, that is to say political freedom, were formed to safeguard."[84]

These theoretical assertions were made in reference to all free states, but above all to the writers' own republic, the *Rzeczpospolita*. That is how freedom was described in the sixteenth century by Orzechowski and also by Wolan,[85] who was much more critical of the Polish reality. During the first free election, the assertion that the "Poles are *gens gentium omnium quaecunque sub sole sunt, liberrima*"[86] was seen as related to their state's form of governance. With time, freedom began to be perceived as the most precious gift that the Polish-Lithuanian Commonwealth gave to its citizens. The link between the Commonwealth and freedom was noticed already in the sixteenth century, and with time became more closely knit. Freedom became a sister of the Commonwealth, its heart and soul, the apple of its eye, its most precious gem and adornment, and at the same time its foundation and hallmark. As Jan Zamoyski said in 1605, "*Fundamentum nostrae republicae libertas est,*" and 100 years later Walenty Pęski wrote about his homeland "*Libertas* is for it *per modum naturae.*"[87] "My freedom is my life," declaimed the personified *Rzeczpospolita* itself in a pamphlet dating from 1697.[88] That connection would not be questioned even after the adoption of certain new concepts of the state in the eighteenth century. The logical conclusion of this conviction, one drawn already back in the sixteenth century, was that the demise of the republic would entail the demise of freedom.[89] This would be reiterated over the next 200 years, almost verbatim.[90]

This leads us to another aspect of the topic in question, one that goes beyond the strict field of the legal order of the state. No analysis of the concept of the *Rzeczpospolita* in the political discourse of the Polish-Lithuanian Commonwealth would be complete without considering the vision of a certain ideal, the supreme political value. We must not forget that participants in the political debate from the sixteenth century almost until the end of the eighteenth century viewed the Commonwealth as something more than a state/community, even in the broadest sense, or its form of government. Rather, the *Rzeczpospolita* was also a certain ideal of a purposeful political order that guaranteed the satisfaction of the needs of the individuals that constituted it.[91] Both in theoretical deliberations and in the course of political disputes, the Commonwealth was described, verbally and in writing, as an "association bound by utility" or good life. In the sixteenth century and in the first half of the seventeenth century, that meant, just like in the antique discourse, that its goals were peace, justice, safety and the satisfaction of the individual needs of citizens. There is no doubt that the Commonwealth was seen by participants of the political discussions of that period as a state that guaranteed their rights and privileges, offered them peace and security as well as enabled them to freely enjoy their property. In one of the *rokosz* pamphlets dating from 1606, the Commonwealth itself is depicted as speaking characteristically to one of its citizens:

> remember that I gave birth to thee in this Crown, that I gave thee liberty, that I loved thee and held thee up, that I enrich'd thee for thy protection and health, that I gave thee the bread from mine own mouth.[92]

Over time, the "benefits" derived from the Commonwealth started to reduce, in extreme cases to only one, namely freedom, but the idea as such remained unchanged – the existence of the Commonwealth was the only guarantee of the satisfaction of the needs of its citizens, regardless of the exact understanding of such needs.

Finally, it seems necessary to attempt to formulate a more synthetic answer to the question that was partially answered earlier: to what extent did the understanding of the concept of the *Rzeczpospolita* change over the more than 200 years of its use in the Polish political discourse? First of all, emphasis must be placed on the durability of the meanings attached to the word. Even in the second half of the eighteenth century, the authors who already used the discourse of the Enlightenment and therefore employed such concepts as natural freedom and social contract still saw the *Rzeczpospolita* above all as a community of free citizens – as much as a country as a society/nation. As Kołłątaj put this, "establishing a republic, in other words establishing a society of free people [...] is the work of the will of the whole nation."[93] Just like for over two centuries, the *Rzeczpospolita* laid down laws and guaranteed the freedom of not only such conservative defenders of the *status quo* as Seweryn Rzewuski and Szczęsny Potocki but also of Montesquieu's follower – Ignacy Łobarzewski.[94] Importantly, that was where the traditional noble discourse, rooted in Roman thought and crystallized in the sixteenth century, met up with the discourse of the philosophers of the Enlightenment, in particular Montesquieu and Rousseau, who rediscovered the antique republican ideals and the classical republican discourse and adapted them to fit the needs of their visions.

Nevertheless, the political language started to change slowly in the 1770s. Those changes did not pertain (at least not directly) to the idea of the state as a community, which proved exceptionally durable, but to the word *Rzeczpospolita* itself, which appeared less frequently, supplanted not only by the name *Polska* (Poland), at the time used in reference to the entire country, but also by such notions as: *rząd* "government" (here in the sense of a political system), *naród*, "nation," *ojczyzna* "homeland," *kraj* "country," and finally *towarzystwo* (here meaning "society"). Apart from the latter word, derived directly from French philosophers, these were not new terms in the Polish political vocabulary – the novelty here lay in their increasingly frequent use and increasingly evident differentiation. Consequently, it was possible to describe the political reality more accurately and separate out issues that had been previously treated as identical (namely the republic and its government), thus describing the crisis of governance more aptly and proposing farther-going programs of reforms. A more moderate use of the concept of the *Rzeczpospolita* had yet another important reason, namely the change of the political language to make it cover the entire society. The term *Rzeczpospolita* was not a good tool for this purpose. Although it could potentially refer to the entire community and the entire state (it played such a role in the statements of some Polish humanists in the sixteenth century), it over time became so closely linked to the noble community that its use almost automatically excluded other inhabitants of the country. In the eighteenth century, that understanding was so deeply entrenched – not only in language but apparently also in the awareness of nobles – that the authors who wanted to include other estates in the national community generally did not polemicize against the exclusive interpretation of *Rzeczpospolita* and simply chose not to use the word in this context.

Only the most preeminent writers wanted to include the other estates into the community denoted by the *Rzeczpospolita*, using that very term: Kołłątaj and Staszic. The former of these two asserted:

> We are everyone, insofar as the Polish land bears us, without any exception, poor and affluent, subjects of the *Rzeczpospolita*. It has the highest power over us, its laws rule over us, its will orders us, its strength defends us, its might tames and punishes us. Through what prejudice can we exclude the most wretched beggar from this highest power?[95]

The latter proposed a very general definition, one already encompassing all of society.[96] However, even they preferred to use different concepts in this respect, mainly "nation." Other authors striving from the 1770s to sketch out a picture of a community that is no longer just a noble community consistently used other terms, such as homeland, nation, and in more theoretical deliberations a new term arose: "society."

Such terminological issues require more in-depth research – for our purposes here, it is important that the late 1780s and early 1790s at least some of the participants of those political debates undertook the task of reforming and reorganizing the political language. An increasingly clear distinction began to be drawn between the *Rzeczpospolita*, as a political community, and the national community, as an object of devotion and care – not always understood in the ethnic sense. Writers and speakers talked less and less about the *Rzeczpospolita*, but increasingly about the homeland, or quite simply about Poland, about its independence, its strength and respect for it shown by other countries. At the same time, however, although this was spoken about in somewhat different words, the state continued to be widely identified with the community of citizens, the only difference being that this was now not necessarily just the noble community. As the concept of the *Rzeczpospolita* had been before, now the concept of homeland was being linked to the ideal of liberty, which guaranteed the existence of a state in which citizens had a share in power, with the difference that the danger to that state was now increasingly espied in external intervention, rather than in despotism on the part of the monarch. Finally, like previously, the state community thus understood was considered to be the highest-ranking value, the sole guarantor of all other goods enjoyed by its participants, including liberty itself. Precisely such an ideal was meant to be made real by the Kościuszko Uprising (1794), although it was meant to be invoked under the notion of homeland, rather than the *Rzeczposoplita*. Ultimately, the concept of the *Rzeczpospolita* lost its significance due to changes not only in the discourse but also in the political reality, together with the fall of the Polish-Lithuanian Commonwealth. The participants of the nineteenth-century uprisings were fighting for their homeland and for freedom, but no longer for the *Rzeczpospolita*.

Notes

1 Bem-Wiśniewska (2007, 15).
2 Bem-Wiśniewska (1998, 170ff., 168); similarly Augustyniak (2004, 53); Olszewski (2002, vol. 1, 7); Pietrzyk-Reeves (2010, 46).
3 Gromelski (2008, 169). The first to note the multiple meanings of the word *Rzeczpospolita* and its fluidity was Stanisław Grodziski (1963, 42ff.); Augustyniak (2004, 52).
4 In addition to the publications cited above, see: Opaliński 1995 (27–38).
5 This has been pointed out in particular by Pietrzyk-Reeves (2012).
6 Opaliński (2001, 193). See also: Backvis (1975, 475, 492).
7 Wisner (1978, 225).
8 Axer (1995, 74; 2010, 51–53), Pietrzyk-Reeves (2012, 190–198).
9 Pietrzyk-Reeves (2012, 200–221 *passim*).
10 Orzechowski, *Dyjalog około egzekucyi* [1563], in Orzechowski (1972, 313).
11 Pietrzyk-Reeves (2012, 46).
12 More on this topic: Maleszyński (1985, 19–46); Herman (1985); Opaliński (1995, 32).
13 Cf. Górska (2005, 138–142 *passim*).
14 "The Commonwealth is a gathering of citizens, bound together by a common law and community of utility, so that it may prevail freely and lastingly in Poland." St. Orzechowski, *Dyjalog około egzekucyi* [1563], in Orzechowski (1972, 314).
15 *Iż na społecznym zjeździe panów rad koronnych w Kaskach*, in Czubek (1906, 244).
16 *Kto zna, co jest R.P. zupełna i cała...* in Czubek (1906, 215).
17 Zamoyski ([1764]/1954, 66).

18 *Głos obywatela dobrze swej ojczyźnie życzącego* (1788, 213). The anonymous author was familiar with Montesquieu's vision of the state and referred to it freely.
19 "Let the Perpetual Commonwealth, represented in its estates, always be prepared to cope with any event," H. Kołłątaj *Listy Anonima* [1788–1789], in Kołłątaj (1954, vol. 1, 273).
20 *Przestroga Rzpltej potrzebna, którą kanclerz on Zamoyski dwiema szlachcicom godnym wiary ukazawszy się niedawno in publicum podać i komu należy odnieść, kazał*, in Czubek (1918, vol. 2, 154).
21 [J. Leszczyński], *Consideratione quibus modis ten domowy ogień uspokoić* [1665], in Ochmann-Staniszewska (1991, 50) – the original is in a mixture of Polish and Latin. Note that the other estates comprising the Sejm mentioned by the author were the king and the Senate, definitely not burghers or peasants.
22 *Rozmowa plebana z ziemianiem* [1641], in Opaliński (1938, p. 47). Here, the author referred to Seneca's *"dum Rempublicam vendunt, etiam vendere."*
23 *List ab anonimo do konfidenta swego pisany die 20 Decembris 1665*, in Ochmann-Staniszewska (1991, 91).
24 J. Leszczyński, *Zdanie o teraźniejszych apartamentach wojennych przeciwko p. Lubomirskiemu*, in Ochmann-Staniszewska (1991, 22).
25 *Rozmowa kruszwicka* [...], in Czubek (1906, 471).
26 According to Henryk Litwin, the king acted as the integrating factor for plebeians: Litwin (2000, 194–195). A different concept was proposed by Andrzej Sulima-Kamiński, who saw the *Rzeczpospolita* as "a civic space" linking not only the nobles but also the citizens of cities (cf. his lecture from a conference organized by the Museum of the History of Poland on 23–24 October 2006, in *Polska na tle Europy XVI–XVII wieku: Materiały pokonferencyjne* (2007, 29–31). Such an analysis is also suggested by: Augustyniak (2007, 23–24).
27 Ohryzko (1859, vol. 1, 89).
28 On the Lithuanians showing a certain restraint in adopting that term and its use in reference to Lithuania itself, cf.: Wisner (2002, 12, 14, 51ff; 2006, 17–28).
29 *Zdanie względem wyboru króla*, in Czubek (1906, 434).
30 The term *Rzeczpospolita* had been used in Lithuanian speeches and writings with reference to the entire Polish-Lithuanian state already since 1571. Cf.: Padalinski (2013, 143–156).
31 Opaliński (1995, 28).
32 *Oświecenie tępych oczu synów koronnych i W. Ks. Litewskiego w ciemnej chmurze rebeliej schizmatyckiej będących* [1653], in Ochmann-Staniszewska (1989, 110). Urszula Augustyniak, using a similar statement, writes that "it starts [...] to sound more as wishful thinking than as a projection of the reality": Augustyniak (2004, 52).
33 That is suggested by Ewa Bem-Wiśniewska's statistical research, which should be nonetheless treated with a certain caution: Bem-Wiśniewska (2007, 25).
34 Cf.: Opaliński (1995, 32ff.); Maleszyński (1985, 23, 24).
35 Olszewski (2002, vol. 1, 10).
36 S. Orzechowski, *Quincunx to jest wzór Korony Polskiej na cynku wystawiony* [1564], in Orzechowski (1972, 574).
37 *Rozsądek o warszawskich sprawach na elekcyjej do koronacyjej należący*, Czubek (1906, 586).
38 [M. Zebrzydowski], *Apologia rokoszu abo sprawa szlachcica polskiego o umowach janowieckich*, in Czubek (1918, vol. 3, 234).

Rzeczpospolita – *The Commonwealth*   37

39 Public letter from Hieronim Jazłowiecki to Stanisław Stadnicki, in Czubek (1918, vol. 2, 170).
40 *Relacyja sejmu 1689 zerwanego*, cited after: Czarniecka (2009, 228).
41 Starowolski (1650, 140).
42 Cf.: Opaliński (1995, 33).
43 J. Chądzyński SJ, *Dyskurs kapłana jednego polskiego/.../* [1657], in Ochmann-Staniszewska (1989, 186).
44 "The Commonwealth has the following powers and rights: firstly, the right and power to enact laws and not to be subject to any laws other than those enacted by the Commonwealth itself [...] fourthly, to elect a king of Roman Catholic religion," *Zasady do formy rządu* [1789], in *Volumina legum* (1889, 158).
45 Cf.: M. Schofield (1999, 63–84).
46 Mager (1991, 239).
47 Mager (1991, 239); Walzer (1989, 214); Pocock (1998, 37); Wells (1995, 100).
48 Grodziski (1963, 43–54). The Renaissance authors placed emphasis on a civic stance understood as subordination to the laws of a specific country; the definition of a citizen as the subject of the monarch was adopted probably only by Aaron Olizarowski, an author who was clearly influenced by Bodin and wrote completely outside the mainstream of the political discussions in the Commonwealth, cf.: Grodziski (1963, 48); Jarra (1968, 197).
49 Wells (1995, 60ff.); Grodziski (1963, 46–49).
50 "Republics, like princes, ruled over subjects who lacked the privileges and positive rights that full citizenship carried," Hörnquist (2000, 112).
51 Aristotle, *Politics*, III, 1.2.
52 *Kto zna, co jest R.P. zupełna i cała...* in Czubek (1906, 216); *Rzecz o mającej nastąpić konwokacyjej*, in Czubek (1906, 216).
53 *Rozmowa Lecha z Piastem*, in Czubek (1906, 44); Ekes (2001, 32).
54 *Jakiego króla Polakom trzeba*, in Czubek (1906, 276).
55 See Chapter 4 for more.
56 Kunicki (1615, fol. C2).
57 "Three estates, that is the king, the senate, and the nobles, form what the Poles call the *Rzeczpospolita*," Nuncio Girolamo Lippomano stated quite rightly, cited after: Kot (1919, 5)
58 Opaliński (1995, 29); Olszewski (2002, vol. 1, 15); Augustyniak (2004, 53).
59 Similar statements were not yet present in the discussions preceding the first free election!
60 Leszczyński ([1737?]/1903, 63).
61 *Naprawa Rzeczypospolitej Koronnej do elekcyjej nowego króla* [1573], in Czubek (1906, 206).
62 *Libera respublica quae sit?*, in Czubek (1918, vol. 2, 403).
63 Leszczyński ([1737?]/1903, 24).
64 *Kto zna, co jest R.P. zupełna i cała...* in Czubek (1906, 214).
65 S. Dunin Karwicki, *Egzorbitancyje we wszystkich trzech stanach Rzeczypospolitej krótko zebrane...*, in Karwicki (1992, 27).
66 *Respons na tenże skrypt*, in Czubek (1906, 463) (a response to the letter: *Krakowski skrypt przeciwko królewicowi francuskiemu*).
67 "A commonwealth was not the antithesis of monarchy, but it was incompatible with tyranny," D. Wotton, *Introduction*, in Wotton (1994, 5).
68 *Gdychżechmy przyszli na ten nieszczęsny wiek...* in Czubek (1906, 158); [P. Pękosławski], *Rytwiański 1607*, Czubek (1918, vol. 2, 161).
69 *Libera respublica quae sit?*, in Czubek (1918, vol. 2, 403).
70 *Naprawa Rzeczypospolitej* [1573], in Czubek (1918, vol. 2, 190).

38   Rzeczpospolita – *The Commonwealth*

71 *Libera respublica quae sit?*, in Czubek (1918, vol. 2, 407)
72 Koranyi (1967, 206–214); C. Backvis, *Jak XVI-wieczni Polacy widzieli Włochy i Włochów*, in Backvis (1975, 515), Grześkowiak-Krwawicz (2007, 67–77).
73 *Wolność polska dla ewakuacyi wojsk egzotycznych, życzy się brać ad arma defensionis* (1733, fol. 340).
74 S. Dunin Karwicki, *Egzorbitancyje...*, in Karwicki (1992, 24).
75 More on this issue: Grześkowiak-Krwawicz (1994, 167–183).
76 The term appears in pamphlets from Zebrzydowski's *rokosz* (1606): "in the free states there was always an asylum of liberty...," *Skrypt o słuszności zjazdu stężyckiego*, in Czubek (1918, vol. 2, 257).
77 Grześkowiak-Krwawicz (1994–1995, 85).
78 Viroli (1995, 19).
79 A. M. Fredro, *Praerogativa popularis status repraesentatur Monarchiam saepius nisi regnanti bonam*, 1668, in Fredro (1668/2015, 724).
80 The issue is discussed more broadly in Chapter 3.
81 [Konarski?] ([1764]: 5).
82 *Libera respublica quae sit?*, in Czubek (1918, vol. 2, 403)
83 Konarski (1760–1763, vol. 2, 166); cf.: Rostworowski (1976, 95ff.); Michalski (1983, 329).
84 H. Kołłątaj (1790, 20).
85 S. Orzechowski, *Mowa do szlachty polskiej* (*Oratio ad equites Polonos*) [1551], trans. J. Starnawski, in Orzechowski (1972, 99); Wolan (1572/1606/2010, 137ff.).
86 *Ślachcica polskiego do rycerskiego koła... o obieraniu króla przemowa*, in Czubek (1906, 278).
87 [Pęski] (1727, 122).
88 *Respons Rzeczypospolitej Polskiej na uniwersał i manifest książęcia Imci Franciszka Ludwika de Borbon de Conti,* [1697].
89 "[S]o that the foundations of the *Rzeczpospoita* be not ruined or disturbed in any way, by the stain of which the whole construct would have to collapse and be destroy'd, thus turning freedom to captivity," *Iż na społecznym zjeździe...*, in Czubek (1906, 245).
90 "[W]hen our Commonwealth and our homeland perishes without council and without Sejms, where will this freedom be?," Konarski (1760–1763, vol. 2, 152).
91 Pietrzyk-Reeves (2012, 34–42, 200–221).
92 *Żałosna mowa Rzpltej polskiej pod Koprzywnicą do zgromadzonego rycerstwa roku 1606*, in Czubek (1918, vol. 2, 97).
93 Kołłątaj (1790, 47).
94 [Łobarzewski] (1789b: 27).
95 H. Kołłątaj *Listy Anonima* [1788–1789], in Kołłątaj (1954, vol. 1, 278).
96 "Where no man has more power and personal will, only as much as the law permits and all owners, without exception, participate in enacting laws, where everyone is only subject to everyone and where only the general might and will – that is, the nation – sets forth the laws for itself. [...] I call this [one] society the *Rzeczpospolita*." Staszic (1787/1926, 49ff.).

2   *Prawo* – The Law

This chapter should start with an important stipulation or reminder: it is not concerned with early Polish legal theories,[1] but rather with the place of law in the political discourse of the Polish-Lithuanian Commonwealth. The two topics may lie close to one another, but they are not interchangeable. In the case of the former, the fundamental issues revolve around definitions and divisions of law, questions about its sources, scope, attempts to organize it and so on.[2] These concepts have been pored over in political reflections, but infrequently, only at certain periods and, generally speaking, only in far-reaching texts with strong theoretical foundations.[3] More importantly, they were not the authors' main concerns and they did not serve as the starting point for further discourse. Of far greater importance was the place awarded to the law in the political universe – the role assigned to it and how it shaped the lives of individuals and communities – and this is the subject of the analysis presented here.

Law is an incredibly important concept in political discourse, not just in the Polish-Lithuanian Commonwealth but across all modern Europe, following in the footsteps of ancient philosophers.[4] It was an important subject of investigation and dispute, as well as being a major element of discussions about the state, society, the relationships between individuals and communities and among individuals comprising each community. Oftentimes it was even the fundamental element. Scholars note that the political discourse that emerged in Western Europe, both during the Middle Ages and the Renaissance, clearly shows a trend in which law is the key element systematizing the political world and serving as the starting point and foundation for contemplations on society and the individual's place within it.[5] This has even encouraged some scholars to argue that it is possible to describe the language of that discourse as jurisprudence language, clearly distinct from that known as republican language.[6] Although this distinction, perhaps too radical, has stirred some controversy,[7] the fact remains that such a position did indeed characterize statements by many sixteenth- and seventeenth-century European authors; moreover, in the seventeenth and eighteenth centuries it contributed to shaping modern discourse about the state as a community of individuals endowed with same natural rights, and therefore the same civil rights, being subordinated to the same government that originated in a certain contract.[8]

The first thing that becomes conspicuous when one analyzes the concept of law in the discourse of the Polish-Lithuanian Commonwealth is the near absence of jurisprudence language and the clear "politicizing" of the question. Polish legal discourse is clearly distinctive in this respect.[9] Even authors who wrote extensively about law as early as in the sixteenth century, such as Andrzej Frycz Modrzewski and Wawrzyniec Goślicki, included it in more far-reaching arguments concerning the system of government rather than using it as the foundation of their ideas. A total subordination of political vision to legal discourse did not happen until the second half of the eighteenth century, when Hieronim Stroynowski wrote his *Nauka prawa przyrodzonego, politycznego, ekonomiki politycznej i prawa narodów* [The study of natural law, political law, political economics and the law of nations] (1785). He was clearly heavily influenced by Western European concepts, mainly those rooted in physiocracy,[10] in his descriptions of the political world written in almost exclusively legal categories. However, he was very much the exception; in any case he was suggesting a brand-new discourse, rejecting many existing concepts.

Although almost no participants in political debate of the Polish-Lithuanian Commonwealth treated law as the foundation and starting point of their vision of the state, the concept remains one of the most important in political discourse in the sixteenth, seventeenth and eighteenth centuries. It could even be said that it is key to understanding the discourse of the time.[11] While certain elements of the vision of law, its interpretation and the role assigned to it turned out to be enduring, the meaning imparted on the concept and the ways of perceiving the functions and goals of law evolved significantly over the two centuries of the existence of the Polish-Lithuanian Commonwealth. They are all the more interesting since they serve as the signal and illustration of the changes which took place in political discourse, and, even more broadly, in the vision of the state and society contained within it, especially during the eighteenth century.

Lex anima respublica

Not only was law ever-present in discourse, it also had a highly significant impact on the political world that discourse helped to shape. Contemporary readers are commonly struck by the universal role that was assigned to the law. Occasionally it was presented as a way of imposing a universal order and drawing a clear distinction between humans and animals: "If laws shall not have their weight, and everyone acts as driven by their desire, then not only shall the *Rzeczpospolita* perish, but there shall be no distinction between human beings and beasts," wrote the anonymous author of *Philopolites, to jest miłośnik ojczyzny* [Philopolites, or Lover of the Homeland].[12] Wolan was of a similar opinion.[13] They both followed classical thought, as the author of *Philopolites* makes clear by referencing Demosthenes. However, such framing is more typical of general statements or those with a more extensive theoretical foundation, and even then it is rare. This is because the role of the law was examined mainly in the context of the fabric of political unity, understood as a state in general, or the *Rzeczpospolita* in specific. It was a hugely powerful, one could say all-embracing, role, which is mainly present in texts from the early part of the period under investigation. In writings from the turn of the seventeenth century, the law creates, animates, infiltrates and unites entire political and social structures.[14] This was in accordance with traditions originating in the antiquity which had a strong impact on how law and its role were perceived in Polish writing of the Renaissance – that is during the time which shaped the political discourse of the *Rzeczpospolita*. This tradition regarded law, inseparably linked with justice, as an element uniting people into a political community.[15] The belief that "laws themselves exist, which seem to join the many people into a single body,"[16] can perhaps be regarded as popular in sixteenth-century statements, although by the seventeenth century the view was less widespread (though not entirely abandoned), since theoretical contemplation was generally less common.[17] It is notable that the general conviction was at times applied to the authors' own *Rzeczpospolita*; they were no longer writing theoretically about the unifying power of law in general but about the equivalent function of their very own laws:

> [...] our ancestors [during the rule of King Jagiełło in the early fifteenth century], seeing that their Crown was being joined by various nations, Lithuanians, Germans or Prussians, Wallachians and many others, made certain that all were under a single law [...] thus they ensured that their ruling kings, namely Władysław Jagiełło, would swear to them the right and privilege that all shall live under a single law and a single freedom.[18]

It is worth noting that this author did not mind certain provinces having distinct privileges, and when it came to Lithuania, even an entire distinct legal system – he perceived the issue on a different level.

This role of law in relation to just the Polish Crown is described particularly beautifully and imaginatively by Stanisław Orzechowski in his *Policya*:

> the populace [here meaning the nobles], the council, the king [...] these people have become a single crown body, by laws and privileges

as though internal veins somehow joined, brought together and unified towards not just a single life, but also a good life.[19]

This vivid image, invoking the organicist concept of the state, describes
law as a factor unifying the political community, yet the author's comparison suggests that it went even further. Not only did it unify and
create the community, but it also gave it life and permeated all aspects of its existence and function. The great significance assigned to
law was symbolized by comparing it metaphorically to the spirit of the
Rzeczpospolita, borrowed from classical authors.[20] In this vision, a
commonwealth without law is presented as a dead body: "to be *abse-
que legibus*, the *Rzeczpospolita* is as though a body without soul, as
Plato and Aristotle state in their *de Legibus* and *de Republica* volumes,"
writes Stanisław Sarnicki in the preface to his *Statut*.[21] The anonymous
author of *Philopolites* described it even more succinctly: "Just as a body,
having forfeited its soul, is obscene, wicked and useless, so too each
Commonwealth not rooted in law standeth waste, having lost its soul
whose power and strength gave it growth and life."[22] The metaphor of
Demosthenes was enormously popular in the sixteenth- and seventeenth-
century *Rzeczpospolita*; it was referenced in serious political treatises
and legal considerations, in political publications, and even – as noted
by Anna Sucheni-Grabowska – in parliamentary speeches, therefore in
the letter of the law.[23] Memory of it lasted until the eighteenth century,
although no longer with strong awareness of its roots in antiquity and
perhaps without a deep understanding of its profound significance.

Participants in political discussions of the sixteenth and early seventeenth centuries saw law as permeating the entire fabric of the body
politic.[24] This is particularly clear when one analyzes political treatises
which feature many references to the law and discuss a wide range of
aspects of the life of a community. However, its role is described most
fully not by a theorist but a participant in a political struggle during the
first interregnum:

> Because everything in the *Rzeczpospolita's* health, respectability,
> renown, pride, royal office, majesty, dignity, peace, liberty, abun-
> dance of all things, security and defense lies in the common law,
> because the law punishes wrongdoing and transgressions, protects
> virtues and innocence, prevents treachery and guile, enforces hon-
> esty with discipline, levels enmities with harmony, aids and recon-
> ciles war, brings peace and defends the liberty of each estate of the
> *Rzeczpospolita*, whichever Lord then abides by these laws, so abides
> by virtue, abides by honesty, abides by justice, abides by everyone's
> freedom, and thereby preserves the *Rzeczpospolita* in its entirety,
> and thereby gains eternal renown.[25]

This anonymous supporter of a Polish-born candidate to become king seems to have captured all the most important functions of law. It created a structure for the system, shaped social order and relationships between individuals, and, in the government-citizen structure, guaranteed liberty and peace, security and wellbeing, shaped attitudes and even personalities of individuals comprising society, and served as a signpost for behavior, indicating good and evil actions. This is also revealed by other descriptions of the role of the law, sometimes drawn from foreign authors, although none are as detailed as the one quoted above.[26]

It can be said that the belief in the far-reaching influence of the law on the lives of individuals and the shape of the political community was widespread in the sixteenth and early seventeenth centuries. This raises the question of to what degree it manifested itself in writings of the second half of the seventeenth and the eighteenth centuries. It certainly did not disappear entirely, and discourse influenced by classical traditions remained faithful to it. As mentioned above, law continued to be occasionally described as the spirit of the *Rzeczpospolita*, using the same classical definitions of its role as during the Renaissance. However, the question was generally marginal and no longer served as an axis or starting point for legal discourse. While during Zebrzydowski's rebellion (1606–1608) political commentaries included extensive references to the all-embracing role of the law, in later years they were few and far between, even in the most comprehensive texts aiming to describe the whole political reality of the *Rzeczpospolita*. This does not reflect a rejection of the concept, however, so much as the low level of political reflection, both in long texts as well as in short publications. Fewer theoretical treatises were written at this time, and even the most interesting ones were generally mainly concerned with the realities of the *Rzeczpospolita*, with the exception of certain publications by Łukasz Opaliński and Andrzej Maksymilian Fredro. As such, references to the law far more frequently concerned the specific aspects of its influence on the functioning of the Commonwealth, rather than the idea as such. The vision of the law as a factor shaping the entirety of social and political life made a triumphant return to Polish discourse with adapted ideas of the Enlightenment. Law became one of the main subjects of interest for scholars of statehood of the time, as well as for their crowned pupils. It is with good reason that the eighteenth century in Europe was known as the Age of Rights.[27] New categories of law and new theories were becoming commonplace, while the idea of human rights, deriving from natural law, was gaining popularity. Most importantly, however, while in many ways these concepts were becoming distant from classical traditions, they continued to ascribe a powerful role to the law. They led Polish discourse to once again focus on a vision of law permeating the entire social fabric, initially in statements by authors who were under very heavy influence of Western concepts, such as Wincenty Skrzetuski, who borrowed a chapter of his book entitled *O zachowaniu praw* [On Preserving Laws] partially from Rousseau's *Discourse on Political Economy*. He wrote:

> Laws must not be violated, so that this chain binding private matters with common happiness, so that the order according to which citizens should embrace social virtues be not muddled; simply so as not to divide the political system which aims to disseminate among society members humankind's virtues, charity, justice, reconcile assistance they have a right to expect of society, allow them to achieve the benefits offered to them by this society.[28]

The sentence, evidently influenced by Rousseau, fits in perfectly with a traditional outlook on law. The author was clearly aware of this, combining it into a single mental thread with Cicero: "Laws are established such that they offer protection to all republics and citizens, to bring equally peaceful, safe and happy lives to all."[29] Skrzetuski's treatise is interesting because it shows that although in certain aspects it is rather distant from classical discourse – such as its use of different notions and its turning partial attention to different functions of law – it retains the belief that the law is one of the foundations of the wellbeing of human society. At the same time, the universe in which law exists is not only limited to the material world but also extends to spiritual and moral aspects in shaping attitudes of individuals living in society. This was also in accordance with classical thought, although in this instance it seems filtered through a contemporary philosophy of statehood. It is also interesting in that it reveals a certain choice of discourse. Although Western scholars of statehood were in agreement when it came to the law's leading role in society, many of them (all those representing the liberal trend and the physiocrats) distanced themselves from its influence on the sphere of morality or social attitudes, which would have carried with it a different vision of the political world and also require a change in political language. A more universal vision of the law as a factor shaping social relationships and attitudes of individuals within society was retained by authors belonging to a trend at times described as republican – including Mably and Rousseau, and to some extent Montesquieu. The latter were the most popular authors in Poland, and they exerted the greatest impact on Poland's political thought of the late eighteenth century and on how statehood was described in Poland. Their influence was greater even than that of the popular physiocrats. This is why Skrzetuski (and other authors) retain the law's instructive or, more broadly, ethical aspect as an element of its role in society. Karol Wyrwicz wrote: "The prosperity, happiness and integrity of all nations bonded by ties of social community depend on laws which are wise, clear, and precisely distinguish justice from injustice, righteousness from wrongdoing, virtue from offence."[30] We will return to this in a moment; here we focus on the wealth of roles ascribed to the law by authors of major treatises of the 1780s and 1790s. In the writings of Józef Wybicki, Hugo Kołłątaj, Stanisław Staszic, Hieronim Stroynowski and Konstanty Bogusławski, the law embraced and shaped all aspects of a society's life. These authors had different views on the concept of the state, in Stroynowski's case going as far as using a distinct political language; what linked them, however, was that their works describe the role of the law the most extensively. This is particularly pertinent when it comes to Wybicki, Stroynowski and Kołłątaj, for whom the law was an element bringing order to the entire social sphere. It is another matter that Wybicki was closer to Rousseau in how he focused on the instructive role of law, Kołłątaj's more independent and eclectic approach was not especially interested in it, while Stroynowski followed the ideas of physiocracy in ignoring it entirely. The fact remains, however, that they all saw the law as the spirit of the "body politic," although only Wybicki continued using this old metaphor.[31]

In a sense, ascribing to the law such a major and far-reaching influence on social life became one of the distinguishing points of discourse of reformers of the Enlightenment. In writings by supporters of the old order – even those familiar with the latest theories of the state – such an image of the law was almost entirely absent; it may be telling to compare the two treatises by Michał Wielhorski and Wybicki, published around the same time. While the former defines the function of the law as very specific, limited to the "former rights" protecting the structure of the *Rzeczpospolita*, for the latter the law is permanently present on the level of a general theory of society and individual considerations of Poland by playing a range of functions and making sense of the world. The discourse of the reformers also included a new element that was absent in previous eras: the law imposed an order upon the world, but it could also alter and shape this order. This was more than just a new component of discourse; it was an element of the era's belief in the ability and need to rationally regulate all aspects of social life. The view was not expressed most widely in general discourse, but rather in discussion of events in Poland in the wake of the Constitution of 3 May 1791. According to statements by its supporters, the Constitution (the *Governing Act*) would become an all-encompassing law which would change everything (for the better, naturally).[32] As the Marshals of the Sejm declared after 3 May: "Our homeland is now saved, our liberties protected, henceforth we are a free and independent nation."[33]

The *Governing Act* was, according to its supporters (and perhaps also its opponents), a law that altered the entire political universe of the *Rzeczpospolita*. More than anything, it changed (or, according to its supporters, improved) the political system, and that was how its role was described. It can be said that the image of the Constitution, which emerged as it was being debated, superimposed two different functions ascribed to the law by Polish discourse: one new, one traditional. Faith in the power of the law as a factor changing reality was a reflection of a new, Enlightenment-based vision of the political world, while a belief that laws are what formed the *Rzeczpospolita's* very governmental foundations and guaranteed its endurance dated back a long way. The phrase "governmental foundations" is something of an anachronism here, since laws shaped and protected the *Rzeczpospolita* per se, understood here as a specific political construct. They determined the specificity, distinctiveness and, of course, excellence of that construct. As early as 1573, the anonymous author of *Naprawa Rzeczypospolitej* [Repairing the Republic] wrote more generally: "*leges* serve republics one way, and serve *regnis* another."[34] This sixteenth-century author's view on the divergence of laws governing commonwealths and monarchies was later repeated by Andrzej Zamoyski in 1764: "The laws maintaining the *Rzeczpospolita* are the bane of the monarchic government, those maintaining monarchy are the bane of liberty," although in his instance this was a reference to tradition as well as to Montesquieu's writings.[35] Even when their views on the surrounding political realities or even on systems of government differed, all those who took part in political debates between the sixteenth and eighteenth centuries held a deep belief that "laws are the prescriptions of government in a nation."[36] The quote originates from the eighteenth century and it is already taking on a format typical of the Enlightenment, yet the vision of the law shaping and maintaining the *Rzeczpospolita's* construction had not changed. As "Senator anonym" wrote in ca. 1570:

> We all know this and in our law and our privileges we see that preserving our *Rzeczpospolita* in its entirety according to the determined and described order depends on none other than the king our lord, and on royal councils.[37]

A few decades later, the author of perhaps the most famous text of Zebrzydowski's rebellion, *Libera respublica*, wrote: "Common law remains as *dignitatem* for HRH, as *gravitatem* for the senate, and as *summam potestatem* for the noble and chivalrous classes."[38] These are just two examples from a vast volume of similar statements. It is notable that while the authors presented very different visions of the surrounding political realities, they were united in regarding the role of the law as that which gives shape to political form. In any case, that role was more complex than it might seem from the above quotes, which mainly refer to the scope of authority of the individual elements comprising the mixed government of the *Rzeczpospolita*. The tasks assigned to the law were not limited to describing how the state should be organized or the rights and responsibilities of its individual components. Until at least the mid-eighteenth century, participants in political discussions saw the intricate network supporting the delicate structural system of the *Rzeczpospolita* as being formed by laws themselves, concerning very different aspects of the functioning of the political community, from fundamental to very detailed in scope. They gave the republic its shape, defined the rights and responsibilities for the estates that comprised it, outlined their operation, protected them against abuse of power and provided guidelines of conduct.

In writings on current affairs, a certain shift started to become evident during the seventeenth century and became prominent in the eighteenth, although it never came to fully dominate the discourse. During the sixteenth century, the law or laws had been discussed in general terms, as providing the foundations of the *Rzeczpospolita*, less frequently enumerating specific solutions.[39] This was an element of a broader vision of the law as the spirit of the *Rzeczpospolita*. Over time, authors started devoting less attention to the general idea of the law as the foundation of mixed government and more to the specific laws that created this construction. Depending on the author's views and the current political needs, different statutes and privileges were described as "the *Rzeczpospolita's* most fundamental law on which all liberty *et formam regiminis nostri* is supported."[40] Over time, this resulted in a canon of fundamental or cardinal laws. To begin with, one of the most important was the *nihil novi* privilege, gradually replaced by free elections in the seventeenth century and later joined by the concept of *liberum veto*. According to one of the participants in the Great Sejm: "As cardinal laws, nothing can be understood in republics other than the laws that ground the entire government." Interestingly, he believed that "in monarchic states they protect civic life and property,"[41] thus bringing them down a level. On the surface the statement was very similar to general reflections on the system-shaping role of law; however, in contrast to them it had a very real goal: to argue that the changes proposed to the sphere of government in 1790 by the *Deputation to the Form of Government* are dangerous and unlawful. This is a clear demonstration of the shift in the political discourse since the sixteenth century. Eighteenth-century discussions on cardinal laws were less concerned about their role in shaping the *Rzeczpospolita* than about the danger it would face if they were to be infringed.[42]

This leads us to the next issue, which can be described as a defense of the old, good laws. The *Rzeczpospolita's* system of government was quickly proclaimed as an ideal: "The *Rzeczpospolita* is *ab origine* so endowed with all laws that whatever all republics the world over can have that is perfect in their laws *et in statutis suis*, still our *Rzeczpospolita totum comprehendit omni ex parte meliori*."[43] However, it was also perceived as very fragile, only enduring because it was supported by a complex network of laws covering myriad aspects of political life. In this instance, the role of laws was rather passive – they were not intended to moderate the system but to protect the balance they themselves created; in a sense they did not have to work, but they simply had to exist, to remain intact.[44] This was not simply conservatism combined with an apotheosis of the status quo; it was a deeper vision of the law as the only protection of the *Rzeczpospolita's* shape: in 1587, an anonymous author quoted Mikołaj Taszycki's preface to his *Statutes*: "The status of the *Rzeczpospolita*, which depends on a healthy understanding and correct preservation of the rights."[45] Since the entire edifice of the *Rzeczpospolita* rested upon law, the infringement of any – even seemingly trivial – law was seen as dangerous. Even the smallest brick could turn out to be a cornerstone; an element whose removal could lead to the collapse of the whole structure, or at least could shake its foundations. This context makes it easier to understand why one of the most important, perhaps even the gravest, political accusations of the time would have been that of breaking the law. This charge was frequently leveled against monarchs, especially during serious conflicts. "But which law did the king break?" asked an anonymous rebel in 1606, and immediately provided an acerbic reply: "Let him show me one he did not! Since of those that could be broken, none have been left whole."[46] From Zebrzydowski's rebellion until the Bar Confederation (1768), monarchs were accused of ruling "following no laws"[47] and of abandoning "ancient laws entirely."[48] At times this meant infringements of the privileges of the nobility, but most frequently it concerned breaking the laws of the *Rzeczpospolita*, although generally speaking almost all decisions taken by monarchs could be interpreted this way. And not just monarchs: having infringed or broken the law was not just a serious accusation, but also a very popular one, waged at all political opponents. By the late eighteenth century, it became something of a "trademark" of conservative supporters of the old order, but it had a long history of having been used by individuals regardless of political views or ties. An infringement of a minor law was sufficient; the mere fact was enough because it caused a "jumble" (*mieszanina*) that was seen as a threat to the *Rzeczpospolita*.

Because the structure of the *Rzeczpospolita* was based on laws, infringement or neglect of them was seen as one of the main reasons for any failures of its political system. As a result, the remedy would be the reinstatement of the law. The good old laws were recalled as early as during discussions preceding the first free election, and even earlier still; the slogans of the executionist movement of the mid-sixteenth century were based on this very idea,[49] although their reinstatement was not seen as the only option. It is notable that during the period when the nobility was working to devise a new shape for their state, this was also reflected in the discourse. Without a doubt theorists such as Modrzewski, Wolan and later Warszewicki and Górnicki[50] were the boldest in their support for amending the law, but even public discussions during the first interregnum had resounded with voices arguing that laws are not immortal and can be adjusted as required.[51] This was not the overwhelming opinion, but even in case of laws passed down by political ancestors, their "reform" or even the need to "repair and discard that which is bad"[52] were frequently mentioned. This soon changed. There is a very clear shift from publications during Zebrzydowski's rebellion, whose main theme was the reinstatement of the old laws, allegedly broken by the king. Throughout the seventeenth century and a major part of the eighteenth century, no proposals to amend the law were made. Even supporters of certain reforms aiming to improve at least some of the gradually failing political system of the *Rzeczpospolita* only mentioned the reinstatement of laws set down by former generations that had gotten forgotten or distorted. This also includes the most eminent authors of the first half of the eighteenth century, including Stanisław Karwicki and Stanisław Leszczyński, whose proposals also were the most extensive. It was only in the wake of speeches by Konarski and later Wybicki that the belief that the law needed to be adapted and created, as well as protected, returned to the Polish discourse. This was undoubtedly a new element of political discussions and it signaled a change that finally came true during the Great Sejm, which featured two approaches to the issue: one conservative, focusing on the protection of old laws, and one more active, allowing or even calling for certain changes. What they had in common is that they were rooted in the traditional belief that it is the laws that create the *Rzeczpospolita*.

Non rex sed lex

The vision of the law as a factor regulating the entire life in the Commonwealth and its components only made sense if one started with the assumption that, to paraphrase Pausanias, "laws place order on people, not people on laws"[53] – or, in other words, that the law rules supreme. The nobility universally accepted this in their discourse in accordance with classical thought, which in any case was invoked following certain concepts inherited from the Middle Ages.[54] Theorists and participants in political debates agreed with Modrzewski's opinion that "Not by royal will, but by written laws the *Rzeczpospolita* must be ruled."[55] In any case, Modrzewski was by no means the first to say this; earlier writers had stressed the function of the law as the highest principle ruling the state, going as far as giving it the ultimate status of "ruling the king and the nation."[56] For the majority of writers, this was more than just a theoretical ideal: it was a belief that this, truly, was the role of the law in their own *Rzeczpospolita*. Scholars have long been pointing out that since the sixteenth century, the Commonwealth had been perceived by the nobility as a state in which the law rules supreme, and, *de facto*, the law is the sovereign, rather than the king.[57] The discourse was in this case influenced as much by the tradition of talking about the state and perceiving the role of the law in it, as by the political reality of the time of the last monarchs from the Jagiellonian dynasty and the first elected kings. It is notable that it was then, during the second half of the sixteenth and the early seventeenth century, that the topic was the most widely discussed. Furthermore, statements of this kind were not limited to theoretical considerations but featured to an even greater degree in political discussions, in particular during the first interregnum. The sovereignty of the law was not seen as an academic question but as an important foundation for developing new governmental models benefitting the noble class. Remarkably, statements about the authority of the law rarely take a general form that refers to its overriding role in society; it is far more common for them to appear in the context of defining the scope of the monarch's rule, or, more precisely, how the law applies to the monarch. In the mid-seventeenth century, Łukasz Opaliński wrote about "free states, where the gravity of the majesty is either equal or lesser *cum authoritate legum*."[58] However, it was a far older vision and in general it only acknowledged the second option of placing the law above the king. The principle "*nec principem supra leges, sed leges supra principem*,"[59] popular as early as the first half of the sixteenth century, became one of the most important political maxims during discussions preceding the first free election. It should be noted that participants in political discussions chose one of two possible interpretations of the principle of the sovereignty of the law. As noted by Anna Sucheni-Grabowska, and more recently Karin Friedrich, the monarch's being a subject of laws did not have to be interpreted as a limitation on his power; indeed, it could serve to legitimize and guarantee it,[60] in particular as the blurring of the boundary between the law and the ruler, who after Cicero was seen as "the speaking law." That was how the question was described by many Western theorists, and the interpretation was also occasionally found in Jagiellonian Poland. This take can be found in theoretical treatises[61] and (more rarely) in political publications. An interesting example of such thought is a paper by an anonymous participant in pre-election discussions. In his starting point he refers to Aristotle, assuming the overarching rule of the law in society, which leads him to the conclusion that since the king's power originates from the law, it follows that obedience to the monarch is equivalent to obedience to the law: "'Tis not man who thus commandeth us, but the law; 'tis not man we obey, but the law."[62] However, this was a rather unusual interpretation.[63] Perhaps the last author to invoke it, clearly for the benefit of readers abroad, was Łukasz Opaliński, explaining in his *Polonia defensa contra Ioannem Barclaium* (1648) that "Laws which simply disallow sin do not detract from the monarch's power, but, on the contrary, increase and define it."[64] However, in Polish discourse the aim of the principle *non rex supra leges*, *sed leges supra regem* was not so much to support the monarch's rule as rather to stress that it is not limitless; that there is a higher power – the law – whose rules must be adhered to by all members of society, the king included. Statements from the early days of the Commonwealth were strongly supportive of this communal submission to the law: "The king under the same law as us,"[65] "The law commands the king as it does the king's subject,"[66] "The lord just as his subjects must avail himself of the law and liberty."[67] This is just a selection of typical excerpts from texts written during the period when the Commonwealth's governmental structure was being shaped. One could get the impression that at the time it was of utmost importance that the monarch was not above the law and that he was bound by it as much as his subjects: "A tyrant wishes to be bound by no laws, whereas the king's power and royal majesty are measured and limited by the law."[68] Of no lesser importance was the fact that the king was perceived as the guardian of the law, but his will could not be its only source. Neither theorists nor (especially) participants in political discussions accepted the principle *princeps legibus solutus est.*[69] If it does feature in their writings, it is only in the context of despotic or tyrannical power.[70] Lew Sapieha wrote in the foreword to the Third Statute of Lithuania: "Since anyone [...] according to their whim rather than our laws would torment us, he would no longer be our lord but a destroyer of our laws and liberties, and we would have to be his slaves." He proudly explained on behalf of Lithuanian citizens: "'Tis our freedom of which we boast to other Christian nations, that we have no monarch above us who would rule according to his will rather than our laws [...]."[71] In this respect, the Crown nobles were in full agreement with the Lithuanian nobility. An accusation that kings desired "that their rule should no longer be subject to written laws, but that they themselves should remain above the law"[72] was the most serious charge which could be leveled against monarchs of the *Rzeczpospolita*. It was a charge the royalists hotly denied, while not denying the actual principle. Justinian's *Digest* was depicted as a significant part of legal education in Europe,[73] but when it came to the principle of *quod principi placuit legis habet vigorem*, this lesson was not learned by the participants in noble political discourse, so much so that it could be said that they deliberately avoided being taught.[74] It seems that in view of those involved in the debates of the time, in order for the law to be accepted as such, rather than as iniquity and usurpation, it could not be simply an emanation of the monarch's will, since it was an institution external both to him and to the entire society.[75]

It may have been external, but it was not abstract. Although Polish political discourse, at least on the theoretical level, adopted the concept of natural law relatively early[76] – and although no one had any doubt that monarchs and subjects alike were bound by divine law – the issue of the monarch being subject to the law was examined almost exclusively in terms of the "common" law, in other words both the customary norms and enacted norms in place in the *Rzeczpospolita*, which set not the theoretical but practical foundations and conditions of his rule.[77] It is significant that election-related writings in 1573 frequently featured the phrase that the king "arrives to find ready laws."[78] In a sense, it could be said that the authority of the law was also rooted in the fact that its rule predated the rule of any individual monarch. It was also significant that – as mentioned above – laws create the system into which a new king would fit, therefore their rules were in equal measures a limitation and a guarantee of his power. The latter was reminded to Sigismund III by rebels, stating "His Royal Highness the King, being unwilling to rule us in accordance with the law, rapidly absolves himself from ruling."[79]

However, discussions of laws the king was to be bound by, held ahead of the first free election, featured another element which over time came to dominate the discourse, leading to a clear shift in attitudes. Many statements discuss in general terms how the king is subject to the Commonwealth's or the "old" laws, but they also frequently added the caveat that they are laws defined by "us": "The king arrives to find ready laws, but it is we who impose rights and laws upon ourselves."[80] Over time, the emphasis shifted from affirming that the king is subject to laws to a conviction that the law is "established and corrected by us."[81] This marked a clear change in the discourse. It could be said that since the rule of law was universally accepted, it was no longer the subject of discussions; however, there was a widespread need to emphasize the authority of "the Commonwealth" understood as its noble citizens. There was no question whether the monarch and the citizens were subject to the law, with the proviso that the law was to be created by the citizens. According to an author writing in the late eighteenth century, "The will of society is expressed through laws."[82] In his instance it was a clear reference to Rousseau, but this was also a far earlier belief that the law is an emanation of the will of the nobility, re-expressed in words of an Enlightenment-era philosopher. Rather than being a departure from the idea of the sovereignty of the law, it served to clarify where the law originated from.

The shift of the focus from a widely understood authority of the law to the rule of law established by the noble "nation" was accompanied by another change. While in the early years of the Polish-Lithuanian Commonwealth the authority of the law was brought to the fore, over time attention gradually shifted to its effects, and, more specifically, to limiting the monarch's power. It was not a radical change and some of the elements of this view on the role played by the law were included in the concept of their sovereignty. Since kings "must not do anything against laws,"[83] it was obvious that laws constituted a limitation of their power, or perhaps served as a boundary they were not permitted to cross. Andrzej Wolan wrote about monarchs from the Jagiellonian dynasty: "Because before they are entrusted with the *Rzeczpospolita*, the very coronation oath binds them to do nothing against the law."[84] Lew Sapieha spoke for Lithuanians in his address to Sigismund III: "So that we create laws as the finest guardians of common liberty, and do not permit greater rule from the monarch, so that laws impose a certain boundary on his rule over us."[85] The limitation was in part because monarchs, just like their subjects, had to submit to the rule of law and laws were the only principles guiding their actions. This was what Orzechowski meant when he wrote: "The Polish eagle sits in shackles."[86] Over time, the "shackles" started to be understood more literally, as specific limitations on the king's power. This is perhaps best expressed by Franciszek Radzewski, writing about ancestors who had "spent so long writing laws for their kings that they removed all their royal power."[87] In this context, the role of the law gradually shifted from that of the overall sovereign, to a guardian of monarchs and a warden of the liberties of their subjects. It is difficult to say exactly when the change occurred, and in any case it was never complete; however, in the eighteenth century monarchs were mentioned far more frequently in the context of this function of the law: "as we have ascribed our kings with the law, so we have accommodated them to liberty."[88] It was as much a change in the function of the law as in the perception of the role and place of the king in the Commonwealth. This interpretation turned out to be enduring and it was still in use at the end of the eighteenth century during the Great Sejm as an argument to allay the concerns of opponents of inherited succession, saying that "a hereditary crown ascribed by cardinal laws cannot be damaging to freedom."[89] On the other hand, these kinds of arguments resulted in the questioning of the role or strength of the law against royal despotism, which was rather unusual in Polish discourse. Wojciech Turski warned, rightly: "My readers would do well to remember that forbidding oppression by law is not the same as preventing oppression."[90] Similar views had been expressed previously, yet the faith in the power and authority of the law was enduring.

All the more so because by the late eighteenth century the theme of "autocracy" of laws[91] made a return to discourse. And it is no wonder, since the concept of the supremacy of law played an important role in theories of statehood of the Enlightenment. It fit perfectly into Polish traditions and it quickly became a part of Polish discourse. The supremacy of laws in a range of contexts was written about by authors influenced by Western theories, including Wybicki, Stroynowski and later Staszic and Kołłątaj. All voices on the subject were conscious of their own tradition of the concept, but they were filtered through political theories of their contemporaries, the physiocrats, Montesquieu and especially Rousseau. The latter was referenced by Adam Wawrzyniec Rzewuski: "In free nations it is law alone that has power and it does not share it."[92] A few of the authors extend the concept combining the tradition of the sovereignty of the law with the modern concept of the rule of law to the whole society; having written that the *Rzeczpospolita's* laws "rule over us," Kołłątaj stressed that this rule encompassed everyone.[93]

Servi legum sumus...

This assertion incorporated something new, stepping beyond the previous narrow understanding of the Commonwealth, but the vision of sovereign law was traditional. Although at times the question of the authority of laws over citizens became secondary to their power over the king, we should also remember the notion that the law "has equal power over the monarch and his citizens."[94] The king and the citizens were bound to obey the law absolutely. Edward Opaliński noted a kind of legalism of the nobility (at least at the level of their declarations) and that "one of the most frequently used political arguments was stressing how one's actions followed the legal norms in the *Rzeczpospolita*."[95] It should be added that this was about more than simply not breaking laws; it stressed acting in accordance with their invectives, and it was this obedience which was seen as one of the fundamental duties of citizens, who were to "always desire what the law demands."[96] This was an obvious truth, oft repeated between the sixteenth and eighteenth centuries. When Józef Wybicki said in 1775: "Every good citizen proclaims himself bound by law,"[97] he confirmed himself to be part of a tradition dating back at least two centuries. It is notable how frequently Cicero's maxim *"servi legum sumus ut liberi esse possimus"* was repeated in political discourse; noble citizens did not hesitate to describe themselves as slaves of the law, its servants,[98] or subjects – concepts they would have been very reluctant to use in relation to their king. Even though, if we were to apply today's standards, we would find they struggled with abiding by the rule of law, the fact remains that they held it to be one of the greatest political values and that, after God, the law was undoubtedly the highest authority. The last statement is particularly worthy of notice, since it captures how differently the law was perceived then and now. In the political discourse of the Commonwealth, the law was assigned more than the passive role of a boundary or wall protecting rights of individuals while limiting their impact on others; it was also an active factor shaping the behaviors, attitudes and even personalities of citizens. The law was depicted as an authority, a "common wisdom" which was supreme and must be followed implicitly. This comparison, rooted in traditions of antiquity and inherited and expanded upon by Christianity, was a favorite of Renaissance authors of political treatises including Wolan, Goślicki and Górnicki.[99] Just as for their idols, Aristotle and Cicero (they rarely quoted St. Thomas[100]), they saw it as an element of a broader discussion on the source of the law, natural law and its links with constitutional law.[101] Such formulas were rare in more contemporary statements, and they were generally penned by authors with a meticulous background in the humanities, such as the author of *Naprawa Rzeczypospolitej*, who explained: "The source of all laws, both natural and those established by people's agreement, is a refined and polished mind."[102] Over time, similar comparisons largely disappeared from discourse, although the belief in the role of the law as a signpost for correct behavior, *secundum quam omnes decet vivere, qui in civitate sunt*,[103] persisted. The image of the law as an indicator of good and evil, of justice and injustice, turns out to have been highly enduring and common in Polish discourse. It was mentioned by participants in political debates between the sixteenth and eighteenth centuries regardless of their beliefs, ties or even background. The burgher Bartłomiej Groicki[104] wrote during the Jagiellonian era that "the law is, thus, a lesson leading to full decency and dissuading from all iniquity," which would be reiterated by one of the first ideologues of a nobility-led Commonwealth, the Catholic Orzechowski[105] who wrote: "With the aid of laws they usher in all that is just." For the Protestant Wolan, law was "a lesson in all decent righteousness,"[106] with Goślicki,[107] Górnicki and later Opaliński, Fredro and other authors of the eighteenth century echoing the sentiment. The definitions listed above sound like more or less direct quotes from classical works, and frequently that is indeed what they are, such as this statement by Górnicki: "True law is right reason in agreement with nature [...] it summons to duty by its commands, and averts from wrong-doing by its prohibitions," quoting from Cicero.[108] The entire discourse was deeply rooted in antique traditions which endured until the eighteenth century, when it encountered ideas devised by philosophers of the Enlightenment, in particular Montesquieu and Rousseau. When Szczepan Sienicki wrote in 1764 "All laws of every republic are the rules for the lives of decent, free citizens,"[109] he was invoking an old vision of law. However, when an anonymous author wrote in 1789 about laws which "are an instruction for citizens in terms of behavior and happiness for all,"[110] it was in reference to Rousseau, as were earlier statements by Wybicki and Staszic. It is another matter that the clear reference to the ideas of the Genevan philosopher in the statement by Staszic that citizens "can rarely be unhappy, and never evil, so long as they obey the law,"[111] fit perfectly with the traditional view of the law. It is unsurprising under the circumstances that the author of *The Social Contract* rediscovered and adapted for his own needs antique republican discourse[112] that formed the foundation of the political discourse in the *Rzeczpospolita*. Although in the late eighteenth century the vision of the law was starting to change gradually and it was increasingly assigned a passive role of limiting and protecting freedom, the concept of law as a factor shaping citizens' attitudes endured partly due to Rousseau's influence.

This was because laws contained not just *rationes honestatis, aequi et iniqui,*[113] but also taught citizens how to obey them: "*Lex pedagogus esto* in everything."[114] The law's role in guiding its citizens is a very important and enduring element of the discourse and the entire vision of the state. Given the rejection of the concept of strong government, the law remained the only power able to force citizens to act for the public good – for the Commonwealth. This was not so much about directly enforcing or preventing certain actions, but more about shaping people's attitudes such that they voluntarily took or avoided those actions. According to the anonymous author of *Philopolites*, the law "suppresses profligacy, anger, impudence, protects innocence, augments virtue, destroys tyranny and establishes freedom, without concern for power."[115] According to Wolan, laws "enforce virtue and generous obligation," while "human nature, in itself inclined to evildoing, is ruled and returned to virtue [by laws]."[116] In Wolan's treatise, as earlier in Modrzewski's writings,[117] it was an important topic and one of the foundations of the entire political concept. Not all authors devoted as much attention to this; however, it seems that the belief in the didactic role of law at the turn of the seventeenth century was universal. It was not even opposed by supporters of bolstering the monarch's power, including Warszewicki,[118] although they focused more on the "execution" of laws, that is, the role of government.

In the seventeenth and early eighteenth century, this element of the vision of the law appears less frequently, or at least it rarely features in extensive discussions (this can only really be found in Łukasz Opaliński),[119] but the belief endured. This is confirmed by direct postulates that the law should instruct citizens; to an even greater degree, it featured in widespread complaints that virtues were disappearing and morals failing because citizens did not obey the law.

This didactic vision of the law remained unchanged in the eighteenth century, as shown in serious treatises and more informal speeches. It is no wonder that in the 1770s, Polish discourse absorbed Rousseau's idea that laws can instruct people. Influenced by the Genevan philosopher, Michał Wielhorski wrote: "All statutes of free government should aim to maintain at once civic courage and obeying the law."[120] Wybicki believed that they already did so aim.[121] Bogusławski, a Catholic priest, was perhaps the most optimistic in his belief in the power of laws: "Good laws can effect anything from people. They direct the human will, and make people just, humane and happy."[122] These were authors with divergent political views, and they used rather different styles of discourse: Wybicki and Bogusławski invoked many new ideas and concepts, while Wielhorski stayed away from them. And yet their perception of the role of the law was very similar. There were also notable differences between the views of Adam Wawrzyniec Rzewuski and Stanisław Staszic – two eighteenth-century authors who explored the idea of instruction by the law. They both took this quite far, proposing some highly restrictive regulations which they believed would shape the ideal participants in society.[123] Rzewuski's goal was to protect the old ways of government, Staszic's to protect the existence of the state. It could be said that Rousseau's influence encouraged the idea of instruction by law, and writings in the Polish-Lithuanian political discourse in the late eighteenth century were surprisingly similar to statements made by the Renaissance humanists.

They are linked by their belief in the active role of the law as a factor shaping the attitudes of its subjects, and by the intertwining of the law and ethics noted by scholars in relation to Renaissance thought.[124] When we read A. W. Rzewuski's claim that laws will become redundant when "customs become complementary to laws, or even replace them,"[125] we might be under the impression that it is a quote straight from Modrzewski: "If any commonwealth were ruled by immaculate upbringing, shame, honesty, pure and untainted customs, laws would be somewhat redundant."[126] The similarity seems superficial, but there is no doubt that both authors are referring to the same tradition of intertwining laws and customs. It was a logical consequence of the assumption that the main aim of the law is to shape good behavior, therefore if people were guided by virtue alone, there would be no need for laws. Opaliński wrote in the seventeenth century: "First there blossom virtue and decency, which in and of itself postulates good deeds," then laws "are established" only when morals start to decline.[127] Here, Polish discourse once again relied heavily on the classical canon, stressed by Opaliński by supporting his statement with a quote from Tacitus' *Germania*.[128] Laws and morals could be seen as profoundly intertwined, mutually influencing one another: on the one hand laws shaped good morals, but on the other laws were described as impotent without good morals. As Łukasz Górnicki put it: "Just as good morals need good laws to remain pure, so do good laws require good morals to remain whole."[129] This sentiment was echoed by Opaliński in the seventeenth century, although – unlike his predecessor – he admitted that he was paraphrasing Machiavelli.[130] This was due to the close ties between the law and ethics, and to the concept of the state in which there was no vision of authority external to society as a factor enforcing the rule of law. This latter concept dominated European perception of statehood until at least the mid-seventeenth century, but its echoes were weak in the *Rzeczpospolita*. And since there was no authority that could dictate and enforce the rule of law, it relied on the attitudes and morals of citizens. Laws should shape virtues, because only virtuous citizens understood that the decisions of the community – laws – must be followed to be letter. Influenced by Rousseau, Wybicki wrote in the eighteenth century: "Laws shape minds such that people know how to establish them. They rule hearts such that they should be obeyed."[131] This provides an apt setting for the proposed rigorous laws that would severely restrict liberty. Although by the end of the eighteenth century we can see a clear influence of the *Considerations on the Government of Poland*, the belief that "free [...] states have no other way of correcting bad morals than by establishing strict and severe laws"[132] dated back far earlier. Goślicki explained the need for rigorous laws to restrain the depravity of evildoing citizens,[133] and his opinion was later shared by Warszewicki and Górnicki.[134]

However, the republican followers of Rousseau, especially the most radical ones including Adam Wawrzyniec Rzewuski, missed an important issue that was noticed by Renaissance humanists and by participants in political discourse throughout the existence of the *Rzeczpospolita*. For Rzewuski, severe laws were proposed as the prime remedy for the Commonwealth's problems, perhaps even as the main conclusion of his disquisition. He assumed that good laws and virtuous citizens formed by them were sufficient for its effective functioning. He did not provide answers who should be responsible for enforcing laws or who should be concerned with implementing even the best legal regulations, although in fairness this question was not being asked at all. Yet it was a fundamental question, as realized by theorists of the state and participants in political discourse as early as the sixteenth century. "What of the law where it is not enforced? Where the law is not executed?"[135] was one of the most serious problems faced by all participants in debates in the *Rzeczpospolita*. In contrast to many Western theorists, for Polish authors it was never simply an academic issue and it was always reflected in the realities of daily life. It seems that this made it all the more difficult to solve. Complaints about citizens disobeying laws and the state failing to implement them were a constant element in Polish discussion, both on the level of major theoretical discourse and in specific clashes. "Not any law, nor royal decrees, nor public resolutions shall enforce anything, because nothing will ever have any effect," sighed an anonymous author towards the end of the reign of Sigismund August,[136] and the view was echoed by participants in political discourse around the time of the first free election.[137] Another anonymous author wrote in the mid-seventeenth century: "One and all write laws, constitutions – yet none are ready to execute them."[138] Similar yearnings are present throughout the seventeenth and eighteenth centuries. As early as during the Great Sejm, Ignacy Łobarzewski addressed republicans in the style of Rzewuski or Rousseau: "For naught shall the most beneficial laws be, when they go unexecuted."[139] Łobarzewski was one of the last in a long line of authors for whom the belief that even the most severe laws "are dead without the executive"[140] was the foundation of their petitions to bolster the monarch's power. He was preceded by Warszewicki, Górnicki, Opaliński, Starowolski, and in the eighteenth century by Pyrrhys de Varille, Popławski and Skrzetuski.

However, it should be stressed once again that in Polish political discourse the idea of strong authority never replaced the concept of the rule of law. The authority of the law remained the utmost and undisputed.

Libertas consistit in legibus

Obedience to the law was all the more important because liberty depended on it. After all, Cicero wrote, "We are slaves of the law SO THAT WE MAY BE ABLE TO BE FREE." From Cicero to Montesquieu, all theorists of statehood – or at least the republican state – were in agreement in that liberty is only realized where everyone without exception fully submits themselves to the law, from the highest monarch down to the lowest, most wretched members of society. Liberty without laws meant enslavement for some and tyranny for others, and it ran the risk of degenerating into unbridled license or anarchy. According to the anonymous author of *Philopolites*, laws "exist to keep human license in check."[141] The law was described as channel to guide the turbulent tide of liberty. In the eighteenth century, Sebastian Dembowski wrote: "By laws, statutes, constitutions is our freedom bridled and defined. Its boundaries and corrals are such that it is not permissible to cross."[142] A belief in this function of the law was shared by scholars of statehood and participants in public life. It was what Wolan was referring to when he paraphrased Cicero: "There is no place for liberty where there are no laws."[143] An anonymous participant in Zebrzydowski's rebellion quotes Cicero almost to the letter: "Liberty hangs on laws";[144] this was repeated by Opaliński and Starowolski in the seventeenth century. All participants in discussions about the *Rzeczpospolita* denounced *effrenam sine lege licentiam*[145] and contrasted it against true liberty which "follows the law"[146] well into the eighteenth century, when their vision was bolstered by opinions of contemporary philosophers; Wincenty Skrzetuski echoed Montesquieu, warning that the free state falls "when people want to be free not according to laws, but against laws."[147]

However, the claim that "in laws is common liberty enclosed,"[148] borrowed from Cicero, had a broader meaning. Scholars have long stressed the close links between liberty and law, both in Polish theory and in how the noble class perceived the questions.[149] According to Stefania Ochmann-Staniszewska, "The defense of liberty is seen as the defense of the law, and vice versa – that is how closely the two are related."[150] This was partly the result of the functions assigned to the law, described above. This particularly concerned protecting liberty in the vertical sense, in the sense of protecting citizens from attempts by authority. Since the king was bound by laws, this inevitably meant that liberty necessarily had to be protected against his intentions. It should also be stressed once again that this concerned positive laws. Although natural law was present in political discourse as early as the sixteenth century, and made a return in the late eighteenth century, in terms of liberty it was usually regarded horizontally – as a way of regulating relationships between individuals comprising society. A vision of natural rights of "the people," in which the king had no authority to intervene as this would amount to nothing short of tyranny, did not appear in theoretical considerations and especially in actual discussions. Although the topic was widely discussed in England during the Civil War and even more so during the Glorious Revolution,[151] it hardly featured in Polish discourse.[152] To a large extent, this was due to the different situations in the two countries – it was far easier for participants in debates in England to appeal to natural laws applying to the entire population than Polish nobles whose rights were protected by exclusive privileges. However, the choice of traditions of thinking and speaking about the state in which common law created liberty as well as protecting it remained significant. During the majority of the existence of the Polish-Lithuanian Commonwealth, natural liberty was barely present in discourse; discussions were dominated by republican liberty which, similarly to that of Cicero, only existed due to laws. This view was shared by the author of *Philopolites* in his quotes from Cicero; similarly, Wolan states: "laws CREATE full and complete liberty for citizens, this fortune bring to all, that all can live securely."[153] Even earlier Orzechowski reminded the nobles: "These benefits given to you by your great liberty, enclosed entirely in your rights and customs"[154]; the view was shared by Warszewicki, although he phrased it more as a general truth.[155] It is worth noting that these authors had very different perceptions of liberty but were in agreement in how they regarded the role of the law in shaping it. The view was repeated by later generations of participants in public debate regardless of their views; like Orzechowski, the majority of them applied it in practice as well as theory. "Our laws which founded Poland's liberty"[156] is a common phrase, resounding with the reality of the nobility's privileges and recalling classical discourse on the ties between the law and liberty. At the level of declarations by individuals directly involved in political struggles, the relationship can be expressed as the phrases "rights and liberties" or "law and liberty." This was not peculiar to Poland, since similar associations can be found in discourse in England, the Netherlands, Switzerland and the German states, in particular at periods of dispute between citizens and rulers. The difference lies in what those phrases concealed. In the Netherlands and England, references to ancient laws guaranteeing liberty were at least in part references to theoretical "ancient constitutions" concerning common law and used to oppose the royal prerogative (the laws of the Britons/Batavians), somewhat subversive and therefore inviolable.[157] In a sense, this semi-mythical character also applies to the references to the fundamental rights of Dutch and English freedom, that is Joyeuse Entrée and Magna Carta.[158] In Polish discourse, there was no such "foundational" law of liberty; however, equally old laws were understood far more precisely as real privileges either granted by monarchs or fought for or bargained from them. Although common law played an important role in the *Rzeczpospolita*,[159] texts on the history of liberty referred to written laws, generally dating them from the rule of Casimir the Great. Walęty Pęski put it well, saying, "Casimir the Great was the first to record and promulgate laws serving as a powerful wall supporting and protecting liberty."[160] It could be said that noble citizens in Poland simply had real laws they could have recourse to in order to defend their liberty, while people in the Netherlands and England were still fighting for those rights and had to justify their demands with privileges some of which might have verged on the imaginary. What they did have in common is the belief that laws are the foundation of liberty, originating in antiquity. It is notable that although in noble discourse the main cluster of laws guaranteeing liberty originated from monarchs, this was no barrier to regarding them as a gift from their honorable ancestors and the inviolable inheritance of their descendants. "Liberty, freedom and our rights/laws [...] as great and honorable as they are, acquired by our ancestors with their noble blood and given into our hands and entrusted to us"[161] – this view, here voiced by an anonymous participant in the disputes of 1573, was widely held until the end of the Polish-Lithuanian Commonwealth.

The notable phrase in the quote is *nasze prawa* – which can be understood as both "our rights" and "our laws" (there being only one word in Polish) – as it indicates an important pattern reaching beyond the political language. The author regards rights as the property of the noble community, as its wealth and heritage. And he was in no way an exception: on the contrary, he represented a running view according to which citizens of the *Rzeczpospolita* believed they were entitled to their rights/laws.[162] This was also reflected in language – the noun *prawa* "rights/laws" was frequently preceded by the pronominal adjective *nasze* "our," as is the case of the anonymous author writing in 1573 and echoed by his contemporaries and future generations. This usually applied to collective rather than individual ownership. Laws shaping and protecting individual liberty were not seen as individual rights, similar to today's human rights, but rather seen as a result of individuals belonging to a certain community: the noble class or the *Rzeczpospolita*.

This was also the framework used to examine the question of equal submission to the law alongside equal legal protection of liberty. The majority of those involved in political discussions agreed with Aristotle, in that "When two persons have equal status in at least one normatively relevant respect, they must be treated equally with regard to this respect."[163] It was the question of equal justice and equal liberty. However, it was only sixteenth-century humanists – and not all, at that – who used it to refer to entire society. When Wolan wrote: "In any commonwealth that serves all its citizens equally by law, they can be called free,"[164] he meant the nobility as well as burghers and peasants. The question of equal provisions of liberty was seen in a similar way (albeit more theoretically) by Goślicki,[165] and to a lesser degree by Górnicki.[166] For the vast majority of those involved, the statement "the law hangs on equality"[167] concerned the noble class only, as did complaints that this equality was not being observed and laws "were only applied to those more wretched, and from spared those more powerful."[168] It is worth stressing here that the difference was not due to a different understanding of the role of the law and its links with liberty/justice, but to a different understanding of the population it was meant to cover and a different understanding of such concepts as "*Rzeczpospolita*" and "citizen." This became very clear by the late eighteenth century when a few authors started to talk about society as a whole. When Kołłątaj postulated, "So that we are all entirely free and under the rule of good laws, the same for the whole population,"[169] he was talking about all members of the national community; however, when Feliks Trojanowski had used similar terminology to say just a few years earlier that laws "are written such that all equally-born citizens draw the benefits of happiness as though from a well,"[170] his concern lies solely with the noble class. The difference between the authors is not how they perceive the function of the law but their understanding of its social reach. The conviction that for liberty to exist, the entire population must be equally protected and bound by the law, rooted in the antiquity, was enduring and widespread, albeit with different understanding of who exactly is included in "the entire population." The reasons why equality was essential was best explained by Wybicki in 1775: "Liberty is the right to do everything permitted by laws: but if one citizen were permitted to do something they forbid, there would no longer be equality because it would follow that the others had the same right" – although he was, however, quoting straight from Montesquieu.[171]

The words of the author of *The Spirit of the Laws* fit perfectly into Polish discourse in terms of the necessity for equality in submission to the law, although in his view the law was not just a guarantee of liberty: its main role was to limit liberty. This was not new in Polish discourse and it had been discussed, in particular when issues of obedience to its decisions were being analyzed. However, this was seen as a limitation on the liberty of a certain group to prevent excessive liberty from turning into anarchy which would endanger the *Rzeczpospolita*. Even when legal limitations applied to the actions of individuals, liberty was seen as a whole; an element on which laws set boundaries for the greater good. There was also an important issue of the function of the law as a boundary between individual liberty – between what is mine and what is yours. Łukasz Górnicki describes it thus: "May your liberty not make for another's bondage."[172] It was an important function, even though it was not as widespread in Polish discourse. The concept that "there is no liberty without the law, which restrains evil citizens when they wish to violate the liberty of their co-citizens"[173] was certainly not invented during the Enlightenment. The principle according to which "the law has put certain shackles on liberty so that things which are unjust are not done, and so that one uses his liberty such that others can also share it and one's liberty not make another's bondage"[174] was shared by all participants in public debate. In more practical declarations, it usually featured as a criticism that the law does not set a high enough barrier against wrongdoing and at the same time does not protect individual liberty from assault from their "equals."

Here we should stress another important question: the political discourse of the *Rzeczpospolita* was never dominated by the liberal concept according to which liberty lies where the law does not apply. In the 1770s the idea of natural liberty was accompanied by definitions stressing that the law was not to shape but "to limit liberty given by nature,"[175] yet this vision of liberty within the boundaries of the law remained just a single element of the relationship between the law and liberty. Even for authors who were heavily influenced by the West, such as Wybicki and Stroynowski, the role of the law was far more active and its relationship with liberty far more multilateral. The Enlightenment enhanced Polish discourse with the belief that any laws laid down must be in accordance with the laws of nature, somewhat forgotten since the Renaissance. Konstantyn Bogusławski wrote: "All laws and political obligations of all societies result from natural laws and natural human obligations."[176] It is important to note that the laws were equally applicable to all. This brought a new concept of "human rights."[177] Although it was not especially popular to start with, it was drawn upon by several supporters of social reform during the Great Sejm.[178] Kołłątaj stated unequivocally: "The liberty of the people is nothing other than human rights."[179] While it was not a widespread interpretation, we can risk stating that the discussion of laws shaping the *Rzeczpospolita* and guaranteeing the liberty of its citizens was being gradually replaced by the idea of a modern nation with the prevailing rule of law.

Notes

1 Karin Friedrich maintains that such theory was not particularly well developed in the Polish-Lithuanian Commonwealth (Friedrich 2007, 220), although on the other hand the work of Eugeniusz Jarra (1968) indicates that Polish state theoreticians did devote considerable attention to the law, particularly in the sixteenth century (Jarra 1968); on old-Polish legal theory see also Estreicher (1931).

2 Hence, I also do not deal with the issue of the hard-to-trace distinction between the concepts *ius* and *lex*. This problem been most penetratingly analyzed by Sapała (2017, 199–241), cf. also Lizisowa (2006, 97–112). The Polish language operates with just one word: *prawo* meaning "law"/"the law"/"a law" as well as "right" (especially in the plural: *prawa* "rights").

3 Cf. Jarra (1931a,b; 1945); Pietrzyk-Reeves (2012, 227–257).

4 Kelley (1991, 66–94); Dagger (1989, 293–308); Mäkinen and Korkman (2006); Pietrzyk-Reeves (2012, 43–49, 129–134).
5 Skinner (2001, 286–295, especially 295).
6 This concept was created and presented in numerous publications by J. G. A. Pocock, e.g., Pocock (1981, 355ff.); similarly Goldsmith (1994, 199–200).
7 Cf. Brugger (1999, 42).
8 Reid (2004 passim).
9 This was linked to another distinctive trait of the noble discourse, at least within the Polish Crown, namely the very poor presence of Roman law. Justinian's *Digest*, which throughout Europe served as a basis for thinking not only about the law, but also about the state, exerted almost no influence on the Polish discourse, and was even rejected by some authors (e.g., Orzechowski). On the nobility's dislike for Roman law, compare Vetulani (1969, 372–386); C. Backvis, *Jednostka i społeczeństwo w Polsce doby renesansu*, in Backvis (1975a: 556–557); Estreicher (1931, 44ff.); Grodziski (2004, 166). It seems that this issue is still understudied with respect to Lithuania, where the influence of Roman law was decidedly stronger, as is evident in the Statutes; cf. Bardach (1999); Godek (2004; 2013); Zakrzewski (2013, Chapter 12 *Statuty litewskie* and Chapter 13 *Prawo w teorii i praktyce*).
10 Opałek (1953).
11 Scholars have long pointed out that the cult of the law and legalism constitute one of the more distinctive exponents of Polish noble culture, cf. Tazbir (1979, 58, 71); Opaliński (1995, 96–97); Ochmann-Staniszewska (1994, 232ff.).
12 *Philopolites, to jest miłośnik ojczyzny, albo powinności dobrego obywatela, ojczyźnie dobrze chcącego i onę miłującego, krótki traktat*, 1588.
13 Wolan (1572/1606/2010, 161).
14 Pietrzyk-Reeves (2012, 239–240).
15 Pietrzyk-Reeves (2012, 84, 239ff.).
16 Wolan (1572/1606/2010, 167).
17 This role of the law was discussed in the seventeenth century by Ł. Opaliński, *Obrona Polski przeciw Janowi Barklayowi* [1648], in Opaliński (1959, 208).
18 Suski (1612/1893, 60).
19 Orzechowski ([1556]/1984, 23).
20 Pietrzyk-Reeves (2012, 234).
21 Sarnicki (1594, foreword, fol. *3v).
22 *Philopolites...* (1588), fol. D 3.
23 The Constitution of 1507, "*Quia cum omnis lex donum Dei sit [...] utpote, sine qua Respublica veluti corpus sine anima, consistere et regi nequit...*," cited after: Sucheni-Grabowska (1994, 73, 107, footnote 72).
24 Ochmann-Staniszewska (1994, 234).
25 [Sz. Budny?] *Elekcyja króla krześcijańska*, in Czubek (1906, 323).
26 This was how Stanisław Sarnicki wrote about the role of the law "under the statutes of Emperor Otto": "*Bonos mores informat, inimicos confoederat, discolos disciplinat, elatos superbire deterret, Rembublicam disponit, lites sedat, amicitias consolidat, mares et foeminas copulat ac foecundat, diuitiasque congregat*," Sarnicki (1594, foreward, fol. *3v), and how Piotr Bogoria Skotnicki presented the role of the law: "*Fundamentum siquides libertatis, fontem aequitatis, mentem et animum et consilium sententiamque civitatis in legibus posita esse*," Skotnicki (1576, fol. C).
27 Cf. Dagger (1989, 300ff.).

28 Skrzetuski (1773, 350).
29 Skrzetuski (1773, 349ff.).
30 Wyrwicz (1771–1772, 20) – this was not an independent text, but a polemic with Rousseau drawn from a foreign source.
31 Wybicki (1775/1984, 52).
32 Michalski (1987, 324).
33 S. Małachowski, K. N. Sapieha, *Uniwersał marszałków Sejmowych z 7 maja 1791*, in Grześkowiak-Krwawicz (1992a: 24).
34 *Naprawa Rzeczypospolitej* [1573], in Czubek (1906, 196).
35 Zamoyski ([1764]/1954, 74).
36 Karpowicz (1786, no pagination).
37 *Senatora anonima deliberacyje o królu, panach, radzie i urzędnikach, sejmie i bezkrólewiu* [1569], in Ulanowski (1921, 171).
38 *Libera respublica quae sit?* in Czubek (1918, vol. 2, 404).
39 Which does not mean that they were not appreciated, cf. Sucheni-Grabowska (1994, 64).
40 [Leszczyński] ([1733]/2007, 23).
41 *Treść pism różnych względem formy rządu i sukcesyi tronu polskiego* (1791, 6); cf.: Friedrich (2007, 222).
42 Cf. Radwański (1952, 44 *passim*).
43 *Refleksyje do następującej elekcyi* (1696, 425).
44 Estreicher (1931, 82).
45 *Krótkie rzeczy potrzebnych z strony wolności a swobód polskich zebranie*, (1587/1859, 68).
46 *Przyczyny wypowiedzenia posłuszeństwa Zygmuntowi królewicowi szwedzkiemu, anno 1607 die nativitatis Joannis Baptistae*, in Czubek (1918, vol. 3, 35).
47 *Racyje przywodzące Confederacyją do wypowiedzenia posłuszeństwa królowi JM.* (1703, leaf 285).
48 *Oda pierwsza rewolucyi polskiej w roku 1767*, in Maciejewski (1976, 18); cf. also: Czarniecka (2009, 127, 177, 227 *passim*); Michalski (1991, 17).
49 Grzybowski (1959, 231).
50 C. Backvis, *Główne tematy polskiej myśli politycznej w XVI wieku*, in Backvis (1975, 483).
51 "*nullae leges sunt immortales: tempori servire debent, saepe refigendae sunt veteres, antioquandae, abrogandae et novae figendae atque in illarum locum meliores subrogandae,*" *Dialogus I de regis Poloniae electione*, in Czubek (1906, 678).
52 *Gdychżechmy przyszli na ten nieszczęsny wiek...* in Czubek (1906, 147), cf. Grzybowski (1959, 231–244).
53 Januszowski (1602/1920, 14).
54 Litwin (1994, 17ff, 22). On the understanding of the sovereignty of the law in early Polish thought, see also Wachlowski (1927, 236–240); Uruszczak (1993, 149–157).
55 Frycz Modrzewski (1577/2003, 325).
56 [Kossobudzki]/Januszowski (1606/1921, 267); Sucheni-Grabowska (1994, 79, 87 *passim*).
57 Opaliński (1995, 107); see also: Wisner (1978, Chapter 3); Ochmann-Staniszewska (1994, 234); Ogonowski (1992, 79).
58 Ł. Opaliński, *Rozmowa plebana z ziemianinem*, in Opaliński (1938, 28).
59 A. Ciesielski, *Oratio ad senatum Regni Poloniae Magnique Ducatus Lituaniae, qua boni proncipis in Republica constituendi modus ostenditur*, in Czubek (1906, 181); this is a quotation from Pliny the Younger's *Panegyricus Traiani*, functioning as a well-known adage throughout Europe.

60 Sucheni-Grabowska (1994, 65); Friedrich (2007, 221); Wyrwa (1978, 368).
61 Wolan (1572/1606/2010, 97, 99).
62 [S. Budny?] *Elekcyja króla krześcijańska* [1573], in Czubek (1906, 325).
63 Even this author was not fully consistent in this, elsewhere clearly stressing the king's subordinance to the law Czubek (1906, 324).
64 Opaliński (1959, 199).
65 Quoted from: Sucheni-Grabowska (1994, 73).
66 St. Orzechowski, *Dyjalog około egzekucyi* [1563], quoted after: Sucheni-Grabowska (1994, 87).
67 Herburt (1570, fol. A 4).
68 [S. Budny?] *Elekcyja króla krześcijańska* [printed 1573], in Czubek (1906, 324); see: Brzeziński (2008, p. 302).
69 On its role as a foundation for the theory of absolutism, see Pennington (1993, 276ff.).
70 Here it is worth citing the treatise of Aaron Olizarowski, although it is hard to recognize it as an example of typical noble discourse, given that this was an erudite university treatise. The author was one of the few theoreticians in Poland familiar with and enamored of the concepts of Bodin, and yet despite this he recognized the principle *princeps legibus solutus est* as the basis not for royal power, but for tyrannical rule, Olizarowski (1651, 305, 307); cf. Jarra (1933, 129).
71 Third Lithuanian Statute (1610, introduction by Lew Sapieha, addressed to the Estates of the Grand Duchy of Lithuania, no pagination); Zakrzewski (2013, 238).
72 J. S. Herburt, *Strzała, którą korona Polska, śmiertelna już matka strażą obtoczona z więzienia swego do dziatek swych stanu rycerskiego wypuściła*, in Czubek (1918, vol. 2, 164).
73 Kelley (1991, 67).
74 Estreicher (1931, 44, 93 *passim*); Wyrwa (1978, 365); a similar approach to the law in concepts described as republican was pointed out by Bill Brugger: "In early modern republican theory, [...] the rule of law was also particularly important in that it was seen as offering a much surer guarantee of security than the rule of a powerful monarch," Brugger (1999, 42).
75 This was already pointed out by Estreicher (1931, 64).
76 This was, however, a concept of natural law in its antique understanding, adopted and developed by Medieval Christian thought – Friedrich (2007, 221); Estreicher (1931, 64); Grzybowski (1956, 193ff.); Pietrzyk-Reeves (2012, 234–237 *passim*); Kochan (2010b: 50ff.).
77 Augustyniak (2007, 17).
78 *Naprawa praw, swobód i wolności naszych*, in Czubek (1906, 187).
79 *Objaśnienie prerogatywy stanu rycerskiego*, in Czubek (1918, vol. 3, 262).
80 *Naprawa praw, swobód i wolności naszych*, in Czubek (1906, 187).
81 This specifically in the context of the struggle against the Jesuits: "We enact and improve the law, not the priests," *Jezuitom i inszym duchownym respons*, in Czubek (1918, vol. 3, 93).
82 *Poparcie „Uwag nad życiem Jana Zamoyskiego,"* ([1788]: 33); "The general law is the will and highest opinion of the nation," Pyrrhys de Varille (1764, 34).
83 [Ładowski] (1780, 65).
84 Wolan (1572/1606/2010, 99.
85 *Third Lithuanian Statute* (1610), foreword by L. Sapieha, dedicated to Sigismund III, no pagination.
86 St. Orzechowski, *Dyjalog około egzekucyi* [1563]. Quoted after: Sucheni-Grabowska (1994, 87).
87 [Radzewski] alias Poklatecki ([1743]: 32).

88 [Pęski] (1727, 82).
89 [Plater] [1790, 39).
90 Turski (1790a: 13).
91 As they were called by H. Kołłątaj *Listy Anonima* [1788–1789], in Kołłątaj (1954, vol. 2, 101).
92 A. W. Rzewuski (1790, part 2, 57).
93 H. Kołłątaj, *Listy Anonima* [1788–1789], in Kołłątaj (1954, vol. 1, 278).
94 *Iż na społecznym zjeździe...*, in Czubek (1906, 244).
95 Opaliński (1995, 97).
96 Leszczyński ([1737?]/1903, 92).
97 Wybicki (1775/1984, 118).
98 "Better then to be free servants of the law, than slaves of absolutism," Sienicki (1764, vol. 1, 256).
99 Pietrzyk-Reeves (2012, 47, 235); on the antique sources of these views, cf. Shklar (1987, 1–4ff.); Spellman (1998, 51).
100 His definition of the law as the rule and measures of behavior was cited by Aaron Olizarowski in his treatise *De politica hominum societate libri tres* (1651, 266), but these were erudite deliberations, not only strongly theoretical but also lying outside the mainstream discourse, a certain variation on Aristotle and Bodin, cf. Jarra (1931a: 33–72).
101 Makiłła (2012, 126ff.); Pietrzyk-Reeves (2012, 232ff.); Kochan (2010a: 59).
102 *Naprawa Rzeczypospolitej* [1573], Czubek (1906, 196).
103 Zalaszowski (1702, vol. 2), the motto of the volume, taken from Demosthenes' oratory against Aristogeiton.
104 Groicki (1559/1953, 21).
105 S. Orzechowski, *Mowa do szlachty polskiej (Oratio ad equites Polonos)* [1551], trans. J. Starnawski, in Orzechowski (1972, 100).
106 Wolan (1572/1606/2010, 89).
107 Pietrzyk-Reeves (2012, 238).
108 Ł. Górnicki, *Rozmowa Polaka z Włochem o wolnościach i prawach polskich* [1616], in Górnicki (1961, 389); Cf. Cycero, *De legibus*, I, 6, 18; Kochan (2010a: 59); Pietrzyk-Reeves (2012, 47).
109 Sienicki (1764, vol. 1, 77).
110 *Poparcie „Uwag nad życiem Jana Zamoyskiego,"* ([1788]: 33).
111 Staszic (1926, 19).
112 Leduc-Fayette (1974); Touchefeu (1999).
113 *Naprawa Rzeczypospolitej* [1573], Czubek (1906, 196).
114 [Dembowski] (1733/1904, 11).
115 *Philopolites...* (1588, fol. K 4v).
116 Wolan (1572/1606/2010, 147, 151).
117 Modrzewski's "idealistic view of the law as a regulator of people's habits and as a moral educator," Friedrich (2007, 221).
118 Warszewicki (1598/2010, 136 in Latin; 278 in Polish).
119 Ł. Opaliński, *Rozmowa plebana z ziemianinem*, in Opaliński (1938, 19).
120 Wielhorski (1775, 257).
121 Wybicki (1775/1984, 122, 140).
122 Bogusławski (1786, 11).
123 A. W. Rzewuski (1790, *passim*); Staszic (1787/1926 36ff, 39, 133ff *passim*); cf. Lis (2015, 341ff.).
124 Pietrzyk-Reeves (2012, 241); Kochan (2010a: 59).
125 A. W. Rzewuski (1790, part 1, 109).
126 Quoted from: Kochan (2010a: 60); Pietrzyk-Reeves (2012, 245).
127 Ł. Opaliński, *Rozmowa plebana z ziemianinem* [1641], in Opaliński (1938, 20).

128 *Plusque tunc boni mores valent, quam alias bonae leges.* Tacitus, *Germania* XIX, a slightly modified quotation.
129 Ł. Górnicki, *Droga do zupełnej wolności* [1650], in Górnicki (1961, 484); cf. Pietrzyk-Reeves (2012, 248).
130 Ł. Opaliński, *Rozmowa plebana z ziemianinem* [1641], in Opaliński (1938, 20), citing the source and the quotation in the original..
131 Wybicki (1775/1984, 122).
132 Ł. Opaliński, *Rozmowa plebana z ziemianinem* [1641], in Opaliński (1938, 19).
133 Goślicki (1568, fol. 40v).
134 Warszewicki (1598/2010, 136 in Latin, 278 in Polish); Górnicki, *Rozmowa Polaka z Włochem* (1616), in Górnicki (1961, 348, 383).
135 Januszowski (1602/1920, 14).
136 *Senatora anonima deliberacyje o królu, panach, radzie i urzędnikach, sejmie i bezkrólewiu* [1569], in Ulanowski (1921, 163).
137 "*Verum etiam ad corrigendas et debitae executioni demandandas leges nostras,*" A. Ciesielski, *Oratio ad senatum*, in Czubek (1906, 339).
138 *Status Reipublicae moderne* [1668?], in Ochmann-Staniszewska (1991, 370).
139 [Łobarzewski] (1789a: 79).
140 Ł. Opaliński, *Rozmowa plebana z ziemianinem* [1641], in Opaliński (1938, 19).
141 *Philopolites...* (1588), fol. D 3.
142 [Dembowski] (1733/1904, 11).
143 Wolan (1572/1606/2010, 89), who also called for stricter laws to "harness" excessive liberty.
144 *Rozmowa synów z matką*, Czubek (1918, vol. 2, 145).
145 [Pęski] (1727, 13).
146 S. Dunin Karwicki, *O naprawie Rzeczypospolitej*, in Karwicki (1992, 110).
147 Skrzetuski (1773, 37); the fragment is a quite faithful Polish rendition of book III, Chapter 3 of *The Spirit of the Laws*.
148 *Philopolites...* (1588, fol. E 4v).
149 Ochmann-Staniszewska (1994, 232ff.); Urwanowicz (1994, 172); Opaliński (1995, 84 *passim*).
150 Ochmann-Staniszewska (1994, 231).
151 Mouristen (2006, 22); Nenner (1992, 90).
152 Although it did sometimes appear, cf. Zwierzykowski (2017, 275); in the seventeenth century a distant echo of this was sometimes audible in statements by Protestants defending their rights, cf. e.g. *Uniżona prośba do Króla Jego M[it]ości i Rzeczypospolitej na sejm MDCXXVII pisana*, in Augustyniak (2013, 389).
153 Wolan (1572/1606/2010, 215).
154 S. Orzechowski, *Mowa do szlachty polskiej (Oratio ad equites Polonos)* [1551], trans. J. Starnawski, in Orzechowski (1972, 100).
155 Warszewicki (1598/2010, 138 in Latin, 282 in Polish).
156 Konarski (1760–1763, vol. 2, 185).
157 Spellman (1998, 87); Van Gelderen (1996, 105); Nenner (1992, 89); Dickinson (1979, 63ff.).
158 Pallister (1971, 3).
159 Estreicher (1931, 63).
160 [Pęski] (1727, 34).
161 *Gdychżechmy przyszli na ten nieszczęsny wiek...* in Czubek (1906, 147).
162 Besides, this was not a Polish pecularity, cf. Nenner (1992, 97).

163 "True *aequalitas* rests upon what Aristotle expressed »Ut omnibus sit jus idem, eadem leges quae non plus unum gravent, quam alterum: non plus uni commodent, quam alteri«," Wieruszewski (1733, 112).

164 Wolan (1572/1606/2010, 107).

165 Goślicki (1568, fol. 41v).

166 Ł. Górnicki, *Rozmowa Polaka z Włochem* [1616], in Górnicki (1961, vol. 1, 388).

167 *Iż na społecznym zjeździe panów rad koronnych w Kaskach*, in Czubek (1906, 244).

168 S. Dunin Karwicki, *Egzorbitancyje…*, in Karwicki (1992, 13).

169 H. Kołłątaj, *Do prześwietnej Deputacyi dla ułożenia konstytucyi rządu polskiego od Sejmu wyznaczonej* [1789], in Kołłątaj (1954, vol. 2, 181); H. Kołłątaj, *Prawo polityczne narodu polskiego* [1790], in Kołłątaj (1954, vol. 2, 222, 245).

170 Trojanowski ([1780]: no pagination).

171 Wybicki (1775/1984, 59); Montesquieu *The Spirit of the Laws* XI, 3; the same fragment is cited in Wyrwicz (1771–1772, 124).

172 Ł. Górnicki, *Rozmowa Polaka z Włochem* [1616], in Górnicki (1961, vol. 1, 356).

173 Bogusławski (1786, 81); Popławski (1774, 251).

174 Ł. Górnicki, *Rozmowa Polaka z Włochem* [1616], in Górnicki (1961, vol. 1, 356).

175 [Łobarzewski] (1789b: 15); similarly: Kaliszewski (1760, 304); Wybicki (1775/1984, 56).

176 Bogusławski (1786, 77); similarly: Stroynowski (1785, 74); Popławski (1774, 53).

177 This approach already appeared with Wybicki, who accused his fellow citizens thusly: "we are excepting the Polish peasants from human rights," Wybicki ([1777–1778]/1955, 117).

178 "Natural rights, human rights," "above all political and civil rights" in *Krótkie uwagi nad pismem JP. Wojciecha Turskiego O królach* (1790, 24); "human rights ensured" in [Jezierski] (1790, 8).

179 H. Kołłątaj, *Ostatnia przestroga dla Polski* (1790), in Kądziela (1991, 116); also: "Human rights, that is the rights of a free people, are surrounded by danger all around"; Kołłątaj (1790, 23).

3   *Wolność* – Freedom

"Let us begin with what Poles are concerned about most – freedom,"[1] Piotr Świtkowski wrote in 1791. I have quoted this assertion a number of times in other works,[2] as it so characteristically captures the significance of freedom in the political discourse of the Polish-Lithuanian Commonwealth. In fact, the significance of freedom stretched far beyond discourse, as a notion much more inclusive, embracing a certain political way of thinking, political culture and ideology of sorts, a certain outlook on the state, society and a place of the individual within it. But even if we focus solely on political discourse, the problem of freedom is of crucial importance. The claim can be ventured that it was freedom that bound this discourse together and constituted its soul, to use an allegory that was popular in the debates conducted at that time. It was also a concept forging a particular view and understanding of the world and, at the same time, one of the highest, if not *the* highest, political value,[3] a fundamental criterion for assessing political proposals and the actions of public figures. Care and love for freedom (or lack thereof) were used as valid arguments in disputes. Freedom was also a political myth, which could become an object of pride, solace or reproof, depending on the given situation.

I intend to demonstrate that some elements of the conception of freedom evolved during the 200 years of the noble republic, but its role in the discourse proved to be stable. Its image first sketched out in the sixteenth century when various factions were still fighting for their vision of the state, under the influence of the political reality of the day and also the ancient tradition and the humanistic vision of the world, largely survived through the Commonwealth period, and perhaps even longer.

One of the essential components of the conception of freedom was the belief that it should be highly valued. This is evidenced by epithets applied to freedom, which was described not only as "golden," but also as "the most precious and the loveliest jewel and treasure," "worldly honor," the most precious gift from heaven or from nature (depending on the author's views and the context), "sacred," "invaluable" and "sweet." The latter expression, echoing the ancient maxim *Libertas patriae dulcissima rerum*, seems to have enjoyed the greatest popularity

from the sixteenth century on. "The sweet fruit of freedom"[4] was valued
not only by its ardent followers but also by critics, one of whom wrote
this in the eighteenth century: "[...] sweet, golden freedom desired by
humankind," simultaneously expressing doubt whether this kind of freedom still existed in anarchy-seized Poland.[5] In writings and speeches by
the Poles, liberty was portrayed not just as a precious value but as the
most precious, as evident in this opinion by Andrzej Wolan modeled on
the ancient tradition: "there is no such thing among all things human
as could equal the value of freedom."[6] This belief was reiterated in various formulations through the centuries to come, but subtle alterations
started to appear with time. Renaissance authors, both theoreticians
and participants of political debates, voiced the opinion that all spiritual and material goods were bereft of any value in a world deprived
of freedom,[7] additionally underscoring that it is freedom that is a prerequisite for these other goods. Treatises were written on the abstract
philosophical and political facets of freedom, but those engaged in current disputes in the sixteenth and seventeenth centuries were primarily
concerned with the link between freedom and security (of one's person
and one's property). Andrzej Radawiecki intimated that "[...] equal and
free is but he who lives in safety."[8] It was emphasized that the Poles
"are free from fear,"[9] that "everyone lives in safety, certain of his own
honorable health and wealth."[10] On the other hand, a lack of safety and
permanent uncertainty giving rise to fear were believed to characterize
countries deprived of freedom. An impressive account of how fear pre-
cipitates the atrophy of social bonds was presented in a 1606 *rokosz*-era
pamphlet inciting sedition, in which life under a monarchy was likened
to life during a plague.[11] The discourse of freedom in the *Rzeczpospolita* did not diverge significantly from what was advocated by Western
admirers of freedom.[12] A fissure between Polish and Western discourse
appeared about the mid-seventeenth century, when freedom began to
appear in the former, at least in the discourse, not only as the highest
value, but almost as the single value (this viewpoint was not necessarily
shared by the nobility). In the eighteenth century, the well-known phrase
"freedom and faith" elevated freedom nearly to the realm of *sacrum*.[13]
Moreover, it began to be presented in opposition to security. In public
speeches liberty and safety became to be increasingly contrasted rather
than juxtaposed. This view may have been underlain by specific theoretical foundations,[14] but it may also have been linked to a certain
change in the situation of the *Rzeczpospolita*. Up to the mid-seventeenth
century Poland had epitomized a close connection between freedom and
safety (of life and property), but the experience of the wars fought under the reign of John II Casimir and even more so the beginning of the
eighteenth century undermined this connection. Importantly, given the
choice between freedom and safety, the Poles – quite unlike Hobbes –
firmly opted for freedom: *malo periculosam libertatem quam quietuum*

servitium. Presented as the most precious value, it compensated for all possible hardships that stemmed from it, making them mere "sweet miseries suffered for freedom."[15] The loss of property or even the loss of life paled into insignificance in comparison with the loss of freedom. Opinions of this kind, more than on any other subject, were often expressed as demagogic proclamations, typically as an argument leveled against legal proposals intended to make state institutions more efficient. To illustrate this, consider the following closing lines from an anonymous letter written during the reign of John II Casimir: "And better to live in misery, awaiting God's mercy, better even to die than to desire this *remedium* for curing domestic dissent by means of even worse *antidota*, which smell of poison to our freedom and liberties."[16] This line of thought became highly popular at the time of the Four-Year Sejm (1788–1792), being the most vibrant political debate of the eighteenth century. Opponents of the reforms, especially supporters of the free election, and later malcontents in the debate on the Constitution of the Third of May 1791, were the last to evoke the idea of freedom as a value above everything else.[17] On this view, as Jerzy Michalski has pointed out, freedom was a fundamental, and frequently the only criterion for assessing systemic political solutions.[18]

At that time, markedly polemical attitudes appeared towards such a vision of freedom. But even in the preceding decades, authors postulating detailed political solutions aimed at salvaging the *Rzeczpospolita* remarked that there were other values equally (or almost so) attractive as freedom. Among these writers were such prominent figures as Stanisław Leszczyński and Stanisław Konarski, for whom the greatest happiness for the *Rzeczpospolita* was afforded by "domestic peace and safety of our citizens, possessions and wealth."[19] This idea, subsequently recast in Enlightenment parlance, was repeated by many authors in the 1770s and 1780s.[20] During the Four-Year Sejm disputes, a clear divide appeared between the advocates and the opponents of political reforms. While in the statements produced by the latter, freedom is characteristically portrayed as the only value, the proponents of political and/or social reforms put it next to other desirable goods: peace, security and the Enlightenment conception of happiness.[21] This stance was a powerful argument in disputes, at the same time marking a change in political language, which in turn reflected a more general evolution of the vision of the state. It has to be emphasized that unlike in the Western European political discourse, where freedom gave way to other values, in Poland it was still holding strong. In a way, the end of the eighteenth century saw a rediscovery of a traditional, somewhat forgotten perspective on freedom.

Equally durable proved to be the belief that freedom exercised by the *Rzeczpospolita* nobles was unique and gave their homeland a special status among other European states. Originating in the mid-sixteenth century, this belief was not an expression of the usual Sarmatian meg-alomania, which manifested itself in the seventeenth century and at the beginning of the eighteenth. It was not a Polish idiosyncrasy either, with similar opinions on liberty being voiced in other free republics. For in-stance, the citizens of the fifteenth-century Florence considered their re-public to be unique and extraordinary due to freedom it guaranteed.[22] The Venetians, and later on the Dutch[23] and the English, held similar opinions on their states. The statement "[...] there is one kingdom on earth where Liberty has taken up her dwelling," was not intended to describe the Sarmatian *Rzeczpospolita*, but rather Hanoverian England, and its author believed that it was his homeland was "the only kingdom, and Britons the only people who can truly say, we are free."[24] Noble cit-izens eagerly subscribed to this viewpoint, and even well before the first free election they voiced the following opinion: "freedom and liberty [...] are so great and worthy in Poland that other nations' liberty, when com-pared to ours, appears nothing more than unbearable slavery."[25] Even authors who were not uncritical admirers of freedom, such as Krzysztof Warszewicki[26] or Andrzej Wolan, admitted its unique position: after all, one of the chapters of Wolan's treatise was entitled *The noblemen's free-dom in our nation others by far exceeds.*[27] During the political conflicts following the death of Sigismund August, the motif of the uniqueness of Polish liberty and its superiority over other nations' freedom was omni-present. It was asserted with pride, if not overt hubris, that "The Poles are *gens gentium omnium, quaecunque sub sole sunt, liberrima*,"[28] and that "no nation in the entire world has greater freedom and liberty than us."[29] The opinion that "there is not a nation under the Sun as free as Poland,"[30] prevailed at least until the 1770s, and its echoes could still be heard in the disputes during the Four-Year Sejm. Most of the time, it was asserted with reverence, but sometimes also with a note of sarcasm, as was done by Józef Wybicki, who once wrote: "[...] the Poles are con-vinced that they are the freest nation amongst all."[31] It seems, however, that the uniqueness of Polish freedom was never to be so strongly and proudly emphasized as it was at the beginning of the Polish-Lithuanian Commonwealth period.

Polish freedom was considered not only unique, but also inherent to the Poles, who had every right to own it. This conceptualization of free-dom as a property belonging to the noble class is a conspicuous element of the noblemen's political discourse, evidenced by the use of the posses-sive pronoun "our," omnipresent in speeches delivered in the Sejm and in local assemblies, and also in political writing.[32] With each speaker or writer presenting himself as a co-owner and co-participant of freedom, rarely was it subject to analysis proper. Unlike in the works of Western European writers, freedom in Poland was not treated as an abstract phil-osophical issue or a problem belonging to the theory of statehood but as a reality surrounding the participants of political debates. Therefore, in the majority of cases it was analyzed "from within."[33] A number of Renaissance writers, including Andrzej Frycz Modrzewski, Wawrzyniec Goślicki and Andrzej Wolan, may have dealt with freedom on a more general level, but for one thing, they were not fully consistent, and for another, their approach was not representative of the prevalent way of thinking. The translation of the title of Wolan's dissertation *De libertate politica seu civilis* as *On the Polish, or noble freedom* in its 1606 Polish version speaks for itself: freedom, which for Wolan was a communal value, available to all members of a society, became tied to a specific *hic et nunc* and a specific social class. It was only in the 1770s and 1780s that some general theories of freedom were invoked by authors influenced by Enlightenment ideas, but even those authors tended to discuss Polish freedom rather than freedom in general.

Having considered the significance of freedom in the Polish political discourse, it is now time to define this concept by addressing the fundamental question of what exactly constituted the highest value, object of pride and concern, as well as the inherent property of Poles. First, it is necessary to systematize terminological issues and to distinguish freedom (*wolność*) in the singular, which will be subject of further considerations in this chapter, from freedoms or liberties (*wolności*) in the plural number. It is no wonder the latter are mentioned all too often in the political discourse, since they signified the noblemen's privileges, guaranteed by a number of enacted laws, therefore becoming the object of deepest concern in political texts and in Sejm or local assembly speeches. Liberties/privileges are an essential component of the discourse, which parallels their role in the socio-political reality. But the key notion that defined the political discourse was *wolność* – freedom. Both theorists and participants of contemporary disputes acknowledged the existence of one, singular and uncountable freedom, alongside, or possibly above, particular liberties/privileges. On this view, privileges were no longer conceived of as liberty (or liberties) but rather as legally guaranteed rights, with freedom providing the foundation for the infrangibility of those rights. It was thus freedom that constituted the highest value and most precious treasure of a Polish citizen[34] and it was freedom that was permanently interwoven into the political discourse. Evoked endlessly, it was however rarely defined or analyzed, being mostly taken for granted. Owing to this practice, some researchers approach freedom as an amorphous umbrella term encompassing all the various rights, institutions and traditions that constituted the noble democracy.[35] A careful analysis of various mentions of *wolność* indicates, however, that this concept was coherent and far from amorphous. It is worthwhile to recall its foundations, as the specific understanding of freedom set the perspective on the political world, on the perception of an individual's rights, and on the relationship between an individual and the community. The concept of freedom underlying uses of this term in Poland from the sixteenth century on was markedly different from its present-day conceptualization, largely shaped by the liberal discourse. It has been pointed out that if present-day notions are applied to the analysis of freedom understood in the Commonwealth terms, elements of both positive and negative liberty can be found.[36] On the one hand, it was a freedom to participate in the political life and to make decisions about the state, fellow citizens and about oneself, and on the other, it was a freedom from interference into a citizen's private sphere of life. As Konarski writes,

> this is what true freedom of the country and its citizens rests upon – to govern yourself, to write laws for yourself, to levy taxes for yourself, to establish government for yourself, to be certain of your fortune, honor, and life.[37]

It has to be underscored that the two kinds of liberty were not seen as separate for a long period of time, but the former was seen as dependent on the latter.

This perspective situates the Polish political discourse and the Polish conception of freedom within what Anglophone researchers dub the republican or Neo-Roman tradition,[38] originating from Aristotle's *politeia* and Polybius' mixed government, and later significantly influenced by the vision of freedom created in the Roman Republic by Sallust, Livy and especially Cicero, who was the best known of the three in the *Rzeczpospolita*.[39] This vision inspired and was developed by the Italian proponents of civic humanism, and later also by advocates of the republican system throughout Europe. It was widely known and accepted in Poland already in the Renaissance period, with Polish theoreticians citing not only renowned Roman writers but also Aristotle's theory of statehood, familiar to the Poles from the works of Stanisław Orzechowski and Sebastian Petrycy of Pilsen.[40] The Polish viewpoint was also influenced by Italian Renaissance writers, especially those who created the myth of the Venetian Republic, among whom Gasparo Contarini[41] was best known. Importantly, the Polish conception of freedom was not merely a theoretical construct, but a working notion commonly evoked in political debates.

The concept of freedom so understood was premised upon the assumption that a free person has the ability to decide affairs for themselves. Servitude in turn denoted not only a specific act of infringement on an individual's rights but also a general possibility of such infringement, that is, being dependent on another person's will, or – in the Roman Law terms – remaining *in potestate domini*.[42] Orzechowski puts it as follows: "a servant is not his own, being all his master's, not having his own will,"[43] and Andrzej Radawiecki explains further that "a slave is he who exists and lives for another, whereas free is he who lives for himself."[44] In the introduction to his statute, Jan Herburt describes the conditions of living under absolute monarchy in the following way:

> Because there they have every abundance, yet they are not owned by those who possess them. And moreover, whenever the supreme ruler so wisheth, thou must present thyself and suffer thyself to be judged as he seeth fit and whensoever thou be'st so ordered; when they order so needlessly, shouldst thou wish to 'scape trouble then mount thine horse.[45]

"Freedom at another's mercy," as it was reportedly referred to by Andrzej Maksymilian Fredro,[46] was completely unacceptable for the participants of the political life in the *Rzeczpospolita* in the sixteenth century and at later times. To be free, an individual had to have a right to decide matters for himself: the frequency of the expressions "his own," "himself" should be seen as symptomatic.[47] In 1573 an anonymous writer confesses that

> Great is the common freedom, that I am not ruled by any lord as he wishes and desires, or by any other frivolous individual, but by my brother (...), and the more agreeable 'tis for me as a free man to bear what I myself and my brother, exalted by me to do so, have consented to bear.[48]

Thirty years later, another anonymous writer and *rokosz* participant explains that the law of a republic is called "common law" because "everyone voluntarily ordains that law upon themselves, so that the law be not burdensome upon him who ordains it upon himself."[49] The belief that freedom primarily involves the self-determination of citizens lasted until the end of the First Commonwealth. In 1775 Michał Wielhorski expressed an opinion very closely resembling the above-quoted sixteenth-century statement, namely that "a Pole's freedom consists in obeying only these laws that were establish'd by himself or by lawmakers he has rightfully elected."[50] The most poetic formulation of this idea was offered in the seventeenth century by Jakub Zawisza of Kroczów, who likened the laying down of laws for citizens by citizens to the earthly image "of heavenly joy."[51]

Freedom so understood was to be guaranteed and at the same time exercised by participation in government. Deliberations on the foundations of freedom in Poland characteristically focused only on selected noblemen's privileges, which indicates that they were not automatically and unreflectively identified with freedom. Among those that were mentioned are the nobles' rights guaranteeing their participation in making decisions about the state and about themselves. A scrutiny of this issue over the whole Commonwealth period reveals its evolution. In the sixteenth century "the finest Polish liberty" was typically identified with "free election of a lord."[52] Elections were considered to be "the foundation of freedom," or "*basis et fundamentum* [...] of all our liberties."[53] It has to be borne in mind that the idea of a nation's sovereignty was absent from the Polish political discourse and theory, nor was it obvious for Western theorists. Judging by the popularity of Jean Bodin's thought, it was the idea of governance conducted by a sovereign individual that had currency.[54] The fact that noble citizens elected their ruler underscored their supremacy over the monarch. Moreover, the right to elect the king had direct ramifications for their second most important power, namely participation in lawmaking, which was the essence of their freedom to decide matters for themselves. This was emphasized both in theoretical considerations,[55] and in the course of current political debates.[56] The significance of free election as one of the foundations and at the same time execution of the noble freedom was being pointed out almost until the end of the Polish-Lithuanian Commonwealth, with the Four-Year Sejm providing the last forum for this issue to be debated. But in the course of time, the laying down of laws in the form of making decisions at the Sejm or at local assemblies – or, as was often the case, opposing decisions by exercising the right to *liberum veto* – became prioritized. Even though other laws guaranteeing individual liberties were also mentioned, especially in the sixteenth and in the beginning of the seventeenth century, such as the privilege *neminem captivabimus nisi iure victum* ("We shall not arrest anyone without a court ruling"), they were discussed less frequently, and, so to speak, ranked lower than lawmaking. The fact that the number of mentions of this privilege in the freedom discourse decreased with time should not be taken as an indication that its importance also diminished. Simply, it resulted from the belief that privileges guaranteeing rights of an individual would not be sufficient without the laws guaranteeing self-determination. As Szczepan Sienicki observed in the eighteenth century: "this and similar rights are all derived from the freedom of deliberations and assemblies."[57]

The civil freedom of the individual, that is, the right "to own [property], serenely and without fear of harm"[58] was not neglected in the political discourse of the First Polish Republic. However, it was only in the 1770s that freedom came to be separated from participation in governance, as took place in the Western European discourse in the mid-seventeenth century through the work of Thomas Hobbes.[59] Participants in the Polish political discussions remained loyal to the antique traditions, seeing freedom as inseparable from a specific form of governance, claiming that the liberty of the individual could be secured only in a free republic, that is, in a state in which the people or the nation (however construed) participated in ruling the country.

There is yet another aspect of freedom being linked with a republic, with the *Rzeczpospolita*, which is essential for understanding the Polish freedom discourse. Simply put, the *Rzeczpospolita* was considered indispensable for freedom to exist. Recall that the noun "freedom" was typically preceded by the plural first-person possessive determiner – it was "our" freedom rather than "my," "thy," "your," or "his" freedom, or perhaps it was "my" freedom because it was "ours" in the first place. The divergence between the noble class discourse rooted in the ancient tradition and the liberal notion of freedom arising out of the law of nature was very clear. In the latter liberty was seen as a natural and inalienable (at least theoretically) property of the individual, regardless of his membership in a given community, whereas in the former, freedom depended on such membership. The noble class discourse has been occasionally criticized on the grounds that it did not make use of the notion of independence (*niepodległość*) until the 1760s.[60] The critique is ill-founded, however, as independence was included within the notion of freedom, inherently hinging on the existence of a free and independent republic. It has to be emphasized, though, that on this conception an individual was not completely subordinated to the community, as envisaged by Jean-Jacques Rousseau in an extreme version of his theory, which had been allegedly modeled on the practices implemented in Sparta.[61] Rather, the community portrayed in the noble authors' writings consisted of free individuals, each of whom decided matters for himself, albeit within the framework of the freedom guaranteed by the community.

This conception of freedom provided an adequate foundation for describing the reality and political postulates put forth by the nobility in the sixteenth century, when a political language was still being forged, and also in the later period of the Polish-Lithuanian Commonwealth. At the same time, it excluded all those who – in the opinion of the participants of political life – did not belong to the noble *Rzeczpospolita* community. The freedom of Poland's non-noble inhabitants was a subject of concern for those Renaissance theoreticians who subscribed to the conception of natural freedom, including Modrzewski, Petrycy and Wolan[62] – in contradistinction to Orzechowski, for whom freedom and the *Rzeczpospolita* were inseparable. No wonder this issue disappeared from the discourse for almost 200 years, the effect being the same as in the case of the notion *Rzeczpospolita*: the reality influenced the political language, which in turn affected the perception and categorization of reality. The revival of interest in the liberties and rights of the other social classes in the eighteenth century was accompanied by attempts to reform the language and to include into it the notion of natural freedom.

Owing to the close ties between freedom, rights and the political system of the *Rzeczpospolita*, freedom was considered extremely fragile. It was dependent not only on the existence of the republic, but also on maintaining the volatile balance of mixed government, being the only guarantee of citizens' liberty and of the state's strength. Following Western thinkers, the Polish participants of political debates from the sixteenth to the eighteenth centuries noted two chief threats to this balance, and consequently to freedom: the ruler had a natural tendency to assume all power and hence become a tyrant, and the people striving to enhance their liberty had a tendency towards unbridled license and anarchy. Inspired by Wespazjan Kochowski, Stanisław Konarski warned: *"Nam ut neglecta libertas in servitutem, ita libertas sine modo in licentiam degenerate"* ("As neglected liberty degenerates into servitude, so too does liberty without moderation degenerate into license.")[63]

Of the two threats to freedom, the king's despotism – the infamous *absolutum dominium* – garnered much more attention, becoming dominant not only in the discourse but also in the nobles' views.[64] The other one, which could be dubbed "freedom as a threat to freedom," was however also highly conspicuous in the Polish discourse. Opinions voiced by Polish speakers drew upon the ancient tradition of treating liberty as a priceless good, which was at the same time to be approached with utmost caution, as it could easily turn from privilege to peril. From the very beginning of the Polish-Lithuanian Commonwealth, and possibly even earlier, good, true and law-constrained freedom was clearly distinguished in political texts from excessive freedom and misrule, or lack of government. At this junction, two notions crucial for the freedom discourse need to be mentioned, namely license and anarchy. Even though both of them denoted degenerated freedom, they were not synonymous. License (Latin *licentia*, Polish *swawola*) concerned chiefly the attitudes of people abusing or misusing freedom, who were disobedient of the laws and placed their own private good over the community's wellbeing. Anarchy (Greek *anarchia*, Polish *bezrząd*), in turn, resulted from such abuse, being a condition of the state in which its basic institutions were malfunctioning or not functioning at all. Despite the fact that both terms had been known since antiquity, it was only in the eighteenth century that the latter gained currency in the writings of authors postulating reforms of the *Rzeczpospolita*'s inefficient political system, with Stanisław Konarski presenting the most dramatic accounts of anarchy.[65] *Licentia* – wanton license, on the other hand, was seen as an inseparable, albeit undesirable companion of freedom already in the sixteenth and seventeenth centuries. It was a dangerous companion, too. Plato's opinion that "too much freedom is too much slavery, in the individual and the state,"[66] was cited and endorsed by Polish authors writing at the time of the nobility's struggle for the rule of Poland, especially by those who were highly critical towards the political reality and the nobility's aspirations.[67] License inevitably leading to anarchy and demise of the state was seen as a threat by Wolan, portrayed with plain disgust by Warszewicki, and sketched with a touch of dramatism by Łukasz Górnicki, whose account may have been inspired by Italian theoreticians:

"What comes after great liberty is license, followed by disdain for the laws, this is then followed by internal altercations, and then comes slavery."[68] A similar path to the fall of liberty was envisioned in the seventeenth century by Łukasz Opaliński and Szymon Starowolski. The latter echoed Seneca in saying that license "to every man, to every kingdom, to every republic, to every house or family, society or assembly will bring bane and disaster."[69]

For some authors, especially Warszewicki, but also Górnicki and Opaliński, this statement constituted an argument for strengthening the monarch's power, but complaints about *licentiosa libertas* were quite frequent in the discourse, even in zealous panegyrics praising the Polish liberty, as was the case of Wojciech Bystrzonowski, who admitted that "in our democracy *libertas* is giving way to *licentiam*," which he accepted with philosophical resignation.[70] The belief that freedom is a precious good but can also be dangerous was widespread, with descriptions of license and later also of anarchy occupying a prominent place in the political discourse up to the eighteenth century. For such authors as Leszczyński, and later for Konarski, the dramatic account of Poland sliding into total anarchy became a departure point for their deliberations on how to remedy its institutions, which bore some analogy to the role played by the accounts of license for the Renaissance writers. It was also a convenient propaganda argument, still much in use in the disputes of the Four-Year Sejm, since the proposed remedies were presented as the restoration of true liberty, which had been destroyed by *licentia* or anarchy. Not infrequently, though, such complaints were simply an expression of helplessness and desperation about the downfall of the nobles' morale resulting in the state crisis. The helplessness can perhaps be best captured in the saying "excessive freedom is still better than no freedom at all." The idea appeared in an anonymous politician's speech delivered during the great interregnum, for whom the statement "I prefer for freedom to lean towards license, than for it to be confined by subjugation" became the "*dictum* of a true lover of his homeland's liberty."[71] What was being referred to as subjugation in this speech and in many others was the strengthening of the monarch's power.

Suspiciousness towards the ruler was one of the dominant elements of the Polish political discourse and political thought in general. Its origins should be sought both in the theory of statehood and in the reality of struggles for power between the nobility and elected monarchs, with the political on-goings in other European monarchies playing a part, too. Accusations of attempts to enhance royal prerogatives at the expense of the nobles' liberties were leveled during the preparations for the first free election, at the time of the 1606 *rokosz* and in the political debates at the Four-Year Sejm.[72] It should be borne in mind, however, that tensions between the royal power and the people's liberty were inevitable, as was apparent not only to the Polish nobility but also to other nations exercising some freedom under the rule of a monarch.[73] Much as citizens strived towards expanding the realm of their freedom even beyond the confines of rationality, monarchs had a natural tendency to introduce absolute power unrestrained by any legal or institutional regulations. "As it is in our natural interest to defend liberty, so it is natural for all monarchs to *deprimere* it," wrote in 1733 the author of *Przestroga braterska* [A Brotherly Warning], for whom it was reprehensible yet perfectly natural that King Augustus II intended to suppress freedom throughout all his reign.[74] What makes this statement ironic is that it was produced by none other than the king-to-be Stanisław Leszczyński, who thereby was actually echoing an opinion voiced at the time of the Zebrzydowski rebellion that "the nature of kings is such: when warring they think of how to acquire what belongs to others, and when idle they wish to rule their country absolutely."[75] This tendency was seen as consequent upon the weakness of human nature, always hungry for power, and also upon the nature of every rule, always striving towards the expansion if its privileges. Attempts to undermine this belief were taken only at the end of the eighteenth century, when the conception of the mixed government was replaced by the idea of the separation of powers. This issue, however, extends beyond the scope of the present chapter.

What is highly relevant for the current discussion is that at some point the fear of freedom being endangered by a king (or any ruler), who could set himself free from the nation's control, started to dominate the political discourse together with an increasingly passive attitude to liberty, which was seen as a good that had to be preserved. Below is a comment by Hans-Jürgen Bömelburg on the influence of the constant fear of tyranny identified with the absolute rule on the Polish political discourse:

> Debates on the absolute rule exercised by a prince over his citizens for their own good are present in the history of political thought of almost all European cultures of that time. But they were not conducted in Poland, where every form of "absolute rule" was evaluated negatively, so there was not a serious discussion on the foundations of this kind of political reflection.[76]

The feeling of impending threat, the "fear about retaining freedom," which was not absent from other nations' discourses either, became a highly prominent motif of all Polish political texts, from speeches to treatises.[77] With the passage of time, it also became the most extensively discussed topic. Expressed in texts originating from the days of the first free election (or even earlier ones), warnings against the demise of freedom became more frequent in later times, with the call *adieu libertas, vale libertas!* virtually dominating the eighteenth-century discourse, from the Saxon rule to the Confederation of Bar.[78] The Poles were no longer just free, but rather "still free," which was indeed a useful propaganda argument implying that a loss of liberty would be blamed on the political opponents bringing such unfreedom on. For the last time, this argument was exploited in a Four-Year Sejm debate by the advocates of free elections, who claimed that even if freedom had not yet vanished completely, it was vanishing. The idea of *liberum veto*, an individual's right to challenge any decision taken by the parliament, fit in well with this conception. On the one hand, it was an extreme manifestation of the political freedom of an individual, who could exercise real influence on the laws, and on the other, protection of liberty from usurpers or corrupted fellow-citizens. As Szczepan Sienicki – one of the last defenders of *liberum veto* – wrote: "the prerogative of freedom is so great that every nobleman has the power and capacity to protect the public good and to prevent all things that could hamper freedom, the totality of rights and liberties of a free nation."[79] As is evident, the protection of the public good was identified with the protection of freedom.

No less evident is the emphasis on the fact that power is exercised by every nobleman, pointing to another element without which the picture of freedom in the nobles' political discourse would be incomplete, namely equality. When defending the rights of Protestants, Hieronim Moskorzowski explained "that the noble estate in the Kingdom of Poland was acquired from the freedom of one's ancestors' blood equally by all. Therefore, reason would not admit some enjoying it more than others in one homeland."[80] Equality of rights, or more precisely equality in submission to the law, as a prerequisite for liberty was discussed in the previous chapter. But there was a political element in equality so understood as well, since it included equal rights to participate in the public life and in making decisions about the community. As Andrzej Radawiecki observed in the seventeenth century, "in Poland one compares equally against others – one law to all and a free equal vote."[81] On the conception of freedom as an unrestrained right to decide matters for oneself and independence of another person's will, it could be indeed achieved only under the condition of legal and political equality of all citizens. Broad and complex as it was, the nobles' "ideology of equality"[82] could not be identified only with political issues, but its link to liberty both in the political discourse and in the perception of its participants cannot be questioned. Researchers have long noted this connection, emphasizing that "the two values were inseparable; both were inscribed in the political system of the state."[83] They were presented in the political discourse accordingly: "This *aequalitas* holds among us and *in ea libertas nostra consistit.*"[84] This opinion voiced by Jan Zamoyski in 1605 was shared by the nobles and by the theoreticians of statehood alike practically till the end of the *Rzeczpospolita*. Andrzej Radawiecki wrote that "free is but he who is equal to others,"[85] Kazimierz Wieruszewski framed it figuratively as "*inequalitas* is but a stepmother and *civium aequalitas* is liberty's true mother,"[86] and Stanisław Konarski warned "the ruin of equality drags freedom behind, and turns it into ruin as well."[87] Similar warnings were issued throughout the seventeenth and eighteenth centuries, accompanied by complaints about equality being breached, which affected freedom too.[88]

As was stated at the beginning of this chapter, both the definition of freedom and attitudes towards it in the political discourse of the Polish-Lithuanian Commonwealth proved to be exceptionally stable, with some elements even outliving the state. This should not, however, be understood as an indication that the conception of freedom did not evolve; on the contrary, it did, with new notions and ideas enriching the political language in the second half of the eighteenth century. These novel notions not only systematized the Polish vision of liberty but also brought about some reformulations within it.

One of the problems of the Polish "language of freedom" was the non-existence of terms enabling distinctions between its various levels. As was mentioned before, the conception of freedom – *wolność* – included both the liberties of an individual and the right to participate in ruling the country. The inventory of Polish political terms did not, however, include items to name the two kinds of liberty, which were therefore seen as two different aspects of one phenomenon. This may have led to terminological and legal confusion: on the one hand, any breach of a nobleman's privilege could be represented as an attempted breach of the nation's prerogatives, on the other, the right to participation in exercising power could be interpreted as mere protection of the freedom of an individual rather than this plus the protection of a free state.[89] Both interpretations occupied a prominent place in the eighteenth-century discourse, leading to a severe impasse of political thought.

A possible way out could be sought in the somewhat forgotten foundations of the liberty discourse, which stated that the only guarantee of liberties was the existence of a free republic, with the traditional idea of "constraining freedom for the sake of freedom itself" providing guidelines for solving the dilemma. This path was followed in the eighteenth century by the advocates of improving Poland's political system, such as Leszczyński and, especially, Konarski, whose argumentation on that issue was really impressive. Towards the end of that century, these ideas were combined with Rousseau's notions and terminology in the writings of Stanisław Staszic, which bore fruit in a most interesting conception of freedom characterized by anti-individualism and focus on collective liberty, a notion highly untypical in Poland.[90] It should be underscored that Staszic was concerned with liberty in a community/society, not with the liberty of noble citizens.

From the perspective of discourse analysis, the systematization of the concept of freedom, clearly divided into civil liberty and political liberty, appears to be more promising. Such distinction was prompted not only by the influence of foreign ideas but also by the development of political

science, which entailed a need to precisely define all fundamental notions, liberty included. It is difficult to find the first occurrence of this
distinction; suffice it to say, then, that it was widely attested in various
political texts of the 1770s, including disputes and Sejm speeches. The
definitions of political freedom did not diverge from the traditional understanding of freedom as self-determination and participation in governance. This is how it was defined by all thinkers deploying this term,[91]
who also subscribed to the traditional view that it can only be achieved
in free states or republics. As Antoni Popławski put it, "glorious is liberty which can be found in a *res publica*, and which is commonly known
as political liberty."[92] A certain novelty, in turn, can be found in the
definition of civil liberty, presented as freedom "which enables everyone
to occupy themselves with their own happiness, without injury to the
public happiness or that of their fellow citizens" in the words of Franciszek Bieliński,[93] who modeled his view on Paul Holbach. It was also
emphasized, much stronger than ever before, that liberty consisted in the
ability to enjoy one's property freely and safely. Konstanty Bogusławski
believed that freedom is "free exercise of ownership under the protection
of law,"[94] where "law" was generally thought of as constituted by citizens. Authors of handbooks and essays dealing with the condition of the
state, such as Bogusławski, Stroynowski or Wyrwicz, who were strongly
influenced by foreign thinkers (chiefly Montesquieu and the physiocrats),
occasionally identified liberty with its negative form, without endorsing
its connection to governance.[95] Stroynowski once polemicized with the
view that liberty and self-determination go hand in hand, saying this:

> [...] contrary to what many may surmise, a citizen's freedom does
> not hinge on his not being subject to the laws which he himself had
> not enacted, instead it hinges on his being subject only to such laws
> that are given by the natural order, that are necessary for his own
> good, and that are good and fair in all their essence.[96]

This opinion, however, clearly stood out from the dominant view on
which civil liberty was guaranteed only by political liberty. By subscrib-
ing to this view, Polish authors could at the same time uphold the republican ideal and criticize its deformations, which they dubbed "false"
or "purported" freedom, postulating their own unblemished construct
instead. The adoption of precise definitions of both freedoms revealed
that a number of the nobles' rights and privileges had nothing to do with
any of them; hence, the persistent protection of such privileges did not
in fact serve protecting freedom. Besides, separation of civil liberty from
political liberty reinforced the distinction between the liberties of an individual and the rights/liberties of a citizen. Last but not least, emphasis
on the protection of liberty from the infringement not only by the ruling
authorities but also – crucially – by fellow citizens, shifted the focus

of discussion and reduced obsessive fear of liberty being threatened by the ruler's machinations. Consequently, the political atmosphere became more open and welcoming to proposals of the institutional reforms intended to protect the liberty of an individual from infringement by fellow citizens. The most complete exploitation of the newly introduced notions can be seen in the work by Józef Wybicki, whose book *Myśli polityczne o wolności cywilnej* [Political Thoughts on Civil Freedom] (1775) was premised upon the assumption that all Polish troubles stemmed from the lack of differentiation between political freedom understood as self-determination, and civil freedom, which, following liberal thought, Wybicki identified with liberty to act within the bounds of law: "each particular citizen can act as a state's laws permit, and he shall not be forced to commit a deed that such laws do not dictate."[97]

The recognition of the two freedoms was intrinsically linked to another important change in the political discourse, namely the introduction of the concept of natural freedom in the 1770s, initially on the level of general considerations. As was mentioned, the concept of freedom as a natural right of the individual appeared during the Renaissance period, but it did not subsequently win appreciation in the freedom discourse, gradually falling into oblivion. It was revived by Wybicki and the group of political writers referred to – whether deservedly or not – as the Polish physiocrats, including Wincenty Skrzetuski, Popławski, Stroynowski and Bogusławski. The interpretation of natural freedom espoused by Western philosophers, including the "French economists," who significantly influenced the Polish physiocrats, provided a foundation for the concept of civil freedom, or to use today's parlance, negative freedom. It was a natural right endowed upon all human beings, regardless of the political system under which they lived; moreover, it existed prior to the origin of society and, *a fortiori*, prior to the origin of political power.

The reintroduction of the notion of natural freedom into the discourse had profound consequences. Authors who concerned themselves with freedom apart from that of the noble estate could avail themselves of a conceptual tool to account for the situation of the other social classes. The statement that freedom is a natural condition implied that it is not an attribute of noblemen belonging to the *Rzeczpospolita* community, but an inalienable right of every human being; one with which every human is born, and which is safeguarded, and at the same time confined, by positive laws to avoid conflict with the rights of others. "As everyone is by nature the owner of his own person, so he is by nature free in this respect and not subjugated to others" wrote Hieronim Stroynowski.[98] Popławski asserted that "in exercising such freedom one citizen shall not exercise it more or less than another citizen, as such inequality would be adverse to the divine laws of nature," whereby "a citizen" he meant every member of society.[99] This viewpoint was shared by his fellow Piarists Stroynowski, Bogusławski and also by Wybicki.[100] Even if deliberations on natural freedom were purely theoretical, as was the case especially of Stroynowski, they obviously touched upon the issue of peasants' freedom. Although the critique of peasants' subjugation, or more precisely excessive subjugation, surfaced in Polish political texts written in the seventeenth and eighteenth centuries, it was mostly concerned with the moral perspective – of power abuse by the noblemen, or the economic perspective – of loss incurred by the state due to the oppression of peasantry, with the political and legal aspects of the problem being largely neglected, except in the writings of Modrzewski and Wolan in the sixteenth century, as was mentioned in Chapter 2. The separation of political freedom from civil freedom, granting the latter the status of a natural right of every member of humankind, was the first step towards including the issue of peasant freedom in the political deliberations. While political freedom was an attribute accruing to each citizen and needed not to extend over all members of society, civil freedom had to be equal among all. This may not have marked a breakthrough in the discourse on freedom, but the credit due to these somewhat forgotten authors for introducing new ideas and terms should be acknowledged. Stroynowski, for instance, changed his political language completely, abandoning the concept of political freedom, bypassing the problem of free people's attitudes, and treating the state as an institution which is external with respect to individuals. Other thinkers did not break away from the traditional discourse and carried on considering social issues and political problems separately, or even, like Wybicki, in separate works.[101]

A successful attempt to create a coherent discourse combining the tradition with novel concepts was undertaken by Hugo Kołłątaj. As a point of departure, he reformulated the old truth that only free rule can guarantee the rights of individuals in a more modern parlance, writing in his *Listy Anonima* [Anonymous Letters] that "All the conditions of free governance come down only to this – for man to be the truly free owner of his own person and property."[102] Kołłątaj's maxim pertained to all inhabitants of the *Rzeczpospolita*, with the author insisting further that "There can be no free government in a country where the hardest-working millions of peasants [remain] in servitude."[103] This assertion followed logically from the assumption that the liberty of a republic arises in virtue of natural law, rather than as a privilege granted by a ruler to a specific group of individuals. Of all Polish writers, Kołłątaj offered the most complete account of freedom drawing both on modern conceptions, mostly adapted from the physiocrats, and the republican tradition. Employing the distinction into political and civil freedom, he reassured his noble readers that the former is intended only for the nobility and burghers – proprietors, whereas the latter appertains to all, peasants included. He also recalled a number of principles of republican freedom, such as that liberties of an individual depend on the strength and efficiency of a free state, that it is necessary to take care of the public good, and that laws must be obeyed, etc. Such harmonious combination of the traditional elements with modern views posited by Enlightenment philosophers rendered Kołłątaj's contribution the most comprehensive work in the Polish freedom discourse.

The conception of natural freedom undoubtedly paved the way for a new approach to liberty, but the question to what extent this new approach was adopted in the political discourse still needs to be addressed. During the Four-Year Sejm, not more than a handful of writings based on the modern conception of freedom appeared in political debates,[104] hardly constituting a real change. Despite the fact that the notions of natural and civil freedom gained recognition not only in treatises but also in political journalism, especially in the tumultuous period 1788– 1792, they did not become commonly accepted. Even those writers who took an active interest in widening the societal scope of liberty did not always feel the need to systematically redefine this conception. Some, like Staszic, simply applied the old terms, such as "people," "nation" and "citizen" in new senses, transgressing the traditional social estate boundaries. In the case of other authors, however, introducing new terms into the discourse did not yield a genuinely innovative outlook, with natural freedom often being evoked merely as an erudite embellishment. In some works, it provided yet another reason to glorify the Polish freedom in its traditional shape, seen as a continuation or consequence of natural freedom.[105] In his defense of the old system of government against what he described as the "coup of the Third of May," Dyzma Bończa Tomaszewski claimed that this government had been "ordained by our forefathers as the most consistent with natural freedom and laws given by God to man together with his soul."[106]

Until the very end of the Polish-Lithuanian Commonwealth, freedom was chiefly seen in the discourse as a kind of political value: what attracted most interest was how it was implemented in the state and what how the citizen-authorities relationship was shaped. Although many participants in political debates adopted a more modern distinction between civil and political freedom and some of them dropped the understanding of freedom based on the estate hierarchy, they still posited their visions of liberty based on the image of a free state, underlain by republican ideals determining the scope of freedom and the duties of those who exercised it. It should be noted that from among all Western theorists of statehood, it was Montesquieu and Rousseau – that is, the thinkers who closely followed the republican values in their models – that gained the greatest popularity in Poland.

It is extremely difficult to speculate about the possible further development of the freedom discourse after 1792, as its shape and the place of new ideas were then determined by the political reality. An analysis of the discourse of the Kościuszko Uprising (1794) indicates that there was a turn towards the classical conception of freedom understood as

88   Wolność – *Freedom*

the right to decide matters for oneself.[107] The liberal conception of freedom as an individual's liberty guaranteed by law and independent of the current rule was completely unfit for a slogan of insurrection against oppressors and was difficult to implement under the partitions. By this token, the reality lent support to the old belief that the liberty of an individual was possible only where citizens did not depend on the will of others, that only an independent and free Republic could guarantee such liberty, and consequently, that the struggle for the independent homeland was at the same time a struggle for the liberty of her inhabitants.

Notes

1 *Uwagi względem Konstytucyi…* (1791).
2 This chapter is largely based on my previous research, presented in the Polish monograph Grześkowiak-Krwawicz (2006) and its shorter English version Grześkowiak-Krwawicz (2012a); cf. also Janicki (2004, 80–92); Gromelski (2013, 215–234).
3 Cf. Opaliński (1995, 83ff.); Urwanowicz (1994, 174ff.).
4 Sienicki (1764, introduction).
5 *List obywatela do wszystkich stanów…* (1776, 15).
6 Wolan (1572/1606/2010, 77, 79)
7 "Without this supreme jewel, all subsequent goods are next to naught" *Krótkie rzeczy potrzebnych z strony wolności a swobód polskich zebranie* (1587/1859, 13).
8 Radawiecki (1625, 32).
9 Ł. Opaliński, *Obrona Polski przeciw Janowi Barklayowi* [1648], in Opaliński (1959, 197).
10 *Libera republica quae sit?*, in Czubek (1918, vol. 2, 407).
11 *Absolutum dominium quid sit?*, in Czubek (1918, vol. 2, 409–413).
12 Bouwsma (1995, 203–234).
13 Maciejewski (1974, 34).
14 Such as in the writings of Machiavelli, cf. Skinner (1990a: 135).
15 Turski (1790a: 5).
16 *Dyskurs wolnego civis a nie interesów obcych albo swoich, ale tylko dobro pospolite upatrującego* [1666], in Ochmann-Staniszewska (1991, vol. 3, 163).
17 Grześkowiak-Krwawicz (2015, 205).
18 Michalski (1977, 19).
19 [Konarski] (1757, 5); Konarski (1760–1763, vol. 2, 129–130).
20 Wybicki (1775/1984, 54); [Bieliński] (1775, 137); *Zdania sprawiedliwego polityka nad teraźniejszą Polski nieszczęśliwością* [1770], in Konopczyński (1928, 198).
21 Grześkowiak-Krwawicz (2015, 207).
22 Viroli (1995, 29).
23 Worst (1992, 154).
24 *An Essay on Liberty and Independency* [1747], cited after Dickinson (1979, 143); on the English as a nation chosen for freedom, cf. also Pocock (1997, 342ff, 398) (amusingly, Pocock claims that the English were unique in their conviction about the exceptionality of their liberty).
25 Herburt (1570, fol. A 4v).
26 In exchange for faithfulness to monarchs, "the Poles gained the privilege of freedom, such as none of our neighbors enjoys," Warszewicki (1598/2010, 199 in Latin, 363 in Polish).

27 Wolan (1572/1606/2010, Chapter 9, 138), the title in Latin is *Libertatem nobilitatis in gente nostra magnam prae multis aliis nationibus praerogativam habere*" (137).

28 *Ślachcica polskiego do rycerskiego koła braciej swej miłej o obieraniu króla krótka przemowa*, in Czubek (1906, 278).

29 *Naprawa Rzeczypospolitej Koronnej do elekcyjej nowego krola*, in Czubek (1906, 190); cf. also: Janicki (2004, 89ff.).

30 [Dembowski] (1733/1904, 7); note that the author himself did not share this view, but he put these words into the mouth of a Pole, as an expression of widespread views.

31 Wybicki (1775/1984, 182).

32 Rosner (1986, 265).

33 This freedom was viewed from outside by those who did not participate in it: such as the burghers from Royal Prussia who wrote about it, Christoph Hartknoch and Gottlieb Lengnich.

34 Opaliński (1995, 83ff.); Urwanowicz (1994, 174ff.).

35 Gromelski (2013, 230).

36 Ogonowski (1992, 78–79).

37 Konarski (1760–1763, vol. 2, 129).

38 The sources of the discussion on this topic include the now-classic work by Zera Fink (1945) and the concept of civic humanism of Hans Baron (1955). The concept of Republican freedom was analyzed in terms of the history of ideas by Quentin Skinner (1998), and in the philosophical dimension by Philip Pettit (1999).

39 Wirszubski (1968, 1–30).

40 Opaliński (2002, 166); Pietrzyk-Reeves (2012).

41 Backvis (1975, 730); Opaliński (2002, 158).

42 Freedom as dependence on one's own will, rather than someone else's, was already understood by Aristotle, cf. Mulgan (1984, 18); Philip Pettit distinguishes the liberal notion of freedom as *non-interference* vs. the republican notion of freedom as *non-domination* (Pettit 1999, 21), and devotes essentially the whole first chapter of his book to analyzing the two notions, especially among English thinkers from the seventeenth and eighteenth centuries (1999, 22–50); cf. Skinner (1998, 41); Brugger (1999, 41).

43 Quoted after Sapała (2017, 216), who points out that Orzechowski is here following Aristotle's lead.

44 Radawiecki (1625, 31).

45 Herburt (1570 fol. A 4v); *Krótkie rzeczy potrzebnych z strony wolności a swobód polskich zebranie* (1587/1859, 11).

46 A.M. Fredro, *O wyższości rzeczypospolitej nad monarchią*, in Ogonowski (1979, 335).

47 Grześkowiak-Krwawicz (2013, 98–99).

48 *Naprawa Rzeczypospolitej* [1573], in Czubek (1906, 202). Interestingly, this passage was purposefully manipulative, as it refers not to the noble deputies, but to the senators, who were by no means "exalted" by their noble brothers, being nominated by the king.

49 *Libera respublica quae sit?*, in Czubek (1918, vol. 2, 403).

50 Wielhorski (1775, 111).

51 "What harvests, what riches could be dearer and more delectable than true, lofty freedom? Not to demand true consolation from some powerful ruler or inaccessible majesty, but only to devote oneself to a just and necessary cause, until it is *firmum et ratum*: such is the image and shape of heavenly joy," Zawisza z Kroczowa (1613/1899, 16).

52 *Krótkie rzeczy potrzebnych z strony wolności a swobód polskich zebranie* (1587/1859, 55); cf. Gromelski (2013, 225–226).

53 Quoted after Opaliński (1995, 8).
54 Prokhovnik (2008, 13–34).
55 Andrzej Frycz Modrzewski already claimed:

> Because Polish kings are not born kings, but are chosen with the sanc-
> tion of all the estates, it thus does not befit them to wield this power
> to act solely according to their will, or to enact laws, or to levy a tax
> on subjects, or to settle some matter for all eternity. Because they do
> everything with the sanction of all the estates or in accordance with the
> provisions of law [...]

cited from: Sucheni-Grabowska (1994, 75).
56 Citing Sejm speeches from the sixteenth century, Henryk Litwin (1994, 33)
    claimed that "participation in lawmaking was understood as the legal con-
    sequence of involvement in election"; cf. also Sucheni-Grabowska (1994, 7).
57 Sienicki (1764, 88).
58 Wolan (1572/1606/2010, 89).
59 Skinner (2008).
60 Konopczyński (1930, 462–475; 1991, 856)
61 Baczko (2009, 311); Touchefeu (2006, 868ff.).
62 Wolan's assertion is indicative: "No wise man hath doubted that freedom
    is most befitting of human nature, because according to it no one is born a
    captive," Wolan (1572/1606/2010, 81).
63 The opening motto of Konarski (1760–1763), which he took from Ko-
    chowski (1683, 314) but did not quote exactly; the actual original is: *nam
    ut sine curam habita libertas proper servitutem est, ita sine modo in licen-
    tiam degenerat.*
64 Opaliński (1983, 800); Augustyniak (1999, 64ff.); Gromelski (2013,
    223–224).
65 In his depiction, the *Rzeczpospolita* was a country "without freedom,
    without counsel, without strength, without money, without justice, with-
    out glory, without governance, without hope for any good" [Konarski?]
    ([1764]: 19).
66 Plato, *The Republic*, VIII, 564 A.
67 Rotundus (1564/2009, 183, 194).
68 Ł. Górnicki, *Rozmowa Polaka z Włochem o wolnościach i prawach pols-
    kich* [1616], in Górnicki (1961, 350).
69 Starowolski (1650, 26); Ł. Opaliński *Rozmowa plebana z ziemianinem*
    [1641], in Opaliński (1938, 20).
70 Bystrzonowski (1730, b.p.)
71 *Wotum w interregnum po Henrykowym z Polski odjeździe*, in Czubek
    (1906, 634).
72 Cf. Opaliński (1983, 800ff.); Grześkowiak-Krwawicz (2002, 49–59).
73 Cf. Velema (2002, 9–25); Dzelzainis (2002, 27–41); Skinner (1998, 65);
    Boulton (1967).
74 "And so one should not be surprised or complain that King August, whilst
    treading upon our necks, elevated himself *ad hunc supremae domina-
    tium gloriae cumulum*, which he assumed throughout his reign, but by
    God's grace did not manage to become the *dominator* of free nations" [S.
    Leszczyński] ([1733]/2007, 21).
75 M. Zebrzydowski, *Fundament rokoszu*, in Czubek (1918, vol. 3, 347); cf.
    Opaliński (1983, 800); Augustyniak (1999, 35).
76 Bömelburg (2011, 251–252).

77 Cf. Rosner (1986, 266–267); note by way of comparison the opinion of a scholar of English liberty: "[in the eighteenth century] a remarkably large proportion of political argument consisted in specifying how liberty might be lost and affirming how it might best be preserved," Gunn (1983, 229).

78 With precisely these words, an opponent to the Saxon candidacy bid farewell to liberty, *Kopia listu od pewnego Polaka będącego w Dreźnie, pisanego do swego przyjaciela* (1729), in Gierowski (1955, *passim*), where the cry is repeated numerous times.

79 Sienicki (1764, 97).

80 H. Moskorzowski, *Racyje, które dla różności nabożeństw chrześcijańskich w Królestwie Polskim pokoju wnętrznego żadnym sposobem wzruszać nie dopuszczają* [1618–1625], in Augustyniak (2013, 342).

81 Radawiecki (1625, 31); it is another matter that he had great doubts about whether such freedom was actually realized. Cf. also Ekes (2001, 36); Urwanowicz (1994, 174–177); Opaliński (1995, 88).

82 As it was described by Maciszewski (1969, 163).

83 Opaliński (1995, 89); "equality (*aequalitas*) appears to be [...] a derivative of freedom, and in a sense its precondition," Janicki (2004, 92); Wyszomirska (2010, 232–235).

84 J. Zamoyski, *Votum... na sejmie warszawskim... 1605*, in Czubek (1918, vol. 2, 92) (version B recognized by the publisher as authentic); cf. Czapliński (1966, 79); Urwanowicz (1994, 177).

85 Radawiecki (1625, 32).

86 Wieruszewski (1733, 139).

87 Konarski (1733, 19).

88 For broader discussion of this issue, see Grześkowiak-Krwawicz (2006, 165–185), the chapter *Wolność i równość*; Grześkowiak-Krwawicz (2012a: 55–59).

89 Although it sounds paradoxical, such an interpretation was (and is!) consistent with the Republican theory of freedom as "non-domination." Already Machiavelli had stated that a people's love for freedom involved not so much a desire to rule, as a desire not to be ruled; later English theorists also agreed with him (cf. Pettit 1999, 28ff.). It is evident here how dangerous was the implementation of theory in practice.

90 "And because to become a citizen is to deprive oneself, that is, to give up one's will and one's personal strength to the whole community, and so no one is born into captivity but everyone is born into obedience. A person loses freedom when he ceases to be obedient. The most important trait of a free citizen is obedience," Staszic (1787/1926, 19).

91 "But if in the civic status, that is, being in a society with others, that same citizen will have the power and right to enter into the governance of the state as a whole, then apart from civil freedom, he will also be served by that glorious freedom as is found in republics, which is commonly called political freedom" Popławski (1774, 251); "apart from civil freedom citizens also have political freedom, because they are members of the body of highest national supremacy, they are participants in legislative power," Wybicki (1775/1984, 85); Kołłątaj (1790, 20, 103). Morski distinguished between three types of freedom: political (the ability to determine the state's foreign policies), legislative, and civil freedom (Morski 1790, 28).

92 Popławski (1774, 251).

93 [Bieliński] (1775, 137), this was a citation from *Politique naturelle*, something the author made no secret of.

94 Bogusławski (1786, 81); Popławski (1774, 251) felt that civil freedom above all entailed the protection of one's life and property and fair courts; for Kołłątaj the basis for freedom was "for a person to be a truly free owner of his person and property" H. Kołłataj *Listy Anonima* [1788–1789], in Kołłątaj (1954, vol. 2, 146)

95 "A citizen living under any government is free, insofar as he is secure from his fellow citizen, neighbor, and the government itself," (Wyrwicz 1771–1772, 144) – this was written under the clear influence of Montesquieu's *The Spirit of the Laws.*

96 Stroynowski (1785, 108).

97 Wybicki (1775/1984, 58).

98 Stroynowski (1785, 25).

99 Popławski (1774, 251).

100 Stroynowski (1785, 25); Bogusławski (1786, 69), both following Quesney; Wybicki ([1777–1778]/1955, 93).

101 Wybicki ([1777–1778]/1955) – natural freedom, the freedom of peasants; Wybicki (1775/1984) – political and civil freedom.

102 H. Kołłątaj *Listy Anonima* [1788–1789], in Kołłątaj (1954, vol. 2, 146).

103 *List do przyjaciela na sejmiki* ([1790]: b.p.) – the pamphlet is anonymous, but there are many signs that its author was Kołłątaj or someone writing in agreement with him; cf. Zielińska (1991, 200).

104 Apart from Stroynowski's treatise and Pawlikowski's booklet, these include the anonymous brochure *Uwagi nad pismem z druku wyszłym pod tytułem Usprawiedliwienie się JW. Dłuskiego* ([1791]), perhaps written by the king himself; cf. Konopczyński (2012, 497, 562, footnote 6).

105 Wielhorski (1775, X, 86).

106 D. Bończa Tomaszewski, *Nad Konstytucją i rewolucją dnia 3 maja roku 1791 uwagi*, in Grześkowiak-Krwawicz (1992a: 163).

107 See also: Grześkowiak-Krwawicz (2012a: 101–120), the chapter: "From Defending Liberty – to Fighting for Liberty"

4   From *Forma Mixta* to the Separation of Powers

Forma mixta, monarchia mixta, regimen mixtum and *mixtum imperium* are not just names for a specific political construct – more importantly, they also refer to one element of a particular vision of the state and of government which, although largely forgotten today, formed one of Europe's fundamental political theories from antiquity all the way until Jean Bodin.[1] That vision constituted a significant, enduring component of political discourse during the Polish-Lithuanian Commonwealth. In this case, the underlying idea – crucial for our understanding of the political world of the time – is more important than its exact name. Without scrutinizing the underpinnings of this concept, it will be impossible to thoroughly understand issues such as how sovereignty and the foundations of power were understood and how participants in political discussions perceived the relationship between the most important elements of the *Rzeczpospolita*'s power system. Additionally, it should be remembered that the concept was fundamental to the existence of the *Rzeczpospolita* or at least one of its aspects, as discussed in Chapter 1. It should be stressed here that when we talk about *forma mixta*, we will use terms "governmental system" or "form of government," even though in the sixteenth and seventeenth centuries speakers and authors saw it as referring to something more, namely the form of the *Rzeczpospolita*, or quite simply the *Rzeczpospolita* itself, comprising the monarchic, aristocratic and democratic elements – the king, the senators and the noble "people." "Mixed government," understood as a term referring to a certain political system, only entered the vocabulary in the second half of the eighteenth century.

Scholars of political thought and political culture among the Polish-Lithuanian nobility[2] paid particular attention to the significance of the concept of a mixed system, especially during the sixteenth and early seventeenth centuries. The most thorough examination has been provided by Janusz Ekes, whose thesis can be described as a starting point for the discussion below.[3] The main topic will be an attempt to examine the concept of a mixed government from the perspective of political language – in other words, to answer the questions of what was understood by *mixtum imperium*, how European traditions were adapted to defining

Poland's political institutions and how this affected the perception of existing solutions and certain fundamental ideas of the system. Another problem is how enduring the concept was, that is, how long it was used as a tool for describing political reality, whether it changed over time and whether/how it was used as an argument in political conflicts.

We should perhaps begin with a certain caveat: although the terms listed at the start of the chapter appeared in discourse as early as the sixteenth century, they were still used rarely and the concept of "a peculiar combination of rule by one, by the select few and by the many"[4] was generally presented more descriptively. Be that as it may, the idea of *mixtum imperium* or *respublica mixta* was nevertheless widely known and understood. Scholars note that all participants in political discourse of the second half of the sixteenth and first half of the seventeenth centuries invoked this concept in their proposals on how to reform the system – ranging from one of the precursors of nobility-led republicanism, Stanisław Orzechowski, to the monarchist Piotr Skarga, from the most dogged opponents of the king during Zebrzydowski's *rokosz* to devout royalists calling for the monarch's powers to be extended.[5] It should be remembered that the concept itself was very capacious and elastic. It could, as in Polybius's classical vision, mean a balance between three elements: monarchic, aristocratic and democratic. However, *forma mixta* was also used to describe constructions comprising just two "simple" components, or even those in which one element dominated over the others. Moreover, filtered through St. Thomas' ideas, and later invoked by Renaissance supporters of a moderate monarchy, it could even be applied to a system in which the monarch was the main element, albeit somewhat restrained by certain advisory bodies.[6]

It should be added that Polish discourse was dominated by the classical vision[7] borrowed from Aristotle, Polybius and Cicero, comprising three basic forms of a "balanced" mixed system, as it was later described by Bartholomaeus Keckerman from Gdańsk in his texts about the *Rzeczpospolita* in the early seventeenth century.[8] The vision was rarely examined in purely theoretical terms. We can find general discussions in treatises by sixteenth-century scholars Andrzej Frycz Modrzewski, Wawrzyniec Goślicki and a little later Sebastian Petrycy[9]; however, they also believed that this vision was being implemented by the rulers first of the Polish Crown and later in the Polish-Lithuanian Commonwealth. Goślicki wrote *Poloniarum monarchia ex tribus Reipub[licae] formis est constituta, ex rege, optimatibus et populo*.[10] Theoretical considerations were less common than deliberations about the examples of states held up by authors writing in antiquity as models of mixed government – Sparta and Rome[11] – and attempts at including the *Rzeczpospolita* in this tradition. Occasionally, this meant drawing comparisons between specific institutions, such as between the ephors in Sparta or tribunes of Rome vs. the deputies to the Polish-Lithuanian Sejm, and – more frequently general statements about the similarities between the systems or efforts to justify proposals on how to reform the Commonwealth by recalling the ancient republics and their systems of government.[12] While Sparta disappeared from Polish discourse by the mid-seventeenth century as an example of mixed government, comparisons with Rome remained popular, with a focus on different elements of the mythical ideal republic at different times, including its mixed government.

The belief that the *Rzeczpospolita* was a successor to those republics and that it brought forward the model of the perfect *forma mixta* dates back to the time before the Polish-Lithuanian Commonwealth (prior to the Union of Lublin) and so it was first only applied to the Polish Crown, but over time it became more entrenched.[13] During the first free elections, the author of one of the texts first introduced three "simple" systems following classical models, and added: "Our ancestors, while shaping these three systems by eliminating that which interfered while preserving that which benefited, devised the *Rzeczpospolita* such that all three orders are included. There is *optimatum status*, there is rule by one, there is *multitudinis*."[14] Thirty years later, another anonymous – and no less learned – *rokosz* participant echoed Goślicki in expressing no doubt that the *Rzeczpospolita* "comprises these three elements of *ex monarchia, aristocratia et democratia*,"[15] while in the mid-seventeenth century Andrzej Maksymilian Fredro praised Poland's system for successfully intertwining three classic systems of government.[16] In any case, Poles were not an exception: similar opinions on their own system of government had been voiced since at least the fifteenth century by citizens of the Italian republics, in particular by the Venetians, who also saw themselves as successors to Sparta and Rome, but north of the Alps also in sixteenth- and seventeenth-century England, the Netherlands, Germany and even France.[17] What made Poland-Lithuania unique was the endurance of this view, held until as late as the 1770s (though the concept was also the subject of heated debate by that time).

It seems likely that this persistence was due to the close links between classical elements comprising the mixed system transposed directly into specific governmental institutions in the Commonwealth: "*Optimatum statum* is held by the councils. *Popularem*, by the deputies of the knightly estate. Ruling authority is held in single hands, those of the monarch," explained the above-cited anonymous author of *Naprawa Rzeczypospolitej* [Repair of the Republic].[18] The *rokosz* rebel quoted above also listed three "means" of government (monarchy, aristocracy, democracy), and then went on to list the corresponding three component parts of the *Rzeczpospolita*: "There is the king, there is the Senate, there is the knightly estate."[19] Writings by authors who were less interested in theory than the political reality around them tended to omit references to classical visions, limiting themselves to listing the three estates of the *Rzeczpospolita*: the king, the Senate and the nobility, "bound to

one another by mutual symmetry,"[20] "upon whom the empire hangs" as
Jakub Zawisza wrote in the seventeenth century.[21] Polish participants
in public debate were not notably different from representatives of other
nations in seeing their form of government as mixed. Their views perhaps reflected most closely those expressed by Venetians;[22] they also re-
sembled them in their perception of their own political system as unique
and perfect.[23]

It should be stressed that although at times this belief took the form
of passive complacency, stripped of any basis, in the beginning it had
powerful, logical roots in political theory. It is also worth remembering
that the mixed system, whose archetype could be found in Aristotle's *politeia*, was regarded as the best possible solution by some of the greatest
minds of antiquity, including Polybius and Cicero,[24] it was approved by
the founder of Christian reflections on the state St. Thomas, and it was
enthusiastically quoted in its classical version by such admirers of Venice
as Francesco Guichardini, Gasparo Contarini, Paolo Paruta and many
other authors popular in Poland. Although Bodin delivered what turned
out to be the fatal blow, it persisted until at least the mid-seventeenth
century, when it was recalled in England during the struggle against
the Stuarts.[25] It is no wonder, then, as Edward Opaliński notes, also in
the *Rzeczpospolita* this solution was considered to be "the finest system
of all that exist in the contemporarily known world."[26] According to
Goślicki, it was a form of government *omnium iustissimam et comunis-
simam.*[27] And since there seemed to be no doubt that this was what the
system was in the Commonwealth, the conclusion was obvious. Recalling Polybius, Fredro explained:

> A mixed system *[mistum statum Reipublicae]* is better than simple
> forms such as monarchy, aristocracy or democracy. Thus we should
> praise Poland's complex political system, which turns out to be at
> once monarchic, aristocratic and to some extent democratic, and
> perfectly intertwines different ways of exercising power.[28]

Other authors were even more outspoken: "This moderation has created
the Crown Commonwealth as ye see it now. Had not man but an angel
found'd it, as about the Jewish republic is written, it could not have
been done more wisely."[29] "Among the political systems for organizing
republics, the formula of the *Rzeczpospolita* as it exists now in Poland,
is the best, the most fundamental, originating from God Himself, requiring no change or adjustment."[30]

In a sense, it could be said that the political discussions held in the
Commonwealth ascribed the benefits of theoretical solutions to their
own system of government, in particular the endurance and guarantee of
liberty. For the founders and later supporters of this concept, the mixed
system appeared to be significantly more stable and enduring than simpler forms. In contrast with the latter, it was not under threat – or at

least not until much later and to a much lesser degree – of degeneration, inevitable in the cases of monarchy (tyranny), aristocracy (oligarchy) and democracy (ochlocracy or mob rule). It also meant it ensured a greater stability of the commonwealth and greater liberty of its citizens. During antiquity, the Laconian Republic was frequently cited as a model example, having supposedly functioned in an unaltered state for seven hundred years; during the Renaissance, Venice was described as a *respublica mixta* dating back 1200 years.[31] Polish participants in political debate also believed in the endurance of the mixed system and extended this belief to constructing their own Commonwealth.[32] Łukasz Górnicki wrote about King Sigismund the Old:

> He saw that a commonwealth is not mighty, nor enduring, nor safe where one ruleth over all, nor where a part of the noble people rule, nor where all rule, but where all rule together, that is the king, the council and the envoys of all. And the king was fortunate that he inherited such a ready, established *Rzeczpospolita*.[33]

Although Górnicki harbored doubts whether this ideal construction had lasted unchanged until his day, that is the late sixteenth century, he echoed other writers in seeing it as the best possible option. Jerzy Lubomirski wrote in 1666:

> [...] such was the foresight of our ancestors in founding the *Rzeczpospolita* that, wishing to see it be eternal in its laws and freedoms, they establish'd its form of government in three estates. This symmetry of parts comprising a single body meant that anyone separating and dividing one from the others maketh an ugly misdeed of political idolatry or atheism and becometh a slayer of his motherland.[34]

Lubomirski's symmetry, creating a single body out of different, not necessarily friendly components, is another element originating from the traditions of antiquity and transferred to the realities of the Polish-Lithuanian Commonwealth. The inventors of the concept of the mixed system, in particular Aristotle, believed that a state can only be enduring if it meets the needs of all the elements comprising it; in Polybius' classical take, the needs of the people, the nobility and the ruler would be met in equal measures. Only then would the community become a unity, a political body capable of realizing another dream of ancient scholars shared by politicians of the noble class: concord. As Cicero wrote, and was later repeated by Goślicki, paraphrasing Cicero:

> as this perfect agreement and harmony is produced by the proportionate blending of unlike tones, so too is a State made harmonious by agreement among dissimilar elements, brought about by a fair

and reasonable blending together of the upper, middle, and lower classes, just as if they be musical tones.[35]

In this context, the mixed government of the *Rzeczpospolita* was something more than a division of power between the king, the Senate and the nobility: it was a construction defining the roles of its components, their relationships and the interplay of interests bringing together the community into a single whole.[36] Fredro wrote about mixed government:

> What is needed here, even essential, is a unity of minds betwixt one man and another, betwixt the upper and lower estates, and more – a love of one for another; and only when it be bound by these ties doth such a community imitate a coexistence of parts, doth it melt into a unity.[37]

Not all authors described the unity resulting from a balance between the three different estates as loftily as Fredro, but they all considered it to be a very important component of their vision of the *Rzeczpospolita*. It is notable how frequently authors invoked the metaphor cited by Lubomirski, of the *Rzeczpospolita* as a physical body, as an overall vision of a somewhat organic whole. "Within it there is the king, there is the Senate, there is the noble class, yet these three estates become the single body of the *Rzeczpospolita*,"[38] wrote a rebel antipathetic towards the monarch in 1606. A few decades later, a royalist supporter of King John Casimir stated that "The King and the *Rzeczpospolita* all *tres ordines* a single body make *et quod dividi nequit – separari non potest*."[39] This comparison was echoed and even elevated to a higher, almost metaphysical level in the eighteenth century by Stanisław Leszczyński, the author of *Głos wolny wolność zabezpieczający* [Free Voice Safeguarding Freedom]; he was one of the last authors to state that the king as the first estate "*componens* with the other two *integritatem indissolubilem* of the *Rzeczpospolita*, which is a symbol of the Holy Trinity: three estates, one *Rzeczpospolita*, and in it the *individua* of three states *potestas*."[40]

It is no wonder that such a construct was seen as a guarantee of the Commonwealth's endurance. It was also a guarantee of liberty. Once again the roots of this view stretched back far into the past: Cicero had written that only a mixed form of government could ensure people's liberty.[41] Undoubtedly the views of classical authors influenced the Polish discourse, although their authority was mainly called upon in this context in longer texts by authors with an extensive education in the humanities. Krzysztof Warszewicki wrote: "Our system was called by Aristotle mixed, that is one which must consider not just the rule of the king but also the liberty of the citizens."[42] He was echoed by the author of *Zwierciadło królewskie* [King's Mirror]: "This way it limits things, since Aristotle demands that *in mixtis rebus publicis* they were limited when the king's dignity and the Crown freedoms remain whole."[43] It is notable that neither of them were particularly keen on the solutions present in the *Rzeczpospolita*; however, they both regarded the idea that a mixed government guarantees liberty as an objective fact. Not all participants in political discourse were followers of Aristotle, but they all noted the inseparable ties between the structure of the Commonwealth and the liberty of its citizens. However, in this instance it was less widely noted that *monarchia mixta* takes into consideration the interests of all those comprising the body politic, which included the desire for liberty by the people, as had been asserted by Cicero. During the second half of the sixteenth century, when the system of the *Rzeczpospolita* was being shaped, far more attention was devoted to the "curbing" of the monarch's power by the other elements of the mixed system, which brought Polish interpretations gradually closer to the traditions of St. Thomas, or – more broadly – to medieval interpretations of the idea of *monarchia mixta*.[44] The author of *Naprawa Rzeczypospolitej* wrote: "The *finis* of the Councils and deputies is such that would the king wish to destroy the common liberties, those councils and deputies should prevent him."[45] Jan Januszowski put it clearly and concisely in the title of one of the first chapters of his book: *Król w Polszcze bez stanu senatorskiego y rycerskiego nic czynić nie może* [The king can do nothing in Poland without the senatorial and equestrian estates], putting an emphasis not on joint rule but specifically on checking the monarch's power.[46] It should be noted that similar statements in the theoretical stratum recalled the theory of mixed government, while on the practical level they referred to the *Nihil Novi* Constitution of 1505, which was seen by participants in political discussions of the time as the legal foundation for implementing the theoretical model in the *Rzeczpospolita*.[47] The element of the monarch's power being checked by a mixed system of government, or – more precisely – by the two lower estates (occasionally just by "councils") is particularly notable during discussions in the sixteenth century, as the Commonwealth's political discourse and overall format was being shaped; that is, in the times when Poland's monarchs held extensive and largely unquestioned power. It is notable that such discussions frequently went hand-in-hand with listing other factors limiting the monarch's power. Janusz Ekes noted the links between Polish (and other) statements on the subject of *monarchia mixta* with an elected crown and the concept of free people for whom "*ex benevolentia rex imperat* and where there is *merum mixtum imperium*."[48] It was common to mention mixed government and the limiting of the king's power by law in a single breath. The anonymous author from the first interregnum who has already been quoted repeatedly above wrote this about the components of the mixed form of the *Rzeczpospolita*: "The order-giving cometh from one alone, namely from the monarch." He added: "The Lord hath not been left unbridled. The customs of order-giving, known as laws, have been imposed upon him."[49] The combination of all these factors was seen as a guarantee of the freedoms of the *Rzeczpospolita's* citizens.

The situation started to change over time, as the focus gradually shifted. In the context of mixed government, authors wrote not so much about curbing the king's power in order to protect the citizens' liberty but focused more on its being counterbalanced by the other elements of mixed government. The factor of the population was increasingly stressed, with the tripartite division being replaced by the dual model of the *Rzecz-pospolita*, described by Fredro as a monarchic-popular or monarchic-democratic commonwealth (*respublica monarchico-popularis*).[50] It appears that he was the only author to use this definition, but the image of a republic mixed with a monarchy was clearly evident in the Polish and Lithuanian discourse, in particular during the seventeenth and first half of the eighteenth centuries. Until Zebrzydowski's rebellion, the view was infrequent, although opinions such as "our *Rzeczpospolita ex uno atque omnibus constat*"[51] had appeared during discussions of the first free election. By the time of the rebellion, this image of the *Rzeczpospolita* became clear. It was undoubtedly a reflection of how certain political issues were being perceived, and to some extent of an actual shift in the political situation. In this context, the balance between the three estates was gradually being replaced by a balance between majesty and liberty; between king and Commonwealth, understood as the general population of noble citizens. This interpretation also fits into the traditional vision of a mixed government. It is another matter that the concept of *respublica mixta*, once highly complex and imbued with meaning, shifted towards an image of constant conflict between the noble population, with their endless quest for complete liberty, and the king, with his desire for absolute power,[52] essentially a conflict *inter maiestatem et libertatem*, which in turn ran counter to the notion of overall unity whose perfect interpretation would be a mixed government.

In a sense, this shift in discourse and, more broadly, in the vision of the system dovetailed with a certain shift in how the Senate's role was seen. This is undoubtedly a highly complex issue, concerning a real political struggle for power in the *Rzeczpospolita* and ideological conflicts that were deeply rooted in social and political realities, but it is worth also considering its linguistic aspect. In statements from the sixteenth century, in particular from during the struggle for the shape of the Commonwealth, the Senate was described as its protector with a high degree of power; as a warden of the king, overseeing that he does not misuse or abuse his royal prerogatives. In some statements (usually by senators), it was depicted as a participant in royal power:

> The king and the *Rzeczpospolita* to rule – this function itself belongs to the senators. And by the same token, a tyrant is unlike a king since a tyrant wields all power by himself, while a king hath

worthy senators, dignified and fair men, and he makes no decisions in the *Rzeczpospolita* without their counsel.[53]

The royal Councils were given the power to moderate all royal undertakings and business, and they are responsible so that the king, through oversight or any other deed, should not go astray.[54]

These statements clearly cannot be seen as impartial because they originate from senators, but even opponents of extensive Senate power were wont to say: "ye are not the *Rzeczpospolita* herself nor her lords," though immediately going on to add, "but her ministers and protectors."[55] This was the result of the tradition of actual royal council power,[56] but it fit perfectly into the concept of the *monarchia mixta*.[57] However, in later years descriptions of the place of the Senate in the tripartite structure of the *Rzeczpospolita* shifted towards stressing that it was situated "between the King and the nobility..."[58] and the term *ordo intermedius* – the intermediate estate – started being treated increasingly literally.[59] In this sense, the Senate was no longer a participant in the power game between elements comprising the mixed *Rzeczpospolita*, or a counsel overseeing the king, but more of an arbiter – a balancing factor between the ongoing struggle between majesty and liberty. In 1606, an anonymous rebel instructed senators that since "*intermedium tenens ordinem* between HRH and the noble class must ensure [...] that no king does not tend *ad tyrannidem*, and the noble class *ad seditionem*."[60] The Zebrzydowski rebellion marked the moment of a clear shift in how the Senate was discussed in comparison with discourse surrounding the election in 1573.[61] Over time, this perception of the Senate's role became widespread. This is how it was described by direct participants in political struggles and authors of more theoretical statements throughout the seventeenth and most of the eighteenth centuries. Fredro explained: the Senate "doth not support either ultimate power against liberty, nor unbridled nobility against royal majesty, but rather observes events, judiciously leading to agreement."[62] The repeating comparisons to a set of scales maintaining the balance between two opposing factors are notable here. It could be said that this was how a place for the third element in the bipartite construct was found, adapting the traditional vision of mixed government to a new image of the *Rzeczpospolita*. This is notable because it reveals that political language, at least during the first half of the seventeenth century, remained faithful to traditional concepts while not becoming ossified, and strove to adapt itself to changes to political realities and visions of the state and its government.[63]

One thing which clearly did not change was the belief in the need for a great care to maintain the balance of the mixed *Rzeczpospolita*; in the tripartite system the elements came together into a harmonious whole, while a bipartite system made for an uncertain balance of largely opposing factors. This should be examined closely because this care was an important component of political discourse. Paradoxically, although *mixtum imperium* was seen as not only the best solution but also the most enduring one, this belief was accompanied by major concerns about potentially damaging its delicate structure. Paweł Piasecki wrote in 1630: "This institution of our *Rzeczpospolita* is very precarious, albeit very good; there is almost no guarantee of security or stability."[64] This concern for maintaining the delicate balance of the three estates comprising the *Rzeczpospolita* was prevalent.[65] However, there were also widespread objections that the balance had already been unsettled, and that the supposedly perfect system was already degenerating.[66]

Throughout the period under investigation – starting from the first free election (and likely earlier) until the eighteenth century – all commentators expressed their grievance over the "rottenness" of the *Rzeczpospolita*, seeing the cause as lying in its "having distanced itself far from its first establishment."[67] At the same time, while their starting point was common, when it came to assessing the problematic elements or identifying individuals who might have breached the foundations of *mixtum imperium* and how, opinions varied wildly; however, they remained in the traditional conceptual framework of the degeneration of originally pure systems. And so the king was accused of striving for tyranny, senators blamed for either supporting this or for oligarchic aspirations, the nobility censured for overstepping the limitations imposed on their class in the mixed system. It should also be remembered that descriptions of the *Rzeczpospolita's* system rarely strove to provide simple, objective diagnoses and lamentations about its crisis practically never had any such objective. Certain theoretical observations were leveled as arguments in political disputes, which frequently turned rather fierce. This meant that although all those involved accepted the tripartite construct of the king, senators and the noble class (or even perhaps the latter's representation in the Sejm), opinions varied dramatically when it came to assigning them privileges and duties, as did any assessments of whether a particular estate might have overstepped its prerogatives.

A telling example of wildly different interpretations of the concept of mixed government, clearly serving as a weapon in political struggles, can be found in two political texts from the time of Lubomirski's rebellion in the mid-seventeenth century: one by an anonymous royalist and the other from the Chief Marshal of the Crown, that is, Lubomirski himself. Both used almost the very same words to describe the "beautiful harmony" of the estates, "which *unus Reipublicae constituit*, such that one without the other cannot *concludere in negotiis Reipublicae*,"[68] and expressed serious concerns for it. However, Lubomirski structured his entire subsequent argumentation around accusing the king of overstepping his privileges in mixed government, that is of infringing on the "symmetry of the estates." He cited not so much the scope of the monarch's power but rather its limitations,[69] harboring no doubt that "*potissima pars regni nobilitas.*"[70] The supporter of King John Casimir, in turn, was equally fervent in his declaration that among the estates "his Majesty the King is the first and the head of the *Rzeczpospolita.*" Interestingly, he was willing to admit liberties and privileges to the nobility while remaining silent on the subject of power.[71] The conclusion seemed obvious: it was the nobility's demands for greater power that were damaging the *Rzeczpospolita's* "harmony."

During the second half of the sixteenth century, when the concept of *monarchia mixta* became one of the fundamental ideas in political discourse of the nobility, it appeared to be an accurate tool for describing the political reality, and – even more importantly – it made it possible to precisely lay forth the political goals of the time to all participants in public life. This vision was also a useful argument in debates, used by individuals with very different views to pursue contradicting goals. As already mentioned, it was a highly capacious and elastic concept, which could be adapted for a range of needs and situations. However, applying it to actual forms of government and the enduring devotion to it eventually led to problems, gradually limiting how certain concepts were perceived, hindering addressing the changing political situation and articulating new concepts.

The difficulties started already with how the existing institutions should be mapped onto the elements making up the theoretical model of mixed government. In a sense, this was an attempt to tailor the reality to match the political myth which was *forma mixta* – which it did not altogether fit. This lack of fit was at its most obvious when it came to the "aristocratic" element, that is, the Senate. This entailed a clash of two political ideals: mixed government and equality of the nobility. Authors in antiquity and their Renaissance successors in Western Europe saw it as obvious that there existed a clearly distinct, affluent group within the state (the *grandi*, peers, aristocrats), who therefore needed to be represented in government. However, the Senate did not fit into this concept, because there was no such group within the *Rzeczpospolita*, at least formally. The concept of equality of all members of the noble class was one of the fundamental tenets of the noble ideology.[72] It was frequently asserted that "*seantorius ordo ex equestri attolitur,*"[73] at least from Zebrzydowski's rebellion. There was an alternative: it was not senators' background, but rather their function that could assign them to an aristocratic class. Janusz Ekes described this as the "aristocracy of public service."[74] The House of Lords was viewed in a similar way in seventeenth-century England.[75] In this context, senators were regarded somewhat as Aristotle's aristocracy of virtue, as (co)governance by the wisest and most virtuous in the state.[76] This vision of the Senate was rather popular during the sixteenth century, largely supported by senators themselves,[77] although they were also supported by theoretical writers, mainly by Goślicki and Warszewicki.[78] The vision mainly came true when the mixed structure was closely tied to the Sejm, in which the Senate provided the aristocratic element and the Chamber of Deputies the democratic element. However, if the democratic element was seen to be the entire noble class – and this interpretation quickly came to dominate Polish discourse – the position of the Senate as an institution and the senators within it became less clear: they were an aristocratic element, but not the aristocracy per se. There were attempts to create a more coherent structure: tendencies to shift the function of an intermediary between majesty and freedom from the Senate to the magnates, present from around the time of Lubomirski's rebellion (and even in part during Zebrzydowski's rebellion). This was accompanied by a belief that the power of affluent families was the only guarantee of the liberty of the nobility that could resist the king's absolutist tendencies. These kinds of statements were mainly a reflection of real changes in the power structure in the *Rzeczpospolita* and political struggles within it, as were their opposing views on senators' oligarchic tendencies, repeated since Zebrzydowski's rebellion throughout the seventeenth century, and suggestions of changing their status by shifting their nominations from the hands of the king to the Sejm – a measure that had been proposed since the early days of the Polish-Lithuanian Commonwealth. However, it is also true that an absence of a clear place for the Senate in the so-cial realities of the *Rzeczpospolita* meant that of the three elements of its mixed government, descriptions of the aristocratic estate were the most ambivalent and its vision in the *forma mixta* structure seems the least clear. It is notable that in the eighteenth century almost all au-thors of broader discussions about the governmental system suggested far-reaching changes to the fundamental structure and functioning of the Senate, in particular making it more subordinate to the "nation" in the name of equality.[79]

This problem with the Senate was the result of difficulties of matching elements of the mixed system, in theory, to the actual institutions of the *Rzeczpospolita*. However, choosing this construct as the basis for discussing the state, and in particular the decision to remain loyal to this concept, were in and of themselves the cause of problems; they also meant that at some point participants in political discussions no longer had the right tools to describe the ongoing changes and the shifting vi-sion of the state. These difficulties first arose during Zebrzydowski's re-bellion, when it turned out that neither the institution of *rokosz* nor the political ambitions of its participants actually fit in within the concept of *monarchia mixta*. From the perspective of the mixed system, a *rokosz* – or even significantly less drastic attempts to secure more power for the "democratic" element – could throw the whole system off balance and tip it towards a popular government, not to say ochlocracy. It should be remembered that the classic vision of *forma mixta* assigned little power to this element, since the original creators of the concept believed that

this system would mainly guarantee people's liberty and their participation in government remained only a means to this end. The concept
was familiar to participants in political discussions in the sixteenth
century. The rhetorical question posed by a participant in the first free
election – *que salus publica sine libertate, que libertas nostra sine auc-
toritate senatus, quae auctoritas senatus sine dignitate regis?*[80] – was
nothing more than a recollection of the classical vision of *forma mixta*.
Although in his case it was a neutral element in a description of reality,
similar statements quickly became an argument in political struggles,
providing a theoretical framework to real disputes over power. Abuses
by the democratic element were stressed by members of senatorial elites
towards the end of the rule of King Sigismund Augustus and in the early
days of elected monarchs.[81] With time, the argument was taken over
from senators by supporters of strengthening the king's power, including Górnicki, Skarga, Opaliński and Starowolski, who complained that
"*populus* is taking over government"[82] and that "they appropriated all
potency of power and rule such that the King and the Senate are simply for show."[83] While similar accusations were previously aimed at the
Chamber of Deputies who, according to senators, were overstepping
their powers, they were later extended to the entire noble class. Debating these kinds of accusations under the framework of the classical *monarchia mixta* was not easy, and eventually became impossible, all the
more so because the nobility increasingly felt itself to be the sovereign of
the *Rzeczpospolita*. The problem was that their political language did
not allow them to fully articulate this. The ancient concept of *forma
mixta* made no allowance for the concept of indivisible sovereignty as
it was understood by Bodin. The term (and concept) of *maiestas* does
appear in Polish discourse of the sixteenth century, but only in relation
to the *Rzeczpospolita*, therefore as part of the limited unity of all three
estates.[84] These categories were insufficient to describe the sovereignty
of the people, even just the noble class.

This kind of being at a loss and attempting to find a new language are
clear in statements from between 1606 and 1608, in particular among
supporters of the rebellion. Notably, these authors rarely recall the vision of three estates comprising the *Rzeczpospolita*, as though they
were aware that their actions contradicted this very framework. While
preserving the external framework of *forma mixta*, however, some authors strived to fill it with new content, such as the author of *Libera
respublica*, who traditionally assigned the king with *dignitatem* and the
Senate with *auctoritatem*, and significantly less traditionally the nobility with *summam potestatem*.[85] The problem was perhaps best handled by Mikołaj Zebrzydowski (assuming he was the author of *Apologia
szlachcica polskiego* [Apology of a Polish Noble], as concluded by the
twentieth-century scholar Jan Czubek), who transferred *absolutam potestatem* from three estates to the nobility,[86] and further identified the

nobility (or, more specifically, participants in rebellions) with the *Rzecz-pospolita*.[87] As such, he stepped away from the classical vision of the *Rzeczpospolita* comprising three estates in favor of the *Rzeczpospolita* as a commonwealth of noble citizens, which fit into traditional discourse as well as being a far better way of describing the situation and the political ideals of the rebels. It could be said, then, that the fluidity of the term *Rzeczpospolita* turned out to be useful in articulating concepts without introducing new terms (in particular sovereignty) and without undermining the concept of *respublica mixta*. The main innovation was the fact that after the rebellion of Sandomierz, discourse increasingly featured a juxtaposition of the king vs. his noble subjects – which translated into the king vs. the *Rzeczpospolita* – alongside the classic tripartite vision of the mixed system.

The debates surrounding Zebrzydowski's rebellion marked the last period, for a long subsequent time, of attempting to adapt ways of describing the *Rzeczpospolita's* system to fit the actual political situation. Throughout the seventeenth century, Polish political thought would be stuck "in an Aristotelian prison" (as Robert Frost has put it[88]) or "in the corset of a schema" (in the words of Urszula Augustyniak[89]) in terms of the way politics was thought about and discussed. Participants in political debate were not only convinced "of the immutability of the *Rzeczpospolita's* system,"[90] but also described it in almost the very same words as their predecessors of the sixteenth century. What had once made it possible to present an accurate depiction of reality and to formulate postulates for the future, and which were the subject of debate and conflict, by the second half of the seventeenth century had become almost entirely ossified. No one questioned the advantages of mixed government or the fact that it comprised the three estates of the *Rzeczpospolita*, but after Fredro these tenets were rarely scrutinized. The only remaining trace of all the former emotion was the almost obsessive fear of the balance being unsettled, in particular by the royal factor, that is by the king striving for absolute dominion. In any case, the conflict *inter maiestatem et liberatem* stirred far greater interest than the *forma mixta* construct, even though the latter was never questioned.

The first person to break the stagnation, and the first to decisively question the advantages of the *Rzeczpospolita's* mixed system, would be Stanisław Karwicki. Although he started his reasoning by repeating the tripartite vision of the *Rzeczpospolita*, familiar "even to the blindmen and to the barbers" as he noted caustically,[91] the way he continued it would have been surprising not just for the beard-trimmers. The author added that it was, in fact, a fusion of two orders, saying, "Here in Poland we have a kingdom and a republic,"[92] which in his view could not be combined. His view may have faintly echoed distant Western European theories, since to an extent his critiques concerned the notion of divided sovereignty, even though he did not make use of this concept. However, in contrast with Bodin and his followers, Karwicki saw this solution not so much as impossible in theory, but impossible to implement in practice. He also questioned the fundamental axiom of balance between the different elements comprising mixed government, and indeed argued that such balance was absolutely impossible in practice. Additionally, he saw senators not as a stabilizing element but, on the contrary, as actually contributing to growing conflict and confusion.[93] This was not yet a radical shift in language, but Karwicki's proposals certain diverged from the *monarchia mixta* traditions. Stepping away from this concept clearly helped Karwicki to diagnose the situation in the *Rzeczpospolita* and posit reforms.

Karwicki's writings would influence the political language, but not until Konarski's work several decades later. If the shape of the *Rzeczpospolita* was discussed at all before then, it was generally done via the classical mixed-form vision, with traditional praise for the harmony of its elements. Even Leszczyński, who had presented the most interesting vision of reforms during the first half of the eighteenth century, continued invoking the traditional vision of "three estates combined" in the classical understanding. At that time, the only sign that something was starting to shift in the discourse was the occasional description of the *Rzeczpospolita's* system no longer as mixed but as a democratic or popular system.[94]

A real change finally occurred in the 1760–1770s. In a sense, it was initiated by Konarski, whose entire program of revitalizing the *Rzeczpospolita* was written with essentially no reference to the term or concept of mixed government.[95] While Konarski's writings omitted the concept of mixed government, Jan Nepomucen Poniński, writing at nearly the very same time, offered a harsh critique of it. Clearly influenced by Western authors, in particular Samuel von Pufendorf, he saw such a solution as irregular,[96] suggesting as an alternative an aristocracy without a king, which "is a natural, simple government, thus providing the best means of governance."[97] It should be noted that the author wrote about aristocracy rather than democracy, and so he noted estates other than just the nobility, perhaps not actually comprising the *Rzeczpospolita* but at least living in the same country.[98] Poniński's text, likely little known, serves as more of an interesting snippet and it should not be regarded as evidence of widespread change in political language. The shift was starting around then, although the concept of mixed government did not altogether disappear from Poland's political lexicon.

In fact it continued to appear in theoretical writings and texts concerning the realities of the *Rzeczpospolita* until as late as the 1770s. Wincenty Skrzetuski wrote in 1782:

> In the wake of all these changes which we have briefly mentioned from our nation's history, the government of the Kingdom of Poland

comprised three estates: the monarchy as personified by the king, the aristocracy in the Senate, the democracy as the noble estate.[99]

Authors of textbooks and encyclopedic publications took a similar view of Poland's political system.[100] The concept of mixed government also appeared during political debates, although it was generally repeated as a rather automatic, traditional description. These formulations reveal one clear change with regard to the classical vision of *forma mixta* described above: they no longer discuss a mixed commonwealth, but rather a mixed government.[101] Even if authors writing during the second half of the eighteenth century reached for the traditional formulation, they were no longer referring to the state per se but the structure of its government. It should be remembered that Montesquieu rejected the term "mixed government," replacing it with the concept of moderate monarchy which he believed was in place in England, Rousseau also rejected this conception; however, many philosophers of the Enlightenment continued using it, including Mably, Filangeri and d'Argenson, who were widely quoted in Poland.[102] Their writings became a form of support for Polish authors of theoretical treatises, whose descriptions of various forms of government usually concluded with a note that mixed forms are also possible.

However, from the mid-1770s onwards authors either outright rejected[103] or (more frequently) simply avoided the term. To put it in a more poetic way, the ossified corset of *monarchia mixta* was starting to burst under the influence of new concepts arriving from the West; this coincided with an enlivened political scene and a search for new ways of discussing problems within the state. One symptom of the ongoing change was the propagation of the terms "free government" and "republican government." These had occasionally appeared in discourse previously, but from the late 1760s they became widespread in general discussions and as descriptions of existing government. At times they were used to describe the classical mixed structure,[104] but authors increasingly focused on the fact that in a free government "not one individual, but the entire nation is the heir to the state,"[105] that the people have a share in the rule.[106] It was not a new concept, and in a way it fit into the traditional vision of the *Rzeczpospolita* as a community of citizens, but now it was increasingly being expressed using tools brought to Polish discourse with the Enlightenment: the concepts of people's sovereignty, the social contract and political liberty.[107] Wybicki wrote about free government, saying that it gives citizens political liberty "because they are members of the body of the highest national suzerainty. They are participants in legislative power."[108] For Stanisław Staszic, a commonwealth existed where:

> [...] no individual holds greater power and personal liberty than the law permits, and all owners without exception participate in

establishing laws, where all are bound by laws and only power and common will, that is the nation, establishes laws by a majority of votes [...].[109]

Not all authors used language as modern as that of Staszic, but from the 1780s the vision of a mixed government of the *Rzeczpospolita* as three estates disappeared almost entirely from political discourse.

And it is no wonder. The term "mixed government" could still be used to describe or classify Poland's political system, but no longer as a tool of extensive analysis of its shortcomings. Tripartite nomenclature was insufficient to make political diagnoses or formulate meaningful reforms. For authors like Wybicki, Kołłątaj and Staszic wishing to describe the entire population rather than just the commonwealth of the nobility, the concept of mixed government in which the democratic element was the "noble people" was a poorly constructed concept that did not follow either the theory or the reality they were describing and they hoped to change. Even for individuals with less radical social views, the traditional concept of mixed government was more of a hindrance than a help in articulating political agendas. One significant problem with the concept was that it did not acknowledge the idea of division of power. Although statements in the sixteenth and seventeenth centuries distinguished between functions assigned to individual the elements comprising mixed government, this was more of a division of roles, tasks and privileges rather than a division of power as was being suggested by Western political authors as early as the seventeenth century.[110] The problems this caused for political theory are clearly visible in all proposed reforms in Poland throughout almost the entire eighteenth century. While Karwicki, Leszczyński and Konarski and authors debating political reforms during the Great Sejm were able to write precisely about the foundations, goals and limitations of the Sejm's power as a legislative organ, they struggled with distinguishing and describing branches of government which would "have the duty of effectively maintaining, protecting, overseeing and executing the laws and decisions enacted by the Sejms, between one gathering and another."[111] This was the result of the political reality in Poland, of how the state and power were perceived, and of the lack of appropriate language to describe these issues. This was not an issue of vocabulary *per se*, because it had long existed in the Polish political lexicon and the "power to execute laws" had been discussed as early as the seventeenth century; however, there was no clear division into legislative and executive power, nor a precise definition of the latter. The shift only started during the 1770s, mainly under the influence of Montesquieu's theories. The first to recall *The Spirit of the Laws* was Andrzej Zamoyski in 1764 in his famous Sejm speech outlining the political agenda of the Czartoryski family's faction. Echoing the French master, he stated: "In each state exists tripartite power, that is the legislative, executive and judicial,"[112] and consistently treated this as a foundation for reforming Poland's political system. In keeping faithful to Montesquieu's triad, Zamoyski was something of an exception. In spite of the popularity of the philosopher's vision of the state, his tripartite division was mainly reflected in textbooks and authors quoting directly from his writings.[113] Very few participants in political discourse took interest in the issue of the judiciary as a separate branch of power, perhaps either because it was not a major subject of debate or because the existence of a supreme court (the Tribunal), run by the nobility and remaining independent of the king, made it something of a moot point. The other two branches of power, which had emerged as part of European theories on the state far earlier, remained significantly more popular. At the same time, while the concept of legislative power was adopted into the Polish system relatively quickly and easily, almost automatically applying it to the nobility assembled at the dietines (*sejmiks*), to their representatives in the Sejm or to the three estates, the situation was far more difficult when it came to the executive, both in terms of who should be implementing it and its scope and limitations. Doubts and conflicts arose concerning whether it should be a collegiate power and, if so, to what extent; whether it should be entrusted to a single individual or institution or shared among several bodies; where its boundaries should lie and how they should be safeguarded; finally, whether it should be subject to legislation and, if so, to what extent. The diversity of opinion is already clear in writings from the 1770s,[114] but it is most clearly demonstrated in discussions of the Great Sejm, starting with the clash over the Permanent Council, depicted by its supporters as a model of executive power and by its opponents as a tool of royal despotism,[115] until the dispute over the *Governing Act*. Speakers in the Sejm often did not fully understand the function and place of this element within the system. Political clashes occasionally brought up curious ideas such as that of an overseeing power, devised exclusively to supervise the executive.[116] There were also occasional voices questioning whether an executive was necessary in the first place.[117] The latter were rare, however, leading us to the conclusion that the concept of division of power had become a permanent fixture of political language by then.[118] Even if they did not fully understand it, it was invoked both by proponents of systemic reform as well as by supporters of the existing system.

Notably, this shift in the political language led to proposals of far-reaching changes in the structure of the *Rzeczpospolita's* government. First and foremost, it made it possible to resolve the problem of the Senate: following the shift away from mixed government and the introduction of division of power, it was no longer seen as an element essential for the functioning of the system as a whole, which meant it was possible either to abandon the institution altogether or to postulate that it should be declared it a second representative body – a second chamber of the Sejm (alongside the Chamber of Deputies). However, the influence of this shift in language on the discussion of the place of the monarch within the system of the *Rzeczpospolita's* structure is even more interesting. In this instance, it was specifically the introduction of the new concept that allowed some authors to completely change how they saw its role and place in the state.

And the change was certainly inevitable. Rejecting the traditional concept of mixed government comprising three elements meant that the king was no longer perceived as an element essential for the functioning and even the existence of the *Rzeczpospolita*. What remained was his image as a rival and constant threat to liberty. One extreme conclusion was the suggestion that the monarchy should be abandoned, put forward first by Poniński in 1763 and then by a few other authors during the Great Sejm.[119] A less extreme but far more common idea was to entirely strip him of his power, as proposed by Karwicki and his numerous successors, going as far supporters of elections and opponents of the Constitution between 1788 and 1792. However, by referring to the idea of division of power it became possible to once again include the king in the system of government, although his role was now described in entirely new terms. He was no longer an essential component of the *Rzeczpospolita* nor its dangerous rival; as described by authors such as Montesquieu, he was simply its executive arm or one of its executive arms – the highest official.[120] Inspired by Montesquieu's doctrine, Popławski and Wybicki[121] attempted to implement this starting in the 1770s, later continued by Kołłątaj, Staszic and less well-known readers of *The Spirit of the Laws* as well as supporters of governmental reform.[122] Kołłątaj wrote that "in a nation which knows its rights, the king is nothing more than the first [co]citizen in legislative power and nothing more than the highest official of executive power,"[123] while Staszic believed that in a republic the king should be "the first functionary and first servant of the nation."[124] This discourse was continued by supporters of the *Governing Act*; Antoni Trębicki wrote "in this sense, the king should be seen as only the first minister of the sovereign master, that is, of the nation."[125] It should be stressed that the vision of the king as a functionary did not come to dominate the discourse, and the widespread concerns over his desire for despotism endured, supported by the distrust in the executive expressed by Rousseau, who was highly popular in Poland.[126] However, it was these attempts to change the perception of the king and the place he held in the power system of the *Rzeczpospolita* that reveal the extent to which a shift in the vocabulary of the discourse affected political concepts, or at least how it could constitute arguments in political disputes. After all, rule by a dangerous rival constantly striving to undermine the liberty of the "populace" was something quite different from rule by a functionary subordinate to this populace.

During the sixteenth century, the concept of *respublica mixta* made it possible to accurately describe the political realities of the time; it also helped participants in discussions articulate their postulates and political goals and devise a vision of the state they would hope to build together. However, to some extent, the concept outlived its usefulness. Inherently tied to a specific political construct of "three estates comprising the Sejm," and lacking new ideas that were being disseminated in Europe throughout the seventeenth century, at some point, it became more of a hindrance in describing the political world and political visions. It became a kind of relic; a legacy from political predecessors who were still highly admired but rarely discussed. It is no wonder, then, that as discussions of the state became more widespread and increasingly open to concepts proposed in Western Europe, the idea became largely forgotten if not rejected outright. It certainly left a legacy as the doctrine of division of power – as described by Montesquieu and his Polish followers – grew out of the concept of mixed government.

Notes

1 Morel (1996, 95–112); Blythe (1992); Van Gelderen (2002).
2 Baturo (1958); Ochmann (1990, 264–278); Opaliński (1995, 40–42); Gromelski (2008, 173–178); Pietrzyk-Reeves (2012, 356–400).
3 Ekes (2001).
4 Orzechowski ([1565]/1984, 25)
5 Opaliński (1995, 41); Augustyniak (1999, 32).
6 Morel (1996, 103–104).
7 Although Konstanty Grzybowski also points out the influence of conciliarist canonistics (Grzybowski 1959, 24).
8 Ekes (2001, 27).
9 Ekes (2001, 15–16); Pietrzyk-Reeves (2012, 356–380).
10 Goślicki (1568, fol. 14, similarly fol. 10).
11 Morel (1996, 97, 101; 1986, 209–219); Rawson (1969, 101ff.); Pietrzyk-Reeves (2012, 66–69).
12 Cf. Grześkowiak-Krwawicz (2014, 25–44).
13 Gromelski (2008, 175); the fact that the Lithuanians at that time, prior to 1569, had different ideals and a different vision of their governmental system is shown by the work of Augustyn Rotundus, who clearly preferred a monarchy and envisioned such a system for Lithuania (Rotundus 1564/2009, 154 and *passim*).
14 *Naprawa Rzeczypospolitej* [1573], in Czubek (1906, 191).
15 *Libera respublica quae sit?*, in Czubek (1918, vol. 2, 403).
16 Fredro (1660/2014, 459).
17 Morel (1996, 102, 105); Nippel (1994, 17); Gromelski (2008, 175ff.); Haitsma Mulier (1987, 187).
18 *Naprawa Rzeczypospolitej* [1573], in Czubek (1906, 191); "The idea was most clearly reflected in the institution of parliament," Gromelski (2008, 174); Pietrzyk-Reeves (2012, 380–400).
19 *Libera respublica quae sit?*, in Czubek (1918, vol. 2, 403).
20 Lubomirski ([1666]: 1).
21 Zawisza z Kroczowa (1613/1899, 40).
22 Conti (2002, 73–83).
23 "The nobility were convinced that the Polish RP was a model mixed state with the optimal form of government," Gromelski (2008, 175); C. Backvis, *Jak XVI-wieczni Polacy widzieli Włochy i Włochów*, in Backvis (1975, 515).

24 "The views of Polybius had been diffused in Italy in the fifteenth century," Fink (1945, 18); Morel (1996, 104ff.).
25 Fink (1945, 101ff.); Scott (2004, 37); "two near synonyms of great importance in the seventeenth century, mixed monarch, mixed constitution," Condren (1994, 54).
26 Opaliński (1995, 42).
27 Goślicki (1568, k. 1v).
28 Fredro (1660/2014, 459).
29 *Naprawa Rzeczypospolitej* [1573] in Czubek (1906, 191).
30 Piasecki ([1631–1632]/1972, 264).
31 Tigerstedt (1965); Rawson (1969, chapters 1–3); Skinner (2001, 209ff.); Haitsma Mulier (1980, 30).
32 Cf. Ekes (2001, 48); the exception was Goślicki, who despite his high evaluation of mixed government felt that the danger of its degeneration was greater, as each of the elements can turn into a corrupted form (Goślicki 1568, fol. 40).
33 Ł. Górnicki, *Droga do zupełnej wolności* [1650], in Górnicki (1961, 483).
34 Lubomirski ([1666]: 64).
35 Cicero, *De re publica*, II, 69, trans. Keyes (1928); Goślicki (1568, k. 10).
36 Januszowski (1600, *Przemowa do łaskawego czytelnika*, no pagination) this is indeed how it was perceived both by the authors of antiquity, and by their Renaissance heirs, cf. Mouristen (2006, 22).
37 Fredro (1668/2015, 716).
38 *Libera respublica quae sit?* in Czubek (1918, vol. 2, 403).
39 *Respons panu Reklewskiemu* [1663], in Ochmann-Staniszewska (1990, 200).
40 Leszczyński ([1737?]/1903, 24).
41 Morel (1996, 101).
42 Warszewicki (1598/2010, 210 in Latin; 378 in Polish).
43 [Kossobudzki]/Januszowski (1606/1921, 223).
44 Morel (1996, 103).
45 *Naprawa Rzeczypospolitej* [1573], in Czubek (1906, 205).
46 [Kossobudzki]/Januszowski (1606/1921, "Dział II," 219).
47 This is how the issue was interpreted by writers such as Wolan (1572/1606/2010, 97, also 143).
48 *Respons na tenże skrypt*, in Czubek (1906, 461); cf. Ekes (2001, 51).
49 *Naprawa Rzeczypospolitej* [1573], in Czubek (1906, 191); similarly Wolan (1572/1606/2010, 97).
50 Fredro (1668/2015, 716), with the caveat that thereafter he invoked more of a tripartite construct, recognizing the intermediating role of the Senate.
51 [J. D. Solikowski], *Rozsądek o warszawskich sprawach na elekcyjej do koronacyjej należący*, in Czubek (1906, 583). This author was generally an advocate of stronger royal power and harshly attacked the idea of resident senators, the Henrician Articles and at the same time the Warsaw Confederation itself, arguing among other things that its participants had no right to enact anything without a king.
52 The functioning of a concept of mixed monarchy understood in precisely this way is described by Ochmann-Staniszewska (1990, 271ff.).
53 *Naprawa Rzeczypospolitej* [1573], in Czubek (1906, 202).
54 *Senatora anonima deliberacyje o królu, panach, radzie i urzędnikach, sejmie i bezkrólewiu* [1569], in Ulanowski (1921, 117).
55 [J. D. Solikowski?], *Prędka rada przed upadkiem*, in Czubek (1906, 253), authorship listed according to the proposal of the tome's editor J. Czubek (1906, introduction, XXVII).

56 W. Czapliński, *Główne nurty myśli politycznej w Polsce w latach 1587–1655*, in Czapliński (1966, 88).
57 Ekes (2001, 38).
58 [Kossobudzki]/Januszowski (1606/1921, 220ff.).
59 Ekes (2001, 41).
60 *Libera respublica quae sit?*, in Czubek (1918, vol. 2, 404).
61 Jarosław Poraziński thought that the change did not occur until the mid-seventeenth century, but it is clearly evident already in the *rokosz* writings, cf. Poraziński (1993, 219).
62 Fredro (1660/2014, 553).
63 Cf. Augustyniak (2015).
64 Piasecki ([1631–1632]/1972, 258).
65 Ekes (2001, 54).
66 "Critical evaluations, quite widespread in written commentaries and also many public speeches, pertained not to the essence of the system itself, i.e. to the *monarchia mixta* concept, but to the widely perceived distortions of public life." Opaliński (1995, 41).
67 Ł. Opaliński, *Rozmowa plebana z ziemianinem* [1641], in Opaliński (1938, 16); for more on Opaliński's views on the mixed system of the *Rzeczpospolita* cf. Pryshlak (1981, 38–42); Pryshlak (2000, 90–91, 104–107).
68 *Respons wolnego szlachcica na list senatora jednego de data 20 Decembris 1665*, in Ochmann-Staniszewska (1991, 110); the same in Lubomirski ([1666]: 1, 64).
69 "So that he should in no way infringe upon the laws, so that he should be fair to each of his subjects […], so that he should not permit himself anything above the law," "as long as he should remember that he rules over a free nation and should maintain that freedom," etc., Lubomirski ([1666]: 1).
70 Lubomirski ([1666]: 2), this was a somewhat distorted quotation from the Sejm Constitution of 1532, also cited by the author of *Libera respublica quae sit?*, in Czubek (1918, vol. 2, 404).
71 "The third *ordo* is the *status equestris*, enjoying freedoms above other nations," *Respons wolnego szlachcica...*, in Ochmann-Staniszewska (1991, 110)
72 Zajączkowski (1993, 94); Urwanowicz (1994, 171); Opaliński (1995, 89).
73 *Respons na paszkwil przeciw zdaniu in scripto podanemu JK Mci wydany* [1663], in Ochmann-Staniszewska (1991, vol. 2, 164); cf. Grzybowski (1959, 30).
74 Ekes (2001, 38).
75 Nippel (1994, 17).
76 This was pointed out by Ekes (2001, 39).
77 A telling example of this is the small treatise by Karnkowski, *Eksorbitancyje i naprawa koła poselskiego*, essentially fully devoted to this issue [Karnkowski] (1596).
78 Pietrzyk-Reeves (2012, 395).
79 Cf. Knychalska (2005, 261–267).
80 [J. D. Solikowski], *Rozsądek o warszawskich sprawach*, in Czubek (1906, 586).
81 *Senatora anonima deliberacyje o królu, panach, radzie i urzędnikach, sejmie i bezkrólewiu.* [1569] In Ulanowski (1921, 143); *Naprawa Rzeczypospolitej* [1573], in Czubek (1906, 205); "*Nam cum respublica nostra tribus maxime hominum ordinibus contineatur, Regia potestate, quae imperat, Equestri ordine, qui paret, et Senatorio inter hos interiecto, qui consulit*," Karnkowski (1574, fol. A 4v).

82 Ł. Górnicki, *Rozmowa Polaka z Włochem o wolnościach i prawach polskich* [1616], in Górnicki (1961, 465).
83 Starowolski (1650, 156).
84 Ekes (2001, 58); cf. also Wachlowski (1927, 223ff.).
85 *Libera respublica quae sit?*, in Czubek (1918, vol. 2, 404).
86 "if this *absoluta potestas* is in the hands of all the estates, then it is all the more so in the hands of the estate which is *potissima huius regni portio* and which *primas parte habet in regno hoc*," [M. Zebrzydowski], *Apologia szlachcica polskiego*, in Czubek (1918, vol. 3, 234).
87 Ibidem.
88 Frost (1990, 54).
89 Augustyniak (1999, 36).
90 Ibidem
91 S. Dunin Karwicki, *Egzorbitancyje we wszystkich trzech stanach Rzeczypospolitej krótko zebrane*, in Karwicki (1992, 25); *O potrzebie urządzenia Rzeczypospolitej (De ordinanda Republica)*, in Karwicki (1992, 91).
92 Karwicki (1992, 26).
93 Karwicki (1992, 29); cf. Michalski (1983, 330); Poraziński (1993, 218).
94 As for instance "*democraticus regendi modus*" in Bystrzonowski (1730, k. K 4) and "*status popularis*" [Radzewski] alias Poklatecki ([1743]: 135).
95 It had appeared in Konarski's *O skutecznym rad sposobie*, when he wrote about the Sejm composed "of the king and of the two other estates" (Konarski 1760–1763, vol. 1, 173 and vol. 2, 230) with clear propaganda objectives, but the whole argumentation was built around a vision of a free *Rzeczpospolita*, "where not one, but more elected from among the people, or the whole people, govern themselves according to the laws and all justice" (Konarski 1760–1763, vol. 2, 166).
96 [Poniński] (1763, 203).
97 [Poniński] (1763, 203).
98 Indeed, he wrote this forthrightly: "we do not have a populace desirous to rule, nor so strong as to force us to entrust it with some share of the highest governance" [Poniński] (1763, 204).
99 Skrzetuski (1782–1784, vol. 1, 41).
100 See e.g. Karpiński (1766, introduction n.p.); Waga (1767, 230); Popławski (1774, 218), although he in fact was inconsistent, elsewhere deeming the governmental system of the Polish-Lithuanian Commonwealth to be aristocratic, because the nobility rules over the populace (Popławski (1774, 223).
101 "The government of the Polish monarchy, consisting of the monarchic, aristocratic, and democratic," Łubieński (1740, 375); this would become a commonplace formulation starting from the 1760s.
102 Morel (1996, 107–108); Grześkowiak-Krwawicz (1992b: 53).
103 Wielhorski (1775) – essentially the entire book is a polemic, written under the influence of Rousseau, with the traditional vision of the three constitutive estates of the *Rzeczpospolita*.
104 "The government in the Polish Kingdom is free. Legislative power is with the king and the senatorial and knightly estates, which they exercise during the Sejm" Mikucki (1776, 48).
105 *Myśl względem poprawy formy rządu* (1790, 9).
106 Rostworowski (1976, 95); Michalski (1983, 327–337).
107 For more on this see Grześkowiak-Krwawicz (2000b).
108 Wybicki ([1775]/1986, 85).
109 Staszic (1787/1926): 49–50).

110 Echoes of Western concepts, especially those of Hugo Grotius, whom he was familiar with, can be perceived in the work of Łukasz Opaliński, postulating that law-making should be separated from the judiciary, in other words for the courts to be thrown out of the Sejm (Opaliński 1938, 49; Opaliński cites Grotius on p. 37).

111 As it was described by Konarski (1760–1763, vol. 4, 165); on Konarski's difficulties in separating out executive power, cf. Konopczyński (1966, 194–195). On the problems of other eighteenth-century authors, cf. Malec (1986, *passim*); on the problems of defining the rule of the executive branch at the beginning of the Four-Year Sejm cf. Szczygielski (2003, 2008).

112 Zamoyski ([1764]/1954, 68).

113 Wyrwicz (1771–1772, 90, 126, outwardly citing *The Spirit of the Laws* book XI, 6); Wyrwicz (1773, 632); [Łobarzewski] (1789b: *passim*); cf. Smoleński (1927).

114 Suffice it to juxtapose the views of Wielhorski and Popławski: Wielhorski (1775, 310–311); Popławski (1774, 174, 177 and *passim*).

115 Grześkowiak-Krwawicz (2000a: 99–108).

116 Szczygielski (2003, *passim*); Łukowski (2010, 176–177).

117 Heading the furthest in this direction was Dyzma Bończa Tomaszewski, in his fierce attack against Article 6 of the *Governing Act*, who indeed identified the executive power with the king (D. Bończa Tomaszewski, *Nad Konstytucją i rewolucją dnia 3 maja roku 1791 uwagi*, in Grześkowiak-Krwawicz (1992a: 175–177).

118 The same conclusion was reached by Smoleński (1927, 81–82).

119 More broadly see Grześkowiak-Krwawicz (2003, 471, 483).

120 Cf. Michalski (1977, 38ff.).

121 Clearly following Montesquieu, Popławski considered "execution" to be the king's "own privilege" (Popławski 1774, 177, similarly 184); Wybicki (1775/1984, 100 and *passim*).

122 Here it is worth citing the somewhat forgotten Jan Ferdynand Nax, who in Smoleński's view had read and understood Montesquieu most thoroughly, cf. Smoleński (1927, 77–79); [Nax] (1789, 85 and *passim*).

123 Kołłątaj (1790, 20).

124 Staszic (1787/1926, 65).

125 Trębicki, *Odpowiedź autorowi prawdziwemu Uwag Dyzmy Bończy Tomaszewskiego nad Konstytucyją i Rewolucyją dnia 3 maja 1791*, in Grześkowiak-Krwawicz (1992a, 238, similarly 226).

126 Michalski (1977, 92ff.); cf. also Grześkowiak-Krwawicz (2003, 478–482).

5   *Zgoda* – Concord

The concept to be analyzed in this chapter, *zgoda*, is perhaps not as fundamental to the political discourse of the Polish-Lithuanian Commonwealth, not as essential in describing how the state or society functioned, as the concepts considered in previous chapters, such as *Rzeczpospolita*, law or freedom. However, it is a notion impossible to ignore if one wants to properly understand the principles or even the foundations by which this state or community operated, as seen by participants in the political discussions of the day. Hence, even if it is slightly – let us stress, only slightly – less important, the notion of *zgoda* is noteworthy as an illustration of how greatly the vision of the political world in those days differed from today's: that vision was less mechanistic, perceiving the functioning of the state organism as more dependent on the attitudes of the participants in the community that formed it.

Before examining more closely what the concept in question meant to the participants of political discussions at the time and what role it was ascribed, we must squarely face a difficult terminological issue posed by this chapter: namely, the fact that the Polish word *zgoda* embraces a range of senses that are not always easy to clearly tease apart or to render well in English. Polish researchers[1] have long recognized that that *zgoda* encompassed at least two different concepts in Latin: both *concordia* and *consensus*. Thus, the same Polish term was used to refer to a certain ideal attitude among community members, as well as a specific constitutional and legal principle, or even procedural solution. In the former sense, *zgoda* may be rendered in English as "concord," in the latter as "consensus" (taking a cue, of course, from the Latin equivalents).

In the sense of "consensus," *zgoda* was an almost technical term that described the way decisions were made in the Sejm and the regional *sejmiks*,[2] and also, in the sense of Latin *consensus omnium* – consent, approval among all – it constituted the political basis of the *Rzeczpospolita*. It is in this sense that the concept of *zgoda* is probably better known and described, if only because it was seen – it is hard to say if rightly so – as the source of subsequent problems of Polish parliamentarism, with the *liberum veto* at the fore. This was also in part because a thorough study of the place of *zgoda*-as-consensus in Polish political thought at the turn of the sixteenth and seventeenth centuries was published by Janusz Ekes.[3]

However, the situation was somewhat akin to that described above with the notion of freedom: alongside, or perhaps even above, the concept of *zgoda* as political consensus among the three parliamentary estates, among the noble envoys to the Sejm, or among the nobles gathered in a regional *sejmik*, there also existed a more general idea of *zgoda* as concord, as a sociopolitical value, as a kind of ideal vision of community life, an ideal that needed to be striven for, despite being difficult to achieve.[4] The notion of *zgoda*-as-concord is in a way more primary, more basic with respect to the notion of *zgoda*-as-consensus. Without the ethical imperative implied by the former, no agreement or consensus could be reached on any matter.

Zgoda – in the more primary sense of concord – was one of the most-cherished political values, and although it did not always attract as much attention as was paid to the other key concepts, there were indeed periods when it was right at the center of interest of participants in political discussions. It also served as an impactful political argument – albeit perhaps not one as popular as the notion of loving one's homeland or loving one's freedom. Participants in subsequent disputes emphasized their efforts to seek consensus, while accusing opponents of "leading the homeland *ad publicam discordiam*."[5] Both noble citizens and their rulers declared "urgent efforts in favor of pleasant concord, which is the surest ground for the well-being of every republic,"[6] sometimes even suggesting that this was their only goal. At least, this was what Stanisław Leszczyński is reported to have said in 1704, explaining that when he had accepted the crown from the Swedish hands, "it was not a desire to rule that motivated him, but wanting thereby to bring about universal concord"[7] – which, we must admit, was quite a bold assertion given the circumstances of the violent conflict over his kingship. Not bolder, however, than the assurances given by the antiroyal rebellion leader Jerzy Lubomirski in 1666, that his intention was "a desire to calm the *Rzeczpospolita* by quelling the animosities between the estates."[8] In this case, however, it is not the sincerity of the authors that is important, but the significance they attached to the value of concord, and their belief that declaring their concern for it would help them win over the recipients of their writings and speeches. Nobody wanted to be seen as a source of "diffidence in the homeland,"[9] and such attitudes and actions were eagerly attributed to political opponents. Although it seems that the place of *zgoda* in the political discourse waned in importance over time, it remained an argument in discussions until the end of the Commonwealth. Interestingly, its role would be recalled at the very end of the existence of the Polish-Lithuanian state in 1791, when supporters of the Constitution of the 3 May 1791 called for unanimous support for the newly adopted *Governing Act*, using almost the very same words that had been used in back the sixteenth century.

Calls urging concord, extolling its virtues and blessed effects, were particularly strongly present in statements from the sixteenth and early seventeenth centuries. Researchers have long highlighted the importance of *zgoda* for political participants during this specific period.[10] Edward Opaliński wrote that "it was seen as the idea upon which the social and political relations of the country were built,"[11] while Janusz Tazbir wrote: "solemn calls for concord and unity in the face of the dangers lying in wait for the Commonwealth were a favorite motif of Old Polish political writings."[12] This held true not only for political writings, but also for speeches made in the Sejm and regional *sejmiks*, sermons (with Piotr Skarga's sermons at the forefront), and also poetry, including that of the highest artistic caliber, such as Jan Kochanowski's poem on the topic. It even appeared in official legal acts. The Act of the Mielnik Union was opened by a declaration that its purpose was to bring about concord, with reference to the famous maxim of Sallust: *Concordia enim res parvae crescunt, discordia maximae dilabuntur.*[13]

This mention of the Act of 1501 forces us to make one important caveat: although the subject of this book is the political discourse of the Polish-Lithuanian Commonwealth, and so it is naturally limited to materials dated after 1569, concord did nevertheless appear much earlier in the discourse as a political, or more broadly social value, and the date of the Union of Lublin or the first free royal election did not change anything in terms of the place ascribed to it in the political universe.[14] In this respect, the political discourse of the *Rzeczpospolita* here forms part of the common European tradition, dating back to antiquity, developed in the Christian spirit by the Fathers of the Church and later recalled by humanism. This common tradition is illustrated by the quote from Sallust, which had indeed also been repeated almost literally by Thomas Aquinas.[15] Extremely popular throughout Europe, it also appeared repeatedly in Polish and Lithuanian statements in the sixteenth and subsequent centuries. Moreover, their authors, especially in the sixteenth century, were fully aware of their participation in the common heritage of the idea of *concordia*, citing not only Sallust, but also Plato, Cicero and Plutarch, as well as (although much less often) theological authorities.[16]

It is concord that was, at least until the mid-seventeenth century, an important element of the vision of the Commonwealth. Its importance for the functioning of the community was unanimously emphasized. It can be said that while the law was considered the soul of the Commonwealth, concord was regarded as its very foundation.[17] Augustyn Rotundus formulated this quite directly: "concord among the citizens is almost the only thing that compriseth the foundation of the Commonwealth and a safeguard of true freedom."[18] But perhaps its function was depicted more accurately by Andrzej Maksymilian Fredro, when he began his considerations of concord with an emblem depicting a stone vault bearing a quotation from Seneca, *casura nisi cohereant*,[19] commenting: "if its citizens lack concord, no republic or kingdom shall prevail."[20] Indeed, concord in political discourse, especially in this earlier period, appears as an element bonding the entire structure of the Commonwealth, and so not so much a foundation as a mortar, without which the building of the state would fall into ruin, and the community would turn into a set of conflicted individuals. "No other virtue hath such power to preserve every city as concord," declared an anonymous participant in the discussion of 1573.[21] Putting it less allegorically, concord was necessary to ensure peace in the social dimension, and therefore the security of the individuals forming the community, as well as the durability and strength of the *Rzeczpospolita*, and in the political dimension, the efficient functioning (or quite simply the functioning) of its institutions.

Over time, peace and the resulting security of both individuals and community began not so much to disappear from the discourse as to occupy a less prominent place in it, giving way to *periculosam libertatem*, but in political discussions during the beginnings of the Polish-Lithuanian Commonwealth it figured as one of the highest values. Often, very often peace was combined with concord: *concordia et pace* was a typical catchphrase in the sixteenth-century political discussion.[22] Similar statements, at least in terms of the authors of more theoretical considerations, were part of the tradition of perceiving the Commonwealth as a community of good life, in justice, peace and "social love," and therefore in concord.[23] It was connected with a humanistic dream of harmony in social relations identified with peace, and unattainable without social concord. As this hope was expressed by one anonymous participant in the pre-election debate in 1573: "let us abandon the bone that has divided you [self-interest], and there shall be love, peace and harmony betwixt us."[24] In part, the authors of similar statements were invoking, not necessarily consciously, the thought of Thomas Aquinas, who had even explicitly equated these two values.[25] Polish participants in political discussions did not always go so far, but in their statements peace, especially internal peace, was closely related to concord, sometimes treated as its inseparable companion, sometimes as its effect. "For has anyone seen that there could be peace in discord?"[26] asked another participant in the political discussion in 1573 – undoubtedly as a rhetorical question.

Discord, disputes between citizens, could lead to neglect of the public good – *quae enim salus publica sine concordia?*[27] – and, even worse, to conflict, riots, in extreme cases even to civil war. As Andrzej Wolan warned: "because confrontations, altercations, and wars commonly arise for reasons, which, having diverted human minds and trampled upon the concord by which alone all human affairs continue, shall undo and overturn every republic."[28] "'Tis discord that maketh for civil dismay / whence such collapse, scarcely any can say," one anonymous and undoubtedly learned author wrote, quoting Virgil in a fairly free translation in a chapter tellingly entitled "On Domestic Unrest, as Being Highly Injurious to the Whole Republic."[29]

Already in the sixteenth century, there were complaints about "this body of the *Rzeczpospolita*, which our ancestors labor'd long to bring to unity, being torn apart [by discord]."[30] However, when writers sought to draw attention to the true dangers of discord, other countries served as better warnings. Sometimes the deplorable effects of discord in the ancient Greek republics and Rome were recalled, but modern events were much more commonly invoked. During a time of religious warfare, it was not difficult to cite examples of "domestic unrest":

> Ye have seen the German lands profusely drenched with blood, ye have seen the English and Scottish betrayals [...], ye have seen peasant wars in the Swiss lands, ye have seen unfortunate revolts by peasants against the nobility, by the nobility against the princes, by the princes against the emperor, ye have long ago seen the Greek slavery, seen the Hungarian lands rent apart.[31]

This grim picture of Europe was meant by its author – an opponent of the Warsaw Confederation – as a warning against "heterogeneity of faiths," but this does not change the fact that it was also a description of the effects of the discord that stemmed from such heterogeneity. However, when illustrating how disastrous the effects of discord could be, the Hungarian example was most often cited. The case of the Kingdom of Hungary clearly confirmed the conviction that a state steeped in quarreling not only failed to guarantee its own inhabitants' internal security, it also lost the strength necessary to defend itself externally. This was an old conviction dating back to antiquity, often supported by an anecdote from Plutarch's *Apophthegmata* about the Scythian (or Tatar, in some versions) King Skilurus and a set of darts – unbreakable when held together in a bundle, but easily breakable individually[32] (an anecdote, incidentally, that functions in various variants to this day throughout European culture). Hungary, however, offered not an allegorical but rather a real proof of the principle linking concord to the strength of the state, and its example was invoked very eagerly. As the research of Janusz Tazbir has shown, everyone – ranging from theoreticians of the state to parliamentary speakers, not to mention also poets and preachers – agreed that "the Hungarian lands were brought to ruin by discord,"[33] a conviction which, moreover, was used as an argument in very diverse political disputes, ranging from religious issues (nonuniformity of faiths as the cause of discord) to the political system (royal election as the cause of discord and unrest), to calls for current disputes to be quelled. The Hungarian defeat resulting from internal conflicts was remembered for a long time, still even being mentioned in the eighteenth century.[34] Irrespective of the specific purposes for which the example was invoked, all the speakers agreed that "the downfall of all kingdoms, and especially that of the Kingdom of Hungary [...] hath its origins in none other than domestic discord."[35] The Hungarian example was a perfect illustration of the belief that "no power and no abundance are so durable as to preserve it [the commonwealth] entirely, where the minds of the citizens are at odds, where they hesitate and are not aligned to one goal,"[36] and at the same time that only concord gives states and nations the strength to defend themselves effectively against an external enemy. Not surprisingly, the example was also used to support calls urging greater consensus and warnings against "being torn asunder," both of which were quite frequently found in the discourse. They are particularly visible in times of tension or political uncertainty, such as royal elections, confederations, or, Heaven forbid, rebellions. *Cum Poloni sumus, magno unanimi et publico consensu regnum Polonorum tradendo*[37] – this appeal was reiterated starting from the first free election. The assertion that "we need honest concord and brotherly love in our homeland"[38] was repeated in the following years, all the more eagerly the less concord there was. In 1666, during Lubomirski's rebellion, the main hero of the conflict publicly stated that the homeland, "coming to its demise through discord, through suspicions [...], only [can] be cured *per contrarium*, that is, through concord and unity of spirits."[39]

Seeing concord as being linked to peace, as well as with the strength and durability of a state or community, was a characteristic combination of the entire European discourse; it could be applied to any state, regardless of its political system, and indeed was so applied. However, when the functioning of a republic was to be decided not by the individual will of a ruler, absolute to some greater or lesser extent, but rather by the collective will, construed in one way or another, the question of concord took on additional significance. Proponents of solutions deviating from the classical monarchical model had to deal with the quite common belief from antiquity that "human society" will "only be mutual when it is governed with a uniform mind and uniform will,"[40] leading to the conclusion that it would be better to allow an individual to rule. One solution to this problem, a way of responding to supporters of the monarchy, lies precisely in the concept of concord – uniting the minds and the will of participants in political life. This is also how the issue was viewed by the sixteenth-century author cited here: his considerations dealt with the generally understood agreement between members of the political community, in other words, with *zgoda*-as-concord. On the level of the political institutions of the *Rzeczpospolita*, Jakub Zawisza from Kroczów best expressed the concept of *zgoda*-as-consensus:

[...] sacred laws, which we follow, in the shape of the divine, stem *ex consensu omnium*: such laws, which are not *ex libitu* of lords, but out of consensus itself – and consensus among all is a heavenly thing – no one can justly rebuke; the difficulty of establishing such laws may be discuss'd by anyone, but *legitime* challenged by none, because those who impose them upon themselves out of sacred concord understand what is healthy for them; and without a doubt 'tis a better law that the *omnium consensus* decides to impose, than what a single tyrant imposes.[41]

This "community of minds" (*animorum societas*) was described somewhat similarly, albeit less concretely and in loftier terms, by Andrzej Maksymilian Fredro.[42] Consensus among everyone was frequently identified with unity, *unanimitas* was on this approach the counterpart of the individual will of the monarch.[43] There is a telling comparison that was used in this context by the above-cited "lover of the homeland," recognizing concord to be the "lady and queen of states and kingdoms."[44] Concord/consensus among participants of political life was an essential condition for imparting real shape to the will of the *Rzeczpospolita*. As one anonymous royalist put it during the time of Zebrzydowski's rebellion: "The Sejm and concord make, ruin, and repair laws."[45] "Let feuds and discord be set aside, because with them we will achieve naught," a senator whose name remains unknown appealed before the Sejm already during the reign of Sigismund Augustus.[46] A separate book could be put together by citing appeals of this sort. From the sixteenth to the eighteenth centuries, pleas for concord were repeated in the *sejmiks*, the Sejm, in instructions for envoys, who were urged: "So that in everything they should abide by concord and love, and avoid quarrels and discord."[47] Just as often, and with time increasingly so, there were laments that such concord was insufficiently present. In nearly the same breath, there was talk of its absence not only in the decision-making bodies, the Sejm and *sejmiks*, but also among citizens averse to one another. These issues were not distinguished from each other, because they could not be teased apart in the concept of a free republic. Even private conflicts between individuals could, in such a republic, lead to lamentable consequences for the community as a whole. This mechanism was most aptly described by Andrzej Zamoyski: "in the government of the Commonwealth, where, due to private interests, disagreements between individuals become, over time, disagreements between their families, and disagreements between families already cause a commotion in public interests."[48] Speaking in 1764, the Grand Chancellor of the Crown was citing the opinions of enlightened philosophers, but this was also an echo of a very old conviction. One hundred sixty years earlier, in 1598, the anonymous author of *Zwierciadło Rzeczypospolitej Polskiej* [Mirror of the Republic of Poland] had complained: "they incite hostilities and feuds between people

[...] so that as the divergence of minds should bring greater divergence on issues of the *Rzeczpospolita*, and with discord should come inevitable confusion."[49] Discord, always dangerous for the state, posed a much greater threat in a situation where the functioning of that state depended on collective decisions made by members of the political community. As one English researcher writes: "republicans generally condemned discord."[50] Let us add that this was not without reason. Concord was not only a guarantee of peace and power of the state, as in monarchies, but the functioning of the political system depended on it. Without it, political decisions could not be made, institutions could not function, and sooner or later the *monarchia mixta* construct had to collapse. Łukasz Opaliński described the effects of discord most penetratingly, warning his countrymen:

> What not even war and violence will force you into, discord itself will bring unto you. On account of which, unable to fare with public matters, without finding any consequence of your consultations, you must cede this governance to someone else...[51]

Warnings about the dangers stemming from discord, threatening the functioning of the institutions of the free *Rzeczpospolita*, and so threatening the republic itself, had been sounded significantly earlier: "in such sunder and discord, by these Sejms of ours, which are called for the good and providence of the *Rzeczpospolita,* we are condemning it to ruin and downfall,"[52] the senator already cited above warned his countrymen, and similar voices would be repeated in subsequent centuries.

This described relatively precisely the meaning of concord for the Commonwealth, as it was perceived in its political discourse, particularly in the sixteenth and seventeenth centuries. One question remains, however, or essentially two: what such concord was, and how it could be achieved. It is perhaps citing here the somewhat lengthier definition of concord proposed by Wawrzyniec Goślicki:

> CONCORDIA, being nothing else than civil amity, is as it were a conspiration of all the estates to maintain liberty, law, justice, fidelity, religion, and tranquility in the commonwealth. The only hope for the preservation of the commonwealth is when all men consent on all things and at all times and consult on their own matters in concord.[53]

We can assume that all the participants of political discussions would agree with such a definition, although few went into such detailed analysis. And to tell the truth, the calculations proposed by Goślicki came down to one thing: concern for the common *Rzeczpospolita* and its freedom. To put it most briefly, concord meant abandoning "private," individual or group interests, in favor of the common good. As one participant in the first free election postulated: "and then the *contemptus* between all the estates would already abate, and the *affectus* of all the estates would have to ensure that we should think uniformly about the *Rzeczpospolita* and about our freedom."[54] Participants of the political debates eagerly declared that they were sacrificing their private objectives or grudges specifically in the name of striving for concord – like the authors of a pamphlet from the times of the Gołąb Confederacy in 1672, who while asserting "it does not have to be demonstrated to us that there needs to be *reunio disunitorum animorum*, because we not only see but *sentimus* the *mala* which *emanarunt* from this division" promised to forgive all private wrongs "*pro bono publico et tranquillitati*" of the homeland.[55] No less often, such sacrifice was urged, or complaints were voiced that "instead of what would be necessary *Rempublicam curare* in unity, everyone would first strive to preserve *rem privatorum*, hence the *partium divisio*, hence the *aemulatio*."[56] These are just sample quotations selected from among a huge number of similar assurances and appeals. As Janusz Ekes aptly notes, the concord understood in this way did not rule out differences of opinion, or even disputes.[57] However, those disputes should not stem from "private interests," but rather from a desire to discover what decisions should be made for the common good. As this was summed up by one of the participants of the political debate in 1573: "and every *civis patriae* should not contribute only the same as another to the good of his homeland, but something of his own, what he considers to be good and useful for his homeland."[58]

Here it is worth pointing out a certain aspect of such an understanding of concord, one that is important but seems to have so far gone underappreciated. Put most succinctly, it is the idea that concord was not a compromise.[59] This may perhaps sound strange with respect to a country whose existence and functioning were *de facto* based on ceaseless compromise. Historians have long been pointing out that, at least during the time when the political system of the *Rzeczpospolita* functioned well, at its basis lay a compromise between the participants of political life. Be it among the three parliamentary estates, among the noble envoys, or among the nobles gathered in a regional *sejmik*, the practice of "working matters out" (*ucieranie materyi*) remained the basis for the process of making political decisions. This does not change the fact that the concept of compromise did not figure in the political language they used. The ideal of political concord/consensus was not to reach an agreement that would satisfy to some degree the various forces participating in the political struggle, but rather to make a concerted decision in the interests of the common good, the homeland, the *Rzeczpospolita*. We can say that the idea of compromise as we understand it today did not fit within the vision of the political world inherited from antiquity, in which the only criterion for evaluating political decisions, and thereby

the only objective of concord, was to be *bonum publicum*. Between political theory and practice, therefore, a distinct gap opened up; in a sense
one may get the impression that the particular political lexicon was itself
one of the factors hampering both the description of the political reality,
and the formulation of proposals for more modern solutions in how the
institutions of the Commonwealth functioned.

   The adoption of a specific concept of concord, although it did not con-
demn disputes *a priori*, nevertheless ruled out lasting divisions between
the participants of political life, taking the form of factions or political parties. These were by definition seen as something bad, blocking
concord for the sake of private interests, and therefore dangerous for
the community. The sixteenth-century "lover of the homeland," when
writing about "factions," warned: "But where one joins with another,
speaks with him and supports him, there the homeland cannot be without danger."[60] One of the most serious accusations in political disputes
was the assertion that the opponent was *civis factiosus*. It was invoked
frequently, with the certainty, it seems, that it would effectively depreci-
ate the adversary.[61] During the first free election, it was warned that "the
Republica should not have *perniciosos cives*, who disturb and violate the
general peace with *practicis et factionibus*."[62] During the Sandomierz
rebellion, there were complaints that the rebels "want to create factions
between us, such as the Guelphs and Ghibellines were like in Italy, which
the noble virtue never allowed in the Crown."[63] Similar charges had
already earlier been leveled against the envoys by the bishop Stanisław
Karnkowski: "the chamber of envoys has given rise to a *monstrum in
Repub[lica] nostra*, which was christened *partisant*."[64] This was not always an argument in a dispute. Often the point was simply to warn
against divisions among citizens. In Krzysztof Warszewicki's opinion,
Hungary had fallen precisely because of this: "in Hungary, where there
were ultimately so many different groups and factions rampaging in the
whole kingdom, could the state remain untouched both internally and
externally?"[65] An anonymous "nobleman" during the rebellion of 1606
saw this as a general rule, concluding that "nearly all other states perished out of discord, factions and *privatis odiis*."[66] Among the factors
that ruing republics or only the *Rzeczpospolita*, factions were mentioned
throughout the whole seventeenth and a significant portion of the eighteenth centuries. Benedykt Chmielowski, in his encyclopedia from the
mid-eighteenth century, listed "discord, factions, dislike" as the second
among causes for the downfall of states (the first was a lack of justice),
writing: "Our Polish Crown could be wealthier and command greater
respect in the world if it were not lacking in the jewel of *unionis*."[67]
In dislike for factions, the noble citizens were somewhat reminiscent of
the English, who spent a long time condemning political divisions with
nearly the very same words, but had coped with the problem conclusively
in the first half of the eighteenth century.[68] In the Polish-Lithuanian

Commonwealth, on the other hand, nearly to the end of its existence, the political language condemned all partisan divisions, specifically as factions, standing in the way of the concord that lay in the common good. Certain changes would only be seen during the time of the Four-Year Sejm. However, it seems that then, too, the political reality of already quite distinctive political factions got ahead of the discourse, in which the notion of political party was used quite cautiously. Perhaps the first author to perceive the advantages of the existence of political parties was Jan Ferdynand Nax, who described "political leagues, which in free nations are formed among citizens with the aim of augmenting the general or private good" – interestingly, he felt that such "leagues" were easier to reconcile, if necessary, in order to achieve unity.[69] However, he did not have followers. It was still better to insist that one was a patriot, not a partisan.[70] If we look at the seventeenth- and eighteenth-century magnate factions or blocs whose main distinguishing feature was having a source of funding from one powerful country or another, it is hard not to admit that such dislike did have certain grounds. But it is a fact that as a result there was a lack of conceptual apparatus making it possible to describe more modern governmental solutions. In some sense, this also applies to the basic issue of *pluralitas* or *unanimitas*. If *zgoda* were to be identified with compromise, adopting the principle of majority voting could be accepted, but if the concept were to be rejected, the only solution protecting against factions was unanimous consensus among all.[71] Of course, we cannot reduce one of the most important problems with how the institutions of the noble state functions merely to the issue of the store of concepts that were then in use. But it remains a fact that the political language did not make it easier to describe possible proposals for far-reaching changes to the procedures for making political decisions. It is no coincidence, it seems, that the concept of *zgoda* (concord) does not appear nearly at all in the discourse of the first decisive advocate of the majority principle, Stanisław Konarski. Jerzy Łukowski ascribed this to Konarski's realism, his recognition of it as an ideal impossible to attain.[72] But also his understanding of the term seems to have been important here, too. Unlike those who came after him, Konarski did not really, despite proposing quite revolutionary reforms, attempt to create a new political language, instead presenting his own concepts within the old conceptual framework. *Zgoda*, in its old meaning of political concord (the only meaning Konarski was familiar with), would have provided more of an impediment than any assistance in formulating his program; hence, he passed over it in silence.

The question of "the majority or acceptance of all" refers to *zgoda* as the foundation of the functioning of institutions, but there was also, as we have noted, *zgoda* as an attitude, as the binding force for the functioning of the entire community of the Commonwealth. As a result, the issues arise of how widely the members of that community could

differ from one another and, potentially, how despite their differences
they could achieve concord within the state. These questions, posed by
political theoreticians since antiquity, were also asked by participants in
the political debate of the Polish-Lithuanian Commonwealth – though
for them it was not just a theoretical, but a very real problem. The answer to the second of the two questions was partly consistent with the
antique tradition, continued by Christianity, and was contained in the
word "love" or "charity" (*caritas*). The concept may not seem closely associated with political discourse, but especially in the sixteenth century,
it does appear often within it. There were appeals "so that we should
maintain courteous love and constant concord among ourselves,"[73] re-
minders that "we need honest concord and brotherly love in the homeland."[74] These citations, chosen from among many similar ones, come
from statements made by participants in specific political discussions.
They are particularly interesting in that they are clearly an echo of the
great philosophical tradition shaped in reference to the thought of Aristotle, in which a social community should constitute a unified whole,
or at least strive towards unity, and the path towards attaining that goal
was specifically love as charity (*caritas*), which "directs many hearts together to one thing."[75] This tradition was drawn upon by the authors of
theoretical treatises – after all, Goślicki's *civilis amicitia*[76] was nothing
other than an reference to the classics, and the same goes for Łukasz
Górnicki's notion of the "amicability" (*sprzyjaźliwość*) of the estates,
where he was drawing upon Plato.[77] Some of them – Wolan, Górnicki –
saw this love/friendship leading to concord as applying to all of society
and all the estates of the Commonwealth.[78] For most authors speaking
out on political topics, however, this was more love between participants in public life, or simply "brotherly love" within the framework of
the noble class. This does not change the fact that, in conjunction with
concord, this was a reference to a classical idea. Such a combination
can be encountered distinctively more frequently in sixteenth-century
statements, most likely due to the humanistic education of many participants in the political discussions. True, the motif of mutual love leading
to concord despite differences between citizens did also appear later,
but it became less frequent. Another aspect of the connection between
love and concord, on the other hand, proved to be more lasting, namely
love for the common good – for the homeland, leading to concord on
the one hand because it was the basis for prosperity, and on the other
because there could be only one *bonum publicum* and so concern for it
was a unifying element. Its consequence should be the *consensus animorum* (the uniting of minds) that appears frequently in the discourse. As
Janusz Ekes noted, in such an approach concord meant the unity of the
will of citizens (to act on behalf of the homeland), but it did not have to
entail unity of their views.[79] Love for the public good will be considered
later on in this book; what is important here is that love – whether it

was a feeling harbored by citizens with respect to one another, or with respect to the *Rzeczpospolita* (which partially meant the same thing) – permitted the belief that concord would be achieved, even despite the serious differences between them, or at least they did not rule it out.

However, there was no lack of opinions that such differences inevitably give rise to conflicts and hamper or preclude the attainment of concord. This was related to increasingly far-reaching postulates of unity. As we have already said, love, especially in the understanding of mutual love among members of the community, was frequently invoked in the sixteenth and in the early seventeenth centuries. With time, its presence in the discourse distinctly subsided. And, its place seems to have been taken by unity, at least to a certain extent. This was not limited to unity in action and in political decisions; it was increasingly also embraced unity of views and attitudes. It could, for instance, pertain to customs, as in the writings of Paweł Piasecki, who recommended:

> to be fond of our own Polish customs above other customs, so that common trust should arise, a unification of minds, and thereby easy concord for the defending of freedom, because everyone would already both love it and defend it.[80]

However, the problem of unity as an essential condition for concord appears most distinctly in disputes over the rights of adherents of other confessions. These discussions serve as an excellent example for observing a kind of clash of two concepts for how concord should be achieved in the Commonwealth. It will be worth pausing for a moment to consider this issue, with the full awareness that even so we will only outline one of the aspects of this significantly broader problem.

The problem of concord in the context of "the diversity of faiths" was one of the more lasting elements of the political discourse of the Polish-Lithuanian Commonwealth. It appeared very early on, practically at the same time as the aforesaid diversity, and would recur all the way until the eighteenth century. However, there were at least potentially two directions of interpretation here. One, which found expression not only in discourse but also in a legal decision, that is, in the Warsaw Confederation (1573), urged for the protection of the freedoms of faiths, in line with the assumption that "difference of faith between us exists, but concord *in Republica* we need"[81]; "This is not an *articulum religionis et fidei*, but *politicus*, because it is *articulus pacis et tranquillitatis publicae*, for us brothers to keep the peace among ourselves and not fight over faith."[82] For its advocates, the Confederation appeared to be nearly the quintessence of concord – while on the one hand it was its consequence: "it is certain that concord, goodwill and love for the Homeland had drawn them into a confederation with one another,"[83] on the other hand, it was a guarantee of concord. It was even presented here as given

by God's grace, as a "means of concord and mutual love between those
differing in faith."[84] The issue of discussion about the Confederation
and the struggle over abiding by its decisions is already the subject of a
vast literature.[85] What is important here is that the freedom to profess
different faiths was presented by its defenders, and more broadly by defenders of the rights of dissidents, as a guarantee of peace and concord
in the *Rzeczpospolita*: "The same freedom of conscience and religious
celebration thus urgently needed by the whole of the homeland, which
is based on peace and civil concord,"[86] an anonymous defender of dissidents' rights wrote in 1627, while another at the same time asserted
that through their persecution "all other countries lost *concordiae decus*
[...]. The Polish Crown alone and the Grand Dutchy of Lithuania lived
moderatione et iuris aequalitate between different religions maintained
peace and concord."[87] It is worth pointing out that in this last statement
one more line of thought appeared, important for the idea of concord as
it was understood in the *Rzeczpospolita* – namely equality, here invoked
as the equality of rights.[88] Concord *inter dissidentes*, as it was described,
is an model example of concord in spite of differences, for the sake of
love of the common good and mutual love of noble citizens. This motif
sometimes resurfaced in subsequent disputes concerning the rights of
dissidents albeit increasingly rarely and less boldly.

However, from the beginning there existed an alternative here, or essentially a powerful rival for such an interpretation. This was the notion
of concord not **in spite of** differences, but rather **thanks to** the lack of such
differences. On such an approach, everything that might bring about divisions among citizens was dangerous: "There can be, Plato says, nothing
better for the city or republic than what unites it, and nothing worse than
what divides it."[89] This thought can be recognized as the leading motif of
most attacks against dissidents. Defenders of religious unity were guided
by the conviction expressed by Rotundus: "If there is anything that unites
society with a bond and tightens ties between people, it is definitely religion."[90] And like him they asked, knowing the answer in advance: "What
kind of concord can there be with a diversity of different and contrary
religious views? What bonds can there be between people? What kind of
love of citizen for citizen?"[91] Here they had the support not only of the
classical authorities, but also the example of the lamentable consequences
of diversity of faiths in the form of the religious wars ravaging a significant portion of Europe. As an anonymous opponent of the decisions of
the Warsaw Confederation wrote, as an appeal and also as a warning:

> Concord, concord is needed, and I believe it is first of all needed in
> faith; where there is no concord in faith, it should not be expected on
> other things and matters. Discord in faith took away the Germans'
> heart, and order, and ancient valor, and it lost Hungary, and also
> Livonia.[92]

We cannot deny that it was not the ideal of concord above divisions, but rather the postulates of "unity in faith" for the sake of maintaining political unity, peace and concord within the state that dovetailed with the European discourse. Catholic advocates of the ideal of religious unity in the *Rzeczpospolita* had a distinctly easier task than their dissident opponents. The conviction that differences of faith lead inevitably to internal conflicts was nearly widespread in Europe, indeed, among representatives of all the faiths. In the Polish-Lithuanian Commonwealth, it was invoked, like elsewhere, by representatives of the dominant faith, that is, the Catholics. That this argument was appreciated is attested to by its persistence. Using nearly the same words as Rotundus, there were calls for "unity of the sacred faith"[93] throughout the whole seventeenth and a significant share of the eighteenth centuries. As the author of *Eclipsis Poloniae* explained at the beginning of the eighteenth century:

> [...] even to preserve the state in close unity, it [religion] should be kept to. What stands behind its being torn apart in diversity are minds contradicting one another on the very same public issues [...] and never will full friendship come to pass between the dissenters and Catholicism.[94]

This view was shared by essentially everyone – from the fervent defenders of the Catholic faith, to the enlightened reformers. "That there can only be one prevailing faith in each individual country is not a chimera, but a clear truth proven in politics," Franciszek Bieliński asserted, basing himself on the authority of Western philosophers.[95] On this approach, besides, this was no longer the old idea of concord, but rather a reference to modern concepts of the homogenization of society as a guaranty of the strength of the state.

This leads to the next issue – what happened to the idea of concord over the passage of time. Although we have occasionally cited later texts here, our analysis of the concept has been based mainly on sources from the sixteenth and first half of the seventeenth centuries; this was not without good reason. Less attention was paid to it in later statements, and neither was anything added to the concept as it was earlier laid out; rather, one gets the impression that with time the notion of concord decidedly became impoverished. Simplifying somewhat, we could say that it did not cease to be appreciated, but lesser and lesser interest was taken in it. The last writer to undertake sincere theoretical analysis of what *zgoda* meant and should mean, and what its function in the state was, was Andrzej Maksymilian Fredro in the mid-seventeenth century. After him, Stanisław Herakliusz Lubomirski would also consider the issue at some length, although in keeping with the spirit of his treatise it was in a paradoxical and strongly ironic way. He was, besides, skeptical about the possibility of achieving it, and even harbored certain doubts as to whether any kind of concord would be beneficial to the Commonwealth: "Insignificance (*Vanitas*): But the *Rzeczpospolita* will fall because of discord. Truth (*Veritas*): More have perished because of lethargic concord."[96] Later authors of more serious analyses of the Commonwealth mentioned it, stressing its virtues and the need for it, but they did not consider its underpinnings, presumably deeming them to be obvious.[97] Mention was made of it in current statements more rarely, particularly in the eighteenth century. Although there was one exception here: complaints about the lamentable consequences of discord. Statements presenting the virtues of concord and appealing for it – at the end of the seventeenth and especially in the first half of the eighteenth centuries – are increasingly supplanted by descriptions of what the absence of concord, in other words discord, would lead to. These descriptions were sometimes quite extensive:

> distrust and mutual hatred spread [during the great northern war of 1700–1709] in such a hideous manner that we were no longer bound by the most sacred ties nor by faith, nor by honor, nor by freedom, nor by kinship, nor by considerations of friendship

– this state of affairs was described by the author of *Zaćmienie Polski* [Eclipse of Poland], an eclipse which in his view resulted from discord, for which he above all blamed the magnates.[98] "Great animosities between the more powerful houses, mistrust between the estates of the *Rzeczpospolita*, duality and differences in the voivodships, lands and poviats, these are blows meant to rock, if not overthrow the homeland" – such was the diagnosis of Wacław Rzewuski.[99] It was in part shared by Jan Stanisław Jabłonowski, who pointed out that the divisions in a free country are much more dangerous than in an absolute monarchy, although he did not in fact blame the wealthy for them.[100] It is worth bearing in mind that all these descriptions were not theoretical analyses, but descriptions of real disputes, and in the cases of Stanisław Szczuka and Jabłonowski – even of civil warfare, underway in the early eighteenth century. The authors of these and other complaints about disputes and divisions in the noble society were convinced that *civilis discordia* was a symptom, and at the same time the cause of a serious crisis of the state.[101] As an anonymous author wrote in 1775: "Steeped in ignorance and luxury, rent by civil strife, Poland itself leaned towards its demise."[102]

The authors of these complaints give the impression of being relatively helpless with respect to the reality they described; in any event none of these or other similar statements provide any deeper reflections about what concord was and how it could be achieved. Instead, they are dominated by quite vapid lamentation. One may get the impression that concord had partly become exhausted as a concept. It could be used to make a political diagnosis, but it did not lend itself to sketching out a positive agenda.

Konarski's decision to avoid the concept in his treatise, mentioned above, is quite telling. This was, it seems, a consequence of a crisis of discourse that was based on a combination of ethics and politics – something that will be discussed again below. And so, while virtue had regained some of its former splendor through the work of Rousseau, *zgoda* – concord – irrevocably lost its role as one of the most important political concepts. This does not mean that its value or the need for it was questioned, especially in a free state. As Ignacy Łobarzewski wrote in 1789: "Republics themselves succumb to all turbulences; in them prudence should prevail, in them discord must be wiped out at its very appearance."[103] Nevertheless, in the latter half of the eighteenth century, concord cased to be one of the key elements of the vision of the state posited by participants of political discussions. Calls for concord, however, did not cease to be a propaganda argument cited in political disputes. Such calls included *Kazanie o zgodzie* [Sermon on Concord] by Father Michał Karpowicz (1784), certain texts published in the journal *Monitor*, in poetry. This was especially true among the royal circle, because a significant share of Stanisław August's propaganda was based on an appeal for concord (and indirectly, for unity stemming from it). The motif put forward in the *Suum cuique* appeared within that propaganda in different variants: "that it is time to set hatred aside, it is time to make joint efforts to work for calming the country, troubled by so many misfortunes."[104] The famous slogan of 3 May 1791 – "king with nation, nation with king" – fits in here somewhat, being as it was as much an endorsement for the actions and person of the king, as a summons for unity and concord. In these times, it seems, the need for the first of these two (namely, unity) was held up more frequently. Although this is a concept that had been present in the discourse of the Polish-Lithuanian Commonwealth for a long time, its growing popularity seems to attest to a change in the political language under the influence of the Enlightenment discourse, which spoke more about the unity of members of society than about concord among them. In the work of such philosophers as Rousseau and his Polish students such as Stanisław Staszic, this was an idea quite distant from the traditional concept of concord. However, in writings and speeches dating from 1791 and 1792, these concepts are used essentially as substitutes for one another, or unity is treated as a consequence of concord. Uniting around the new *Governing Act* was one of the main slogans of pro-Constitutional propaganda.[105] Such a direction was already pointed out by the universal proclamation of the Sejm Marshals dated 7 May 1791:

> Good citizens! Keep in mind that only unity alone can save us from unjust foreign greed; all your happiness, the strength and power of the nation are attached to it. As long as the nation is with the king and the king with the nation, no power will dare to violate our freedoms and our integrity.[106]

An appeal was made for national concord to the nobility gathered for the *sejmiks* in February 1792: "Notice what your country is today, and what it would be if it were disturbed," "unity, concord, love for the government is your happiness."[107] Its achievement was praised when the *Governing Act* was backed by the general nobility, when "a consensus of all the lands and voivodships, in a word the unity of the whole nation, was found for the new Constitution."[108] Concord and unity were called for in the dramatic moment of the Russian danger.[109] Although it did not become a subject of deeper reflection, as it had in the sixteenth century, its importance for the community was pointed out nearly with the very same words as at the beginning of the noble republic.

Notes

1   Ekes (2001, 75 *passim*).
2   Opaliński (1995, 94–95).
3   Ekes (2001), the whole second part of which is devoted specifically to the concept *zgoda*. See also the recent work by Beata Raszewska-Żurek (2016) on the same topic from a purely linguistic standpoint.
4   This is pointed out both by Ekes (2001, 76) and Opaliński (1995, 94–96).
5   *List prawie senatorski do jednego z wielkich urzędników koronnych podczas elekcyjej confidenter pisany* [1648], in Ochmann-Staniszewska (1989, 17).
6   *Dyskurs o zawziętych teraźniejszych zaciągach skąd in Republica urosły, i o postępku sejmu 1606*, in Czubek (1918, vol. 2, 373).
7   [Szczuka?] (1709/1902, 107), this is a fragment cited by the author of Leszczyński's speech to regular army units (*wojsko kwarciane*).
8   Lubomirski ([1666]: 121).
9   "[L]etters, epistles and speeches are circling around the voivodships, full of rumors and angers, which by multiplying diffidence in the homeland, precipitate ruin to our nation," *List pana Reklewskiego cześnika sendomierskiego 27 octobris 1663*, in Ochmann-Staniszewska (1990, 190).
10   Opaliński (1995, 94–96); Ekes (2001).
11   Opaliński (1995, 94); Ekes (2001, 67).
12   Tazbir (1992, 153).
13   Ohryzko (1859, vol. 1, 131 (285)).
14   Cf. Węcowski (2013, 169–183).
15   Jarra (1968, 130); Sallust, *Bellum Iugurthinum* I, 10; Thomas Aquinas, *Summa Theologica*, 2.2, question 37, art. 2, 3 ("*concordia magnae res crescunt et per discordiam dilabuntur*").
16   Alongside Sallust, the most frequently cited work was Plutarch's *Apophtegmata*; references to the Holy Bible and to the Fathers of the Church appear very infrequently (apart from sermons). As exceptions to this, however, we should recognize the work sometimes ascribed to Szymon Budny, *Elekcyja króla krześcijanska* (1573), whose author cites the Bible and Gregory of Nazianzus, and alongside this provided a whole review of classical praises of concord, from Plato to Empedocles to Gorgias to Cicero. In Czubek (1906, 292–294).
17   Ekes (2001, 67ff.); as this was presented by Jan Januszowski (1613/2009, 524), describing the body of the *Rzeczpospolita*: "the legs of this body and the head, by which they move and stand, are concord and love."
18   A. Rotundus, Letter to Wolan, in Wolan (1572/1606/2010, 263).

19 Fredro (1660/2014, 2014, 735), compare note 416 from the publishers on p. 830.
20 Ibidem, p. 736, 738.
21 [Budny?] *Elekcyja króla krześcijańska*, in Czubek (1906, 292).
22 Opaliński (1995, 96); besides such a combination had been very popular earlier, cf. Węcowski (2013, *passim*).
23 Pietrzyk-Reeves (2012, *passim*).
24 *Rozmowa senatora koronnego z ślachcicem*, in Czubek (1906, 543); on the ideal of peace see Kąkolewski (2007, 123).
25 Thomas Aquinas, *Summa Theologica*, 2.2, question 29, art. 1.
26 S. Reszka, *Konfederacyjej w Warszawie roku 1573 in interregno uczynionej a starym poprzysięgłym przeciwnej rozbieranie*, in Czubek (1906, 574).
27 *Cum in convocatione Varsoviensi*, in Czubek (1906, s. 561).
28 Wolan (1572/1606/2010, 111).
29 *Philopolites...* (1588, fol. O); Virgil, *Eclogae*, Ecloga I also given in Latin.
30 [Grabowski?] (1598/1859, 7). Here the author was writing specifically about discord stemming from a lack of understanding between voivodships, as a consequence of the abolishment of general *sejmiks* (joint gatherings of nobles from a whole province).
31 *De confoederatione Varsoviensi in causa religionis Christianae et patriae salutis cupida sententia*, in Czubek (1906, 559).
32 Goślicki (1568, fol. 63v); [Budny?] *Elekcyja króla krześcijańska*, in Czubek (1906, 325) describes "Skilurus the Tatar"; *Philopolites...* (1588, fol. B2 i B2v), speaks of "the Tatar King Scylurus" with a reference to Plutarch, Skarga (1597/1999, 78) mentions "Sylvius the Scyth" with a reference to Plutarch; *Considerationes de exeptione Ich M|iłoś|ciów Panów duchownych contra securitatem dissidentium in religione po sejmie anno 1632*, in Augustyniak (2013, 607) – here the figure is named Misyp, but the story is the same.
33 Tazbir (1992, 147–161).
34 "The spirit of discord deprived the huge nations of the Hugarians, Czechs, Greeks of that freedom which unity and bravery have given to the Swiss..." Karpowicz (1786, fol. Dv).
35 *List pana Reklewskiego cześnika sendomierskiego 27 octobris 1663*, in Ochmann-Staniszewska (1990, 190).
36 *Philopolites...* (1588, fol. B2)
37 *De rege novo ex sua gente eligendo oratio*, in Czubek (1906, 347); similarly *Zebranie różnych sentencyi na propozycyją uniwersału kaskiego*, in Czubek (1906, 234), [Budny?] *Elekcyja króla krześcijańska*, in Czubek (1906, 293), and many other such appeals.
38 [Solikowski] (1596/1859, 10).
39 Lubomirski (1666, 112).
40 *Philopolites...* (1588, fol. B2v).
41 Zawisza z Kroczowa (1613/1899, 14–15); Ekes (2001, 82).
42 Fredro (1668/2015, 716).
43 Cf. Ekes (2001, 82).
44 *Philopolites...* (1588, fol. B 3).
45 *Dyskurs o zawziętych teraźniejszych zaciągach skąd in Republica urosły, i o postępku sejmu 1606*, in Czubek (1918, vol. 2, 391).
46 *Senatora anonima deliberacyje o królu, panach, radzie i urzędnikach, sejmie i bezkrólewiu* [1569], in Ulanowski (1921, 174).
47 [Grabowski?] (1589/1859, 20), a proposed set of instructions for envoys.
48 Zamoyski ([1764]/1954, 71).

49 [Grabowski?] (1589/1859, 8).
50 Brugger (1999, 38), of course, with the exception of Machiavelli, which seems to be a decent argument for those opposed to his being recognized as a republican; on the meaning of concord in the republican vision of the state cf. also Koenigsberger (1997, 44).
51 *Rozmowa plebana z ziemianinem* [1641], in Opaliński (1938, p. 6).
52 *Senatora anonima deliberacyje o królu, panach, radzie i urzędnikach, sejmie i bezkrólewiu* [1569], in Ulanowski (1921, 174).
53 Goślicki (1568, fol. 63v).
54 *Przestroga z pokazaniem niepożytków z wzięcia pana z pośrzodku siebie*, in Czubek (1906, 395).
55 *Krótko zebrane praeiudicia Reipublicae universae* [1672], in Kluczycki (1880–1881, vol. 2, 1210).
56 *Refleksyje A.S. Dembowskiego biskupa płockiego* [June 1742], in Skibiński (1913, 33); for Dembowski this was an argument against forming a confederation.
57 Ekes (2001, 70) distinguishes between concord as an act of will and unity as a state of minds.
58 *Rzecz o mającej nastąpić konwokacyjej*, in Czubek (1906, 216).
59 For more broadly on the latter concept, cf. Fumurescu (2013).
60 *Philopolites…* (1588, fol. O); cf. Ekes (2001, 71–72); previously Goślicki, when describing the foundations of a fortunate republic, listed among other factors "*si cives […] invicem amici, et nullis factionibus distracti,*" Goślicki 1568, fol. 44).
61 Ekes (2001, 71) points out that this term meant at the same time both "citizen-troublemaker" and "citizen belonging to a faction."
62 *Iż na społecznym zjeździe panów rad koronnych w Kaskach*, in Czubek (1906, 247).
63 *Hieronim Jazłowiecki do Stanisława „Diabła" Stadnickiego, 24 Junii 1606*, in Czubek (1918, vol. 2, 170).
64 [Karnkowski] (1596, fol. B 2).
65 Warszewicki (1598/2010, 207 in Latin, 374 in Polish).
66 *Votum szlachcica polskiego na sejmiki i sejm roku pańskiego 1606*, in Czubek (1918, vol. 2, s. 231).
67 Chmielowski (1745, 456).
68 Dickinson (1979, 179–180 and *passim*); cf. also: Koenigsberger (1997, 44).
69 Nax (1789, 373–375).
70 As the title of a pamphlet from 1776 announced: "The thoughts of a citizen-patriot, not partisan" (*Myśli obywatela patrioty nie partyzanta 1776 anno*, n.d.); cf. Michalski (1998, 42ff.).
71 "And now people easily perceive the inconvenience of *pluralitas*, in that it provides a basis for factions…," a speech by Szczęsny Herburt to the Sejm in 1593, quoted after Ekes (2001, 113).
72 Łukowski (2014, 181–196, 185); Konarski (1760–1763, vol. 2, 91, 102).
73 [Budny?] *Elekcyja króla krześcijańska* [1573], in Czubek (1906, 293).
74 [Solikowski] (1596/1859, 10).
75 This is actually a phrase from Thomas Acquinas, *Summa Theologica*, 2.2, question 37 "*Discord*" (transl. by the Fathers of the English Dominican Province: http://www.documentacatholicaomnia.eu/03d/1225-1274,_Thomas_Aquinas,_Summa_Theologiae_%5B1%5D,_EN.pdf.Cf.Andrzejuk(2007,51); Augustyniak (1981).
76 Goślicki (1568, fol. 63v).

77 "Plato says that a republic in which the estates are not amicable is poorly constructed, and a legislature is not good if it does not consider that all the estates of the *Rzeczpospolita* [here understood socially] are preserved in concord and love," *Rozmowa Polaka z Włochem o wolnościach i prawach polskich* [1616], in Górnicki (1961, 349); cf. also Jarra (1968, 104).
78 Wolan (1572/1606/2010, 111).
79 Ekes (2001, 70).
80 Piasecki ([1631–1632]/1972, 252), the subtext contains an allusion that the blame for discord rests with foreign customs, because each person wishes to emulate a different model, which as a result leads to disputes.
81 *Ślachcica polskiego do rycerskiego koła braciej swej miłej o obieraniu króla krótka przemowa*, in Czubek (1906, 287).
82 *Rozmowa o rokoszu*, in Czubek (1918, vol. 2, 135).
83 *Głos anonima ewangelika do Króla Jego M[ił]ości i do stanów Rzeczypospolitej na sejmie anni 1631 zgromadzonych*, in Augustyniak (2013, 480).
84 *Krótkie rzeczy potrzebnych z strony wolności a swobód polskich zebranie* (1587/1859, 53).
85 Korolko (1974); for the most complete and up-to-date list of such publications see the bibliography of Augustyniak (2013).
86 *Racyje tego, iż pax et tranquillitas inter dissidentes de religione ma być nienaruszenie zatrzymana* [1627], in Augustyniak (2013, 438)
87 *Uniżona prośba do Króla Jego M [ił]ości i Rzeczypospolitej na sejm MD-CXXVII pisana*, in Augustyniak (2013, 390).
88 Opaliński (1995, 94).
89 This quote is from *Egzorbitancyja powszechna która Rzeczpospolitą królestwa polskiego niszczy, zgubą grożąc* (1628/1858, 7), indeed from the very beginning of the text. The author feels that people are united by God's love, obedience to the ruler, and mutual justice.
90 A. Rotundus, Letter to Wolan, in Wolan (1572/1606/2010, 263).
91 Ibidem.
92 *Komornik a burmistrz*, in Czubek (1906, 652).
93 Actually, a term from Starowolski (1650, 6).
94 [Szczuka?] (1709/1902, 131).
95 [Bieliński] (1775, 156).
96 Lubomirski (1699/1916, 75). Could this be an echo of Machiavelli? Cf. also Probulski (2014, 309).
97 It was quite often mentioned by Leszczyński, above all in the context of "general concord and harmony *inter status*," Leszczyński ([1737?]/1903, 7, 30, 53). [Szczuka?] (1709/1902, 111); [W. Rzewuski] (1756, fol. B2, D 2v); "Unity of citizens is the strongest shield and buckler against all attacks by unfriendly powers" Sienicki (1764, 10).
98 [Szczuka?] (1709/1902, 11, 137, 159 *passim*).
99 [W. Rzewuski] (1756, fol. B 2v).
100 [Jabłonowski] (1730, 8).
101 As the first "sign" that the free republic was headed towards downfall, Walenty Pęski recognized *civilis discordia* [Pęski] (1727, 40).
102 *Rada patriotyczna dla teraźniejszego stanu Polski od dobrze życzącego krajowi swemu publico podana* ([1775]: 3).
103 [Łobarzewski] (1789b: 228).
104 *Suum cuique* [1771?], fol. B 2v; cf. Ślusarska (1997, 206).
105 Michalski (1987, 317–329).

106 S. Małachowski, K. N. Sapieha, *Uniwersał marszałków Sejmowych z 7 maja 1791*, in Grześkowiak-Krwawicz (1992a: 27).
107 *Do obywatelów mających się zebrać na następujące sejmiki* ([1792], folio 3v and 4v).
108 [A. Linowski], *Doniesienie pilne współobywatelom z Warszawy*, in Grześkowiak-Krwawicz (1992a: 275).
109 "Unity is now the most important good for us, through disunity you have suffered harm and shame; do not lose this from memory," A. Linowski, *Doniesienie*, in Grześkowiak-Krwawicz (1992a: 280).

6 *Cnota* – Virtue as Advice for the Commonwealth

Attempts to situate the concept of virtue within the political discourse of the Polish-Lithuanian Commonwealth pose a certain paradox. If we were to judge the significance of this term solely by the frequency of its occurrence, we might be inclined to think of it as much less important than the concepts discussed earlier. The word virtue (*cnota*) does certainly appear in Polish statements from the sixteenth to the eighteenth centuries, often in complaints about a lack thereof, yet it does so much less frequently than law, freedom or Commonwealth. However, if we treat this word as a catchphrase nested within a whole network of concepts and ideas, together forming a consistent vision of mutual interconnections between individuals and the community, we will conclude that virtue was one of the most important aspects of talking and thinking about the state, without a thorough understanding of which the political discourse would be incomprehensible and any attempts to interpret it would lead us astray.

Researchers have long noticed that the issue of the character, customs, morals and attitudes of participants in political life was an integral component of Polish political discussions. Likewise, they have long pointed out what was sometimes referred to as "a moralistic perspective on governmental issues" present in the political discourse.[1] Sometimes, especially with reference to the eighteenth century, this perspective was linked to the increasingly barren Polish political thought, bogged down in passive moralizing and unable to propose institutional reforms.[2] However, this is a much broader issue, one that was first noticed by Claude Backvis and further elaborated upon by Dorota Pietrzyk-Reeves, Sławomir Baczewski and Benedict Wagner-Rundell in their recent publications.[3] The Polish political discussions fit into the antique traditions of deliberations on the state, in which the attitudes of the individuals who formed the community were no less important than the structure of governance, in which the shaping of people was no less important than the shaping of institutions, and in which ethics remained closely linked to politics or in fact remained one of its crucial components.[4]

This was partially a reference to the great traditions of the state as a community of good life. In line with the traditions that dated back

to Aristotle and were continued by Christian thinkers, in particular
Thomas Aquinas, both Polish theorists of the sixteenth century and humanists in the whole of Europe saw the state as an ethical undertaking,
a place where citizens could enjoy a "good" life, and the achievement of
such a good or even "blessed" life became its fundamental goal.[5] Such
a vision of the republic was developed by Modrzewski, Wolan (in the
context of freedom) and Petrycy (strongly linked to Aristotle's thought),
but it was accepted by all authors of broader deliberations on the state
in the second half of the sixteenth century.[6] Its echoes could be heard
quite clearly in the political commentaries of that period, when definitions of the republic or the Commonwealth took into consideration
the ethical aspect of life in the community formed *ad unam pacem et
unam salutem ut bene beateque vivatur.*[7] As the anonymous author of
Naprawa Rzeczypospolitej [Repairing the Republic] put it:

> [...] the objective which all republics strive for is that man, being an
> *animal civile*, is drawn towards common life and desires to live his
> life as befits an honest person, in concord, love, peace, justice, and
> abounding in all things needed.[8]

The anonymous author of those words, undoubtedly a well-educated
man, was clearly taking a cue from Aristotle in this respect. However,
similar conclusions could be drawn through references to Christian ethics, with Bishop Karnkowski presenting the blessed life of a citizen of the
Commonwealth in the following way: "*Beata civium vita, ut sit opibus
firma, copiis locuples, gloria ampla, virtute honesta*, as the Christian
order teaches us, *ut in sanctitate et iustititia, tum libertate et pace christiana, coram Domino Deo vitam degamus, omnibus diebus nostri.*"[9]
These words reveal a characteristic emphasis placed on ethical aspects:
life in the state community was expected to be a life of peace and justice,
a life that was honest or, in other words, virtuous. In Górnicki's words,
"Virtues render happy and blessed not only a man, but also the Commonwealth."[10] In this sense, a dearth of virtue openly made it doubtful
whether it was at all possible to talk about a republic, understood as a
state community. It is another issue that none of the Polish authors took
this as far as the ancient philosophers. An absence of virtue was seen
as a serious threat to the Commonwealth, but not as the negation of its
very essence, because this issue was viewed on a different level. Strongly
theoretical and rather abstract, the concept of the state as a community
of people who strove to achieve a good life had a strong impact above
all on the deliberations of the Renaissance humanists[11] and – despite appearing in ongoing political discussions – it did not influence the Polish
"discourse of virtue."

We must not forget that a different and much more concrete vision
of the Commonwealth functioned in parallel, one depicting it as a

community of free citizens, and this other vision also had its roots in antiquity and was also invoked in humanistic thought, particularly in Italy.[12] Over time, this more concrete vision would come to dominate the Polish political discourse. On this approach, the matter of virtue was no less important, but it occupied a somewhat different place – it was no longer the purpose of the existence of the state, because that purpose was above all freedom, treated as both the possibility of deciding affairs for oneself and the ability to safely enjoy one's property. In this light, virtue, understood as certain attitudes of individuals towards the community and the common good, was a fundamental means to achieve this end. It determined the functioning, security and finally existence of the civic community. "The *Rzeczpospolita* will persevere only as long as virtues and sacred principles persevere within it," a sixteenth-century author stated resolutely, describing the role model of a good citizen.[13] Although not everyone formulated this conviction in an equally straightforward manner, it was common and extremely durable and, as I will discuss below, lasted until the end of the Polish-Lithuanian Commonwealth's existence. Western researchers point out that in Italian humanist thought, virtue was expected to protect the community from – or at least delay – the demise that inevitably stemmed from the cyclical history of countries and communities. In the opinion of some historians, this was the idea of virtue as the individual's only defense in the struggle against ways of fate/fortune, influenced by the Stoic philosophy – only shifted instead onto the level of the whole society.[14] A similar interpretation can also be found in certain Polish statements. Górnicki, for example, wanted to halt the wheel of fortune and inevitable decay, which in his opinion had already set in within the Commonwealth, specifically by invoking virtue.[15] However, it appears that this problem was generally considered less allegorically and more concretely in the context of the functioning of the civic community, whose individual members participated in the life of the Commonwealth, made political decisions and had influence over the functioning of the community. At the same time, it was stressed strongly that they voluntarily took, or refrained from taking, any actions and decisions, because there was no external factor, apart from the law, that could force them to behave in a specific way.[16] In this situation, the issue of the attitudes of participants in public life became a matter that was by all means political. It was their care for the public good that determined whether the Commonwealth would safely withstand all dangers, both external and internal ones. "Remember your duties, that the homeland rests upon you," Kunicki told a "son of the crown," stressing elsewhere about the homeland that "all of its happiness and life depended" upon the noble citizen.[17] Influenced by the Enlightenment-age theorists of the state, Wybicki explained in the eighteenth century: "The fate of a monarchic kingdom hinged upon the ruler's way of thinking; the good fortune of the Commonwealth on the spirit of its citizens."[18]

In this situation, an absence of virtue on the part of individuals could lead to the degeneration and demise of the community, also because it led to the degeneration of freedom as the fundamental value guaranteed by the Commonwealth and its distinctive feature. Without virtue, freedom would turn into wanton license (*swawola*), dangerous both for the state and for citizens. As Górnicki warned, "Freedom with virtue is good, without virtue, there is excess license."[19]

It therefore comes as no surprise that the issue of the attitudes of those making up the Commonwealth's community became permanently established as one of the fundamental elements of political deliberations. Long before Montesquieu, virtue was regarded in these deliberations as a principle of the republic in line with the antique tradition, in particular Cicero, and the concepts of civic humanism.[20] The combination of ethics and politics proved extremely durable in the Polish discourse, even more so than in the European discourse. However, we can see that over time the treatment of these issues underwent certain changes, which nonetheless involved more a shift of focus rather than attempts to introduce new concepts. In order to illustrate as concisely as possible what these changes involved, we can structure our discussion around three somewhat arbitrary catchphrases – namely, virtue as the foundation of the Commonwealth, the demise of virtue and virtue *rediviva* – ascribing them accordingly to the period from the mid-sixteenth century to the first decades of the seventeenth century, the period from the turn of the seventeenth and eighteenth centuries to the 1760s, and lastly the final decades of the eighteenth century, starting from the 1770s. This may be a rather far-reaching simplification, but these catchphrases do appear to capture well certain dominant or at least characteristic trends in each epoch.

Virtue as the foundation of the Commonwealth

It is worth noting that the quotations presented above predominantly come from the first of these three periods, and this should be no surprise. It was in that period that certain model attitudes were first sketched out, to which references were subsequently made, practically until the end of the Polish-Lithuanian Commonwealth and, more importantly, it was in that period that a language was created that would be used with what were only minor changes to describe these model attitudes in the following two centuries. It was likewise in that period that the most important treatises on the theory of the state were written, incorporating issues related to the sphere of ethics into deliberations on the system of government as their integral component.[21] Writings that combined these two spheres so consistently, and simultaneously so creatively, would be difficult to find in the following periods, up until the 1770s. At the turn of the sixteenth and seventeenth centuries, the problem of the attitudes of participants in public life aroused great interest, also on the part of those participants, which was clearly reflected in statements on ongoing political topics that discussed very frequently the issue of virtue, its lack, desired and undesired behaviors, and their consequences for the community, sometimes in the form of quite long deliberations, but more often than reduced to short mentions, treated as certain slogans. Indirect proof of that interest was offered by the popularity of the civic *Mirrors*, known in Latin as *Specula*, which could be described as guidebooks on the virtues of participants in political life. The popularity of the genre was also noticed by Teresa Bałuk-Ulewiczowa, who wove the Polish *Specula* into the European literary traditions.[22] Nevertheless, the significance of this phenomenon is not only literary but also political, because it shows the importance of the issue of the personal characteristics and behaviors of citizens. Although the authors of such deliberations had quite divergent visions of virtue,[23] what they had in common was the embedding of the role models described in their treatises in the context of the functioning of the community. Such works as *Philopolites, abo miłośnik ojczyzny* [Philopolites, or Lover of the Homeland] or Kasper Siemek's *Civis bonus* described not only the role model of an upright man, not the virtues of a nobleman as an ideal representative of his estate, but the ideal of an active participant in the political community upon whom the good existence of that community depended. Even Kunicki, when sketching out his picture of a nobleman, presented him as the one "upon whose shoulders the homeland rests, who constantly guards its health."[24] In the mid-seventeenth century, such writings were rather unlikely to appear,[25] and they could be found to some extent in the eighteenth century in Konarski's speech *De viro honesto et bono cive* [1754] and later in the *Catechisms* of a good citizen,[26] modeled on foreign texts.

When discussing the *Specula*, we should also note a certain interesting aspect of the "discourse of virtue" that was reflected in one of these writings, namely Goślicki's deliberations on the perfect senator. Previously, discussions pertained in general to the attitudes of the members of the community forming the Commonwealth, which in fact meant noble citizens. Indeed, they were the addressees of the aforementioned *Specula* and it was usually with them in mind that authors of political letters wrote their texts. However, in the period of the greatest interest in these issues, statements appeared that narrowed the issue of virtue to only one class in the noble estate, namely the one formed by those holding the highest offices in the state, or distinguished between the requirements made for senators and those made for the nobles in general. Senatorial virtues were described by Goślicki,[27] listed by Warszewicki[28] and discussed at length by Karnkowski.[29] In their writings, we could hear distant echoes of the concepts of those Italian authors who had created separate canons of virtues for the aristocracy and for the popular component of mixed government.[30] However, this appears to have followed to a greater extent from the concept of government chosen by the authors listed above. We must not forget that political virtues were only needed by those who wielded influence over political decisions and were only considered in their context – hence the popularity of the royal or ducal *Mirrors* in Western Europe.[31] All of these authors advocated strengthening the aristocratic factor in the *monarchia mixta*, specifically by strengthening the Senate, so it comes as no surprise that they attached more importance to the virtues of its members. Political virtues were ultimately not divided in the noble political discourse. Even the magnates who held the highest offices were required to demonstrate (at least in discourse) the same attitudes as noble participants in political life, and they were expected to have the same virtues as nobles, while the lack of such attributes was held against them in the same way it was held against nobles.[32] Interestingly, this did not change even in the seventeenth century and the first half of the eighteenth century, or in the period when divisions in the noble society became very clear and the political influence wielded by the magnates became incomparably greater than at the end of the sixteenth century.[33] If all nobles continued to form (at least in theory) the community of the Commonwealth, they were required, even if only verbally, to exhibit the same virtues.

At this point, it is necessary to answer one fundamental question: Exactly what attitudes were members of the political community expected to have? Undoubtedly, the most important of all virtues was the love of the homeland and of "the common good," the treatment of individual actions and decisions as subordinate to the needs of the Commonwealth. Essentially, this virtue subsumed all other virtues or other virtues were expected to serve it. It is such an important virtue, in fact, that it will be discussed at length in a separate chapter of this book. Here in this chapter, it is worth looking in more detail into these components, which could be referred to as a catalog of virtues invoked in political statements, with the important proviso that the purpose of these considerations is not to describe the role models of noble citizens but merely to attempt to understand the meaning of the phrases "a good son of the homeland," or *civis patriae*, as well as "a righteous nobleman" in the political language.

In the most general sense, such a man could be described as having the virtues needed by someone who had influence over the future of the community that he co-formed, made political decisions and participated in public life. More often than not, catalogs of such virtues were quite long, in particular in the civic *Specula*, but the most important of these were the four classical virtues of a citizen, identical with the four cardinal virtues of Christians: courage, prudence, justice and temperance.[34] As Górnicki explained, "From these main virtues, other virtues follow, walking as handmaidens behind the eminent virtues."[35] This classical quartet, present in the treatises of humanists, was reiterated until the eighteenth century. One of the last to invoke it, quite conventionally at that, was Szymon Majchrowicz in 1764.[36] Perhaps the last who not only described the four civic virtues in his writings but also used this description as a political argument, for that matter somewhat perversely, was Stanisław Leszczyński, who (hypothetically) ascribed the four virtues to the four highest-ranking offices in the Commonwealth, after which he stated immediately that it was impossible to achieve them, so the system of government should be changed.[37] At the same time, he made an important modification by replacing justice with vigilance, concern for the public good. Such a change is quite characteristic. The virtue-of-virtues in Aristotle's (and Thomas Aquinas') understanding, namely justice, though held in high regard as a political value and often linked to the law, was less likely to be found in the context of civic attitudes, and the same held true for moderation/temperance. It was the most important of all virtues only for the Renaissance theorists, in particular Modrzewski,[38] but even then it appeared less frequently in more ongoing statements. It was listed among other virtues above all by authors of more extensive descriptions of virtues, which means authors of treatises and *Specula*.[39] Some of them, for example Górnicki, invoked all four virtues, yet ultimately focused only on courage and wisdom.[40] Of the four political virtues, the discourse of the Polish-Lithuanian Commonwealth clearly placed greater emphasis on these two virtues, namely *fortitudo* and *prudentia*, which were in most cases inseparable, perhaps because they overlapped with the fields of activity expected of noble citizens, who – as I will discuss below – were expected to defend the homeland and deliberate its fate. Or perhaps because these specific virtues were achieved in action in a more obvious way than other virtues – after all, action and participation in public life were a fundamental imperative for citizens of the Commonwealth.

It is worth pausing for a brief moment to consider prudence. In the analyses of the personal ideals of the nobles, this virtue is usually somewhat underestimated, with researchers more likely highlighting "knightly virtues," above all military courage.[41] Meanwhile, prudence was valued highly in the political discourse – during Lubomirski's rebellion, the defender of the marshal, who wanted to clearly stress his advantages, wrote that he "achieved more with the advice he offered than with his sabre."[42] We must not forget that a noble "knight" was also a citizen and was depicted as one.[43] In the sixteenth century, we could find even apologias of prudence, for example the exceptionally erudite deliberation of an anonymous supporter of a Polish candidate for the crown in 1573, whose author concluded that it was the mother of all virtues.[44] In turn, the author of a royal *Mirror* from the turn of the sixteenth and seventeenth centuries argued that "those in this sense are very much ineffective, who only cherish those that demonstrate valor in war, rather than those who wisely counsel at home for peace and for a

good *Rzeczpospolita*."[45] Participants in political disputes in the period
of Zebrzydowski's rebellion appreciated prudence, and it was not forgotten in the period of Lubomirski's rebellion. The question remains, was
it valued equally highly also in subsequent periods? It appears that although it was discussed less frequently, because in general less attention
was paid to a detailed analysis of the virtues of noble participants in political life and the focus was shifted towards somewhat different aspects,
the need for this virtue was rather unlikely to arouse any doubt.[46] One
telling example was the comment made by Pęski:

> What will you achieve here without reason? By virtue and honesty
> alone you will protect yourself little, by valor you will only defend
> yourself for a time and not always, if this does not go together with
> cautious prudence, probably *decus libertas in difficili et lubrico* will
> remain.[47]

The virtue of prudence, though somewhat forgotten, would return to
the political discourse in the second half of the eighteenth century in
a somewhat changed interpretation, namely clothed in reason, knowledge, and finally enlightenment.[48] After all, Kołłątaj demanded prudence when he wrote that "when one lives under free rule, all the more
enlightenment is needed, so that one can persuade oneself and others
about everything that concerns both individual good and the common
good of all."[49]

As for the other of the two main virtues, namely courage, the border
between the ancient *fortitudo* and the knightly *virtus bellandi* is very
fluid in Polish statements, which is illustrated well by the role models
invoked in such statements – in addition to brave knights from the past,
references were equally eagerly made to the virtuous Spartans and above
all the citizens of the Roman Republic, with figures such as Brutus,
Scaevola, Cato and so on as being often invoked alongside the Polish
hetmans Stanisław Żółkiewski and Jan Karol Chodkiewicz.[50] This issue
is undoubtedly worthy of further research, but even a quite superficial
analysis appears to confirm that the myth of a "Sarmatian knight," albeit popular in the second half of the seventeenth century, did not dominate the political discourse in any period, and it was always at least
coupled with a courageous citizen who could not only show courage in
the battlefield but also make utmost sacrifices for his homeland. However, courage could be shown in every field, not only against the external enemies of the Commonwealth but also through the defense of the
Commonwealth and its values from internal attacks. Opponents of the
king in consecutive disputes from Zebrzydowski's rebellion to the Confederation of Bar and even the Constitution of the Third of May 1791
presented themselves as courageous defenders of the homeland and liberties. Besides, we can see a certain mutual reinforcement here: courage

was a virtue necessary for free citizens, but only free citizens were capable of showing it.[51] This depiction of courage, which invoked ancient ideals, proved very durable – supported by phrases borrowed from the Enlightenment-age admirers of the republic, Rousseau, Louis de Jaucourt and Mably, it would survive the fall of the noble Commonwealth and become one of the leading slogans of the Kościuszko Uprising, whose participants fought "with courage found only in a free man."[52]

As we noted above, direct references to the classical canon of virtues were rather unlikely in the second half of the eighteenth century, when other words were used to describe the characteristics and attitudes required of good citizens. For example, a good citizen should be "faithful in counsel, just in judgments, useful in office, zealous in service, and diligent and constant in work."[53] However, this was a change of terminology rather than ideals. We must not forget that reducing the requirements made for citizens in the political discourse to the two most important virtues or even all four of them would create a rather poor and incomplete picture, also with reference to the earlier periods. As I wrote above, those were only certain component parts, or perhaps rather tools for describing the desired attitude of a "lover of the homeland." Those virtues were by no means considered in the abstract – prudence in fact meant knowledge of the affairs of the Commonwealth, or *reipublicae cognoscere* as Kasper Siemek put it,[54] and wise decisions about its fate, and courage meant defense of the homeland and its rights and liberties. Without the context created by the good of the Commonwealth, virtues ceased to be virtues – courage turned into insolence and bravado, wisdom could become cunning or "perfidious subterfuge."[55] In reality, all of them were included in the virtue of love of the homeland understood as acting in the interests of the community and for its good, putting the "common good" above "self-interest" (*prywata*). In this respect, the Polish discourse fits into the tradition of civic virtue sketched out by civic humanism based on classical models.[56]

This leads us to two questions that perhaps result not so much from the tradition of civic humanism as from the characteristics that researchers ascribed to it under the influence of the analysis of the writings of Machiavelli and his students. These include first of all the links (or their absence) between civic and moral virtues and the relationship between the duties of a member of the state's community and the religious community, something that could be referred to as Christianity/Catholicism versus civic spirit. Machiavelli, as we know, distinguished clearly between the virtues of a man and the virtues of a citizen. Likewise, he did not think much about Christianity's influence on *virtù*, which in his opinion was molded much better by pagan religions.[57] Besides, it appears that some researchers focused too much on the thought of the author of *Discorsi* and his most faithful English students, and therefore clearly overestimated the role played by these two issues in the whole of the way of thinking called republican.[58] It can be said outright that similar views were practically not reflected in the Polish discourse, the only exception being the voice of Goślicki, who argued that the virtues of a good man and those of a good citizen were different. Such a point of view might be regarded as influenced by Aristotle, who was the first to propose this differentiation,[59] but further analyses nonetheless point out to Machiavelli: "a good citizen is astute, diligent, spirited in the service of the state, not a just, temperate, strong person."[60] It is a separate issue that Goślicki attributed this differentiation above all to democracy (*status popularis*) and did not think of this situation as good.[61] Besides, he required a senator to have the virtues of both a man and a citizen.[62] Theorists of the state who were Goślicki's contemporaries did not treat these issues as separate. Sometimes, like Modrzewski and Wolan, they linked the analysis of attitudes in the moral and political aspect. Sometimes, however, they only focused on the latter issue yet not in opposition to moral virtues but in a sense alongside them. No one doubted that a bad man could not be a good citizen.[63] The problem of customs was situated at the intersection of these two spheres, regardless of whether those where "good" customs or "former" ones, which practically meant the same thing. As the anonymous participant in the pre-election battle in 1573 put it: "A republic becometh enduring by means of two things: customs and men. Because in a well-formed republic, men become good, and from good men, there arise good customs."[64] This was in a sense reference to what was at the time a popular quote taken from Ennius, opening Book V of Cicero's *De re publica*: "*Moribus antiquis res stat Romana virisque.*" Those customs may have meant civic virtues, but they may be interpreted more broadly – the most eagerly invoked, in particular in earlier discussions, were the simplicity of former customs[65] and old-Polish candor.[66] Over time, the discourse was dominated by the bemoaning of lost customs and of corruption, which may have referred only to attitudes in the public sphere or perhaps also covered the sphere of what could be referred as morality that could be described as more private or situated at the intersection of these two spheres. We may sum up this issue with the words of the priest Majchrowicz:

> [...] the most important is for people to be good, they will keep the laws, the laws will bring order, and order happiness [...]. If people become rotten, what can come of deliberation and the best of laws? They will lie in the books, but not in the heart, nor in human customs. They will be guarded by moths, but not by the sons of the homeland.[67]

It could be said, quoting the title of Konarski's speech on the upbringing of young people, that a noble member of the *Rzeczpospolita*'s community should be both *vir honestus* and *bonus civis*,[68] although the attitudes of a citizen were the main topic in the discourse.

Besides, separating the moral aspect and the political aspect, especially by treating them as opposites, in a sense means applying criteria that were foreign to the discourse of that period. This holds true to an even greater extent for matters described as religious. None of the Polish researchers have gone so far as to completely ignore the religious aspect of the Renaissance humanists' political deliberations. However, attempts are sometimes made to clearly divide the discourse of virtue into the earlier, civic discourse and the later moral and ethics discourse (from around the mid-seventeenth century).[69] Indeed, in the second half of the sixteenth century, some of the authors who described civic attitudes omitted the religious aspect, as was the case for the anonymous *Philopolites*, for Górnicki, and before him for Wolan. However, we must not forget that the works of such authors as Orzechowski were not written much earlier, and they included the attitudes towards God and Church very strongly into the political discourse. This issue was present also in more topical statements. As Stanisław Stadnicki, called "the Devil," explained in 1606 to Hieronim Jazłowiecki and numerous readers of a letter that he made public, what "old-fashioned virtue" was involved "to praise God honestly and according to his command, not according to human inventions, to defend the full rights and liberties, to serve the common good, and to scorn self-interest for the sake of the common good."[70] In a sense, it could be said that piousness was perceived there as one of the virtues of a good citizen.[71] As early as in the sixteenth century, participants in political disputes, regardless of their confession, not only believed that Christian virtues complemented the political ones but also expressed the belief that love of God (regardless of how it was understood) provided an excellent basis for the love of the common good. As the Reformation receded, a change occurred that involved the conclusion that Catholicism was "the only right" religion, but the way in which this issue was treated did not change. Throughout the whole of the seventeenth century and a large portion of the eighteenth century, it was stressed that "the zeal of faith" helped shape active members of the free community, good – or virtuous – citizens. As Stanisław Leszczyński put it in the eighteenth century, "Holy faith and divine commandments alone should teach us political virtues, so needed for good governance of the kingdom."[72] Jabłonowski went further, in a sense reversing this track of thought and regarding political sins as sins also in the theological sense.[73] Interrelations between faith and civic virtues were noticed until the end of the free Commonwealth, with Adam Wawrzyniec Rzewuski, one of the ardent republicans of the Four-Year Sejm, stressing resolutely – essentially in defiance of his master Rousseau – that "religion is the source and ground for virtue, which alone makes nations happy."[74]

At this point, it is necessary to make one proviso: "perseverance in the faith," albeit very important, did not dominate descriptions of the good son of the homeland in the political discourse in the seventeenth century or in the first half of the eighteenth century. Both in statements made by participants in ongoing disputes and in longer treatises, one could easily find texts limited to strictly political virtues. Those were by no means attempts to undermine the role of religion – simply put, their authors focused on other problems. More importantly, for the authors who included the aspect of faith in their statements, this was one of the elements of the picture of a "righteous nobleman," but not the only one. Even those particularly involved in the propagation of virtues in the religious sphere, for example Starowolski, expected a noble citizen to be virtuous to the same extent in the religious sense as in the political sense. Most participants in discussions regarded virtue in the religious sense as a necessary yet not sufficient characteristic of a noble citizen – it had to be coupled with or lead to attitudes required for the functioning of the Commonwealth.

Why are researchers convinced that the discourse of virtue underwent a visible change that involved in particular the disappearance of civic ethos? Partially because the issue of the desired attitudes of the members of the community stared to occupy less space in discourse starting from around mid-seventeenth century. This applies in particular to ongoing political disputes – if we compare the commentaries from the period of the first interregnum or Zebrzydowski's rebellion with the writings from the reign of King John II Casimir collected by Ochmann-Staniszewska, we can see that the deliberations on moral and religious issues included in the latter works are not very extensive, although they were a major aspect of the rebellion (and anti-rebellion) letters forty years earlier.[75] However, this does not mean that the discourse changed to any radical extent or started to attach less importance to the attitudes of the people who formed the *Rzeczpospolita*'s community. This is a broader issue – discussions held in that period focused on topical issues and current events, and less attention was paid to more general issues related to the system of government or the foundations of the functioning of the community. Obviously, these issues also appeared, but they were less frequent and had the nature of slogans to a greater extent than during fierce battles over the shape of the Commonwealth and its government. In that situation, it was natural that the issue of civic attitudes as one of the elements of deliberations on the system of government occupied proportionally less space. Also, civic attitudes started to be discussed in a somewhat different way than before.

The demise of virtue

It appears that this change, which took place in the second half of the seventeenth century and was perhaps particularly visible in the first half of the eighteenth century, influenced the aforementioned view holding that the language of civic virtues came to be abandoned. At some point, the noble political discourse started to discuss increasingly frequently not virtues *per se*, but rather their absence – instead of descriptions of the desired attitudes of the members of the community, complaints were voiced that these attitudes were not put into effect. If we look more closely at this aspect of discussions on the Commonwealth, it turns that civic attitudes did not generate less interest at the turn of the seventeenth and eighteenth centuries than before, but this interest was aroused in a sense *à rebours*, pertaining not to the characteristics of desired behaviors or role models but to bemoaning of the widespread corruption and its descriptions.

It appears that this element of the discourse has been so far somewhat underappreciated and treated rather superficially, as being just barren lamentation that proved the demise of the Polish political culture and thought at the turn of the seventeenth and eighteenth centuries.[76] In reality, it was an important element of the descriptions of the political reality in that period and an at least equally important argument in political disputes – as such, it should not be judged but analyzed more carefully so as to facilitate understanding of its meaning and functions.

Despite being very characteristic of the statements from the turn of centuries and practically the whole of the Saxon period, this issue was nonetheless nothing new. The accusation of a dearth of virtue was an important weapon in attacks on political opponents in the disputes waged from the sixteenth century onwards. This comes as no surprise – at the time, virtue was a fundamental element of a citizen's image that was simultaneously desired and valued highly, so its absence was a very serious indictment to discredit adversaries in the eyes of listeners or readers. Consequently, abhorrent pictures were sketched out, depicting "people of a kind that very much disgusted our forebears [...], being disgusted by excessive concern for vile self-interest and foul lack of love for the homeland,"[77] and it was exclaimed in horror, obviously with the opposing side of the dispute in mind: "what pride, what covetousness, what ambition, what practices, what diffidence and insincerity in people!"[78] These and similar accusations could be leveled against anyone, and a list of those whom they did get addressed to and for what purpose could make for a quite long publication. Doubts were voiced about the virtuousness of specific individuals as well as entire factions and groups. For example, those who advocated boosting the role of the Senate in the sixteenth century accused parliamentary deputies of "obstinacy, obduracy, arrogance, presumption, hubris, and multiloquence,"[79] while those unfavorably disposed to senators were astonished by their "greedy and shameless avarice [to] the detriment of the Commonwealth *ad officia et dignitates*"[80] – importantly, they were accused of "unvirtuousness" (*niecnota*), not incompetence or ineffectiveness of action. In the following centuries, opponents of the king openly described the corruption in the king's entourage and the court's disastrous influence over the virtuousness of citizens, and such writings also included the well-known issue of corrupting citizens through the king's right to grant offices and assets. Participants in rebellions, all the way to the Confederation of Bar, and royalists accused one another of lacking virtue, the representatives of the "factions" of magnates and in the late eighteenth-century political parties accused one another of all possible vices, and the nobles accused magnates of being unvirtuous. The latter issue falls outside the scope of these considerations and pertains no longer to the political language but to social and political relations within the noble estate – here, it is important that references to ethics, or strictly speaking its lack, were an important and popular argument.

Although the somewhat Pharisean bemoaning of lost virtues on the part of political opponents were a very important propagandist argument, they merely represented a fragment of the broader issue of the moral demise of citizens of a free republic and its consequences for the community. The problem of the corruption and ways of avoiding it had been raised practically by all authors of deliberations on the state since ancient times, especially those who sketched out visions of free republics in which the people also participated in governance. Laments on the demise of morals among contemporaries as opposed to ancestors, who were ascribed all virtues without reservation, were a certain convention that also applied to participants in the political debate of the Polish-Lithuanian Commonwealth. "*Nostris enim vitiis, non casu aliquo, rem publicam verbo retinemus, re ipsa vero iam pridem amisimus*"[81] – this was not a complaint made by an embittered noble statist, but rather the words of Cicero, known very well also to readers in the Commonwealth. They fit their political language so well that they sometimes quoted the phrase directly, automatically transferring the diagnosis of the situation in the Roman Republic onto their own community, as did the anonymous author of *Naprawa Rzeczypospolitej* [Repairing the Republic] (1573), who repeated after Cicero:

> Hence anyone can see that we are perishing through our bad customs, not by any adventure or happenstance (although this did not begin during our age), so that we have a republic only by name, whereas in fact we have lost it.[82]

The complaints that "we have replaced virtue with all of *vitia*"[83] were repeated in ongoing political disputes from the sixteenth century onwards; at the time, they were also an important fragment of longer political deliberations by Modrzewski, Rotundus, Wolan, Warszewicki and, partially, Górnicki. In the sixteenth century, statements started to appear whose authors analyzed cases of abuse in the Commonwealth, focusing above all on the attitudes of its citizens. One such little work was

Zwierciadło Rzeczypospolitej Polskiej na początku roku 1598 wystawione [Mirror of the Polish Commonwealth, Set Forth at the Beginning of the Year 1598] whose author listed the diseases "in the body of the Commonwealth," restricting himself only to issues related to virtue and above all its absence. He lamented that God "he defended us wonderfully from enemies, who having overwhelmed us wanted to devour us yet set us ourselves against us, having given some a stupid heart, others a careless one, and others a heart malevolent to the homeland."[84] A similar judgment, though accompanied with a less detailed description of the flaws of his compatriots, was expressed thirty years later by the author of *Egzorbitancyja powszechna która Rzeczpospolitą królestwa polskiego niszczy, zgubą grożąc* [Widespread Exorbitance which is Destroying the Polish Kingdom, Threatening Ruination][85] – its title alone showed what harm could be done by the abandonment of virtue by citizens. One may get the impression that at the turn of the sixteenth and seventeenth centuries the most extensive analyses of the deplorable consequences entailed by the corruption of virtue were performed above all by the authors who supported certain restrictions on the power of noble citizens (Warszewicki, Górnicki, Skarga) or were at least favorably disposed to the monarch (the authors of both *Zwierciadło* and *Egzorbitancyja*), so for them this was in a sense an argument in the dispute. However, the crisis of civic attitudes was bemoaned by everyone.

That said, it would be difficult to assert that similar opinions dominated the political discourse at that time. Although complaints about the corruption of virtue were quite common, apart from few exceptions they were not what built the narrative. Just like ancient authors and Italian humanists, those who made their voices heard in the political debate in the Commonwealth still found the description of attitudes beneficial for the Commonwealth and ways to achieve them more important than laments on their absence. What is more, those complaints did not mean passivity or helplessness in the face of the situation that they described – they were often linked to proposals of rather far-reaching reforms that pertained not to attitudes but to the functioning of institutions.

A change appears to have taken place in the period of the crisis in the mid-seventeenth century. It could be observed in the political commentaries of that period. Descriptions of the corruption of virtue started to play (at least partially) a different role than in similar earlier statements, which treated the issue of a dearth of virtue above all as an argument in disputes and an accusation leveled against opponents, which could be seen perfectly well for example in the disputes in the period of Zebrzydowski's rebellion. It was also used in this way in later periods, essentially until the end of the eighteenth century,[86] but similar descriptions were increasingly likely to serve the purpose of no longer discrediting adversaries but explaining the causes of the current bad situation of the Commonwealth. Its woes were seen as God's punishments for sins against the homeland and fellow brothers and even (though on very rare occasions) against the subjects,[87] but these troubles were likewise analyzed in political terms, as demise caused by the abandonment of the virtues of ancestors, a failure to care for the common good. As the anonymous royalist bemoaned after the disrupted Sejm in 1666: "having forgotten churches, the homeland, the preservation of the laws [...] eclipsed by wholly private interests, we are headed *in interitum*."[88] Those views were echoed by anonymous opponent of King John II Casimir, in turn, who predicted that the nation would suffer an imminent demise "since you have transformed in virtue and customs and started to be dishonest courtiers, simply put, treacherous people, greedy privateers, unvirtuous counsellors [...]."[89]

It was not the only change. To simplify things somewhat, we could say that virtue was mentioned less frequently as the foundation of the Commonwealth, while unvirtuousness was discussed more and more often as the reason for its demise. The trend was supported not only by numerous mentions in political commentaries but, for example, also in Starowolski's elaborate deliberations included in *Reformacyja obyczajów polskich* [Reformation of Polish Customs] and *Lament utrapionej matki Korony Polskiej* [Lament of the Distressed Mother, the Polish Crown]. In a sense, this is where we can see one of the differences between the discourse of the European "republicans" and the discourse that functioned in the Commonwealth. The former generally considered theoretical issues and therefore focused on descriptions of the attitudes that they urged as necessary in the free republic and the question of what should be done to achieve them. By referring to a specific political reality and noticing an escalating crisis, the participants in Polish debates in a sense drew conclusions from theory, attributing the crisis to corruption on the part of individuals who formed the political community and describing that corruption.

But what did they perceive as its manifestations? Descriptions of "unvirtuousness" were no shorter than lists of virtues and sometimes even more detailed. At the same time, vices against the homeland, just like virtues, were seen essentially in the same way throughout the whole of the period under study. Those who spoke out in discussions in the eighteenth century would have probably have agreed with the author of a sixteenth-century *Speculum* that "the zeal of praising God has ceased to burn" among his compatriots, "we have lost that fatherly heart for impassioned service to the homeland," the Poles have abandoned the customs of their ancestors, disdained "the supremacy of laws and offices," they were greedy, extravagant, and divided, and finally

> even the freedom that the Lord God honored us with above other nations, we so *obutimur* that we use it to insult his majesty, to besmirch the homeland, to wrong good and peaceful people, to the downfall of modesty and good customs.[90]

I have permitted myself to quote longer fragments from this pamphlet, because they list almost all the main transgressions against virtue that would be invoked in the following centuries. After all, this is what its anonymous author wrote about by describing the crisis following the death of King Augustus III, when he stated, "we are without power and without unity, national freedom is an empty word, the freedom of citizens is license, faith is superficiality, love of the homeland is self-interest, virtue is vice."[91] Nearly 200 years after the author of the *Zwierciadło* quoted here, Kołłątaj told his compatriots: "the valor of your fathers has completely extinguished in you, religion has become a vacuous rite, customs corrupted, licentiousness has taken away your health."[92] Words that were only slightly different were still being used to describe the same thing, that "the old character of the Poles has changed in many attributes"[93] and former virtues were replaced by vices. As was the case with the desired attitudes of citizens, all these flaws boiled down to a common denominator: putting private interests above public ones (the infamous *prywata*, or self-interest) and disobeying the law. From the sixteenth century onwards, warnings were made that the absence of virtue understood in this way was driving the country to ruin.

Laments on the demise of morals among nobles, the disappearance of civic attitudes and disobedience of the law, which had been growing in strength at least since the Swedish Deluge and Lubomirski's rebellion, reached their apogee in the Saxon period and continued to emerge in ongoing disputes.[94] In this case, however, an analysis of longer treatises, which had the ambition to present the reality in a more detailed manner, is more interesting, because they show how important this problem was already at that time. Some even saw it as fundamentally important – the person who went farther than others in this respect was Stanisław Szczuka, (assuming that he was the author of *Eclipsis Poloniae*). While it is true that his pamphlet was above all an attack on the magnates, not an objective attempt to pinpoint the causes of the crisis, it was based in whole on the discourse of virtue, or strictly speaking corruption, with the author painting a very gloomy picture of the reality. No one went that far, but the problem of what could be referred as an "ethical crisis" occupied a lot of space in the letters of Jerzy Dzieduszycki and Franciszek Radzewski (to a somewhat lesser extent).[95] Views closest to Szczuka were probably expressed by Jabłonowski, who nonetheless attributed the aforementioned vices and cases of abuse not to the magnates but to the nobles. Jabłonowski's deliberations are interesting in that they are a mirror of citizens, describing not their desired virtues but their actual vices, or as the author called them "the sins that the devil tended to clothe in the mantle of politics, *status*, freedom, honors, and fortune."[96] In a sense, this was still a language of virtue, one in which ethics and politics continued to be linked inseparably, although it would now make more sense to call it a language of the corruption. Contrary to what some researchers believed, this was not necessarily the political language of those who were completely passive and had no proposals of institutional reforms.[97] Some of them, for example the author of *Projekt uszczęśliwienia ojczyzny* [Project to Make the Homeland Fortunate], managed to use it to formulate an interesting (though not necessarily realistic) concept of changes in the system of government. However, there was indeed a certain danger hidden there. When the foundations for the noble Commonwealth were being laid in the sixteenth century and when the power struggle was ongoing at the beginning of the seventeenth, the problem of the attitudes of members of the political community, which formed an integral part of the discourse, was simply one of the elements of the description of the situation and proposals related to the system of government. Over time, the change described above took place, with the language of the corruption of virtue, which attempted to answer the question about the sources of the crisis, being less suited for the formulation of a positive program of changes, although – let me stress this once again – this was not out of the question. Contrary to the accusations that were sometimes leveled against it, a political language that uses ethical categories is neutral and allows a completely passive description of the situation as well as the formulation of proposals of reforms. However, it became an alibi for passivity for at least some participants in the political discussions in the first half of the eighteenth century. The direction was defined by Fredro's statement from the mid-seventeenth century:

> [...] the laws are good, but it is we ourselves who are bad; very nearly have we overturned God's commandments. I would praise not him who wants to [reform] the *Rzeczpospolita*, but him who endeavors to improve us ourselves, because by allegedly improving the laws we are ruining them further, whereas for our own ruination we seek not remedy...[98]

Fredro's words partially fit into the former tradition that has been discussed above. Many years before him, Warszewicki prophesied: "I believe that the fall of the Commonwealth [...] will be caused not so much by absurd laws or ridiculous statutes but specifically by the demise of the morals of citizens and heresy."[99] However, this did not prevent him from making a far-reaching proposal of changes in the system of government. The difference lay not so much in the political language as in the conclusions drawn from the opinions formulated in this language.

At some point, the phrase "the laws are good – we are bad" and the conviction that it was true became a trap that defenders of the old solutions could not escape (and, truth be told, most probably did not want to do so), repeating like a mantra: "Everyone must admit, after all, that nothing has gone bad in our country, only preservation of the law."[100] This was excellently visible during the discussions on the *liberum veto* in the 1760s. In a sense, the whole of the concept of the *liberum veto* as an objection voiced by an individual could not have functioned or at least would have been impossible to describe without the category of virtue. In principle, such a solution or at least its consequences were closely linked to the attitudes of the individuals who exercised that right, and that was also how its supporters presented themselves, starting from Fredro.[101] One telling example was Sienicki's statement:

> [...] the laws of our freedom libertas *sentiendi et ius vetandi* [...] they have no basis other than special love for the homeland [...], and also the indivisible, the mutual love of all citizens, because let just one person be hateful to it, and that one can ruin the whole homeland, because one person is able to overthrow all public debate...[102]

Over time, the focus shifted to this absence of love of the homeland, this unvirtuous use of the *liberum veto* for personal gain, not for the common good.[103] This provided the starting point for Sienicki's book, which was an extensive several-volume polemic against the attack on the *liberum veto* mounted in Konarski's *O skutecznym rad sposobie* [On the Effective Means of Counsel]. On this interpretation, the problems of the efficient functioning of state institutions proved in a sense secondary to the issue of the attitudes of the citizens who used them. For Sienicki and Konarski's other adversaries, a fundamental problem was posed by how they should differentiate "just contradiction, maintained particularly for the common good, from improper contradiction, deriving from self-interest, out of nefarious passion for one's own respect"[104] and what could be done to prevent the latter. In their deliberations, this question translated into an entire array of ideas of what could be done to make sure that the *liberum veto* "could only be used for the good of the homeland, not to cause it harm."[105] One of these ideas that was by no means the least important was the proposal of an oath that the individual using the *liberum veto* should take, swearing that he was guided only by the common good, and of criminal liability for those who broke this oath.[106] The trend would be continued, though unwittingly, by Rousseau with his ideas about the death penalty being imposed for the unjustified use of the *liberum veto*.[107] Unlike the Genevan philosopher, Polish defenders of the *liberum veto* essentially proved completely helpless against problems of governance and became bogged down in increasingly complicated safeguards of the "virtuousness" of individual vetoes. It appears that this was symptomatic of a more general phenomenon, namely the increasingly barren language of virtue, or perhaps the exhaustion of this language. As a useful tool for making political proposals and an important element of concepts related to the system of government at least until the mid-seventeenth century, this language did not disappear from discourse, unlike what happened in the west of Europe. However, it started to lose its functions and hinder efforts to articulate new political visions or assess and understand the political reality, instead of facilitating them. Importantly, the most prominent political writers of the first half of the eighteenth century used this language with moderation. Such issues were almost completely ignored by Karwicki, while Leszczyński and Stanisław Poniatowski were economical with statements on the attitudes of citizens. When writing about economic and social issues, Stefan Garczyński used a completely different discourse. Konarski went further than other authors – he was the first to clearly separate politics from morality in his most important work, in a sense moving the latter to a different system:

> I therefore always assert one thing – what we need to make better is the form of deliberations, not people, who always were, are, and will be of the same nature, always good and bad, some of them good, others bad, but making them better [...] should be left not to the Commonwealth, not to human minds, but to God himself and religion.[108]

He repeated on numerous occasion in his treatise that he wanted to make better "the form of deliberations," and not the people.[109] He did not rule out the fact that the changes that he proposed would also influence (in a good way) the attitudes of participants in political life, but for him this was an issue of secondary importance.[110] The main problem that he wanted to resolve was posed by the question of what should be done to make institutions independent of people's attitudes. It is impossible to rule out that he was influenced in this respect by Montesquieu, well-known to him, who despite regarding virtue as a "principle" of republics in *The Spirit of the Laws*, nonetheless showed that maintaining the freedom and strength of a state required not virtue but procedures and institutional solutions.[111] However, it appears that more importance should be attached to the fact that Konarski regarded virtue as a needless, perhaps even dangerous category in his description of the crisis of institutions and proposed ways out of this situation.

Virtue *rediviva*

One might believe that this shift away from moralizing would be a permanent trend and Konarski's book, extremely popular and quite commonly appreciated, would contribute to the ultimate disappearance of the language of virtue from the Polish discourse. But that did not happen. Furthermore, in the final decades of the Commonwealth, several major treatises were written that included the issue of attitudes of citizens in political deliberations probably in a more integral and extensive manner than anyone else since the sixteenth century. What had a decisive influence on those writings were the works of two Enlightenment-age theorists of the state – Montesquieu and Rousseau. Both of them, albeit to various extents, referred to civic virtue, and both were extremely popular in Poland.[112] In particular, the latter used a political language that linked morality and politics very closely and was therefore extremely close to his noble readers. What is more, he did so in his *Considerations on the Government of Poland*. However, in the 1770s, it was not Rousseau but Montesquieu and his works that revived the Polish discourse of virtue, which drew not only from *The Spirit of the Laws* but also from *Considerations on the Causes of the Greatness of the Romans and their Decline*.[113] Such references were not just merely inspirations but open borrowings, as was the case with Skrzetuski, who based his entire speech *O cnocie, duszy wolnych rządów* [On the Virtue, Spirit of Free Governance] directly on Book III of *The Spirit of the Laws*, without making any secret of this fact.[114] Both Montesquieu's definition of virtue as love of the homeland and its laws[115] and his line of argumentation fit perfectly into the traditional political discourse yet went beyond hackneyed platitudes and barren laments. Civic attitudes became again a subject of in-depth analyses and one of the elements of political programs. Wybicki's 1775 book on civil freedom would show best that the language of virtue did not prevent proposals on the system of government or apt judgments of the reality. The author used this language in two out of the three parts of the book (I & II). In line with Montesquieu as well as earlier traditions, he concluded that "virtue itself has the capacity to maintain nations" and republics were powerful for as long as citizens were virtuous.[116] Wybicki was undoubtedly influenced strongly by the two works by Montesquieu, but he was a lot more independent as a writer than Skrzetuski and he included the French philosopher's concepts into his own proposals, creating a consistent vision of the state based on the virtuousness of citizens. It must be stressed, however, that although he regarded the lack of virtue as the main cause of the fall of republics ("free nations that depart from virtue come to demise, having embraced rotten customs"),[117] he did not restrict himself to proposals to improve those customs, but presented a bold and elaborate concept of political reforms. Wybicki's use of the language of virtue, in such a committed way at that, is interesting in that he was probably the first Polish political writer who used with such ease the new conceptual tools derived from the theories of the state of his contemporaries, which means the categories of society (*towarzystwo*), social contract, as well as natural freedom vs. "social" freedom, civil freedom, political freedom, etc. As it turned out, virtue fit this discourse perfectly. Although the way of talking about virtue was influenced clearly by Montesquieu's works, this language was still close to traditions and surely understandable to readers.

The same holds true for what could be referred to as dialogues with the Genevan philosopher conducted at least by some of those who spoke their mind on political and government issues in Poland. Such dialogue did not emerge until the late 1780s and early 1790s. Although references to Rousseau's works were also made earlier, they had little in common with issues related to the attitudes and duties of citizens.[118] Even Michał Wielhorski, who undoubtedly knew *Considerations on the Government of Poland* very well because they were written at his behest, did not go beyond the stereotypical bemoaning of the lost "old-Polish virtues."[119] In a sense, it could be said that, just like his predecessors, he concluded that the language of virtue was not a sufficient tool for talking about politics, without seeing the possibilities offered by Rousseau's proposals. These proposals were noticed by the participants in the political debate of the Four-Year Sejm, in particular Staszic and Adam Wawrzyniec Rzewuski. Their visions of virtue deserve to be discussed separately – here, I restrict myself to certain general comments. Rzewuski essentially built the whole of his treatise on the description of civic virtue, which he identified with actions taken for the good of the community,[120] and ways to achieve it. He thus created a consistent proposal, one in which even the weakness of the ideas related to the system of government was in a sense inherent to the assumption that common virtuousness would obviate the need for laws, when "customs complement laws, or rather supplant them."[121] He was in certain aspects closest to the language used by Rousseau (though not necessarily his concepts). However, it is impossible to resist the impression that he used that language to describe former ideals and the noble society, without noticing the possibility of going beyond the traditional discourse. If this was Rousseau, it was the Rousseau from the *Considerations*. This becomes evident when we compare his way of talking about virtue with Staszic's statement. The latter made very high requirements for citizens of the republic (because he also agreed that virtue was only possible in a republic),[122] partially similar to those set by Rzewuski. However, his manner of talking about virtue differed markedly from Rzewuski's approach, partially because he had a completely different vision of society and used more modern concepts, treating virtue as part of this discourse, also because virtue, albeit important, was not the center of his deliberations. Most importantly, however, he followed Rousseau more consistently yet in the context of not *Considerations* but *The Social Contract*. For Staszic, virtue meant not only acting for the benefit of the community but also melting completely into this community or identifying with it: "society is one moral entity, the members of which are citizens. Thus, the true own good of each of them does not differ from the good of the whole society."[123] This was no longer the antique idea of care for the public good in one's own interest, but rather Rousseau's concept of the complete melting of the will of an individual into the will of the community.[124]

What these two authors had in common, undoubtedly influenced by Rousseau's concepts, was the demand that citizens should be molded by a system of prohibitions, orders and rewards. The idea of civic upbringing was a lot older, but it was rather invoked in the context of the education of the young in line with the principle expressed by a participant in the discussions in 1573: "if we wish to repair the *Rzeczpospolita*, then let us begin: let us sow in the hearts of young people *semen bonorum morum*, let us reform the schools, colleges, for the honest upbringing of young people."[125] It was not without reason that Modrzewski included a book devoted to education in his treatise on the Commonwealth and Starowolski gave one of the chapters in his book the telling title "On Instructing the Youth, Whose Poor Behavior Greatly Harms the Commonwealth."[126] The deep conviction that "such will be the republics as is the upbringing of their youth" was derived from classical authors, and so was the opinion that a republic required different education than a monarchy.[127] This issue, which generated considerable interest in the sixteenth century as well as at the turn of the sixteenth and seventeenth centuries, returned to political discussions in the eighteenth century under the influence of the Enlightenment-age ideas, occupying a lot of space there from the 1770s,[128] with such authors as Kołłątaj[129] devoting a lot of attention to this issue in the period of the Four-Year Sejm. Taking their cue from the Genevan philosopher, however, Staszic and Rzewuski (the latter to an even greater extent) wanted to influence citizens throughout all of their lives, simultaneously proposing far-reaching limitations of their personal freedom. This was something new in the Polish discourse. The ideas of Machiavelli and his students, which contemporary researchers call "being forced into virtue,"[130] echoed very poorly in the Commonwealth – we could find them in the statements of Wolan, Górnicki and Łukasz Opaliński, but even there they were not major issues, and they were not continued. The vision of influencing citizens permanently and forcing them to act in the interests of the general community would be sketched out under Rousseau's influence. Besides, this was an exception in Polish political discussions.

None of the participants in the political discussions in 1788–1792 went that far in following Rousseau, although his influence can be noticed both in Kołłątaj's statements and in the letters of anonymous authors of different political views, apparently somewhat more often among defenders of former solutions in the sphere of government.[131] Likewise, none of them built their political vision on virtue, but many of them nonetheless believed that it was an important element of the political language and the vision of the state. This is clearly visible in the writings of Kołłątaj, who treated the attitudes of citizens as an important component part of his statements (despite devoting less attention to this issue than Staszic and Rousseau) both when he lamented lost virtues and (more frequently) when he urged specific attitudes in line with the following conviction:

> The nation's salvation rests in its own hands. Thus it will either lift itself up and stand at the summit of upright power, or fall and place

its hands voluntarily in the fetters of a slave, as unworthy of enjoying the gifts of freedom such as heaven is accustomed to rewarding virtuous society with.[132]

Virtue, understood as specific civic attitudes, remained an important element of the political language and a political value that was invoked even by authors who were rather far from noble ideals and the noble discourse.[133] It was still an important propaganda argument, one that was in a sense traditionally used to discredit opponents or stress one's own achievements – it was eagerly mentioned by faithful supporters of Russia – the "virtuous hetman" Seweryn Rzewuski and his supporters and the no less virtuous citizen Szczęsny Potocki[134] as well as many other well-known or obscure participants in political discussions. It was in the course of the most heated disputes of that period, especially the dispute on the question "succession or election," that virtue was surprisingly set against reason. Opponents of succession to the throne and later the Constitution of the Third of May 1791 started to present themselves as simple yet virtuous people who were in opposition to their perhaps more enlightened yet vile adversaries.[135] This was a novelty in the political discourse. From the sixteenth century onwards, authors expressed their yearnings for the "simplicity" of their ancestors, but this meant the simplicity of old customs as opposed to the ongoing demise of morals, not the virtue–reason antinomy. This situation may have been influenced by Rousseau, who used a similar opposition,[136] but it appears to have followed to a greater extent from the fact that enlightenment and reason were not only highly appreciated values but also a propaganda argument used by supporters of reforms, who suggested clearly that only a person of "wretched mind"[137] could oppose them.

Here, I must make one important proviso: at that time, in the late 1780s, the language of virtue was an important yet no longer a necessary element of the political discourse. From the 1780s onward, there was an alternative way of talking about the state. One example was the treatise written in 1785 by Hieronim Stroynowski, who considered the links between individuals and the state (identified with authority rather than with the community) in terms of mutual rights and obligations, and even when he used the concept of virtue, he understood it differently from his predecessors.[138] Stroynowski did not wield much influence over the political discourse – besides, he was not very independent, and he drew heavily from the theories and language of the physiocrats. However, he was not the only author who excluded traditionally understood virtue from his elaborations. This held true for at least several other authors from the period of the Four-Year Sejm, whether anonymous or not, such as Jan Ferdynand Nax and Jan Baudouin de Courtenay, to some extent also Łobarzewski, who was perhaps the most faithful Polish student of Montesquieu, but what he took over from his French mentor was rather the idea of the separation of powers than the concept of virtue.[139] This was not a visible turning point but rather a signal that at least some of the participants in the political discussions in 1788–1792 had noticed the possibility of choosing a different political language.[140]

It is hard to say in what direction these changes would have headed under normal conditions. Given how the situation progressed, with the loss of independence and the fight against an external enemy, the language of virtue – understood as the utmost sacrifice for the homeland – proved the best tool for articulating the political goals of those who were involved in that struggle, and it would come to dominate the discourse again during the subsequent Kościuszko Uprising.

Notes

1 Michalski (1977, 108); "we encounter the concept of virtue in nearly every small writing, in every brochure and pamphlet of the sixteenth and seventeenth centuries" Freylichówna (1938, 12); cf. also Suchodolski (1927, 5–6).

2 Konopczyński (1966); Łukowski (2010, 13–31 and *passim*).

3 Backvis (1975, 549–550); Pietrzyk-Reeves (2012, 291–334); Baczewski (2009, 67) states that in the sixteenth century, "virtue became the central component of state ideology in the political dimension"; Wagner-Rundell (2015, 11 and *passim*).

4 "For all early modern republicans, virtue/*virtù* was of paramount importance" writes Brugger (1999, 39); cf. also Bouwsma (1995, 215); MacIntyre (2006) especially part 1, "Learning from Aristotle and Aquinas."

5 Honohan (2002, 13 and chapter 1).

6 Pietrzyk-Reeves (2012, 294–298, 304–306); on the earlier fifteenth-century Polish tradition of looking at the state in this way, cf. Korolec (2006, 178).

7 *Kto zna, co jest R.P. zupełna i cała...*, in Czubek (1906, 215); similarly, with reference to Cicero: *Iż na społecznym zjeździe panów rad koronnych w Kaskach"* in Czubek (1906, 244).

8 *Naprawa Rzeczypospolitej* [1573], in Czubek (1906, 191).

9 [Karnkowski] (1596, foreword, no pagination).

10 Ł. Górnicki, *Rozmowa Polaka z Włochem o wolnościach i prawach polskich* [1616], in Górnicki (1961, 453).

11 Lasocińska (2010, 21–50).

12 "For Machiavelli and Harrington the primary value of the republic is freedom, and virtue is understood in narrower, or more instrumental, terms," Honohan (2002, 13 and Chapter 2) – the author lists here only two authors, but this was an approach characteristic of the whole way of thought she describes as *civic republicanism*.

13 *Philopolites...* (1588, fol. P 2).

14 See *inter alia* Pocock (1981); Skinner (1978, 84–100 and *passim*); Skinner (2002, 160–184); Brugger (1999, 29).

15 Ł. Górnicki, *Droga do zupełnej wolności* [1650], in Górnicki (1961, 480ff.).

16 Ł. Opaliński, *Obrona Polski przeciw Janowi Barklayowi* [1648], in Opaliński (1959, 197).

17 Kunicki (1615, fol., G 2, D).

18 Wybicki (1775/1984, 232), similarly Kołłątaj *Listy Anonima* [1788–1789], in Kołłątaj (1954, vol. 2, 19).

19 Górnicki, *Rozmowa Polaka z Włochem o wolnościach i prawach polskich* [1616], in Górnicki (1961, 333); similarly, S. Starowolski, *Prywat Polską kieruje*, in Starowolski (1990, 274).

20 A summary of research on civic humanism and the role of virtue in it can be found in the collection *Renaissance Civic Humanism: Reappraisals and Reflections* (Hankins 2000); the introduction (pages 1–13) offers a review of earlier discussions on the issue.

21 Pietrzyk-Reeves (2012, *passim*).

22 Bałuk-Ulewiczowa (2009, 35–82).

23 Suffice it to juxtapose the *Philopolites*, clearly rooted in stoic ideals, or Kasper Siemek also rooted in antique traditions, against Kunicki, definitely more leaning towards moral and religious aspects.

24 Kunicki (1615, fol. C 4); cf. Stasiewicz (2003, 555–569).

25 The personal models then posited have either a distinctly moral dimension, or focus more on chivalrous virtues, like Szymon Starowolski's *Prawy rycerz* or Upright Knight (Starowolski 1648/1858): see: Baczewski (2009, 203–207).

26 Czartoryski (1774); [Dmochowski] (1787); *Katechizm narodowy* (1791), etc.

27 Goślicki (1568, fol. 43ff.), although elsewhere he speaks mainly about civic virtues (fol. 17, 20v and *passim*).

28 Warszewicki (1598/2010, 179 in Latin, 339 in Polish).

29 [Karnkowski] (1596 fol. B 4v).

30 Pocock (1975, 88–91, 117–155).

31 Kąkolewski (2007, *passim*).

32 Here we should note an important caveat: the virtue of magnates was treated differently in panegyrics and posthumous praises, but in statements made in political discussions such a distinction is not really observed.

33 This was pointed out by Tazbir (1976, 789).

34 *Fortitudo, prudentia, justitia, temperantia–* instead of *fortitudo*, in Polish and European statements there sometimes appears *magnanimitas*, a more extensive virtue, the main element of which was valor, but which also comprised generosity, lavishness, a kind of nobility of conduct. In the West this virtue was required especially from rulers or powerful people, in the Commonwealth it also appears as a civic virtue. On the virtue of "magnanimity" in the Polish literature, cf. Lasocińska (2002, 97–115).

35 Ł. Górnicki, *Rozmowa Polaka z Włochem o wolnościach i prawach polskich* [1616], in Górnicki (1961, 453).

36 Majchrowicz (1764, part 4, 345), alongside theological virtues.

37 Leszczyński ([1737?]/1903, 27).

38 D. Pietrzyk-Reeves (2012, 303 and *passim*).

39 *Philopolites...* (1588, fol. D 2); Kunicki (1615, fol. A 2) (although the main virtue for him was the fear of God, *timor Domini*).

40 Ł. Górnicki, *Rozmowa Polaka z Włochem o wolnościach i prawach polskich* [1616], in Górnicki (1961) – on page 453 he lists four virtues and on page 329 he describes "military men of valor, and learned men of reason."

41 Rok (1984, 347).

42 *Skrypt pewny niewinność jm. pana Lubomirskiego ukazujący* [1665], in Ochmann-Staniszewska (1991, 41).

43 Cf. Choińska-Mika (2007, 20).

44 [S. Budny?] *Elekcyja króla krześcijańska*, in Czubek (1906, 295); the author was here following Bion of Borysthenes, also citing the opinions on

prudence of Plato and the Stoics, he cited Cicero, Scipio Africanus the Elder and Seneca.

45 [Kossobudzki]/Januszowski (1606/1921, 255).
46 A very interesting analysis of how the virtue of prudence is understood in the treatise by Stanisław Herakliusz Lubomirski, written at the turn of the seventeenth and eighteenth centuries (Lubomirski 1699/1916), has been proposed by Andrzej Probulski (2014).
47 [Pęski] (1727, 9).
48 Grześkowiak-Krwawicz (2006, 269).
49 H. Kołłątaj, *Prawo polityczne narodu polskiego* [1790], in Kołłątaj (1954, vol. 2, 246).
50 Like for instance K. Siemek (1632, *passim*, e.g. fol. D 3–E), first lists illustrious Roman men of valor, then admits that the virtue of valor is also possessed by the citizens of Poland, Venice and Holland (therefore, of republics), to later switch to Cardinal Oleśnicki, boldly criticizing King Kazimierz.
51 Grześkowiak-Krwawicz (2006, 283ff.).
52 *List ob. Wybickiego pełnomocnika, do RN o potyczce pod Błoniem*, in *Gazeta Rządowa* dated 9 July 1794, no. 9; for more see Grześkowiak-Krwawicz (2006, 345ff.).
53 Kaliszewski (1760, 309).
54 *"Reipublicae cognoscere"* *"tantum ingenia rebuspublicis vero existiose sunt, eo dementia ventum sit, ut eam solam sapientiam aliqui appelent,"* Siemek (1632, fol. E 2v).
55 *"Prudentia,*which*non degenerat*in political and sometimes perfidious subterfuge," Leszczyński ([1737?]/1903, 27).
56 Vetterli and Bryner (1996, 20); Pangle (1988, 67); Opaliński (1995, 92ff.).
57 Skinner (2002, 1990, 169ff.).
58 Above all Skinner and his pupils. This was pointed out by Vetterli and Bryner (1996, 22), showing how strong an influence Christianity exerted on the Renaissance concept of civic virtue; on the atypicality of Maciavelli's views on virtue and the meaning of moral virtues in republican ideology, see also Brugger (1999, 34–36). Indeed, this also follows somewhat from the earlier chapters of Skinner's classic book (Skinner 1978, vol. 1, 84–94).
59 Aristotle, *Politics*, Book III, 1276b.
60 Goślicki (1568, fol. 20); this was pointed out by Baczewski (2009, 48).
61 Goślicki (1568, fol. 8v and 9).
62 Goślicki (1568, fol. 20).
63 *Philopolites...* (1588, fol. L).
64 *Iż na społecznym zjeździe panów rad koronnych w Kaskach*, in Czubek (1906, 247).
65 "That old-Polish simplicity, which is aptly known as virtue," *Philopolites...* (1588, fol. r 3v).
66 Ł. Górnicki, *Rozmowa Polaka z Włochem o wolnościach i prawach polskich* [1616], in Górnicki (1961, 454); *Libera respublica quae sit?*, in Czubek (1918, vol. 2, 409) (both about the honesty of the ancestors); [Pęski] (1727, 9); Leszczyński ([1737?]/1903, 37).
67 Majchrowicz (1764, part 3, 39).
68 "Between the idea or concept of an honest man and a good citizen, let us make only this distinction that we will call an honest man a person in and of himself, and a good citizen to be a person with respect to other people, with respect to human society," S. Konarski, *Mowa o kształtowaniu człowieka uczciwego i dobrego obywatela* [De viro honesto et bono cive ab ineunte aetate formando], in Konarski (1955, vol. 2, 113).

69 Baczewski (2009, 207 and *passim*).
70 Publicly distributed letter by S. Stadnicki to H. Jazłowiecki, in Czubek (1918, vol. 2, 179).
71 Fredro included it into the canon of "great" political virtues, listing: "*justitia pietas, fortitudo, prudentia,*" Fredro (1660/2014, 572).
72 Leszczyński ([1737?]/1903, 9); cf. E. Rostworowski, *Respublica Christiana i republikańsko-pacyfistyczna myśl oświecenia*, in Rostworowski (1985, 44 ff.).
73 [Jabłonowski] (1730, 7).
74 A. W. Rzewuski (1790, part 1, 122); more broadly cf. Butterwick-Pawlikowski (2017a, 175–195).
75 This was pointed out by Baczewski (2009, 135).
76 An exception is the above-cited book by Wagner-Rundell (2015), where he tried to analyze the "discourse of virtue" (and the lack thereof.) without succumbing to the temptation of making rash evaluations.
77 *Gdychżechmy przyszli...* in Czubek (1906, 147).
78 *Mowa Jana Zamoyskiego na sejmie* (1605) [version D, which the publisher considers a *rokosz* falsification], in Czubek (1918, vol. 2, 93 (opinion about the king's supporters).
79 [Karnkowski] (1596, fol. Dv); similarly, Warszewicki (1598/2010, 177 in Latin, 336 in Polish).
80 *Gdychżechmy przyszli...*, in Czubek (1906, 147).
81 Cicero, *De republica* 5.2.
82 *Naprawa Rzeczypospolitej* [1573], in Czubek (1906, 195–196).
83 *Rozmowa senatora koronnego z ślachcicem*, in Czubek (1906, 541).
84 [Grabowski?] (1589/1859, 13).
85 *Egzorbitancyja powszechna...* (1628/1858, 7).
86 This role in disputes under the reign of August II was pointed out by Wagner-Rundell (2015, 44): "the political language of corruption has frequently been deployed merely as polemical tool in factional conflicts."
87 A beautiful example of this latter interpretation can be found in the argument of Father Chądzyński, that the Lord God is punishing the Poles not for heresy, because they are "after all more Catholics," not for drunkenness, because others drink as well, but for vices such as "wanton license, especially among the noble estate, oppression of subjects and the more impoverished nobility itself, wrongs and injustices" J. Chądzyński SJ, *Dyskurs kapłana jednego polskiego[...]*[1657], in Ochmann-Staniszewska (1989, 185).
88 *Relacyja prawdziwa sejmu... zerwanego 23 Decembra 1666*, in Ochmann-Staniszewska (1991, 177).
89 *Instrukcyja [...] na sejmiki teraźniejsze wszystkie posłana [...]* [1667], in Ochmann-Staniszewska (1991, 256).
90 [Grabowski?] (1589/1859, 10–12).
91 [Poniński] (1763, 195).
92 [H. Kołłątaj], *Krótka rada względem napisania dobrej konstytucyi rządu* (1790), in Kądziela (1991, 154).
93 [Kwiatkowski] (1791, introduction, no pagination).
94 Wagner-Rundell (2015, *passim*), essentially the whole book is about this.
95 Dzieduszycki (1707/1906); [Radzewski] alias Poklatecki [1743].
96 [Jabłonowski] (1730, 5).
97 This was convincingly demonstrated by Benedict Wagner-Rundell (2015).
98 A. M. Fredro, *List do poufałego przyjaciela* [1667], in Ochmann-Staniszewska (1991, 237).
99 Warszewicki (1598/2010, 188 in Latin, 349 in Polish).

100 *Opisanie krótkie niektórych interesów...* (1762/ 2011, 14).
101 More broadly see Grześkowiak-Krwawicz (2004).
102 Sienicki (1764, vol.1, 25).
103 "Initially, the kings were opposed but the Sejms were not broken off; there were animosities but when the homeland was in need they were forgotten. Sejms continued to be broken off, but on the grounds of good or contrived laws; [...] ultimately Sejms were broken off at the very beginning, without even stating an honest reason for it," [Poniński] (1763, 197).
104 Sienicki (1764, vol 1, 140).
105 [W. Rzewuski] (1764b, fol. B).
106 [W. Rzewuski] (1764b, fol. B 2); [W. Rzewuski] ([1764a], fol. A 3ff.).
107 Rousseau (1966a, 997–998).
108 Konarski (1760–1763, vol. 3, 252).
109 This was pointed out by Jerzy Łukowski in his articles (Łukowski 1994; 2014).
110 He strongly stressed that it was not anarchy that is a consequence of a lack of virtue, but rather a lack of virtue that is a consequence of anarchy; this was besides also a reference to traditional republican theory, cf. Goldsmith (1994, 202).
111 Shklar (1987, 4). While it is true that Konarski exclusively referred to *Considerations on the Causes of the Greatness of the Romans and their Decline*, he makes certain mentions in his work that lead to the conclusion that he was also familiar with the deliberations in *On the Spirit of the Laws*.
112 On the Polish reception of the governmental ideals of both authors, compare: Szyjkowski (1913); Leśnodorski (1967); Smoleński (1927); Matyaszewski (2012; 2018).
113 The translation of Montesquieu's *Considérations sur les causes de grandeur des Romains et de leur decadence* by Antoni Wiśniewski was published in Poland under the title *Uwagi nad przyczynami wielkości i upadku Rzeczypospolitej Rzymskiej*, Warsaw 1762.
114 Skrzetuski (1773, 39).
115 "This political virtue is as crucially needed for maintaining free government as the soul is to enliven the human body, as is love for the homeland and native laws," Skrzetuski (1773, 34).
116 Wybicki (1775/1984, 112, 121 and *passim*); "For Montesquieu, the major cause of Rome's fall, as of her rise, is to be found in the character of the Romans," Oake (1955, 44).
117 Wybicki (1775/1984, 121).
118 Indirectly, Skrzetuski's *Mowa o miłości ojczyzny* [Speech on Love for the Homeland], being an adaptation of an article by Jaucourt in the *Encyclopédie*, whose author clearly was inspired by Rousseau's concepts; Skrzetuski (1773, 302–321).
119 "Scorn for fundamental laws, neglect of the old honesty and virtuous simplicity, by slightly violating the foundations on which the government had seemed to stably rest, lean it towards its downfall," Wielhorski (1775, XI).
120 "What is virtue, if not the constant custom of deeds useful to society?," A. W. Rzewuski (1790, part 1, 29).
121 A. W. Rzewuski (1790, part 1, 109).
122 Staszic (1787/1926, 182).
123 Staszic (1787/1926, 18).
124 "To become a citizen is to relinquish, to give up one's will and one's personal power to the whole society," Staszic (1787/1926, 19).
125 *Naprawa Rzeczypospolitej* [1573], in Czubek (1906, 196).

126 Starowolski (1650, chapter IX).

127 As the anonymous author of *Egzorbitancyja powszechna...* (1628/1858, 8) wrote, still citing the antique anecdote: the Spartans refused to give the Persians their youths to raise, out of a fear that "having gained different edification, they could easily become degenerates to their own forefathers, who had put up resistance to powerful enemies when free."

128 Grześkowiak-Krwawicz (2006, 264–266).

129 H. Kołłątaj, *Listy Anonima* [1788-1789], in Kołłątaj (1954, vol. 1, 202, 245; vol. 2, 84ff.).

130 Skinner (1990b: 305ff.); Gardiner (1984, 96, 98); Viroli (1987, 173).

131 His thoughts on virtue were clearly being referred to by the author of the anonymous *Bezstronne zastanowienie się nad proponowaną ustawą następstwa tronu w Polszcze* [1789]; Rousseau's influence was also quite clearly evident in the work of Leonard Wołczkiewicz Olizar [1790], who devoted much space to political education in the republic; also Turski (1790b).

132 H. Kołłątaj *Listy Anonima* [1788-1789], in Kołłątaj (1954, vol. 1, 259).

133 [Pawlikowski] (1789, 1–18, the chapter "*Co rada dla kraju.*").

134 Rzewuski (1789, 4); Sz. Potocki ([1790]).

135 Grześkowiak-Krwawicz (2000, 349–351).

136 Clearly following him was A. W. Rzewuski: "Let them hate tyrants, [...] let them value their freedom and homeland above their blood [...], it is a lesser thing that they will not be educated" A. W. Rzewuski (1790, part 1, 102).

137 Cf. Grześkowiak-Krwawicz (2000, 347–348).

138 Stroynowski (1785, 234).

139 Although he did mention the latter: [Łobarzewski] (1789b: 64–65, 242–243).

140 Here it is worth pointing out that at least some of them were not noblemen – Nax, Baudouin, although it is hard to speak of any rule here, given that one of the most outstanding restorer of the language of virtue was Staszic, hence also a burgher.

7   *Amor Patriae* – Patriotism

The contemporary word "patriotism" (*patriotyzm*) appeared relatively
late in the Polish political discourse, and indeed also in the Polish language in general. It is still absent even from Michał Abraham Trotz's
mid-eighteenth-century dictionary of Polish (although perhaps it was a
bit behind the times in this respect).[1] The term was used by Stanisław
Konarski in the early 1760s, and its frequency later increased in political
speeches delivered under the reign of king Stanisław August, to reach
its peak in Four-Year Sejm disputes, as testified indirectly by Franciszek
Salezy Jezierski's sarcastic remarks that it was being much abused.[2] The
lack of a specific word, however, cannot of course be taken as clear evidence that the underlying concept itself was not around. On the contrary,
in this case, the problem of one's obligations towards the homeland was
indeed one of the key issues that had been raised in political speeches
already in the sixteenth century. Despite the fact that the participants
of political debates in the sixteenth and seventeenth centuries could not
avail themselves of the present-day term, they did not seem to be short
of expressions to refer to the desired stance that citizens of the *Rzeczpospolita* should take towards their state. Their linguistic repertoire in
this respect was in fact quite rich, and included such terms as "love for
the homeland," which was the most popular, as well as "courtesy to
the homeland," "benevolence towards the homeland," and a number of
Latin phrases, such as *amor patriae, charitas patriae, pietas in patriam,*
and *zelus patriae*. The still non-existent "patriot" (*patriota*) was instead
described as a "lover of the homeland," as a "faithful" or "good citizen
of the homeland" (sometimes also as its Latin predecessor *bonus civis
patriae*), or otherwise as a "benevolent son of the homeland," or "citizen
wishing the homeland well."[3] This list is not exhaustive, as the aim here
is merely to showcase the variety and number of these expressions, at-
testing to the importance of the underlying idea they stood for.

There is no doubt that the love for the homeland was one of the
highest values of the noble discourse. The author of a 1588 treatise on
this subject wrote that "love for the homeland transcends all love for
earthly things,"[4] which was clearly inspired by Greek and Roman writers. The statement *"caritas patriae omnes caritates complecti debet"*[5]

was generally accepted among all participants of the political discourse in the period spanning from the sixteenth to the eighteenth centuries, regardless of whether they derived it from ancient thought or not. The assertion that a good son of the homeland owed to his country "more than to his wife, more than to his daughter, more than to himself"[6] was much reiterated in the discourse. The significance of love and respect for the homeland can also be appreciated on the basis of numerous declarations voiced by political speakers, repeated almost in the same form for over 200 years, stating that their actions and words stem from their care for the common homeland, or are intended to enhance its glory. Each participant of the public debate presented himself as a "faithful and benevolent member of our homeland,"[7] and each person who joined in the political struggle "declared his love for the homeland"[8] reassuring others that his words and deeds were motivated by such "kind love."[9] Very similar declarations to those quoted above from the sixteenth- and seventeenth-century sources continued to be put forth by public speakers proclaiming their "assiduousness to do good for the homeland"[10] until the Four-Year Sejm. The way in which the authors signed their texts were also symptomatic in this respect, for example, "a Pole favorable to his homeland,"[11] or "a Polish nobleman faithfully loving his country."[12]

When the adjective "patriotic" (*patriotyczny*) did appear in the eighteenth century, it was eagerly used in the titles of speeches: "A Patriotic Voice...," "Patriotic Thoughts on...," "A Patriotic Letter to...," and others of that ilk. By this token, a declaration of love for the country became an obligatory element of public speeches, often becoming a conventional rhetorical device or even a truism. This did not pass unnoticed, with accusations of hypocrisy often being leveled against political opponents. At the time of the Sandomierz *rokosz*, Zygmunt Myszkowski wrote this in his open letter to Mikołaj Zebrzydowski:

> Thy love for the homeland did not flourish such until the Lord ceased to indulge thee in some way. Alas, it was only after a conflict over thy estate that the *Rzeczpospolita* started to decline, ill counsel was revealed and titles proved unjustly granted.[13]

Such allegations of declaring one's patriotism opportunistically were also made later, mostly by the royalists, especially during one of the *rokosz* rebellions (Zebrzydowski's, Lubomirski's and the Bar Confederation). This is not surprising since rulers were invariably attacked under the slogans proclaiming concern for the homeland or an outright need to protect it. The excess of patriotic clichés was succinctly remarked upon by the priest Konstantyn Bogusławski in the eighteenth century: "so much patriotism in words, and so little in deeds,"[14] and Stanisław Szczuka was even more pessimistic about the honesty of patriotic declarations, saying: "It so happens that the greater devotion we proclaim for the homeland, the deeper is the abyss into which we thrust it."[15]

The value of love for the homeland is also proved by frequent accusations against those who did not exhibit it. This was undoubtedly a major offense and an effective and oft-used propaganda argument in the political disputes throughout the sixteenth to eighteenth centuries. Lecherous, infamous and shameful "unlove for the homeland,"[16] and even simple "lack of benevolence"[17] disqualified someone, at least in theory, from participation in political life. "Therefore thou art not *cives, sed profanatores patriae*,"[18] an anonymous speaker in the pre-election debate addressed his adversaries in 1573, and 200 years later Seweryn Rzewuski declaimed "Out with you, degenerate sons of the homeland,"[19] postulating that all those who did not subscribe to his views be declared *pro hostis patriae*.[20] When political tension and the speakers' temperament reached a climax, accusations of treason could be leveled, too,[21] but such situations were infrequent. "Unlove for the homeland" (*niemiłość*) however, surfaced in the political discourse almost as often as love (*miłość*), if not in argumentation, then in speeches lamenting the conduct of fellow citizens lacking "in respect for the good and peace of the country,"[22] and in concern for the "beloved homeland," often evoked in Latin as *caritatis patriae*. This was believed to be one of the main causes of the tribulations experienced by Poland, "abandoned by her sons."[23] Such opinions appeared during the time of the first free election, probably stemming from earlier complaints, and lingering in various forms until the end of the Commonwealth. Despite the temptation to relegate this issue to the level of rhetoric and treat it as a commonplace deprived of any reflection, it should be borne in mind that it did stand for a certain model of the state and a system of political values. In what follows, these values will be scrutinized in more detail.[24]

The most fundamental questions concern the meaning of the term "love for the homeland." What did this feeling involve, if it was a feeling at all, and what was or what was supposed to be its object? Answering the latter question is far from simple, if only for the reason that despite being quickly linguistically assimilated as speakers of Polish, the Lithuanian nobles nevertheless retained a profound sense of their separate identity and tradition, and used the phrase "love for the homeland" in reference to the Grand Duchy of Lithuania in the sixteenth and seventeenth centuries.[25] The referent of "homeland" in the phrase in question could also be a province, especially in areas having a long tradition of independence, such as Royal Prussia.[26] Apart from such a narrow understanding of this concept, there is a more inclusive reading of it, referring to the common homeland of the noble nation, that is, to the Polish-Lithuanian Commonwealth. It was not long after this state came into being that the participants of the political debate talked about "our homeland *Rzeczpospolita*," having in mind not the Crown but the Commonwealth, and demanding from their fellow citizens "love and faith duly offered to our homeland, our true mother *Rzeczpospolita*."[27] Commenting on the sixteen and seventeenth centuries, Edward Opaliński wrote that "love of the homeland was a value that, like brotherhood, drew the diverse noble society together ideologically, ensuring the unity of the Commonwealth state."[28] A claim could be ventured that much as the homeland could not always be equated with the whole *Rzeczpospolita*, the latter always was the homeland. The two interpretations of the concept were not mutually exclusive but complementary in the noble discourse,[29] complying with the ancient tradition, and more specifically with Cicero's statement that a man has two homelands: one by place of birth, the other by citizenship.[30] This quote was very well known to speakers participating in political debates, at least in the sixteenth and the beginning of the seventeenth centuries.

Love for the homeland – for the *Rzeczpospolita* – is the main subject of this chapter. As far as it can be estimated without carrying out quantitative analysis, it certainly seems to have been the most frequently invoked concept in the political discourse, at least in the works discussed here, that is, political treatises and pamphlets.[31] It was the concept that received the most extensive descriptions and analyses. Last but not least, the identification of the *Rzeczpospolita* with the homeland represents the key to understanding the vision of patriotism dominant in the political discourse. Because the term *Rzeczpospolita* corresponded to a number of referents (as discussed earlier in this book), the imperative to show concern for it applied to the state as a political construct, to its territory, to the nation as a community constituting this construct and inhabiting the territory, and also to the values enshrined by the *Rzeczpospolita*, as will be elaborated upon later. The complexity and at the same time stability of this approach to patriotism is best captured in a statement, made as late as 1794, explaining the causes for which the Kościuszko insurrectionists fought: "for their rights, freedom, and liberties [...] for the homeland, nation, integrity of the borders, independence of the governance, for their own laws, common to all."[32] At that time the concept of *Rzeczpospolita* in its traditional rich meaning was gradually waning in the political discourse, but for the forefathers of Kościuszko's insurrectionists, all the above-enumerated causes would have been subsumed under this single concept.

This kind of approach derived from the ancient, especially Roman, tradition of political thought, underscoring the relationship between an individual and the state/community; the Latin expression *amor patriae* in the title of this chapter is intended to highlight this connection. At the beginning of the Commonwealth, when its political discourse was still being molded, the ancient influence was reflected even on the level of terminology, in which Polish and Latin expressions coexisted. Moreover, many Polish terms were literal translations from Latin, with "faith in the *Rzeczpospolita*" – *pietas in patriam* – having perhaps the greatest allure.[33] Despite the fact that native expressions gradually won out over Latin ones, the ancient vision of *amor patriae*, or perhaps *charitas patriam*[34] was still upheld. Love was understood as citizens' concern for the self-determined state/community.[35] The word "citizens" needs to be emphasized here, as the whole discourse which could be called patriotic was about them.[36] The full title of a small treatise on patriotism from 1588 (repeatedly discussed in previous chapters) is characteristic in this respect: *Philopolites, or Lover of the Homeland, or the Duties of a Good Citizen, Wishing Well to and Loving his Homeland: A Short Treatise.*[37] Much as this comparison may seem anachronistic (and the book itself did not even belong to the political discourse), it should be noted that still in Samuel Bogumił Linde's influential dictionary of Polish from the beginning of the nineteenth century the entry "patriotism" was defined as "citizenship," and the entry "patriot" was explained as "a citizen devoutly engaged in the cause of his homeland's good, clinging to his homeland in the same manner as to his own property."[38] The conclusion that the vision of patriotism did not evolve at all during the over 200-year period would of course be a gross oversimplification and is by no means intended here, but the striking superficial similarity of the formulations should not be disregarded, either, lending support to the claim that throughout the period under discussion, love of the homeland was primarily defined in terms of citizenship.

The noble citizens went even further than that, insisting that absolute monarchy and patriotism were practically mutually exclusive. Their speeches were premised upon a deeply entrenched belief that patriotism is possible only in a state in which free people decide affairs for themselves and for their country – in other words, only citizens were capable of loving their homeland and making sacrifices for her. In states cultivating servitude, which, in the opinion of the nobility, included all absolute monarchies, *amor patriae* was not possible, simply because inhabitants of such states did not have a homeland. In the words of Wacław Kunicki, where "a tyrant rules in a *dominium absolutum*, people fight not out of love for their homeland, but out of greed […], or because they have to…"[39] This view, visibly influenced by ancient philosophy, was voiced in the sixteenth century, and then evoked again in the mid-seventeenth by Łukasz Opaliński, in his defense of the *Rzeczpospolita* and its government from the critique by John Barclay.[40] But it was in the second half of the eighteenth century when such views enjoyed the greatest popularity, resonating as well with the opinions put forth by French philosophers. The opening of Wincenty Skrzetuski's *Mowa o miłości ojczyzny* [Speech on Love for the Homeland], which asserts "there is no homeland under the yoke of tyranny," sounded very much like a quote from the *Encyclopédie* – and it in fact was one, with the whole text of the speech being a free adaptation of the article *Patrie*.[41] The views of the Encyclopédistes and also of Rousseau, Mably and, to some extent, those of Montesquieu[42] matched the Polish tradition of understanding patriotism so closely that it can at times be difficult to separate an author's own opinion from a quote. When Adam Wawrzyniec Rzewuski wrote that in a monarchy "there is no nation, the sweet name of the fatherland fears and flinches to come to the mouth of the slave," he undoubtedly expressed his heart-felt conviction, but at the same time he echoed Rousseau's views.[43] Rzewuski was a zealous follower of republican ideology, but his standpoint does not appear to be extreme against the background of others. A similar view was espoused by the modern republican Staszic, very likely to be influenced by Rousseau, too, and the priest Józef Puszet – a relatively moderate supporter of the monarchy. The latter claimed that "subjects in an autocratic state commonly do not consider the country their homeland, only insofar as it is the country of their birth or of the property they possess in it."[44] A man who could not decide affairs for his country was not free, therefore, he did not have a homeland.

What can be inferred from the political speeches produced at the time of the Commonwealth is that patriotism and participation were not separately distinguished, unlike in the political discourse of Western Europe, in which these two notions became individuated in the seventeenth century.[45] A citizen's duties to the homeland are that citizen's duties to the community. Their descriptions can be found in political speeches from the sixteenth to the eighteenth centuries. *Civis* – a citizen, was not only a son, but also a "faithful and benevolent member of our homeland,"[46] somebody who cared for the homeland not only because he owed everything to her, but also because he would have lost everything should he lose his homeland: being an element of the *Rzeczpospolita*'s body, he could not exist without it. This relationship was succinctly captured by Antoni Popławski, who put forth the following motto in the eighteenth century: "By loving yourself, love your homeland."[47] Also quite symptomatic was the popularity of an old allegory, having its roots in Aristotle's theory, portraying the *Rzeczpospolita* as a boat which could be driven to a harbor only by a joint effort of the crew and passengers, but if it sank, everybody would drown with it. In 1573 a participant of the political debate gave the following advice to his fellow citizens: "And so should *cives Reipublicae* act, as to preserve the health of the *Rzeczpospolita* during perilous times, as if it were a boat with us aboard, since her health is the health *privatorum*, its downfall is the downfall *privatorum*."[48]

Crucially, love for the homeland so understood was much more complex than an unreflective feeling or sentiment for the place of one's birth. The motif of natural and unconditional love for the country and nation did appear in political texts but was not prevalent. It was skillfully handled during the first free election by one supporter of a Polish-nationality king, who argued that such a candidate would be ideal "as it is a natural thing to love thy homeland's tradition and to love thy natural tongue, and as of foreign traditions and strange tongues, they are detested and look'd down upon."[49] This perspective drew from the ancient tradition, specifically from the conception of *pietas in patriam*, which advocated that the homeland be forgiven the harm that it had inflicted upon a citizen, with the story of Veturia and Coriolanus being sometimes recalled as an example.[50] As was mentioned, this line of thought did not prevail, and the motif of instinctive love for the language and culturally homogeneous nation as an alternative to the traditional conceptualization of love for the *Rzeczpospolita* appeared only towards the end of the eighteenth century, in texts by Staszic, Jezierski and other authors writing during the Four-Year Sejm, and was accompanied by significant changes in the discourse. But before that period, this motif could be seen as peripheral, providing a counterpoint rather than an alternative to the dominant vision.

The dominant conception of *amor patriae* in the Polish discourse was founded upon love for the homeland seen not as a feeling but as a civic virtue, demeanor, duty, obligation or a rational action underlain by the need to protect one's own interests, and consequently as a *quid pro quo* transaction.[51] First of all, as was indicated before, the idea was deeply ingrained in the political discourse that there was an inextricable bond between the homeland and its citizens, and between the condition of the former and the latter. Łukasz Górnicki put it in the following way: "what ails all people cannot be good to thee, as thou art in all embodied."[52] This argument was repeated in the subsequent centuries, with the belief that "whatever atrocity may befall the *Rzeczpospolita*, threatens equally her sons,"[53] being expressed both under imminent threat and in ordinary discussions on the needs of the country. Stanisław Konarski summed it up as follows: "no one can be fortunate when the homeland is lacking in good fortune; no one can feel secure when the *Rzeczpospolita* is weak and endanger'd,"[54] adding "who thus perishes when the homeland perishes: we perish, as we are the homeland's substance."[55] For Konarski, this assumption provided a foundation for his idea of reforms: what was beneficial and contributed to the security of the homeland, was *ipso facto* beneficial for the individuals that comprised it. His standpoint was exceptional in that similar premises were mainly deployed in deliberations on citizens' duties and obligations, whereas Konarski used them in postulates to improve the efficiency of institutions. Common to both strands was the belief that the only rational stance was to support the cause of the homeland, which guaranteed all tangible and non-tangible goods her citizens could possess. If love for the homeland was to be seen as a feeling of some sort, it was a feeling of gratitude for all goods it bestowed upon her sons. In the sixteenth century an anonymous writer known only as a "Lover of the homeland" wrote this (taking his cue from Plato): "each must comprehend that he owes help, salvation and support to the homeland at all times, bearing in mind the goodness she gives him."[56] It is worthwhile to consider the plea made by the *Rzeczpospolita* herself to her own citizens in one of the *rokosz* pamphlets in 1606:

> Remember that having birthed thee in this Crown, I bequeathed thee (...) with freedom, I gave thee love, I raised thee and strengthened thee for defending me and my health, that I took the bread from my own mouth and gave it unto thee; do not now let me perish disgracefully and miserably.[57]

As is evident, the homeland did not demand disinterested support, but rather had well-founded claims to a citizen's gratitude. This idea was represented in numerous texts, providing the main line of argumentation for Szymon Starowolski, who in 1655 described in his "Lament of the Tormented Mother, the Polish Crown, now Expiring, about her Wayward and Negligent Sons" how the motherland rebuked ungrateful children by meticulously enumerating her sacrifices for them.[58] In the eighteenth century, gratitude to the "good mother" appeared in Stanisław Leszczyński's[59] and Enlightenment-inspired authors' writings.[60] It should be emphasized again that the gratitude was seen as being in the citizen's own interest. "Remember, gentrymen and landlords," one participant of the 1606 *rokosz* appealed to his countrymen, "that after God, whatsoever ye have, ye have from your homeland; it raises you, it feeds you, it gives you all abundances; let it also be so dear to you because if it perishes, we all must perish with."[61]

In 1780, the priest Michał Karpowicz formulated this idea in the Enlightenment style, writing that "The homeland (...), through sweet liberty ensuring happiness and safety to all, virtually itself instils love in its own citizens."[62] This love was not unconditional, though. The principle of reciprocity was stated by an anonymous author in 1776:

> I know what it means to be a citizen of my homeland; I owe her assistance and protection; I abide by the laws she imposed upon me, and I fulfill my duties; she in turn safety and all things SHALL ENSURE.[63]

This author's way of thinking was presumably affected by the Enlightenment discourse, but the same issue appeared in much earlier texts. For instance, it was discussed in 1628 by an anonymous author complaining about "exorbitances" in the *Rzeczpospolita*, and additionally warning about the consequences of the homeland not fulfilling her obligations:

> [...] what an incentive against the enemy it is to love and cherishingly enjoy what it is he wants to take away, which is freedom, justice, peace; but where there is bondage, unbearable wrongs and unrest

among countrymen this incentive weakens, as many may think: who knows whether a foreigner having conquer'd us might give us what we cannot attain among ourselves."[64]

There were a few authors, though they were rare, who drew conclusions from this reasoning regarding the situation of the underprivileged classes, especially the peasantry. One of them was the priest Jan Chądzyński, who put it very plainly during the Swedish invasion, arguing that the obligation to protect the homeland rested upon her sons who obtain profits, such as "liberties, gratifications, honors," and not on farmhands, stating directly that "the peasants have little to lose and they might even get better lords and get liberated from the slavery should they find themselves under a different, fairer rule."[65] In the eighteenth century, this logic was sometimes reversed by the proponents of rights being granted to the non-noble classes, leading to the conclusion that since these classes did have their merits of service to the homeland, possibly even greater than the nobility, the homeland was obliged to return the favor to them and offer them some benefits as well. Among the first thinkers to employ this argument were Leszczyński in his *A Free Voice Ensuring Freedom*[66] and Stefan Garczyński in his *Anatomia* of the *Rzeczpospolita*. Having observed that "paupers" are "not privileged by any protection by the homeland," Garczyński devoted much space to proving that they fulfill their duties to the country better than the nobility.[67] Initially, however, such voices were marginal and it was only in the King Stanisław August era, especially during the Four-Year Sejm, that the issue of granting rights to the underprivileged classes, mostly the bourgeoisie, appeared in debates. It was exploited both by supporters and opponents of social reforms, with the former underscoring the merits of the "plebeians," and the latter denying any rights to the bourgeoisie precisely because of their alleged indifference towards the homeland. One of the authors averse to the idea of granting rights to town dwellers wrote about them that "their goal is their own welfare," adding that in contradistinction to that, a nobleman is concerned with the "happiness of the nation."[68] Occasionally, the principle of mutual obligations was directly evoked, from which the conclusion was derived (*à la* the priest Chądzyński), that since the homeland fails to fulfill her duties to the lower classes, they should not be expected to care for her. "Give freedom to the subjects," an anonymous author appealed to lawmakers at the beginning of the Four-Year Sejm, "when you turn them into citizens, and give them a homeland, which hitherto was not a mother but a cruel stepmother to them, they will show you their strength, which will suffice to fight back the most enormous foe."[69] Still, this problem did not garner considerable attention, and the identification of the homeland with the *Rzeczpospolita*, and of patriotism with citizenship, was responsible for the fact that love for the homeland was seen as pertinent only to the group that constituted it, with the sole exception of sixteenth-century humanists and Enlightenment reformers, who saw things differently.

The question arises about the place of the king in this close relationship between the homeland and the nobility. Was the king part of this relationship? The answer is far from simple, as it evolved over time and was dependent on the political situation in Poland. At the turn of the sixteenth and seventeenth centuries, the feelings for the state and the ruler tended to be treated jointly rather than separately, and love for both was declared as in the olden times, when noble forefathers showed "bravery and shed blood for the lords and homeland."[70] It was still for Jan Zamoyski that services for the king and for the homeland were inseparable.[71] As indicated by studies conducted by Edward Opaliński, at least during the reign of the first two Vasa monarchs, the link between the king and homeland was often brought to the fore in many speeches at the Sejm and *sejmik* assemblies, with the homeland being portrayed as mother and the king as father, and the noble subjects loving them both.[72] But even in such speeches, this vision was not exclusive.[73] It can be hypothesized that the link between the homeland and king was largely taken for granted in the Jagiellonian era,[74] but from the time of the first interregnum on, it ceased to be obvious. This situation resulted from the juxtaposition of two visions of the *Rzeczpospolita*, and, as was mentioned before, the king was a necessary element only in one of them. Love for the homeland, understood as a community in which citizens' needs were catered to, could, but did not have to, include a king, as clearly evidenced by the treatise on love for the homeland cited above in this chapter, in which this issue was completely ignored.[75] What is more, loyalty and love for the homeland were likewise demanded of kings, with the imperative to "cherish this homeland of ours" addressed to successive monarchs, since "kings, too, whatsoever they may have, they have from the homeland, and whatsoever they give, they give from its riches."[76] Kings could also stand accused of being unloving to the homeland. Especially prone to such accusations were rulers conflicted with the nobility, such as Sigismund III or John II Casimir, with Stanisław August topping the list as the one who was the most severely attacked for a lack of patriotism, and even accused of downright treason. Paradoxically, he was the first to actively project his own image as a patriotic king, with this image being also cultivated in the press and poetry written by his supporters.[77] When conflicts and tensions became intense, opinions that the homeland can be loved without necessarily the ruler being loved were voiced with great confidence. A clash between *amor patriae* and *amor regis* can be noticed in texts originating in the Zebrzydowski *rokosz*. In a pamphlet by Jan Szczęsny Herburt, the homeland – or here, we should write: the motherland – asked her children a dramatic, and undoubtedly rhetorical question: "And who, my dear children, should ye love more: me, your mother who gave you birth, or a newcomer, a step-father who strips you of your proud freedom?"[78] In the speeches of the most ardent *rokosz* participants, a "sweet death for the homeland" meant dying in a clash against the king, while defending the privileges.[79] In subsequent conflicts, the opponents of the ruling kings likewise presented themselves as defenders of the homeland, with the love and protection of freedom becoming more prioritized with time. That said, although this vision did not become unanimously accepted in the political discourse,[80] love for the homeland was not identified with love and loyalty for a ruler or dynasty, and with time the two were being perceived as increasingly divergent.

The catchphrase *rex et patria* largely came to be replaced by *patria et libertas*. The latter became the second most frequently used slogan in the Polish political discourse (following *lex et libertas*). However, it seems that, at least up to a certain moment, "homeland and liberty" was not intended to be polemical with respect to the king-and-homeland combination. In sixteenth-century texts, the slogan *patria et libertas* emphasized the most precious value guaranteed by the *Rzeczpospolita* and continuity with the ancient – especially Roman – tradition, in which the homeland and liberty were inextricably linked. An opposition drawn between loyalty to the ruling authorities vs. loyalty to common liberty arose in texts written during the Sandomierz *rokosz*. It is telling to juxtapose two texts from this period in this respect – one royalist, addressed to all "loving the homeland and the king,"[81] and the other rebellious, addressed to those to whom "liberty and the homeland is dear."[82] The latter phrase became widespread in *rokosz* texts and entered the general political language, whereas the previously mentioned declarations of concern for "the good of the kind homeland" started since that time to be accompanied by equally passionate declarations of concern for liberties.[83] Some of the participants of this debate went even further in identifying love for the *Rzeczpospolita* with love for freedom and the protection of the homeland with the protection of citizens' rights and liberties. The anonymous author of a *rokosz* pamphlet advised that "everyone (...) should fully do their foremost duty to the homeland: to defend its rights and liberty."[84] The opponents of Sigismund III did not initiate this line of thinking, as it had already appeared in the sixteenth century.[85] In fact, it ultimately derives from the Roman tradition, where the link between the homeland, rights and freedom was put forth in the works of Cicero and Sallust, and was eagerly followed by the advocates of republican freedom in Renaissance Europe.[86] It continued to be voiced in the seventeenth and eighteenth centuries, reverberating also in the work of Rousseau,[87] who was highly influential in Poland. With time, however, the Polish interpretation of this idea started to become characteristically biased. When the political discourse of the nobility acquired its form in the sixteenth century, all of its participants, drawing on their ancient predecessors, expressed the view that since the free homeland is the only guarantor of liberties, then, love of freedom was *de facto* tantamount to love for the homeland, implying respect for her rights as well as concern for her strength and safety. Later, however, as can be observed already in the Zebrzydowski *rokosz* texts, the main emphasis in the "homeland and freedom" juxtaposition began to be put on "freedom." As such, love of freedom, understood mostly as rights guaranteeing liberties for noble citizens, started to overshadow, or even supersede love for the homeland.[88] It may be difficult to prove this point without statistical analysis, but there are good grounds to assume that love for the homeland, still mentioned very frequently in 1606–1608, gave way to freedom several decades later, during the Lubomirski *rokosz*. Even the Bar confederates in the eighteenth century, who fought against foreign oppressors, referred to themselves as defenders of religion and freedom much more often than as defenders of the homeland.[89] A "true Pole" simply had to love liberty to be deserving of that name. Accusations of insufficient admiration for liberty, often advanced in polemical texts in the seventeenth and eighteenth centuries, were equivalent to accusations of a lack of patriotism, thereby becoming an effective weapon against political opponents.

A claim could thus be ventured that at a certain point a change in the hierarchy of values took place, and it was no longer the homeland that was perceived as a guarantor of freedom, but rather freedom that became a necessary condition for a country to be considered a homeland. This standpoint harked back to the classical link between the homeland and freedom, and simultaneously drew on the conception of patriotism as mutual obligations of the citizen and homeland, from which it followed that when the homeland ceased to fulfill its fundamental obligation to guarantee freedom, the citizen was exempted from the duty to love his country. Such views were by no means confined to the Polish environment, as similar ideas can be found among the Italian humanists, who, in turn, echoed the ancient tradition.[90] On a different note, it can be observed that during the period when the Polish discourse was strongly influenced by ancient thought, the motif of a broken contract was rarely mentioned. It appeared towards the end of the eighteenth century and was exploited to the fullest by the advocates of the conservative solutions during the Four-Year Sejm. This faction drew extreme conclusions from the conception on which patriotism was identified with the protection of individual liberties, rather than with love for a free state.[91] Each attempt to constrain freedom was interpreted by them as an attack on the common homeland, if not as an act of treason: "he who was born free, shall die free and he who wanted to cease being free cannot be merely seen as a degenerate but as a traitor to the homeland, should he dare lead others to slavery," wrote Seweryn Rzewuski about the proponents of a hereditary monarchy.[92] When deprived of freedom, the homeland ceased to be what it was: "What use would be the name of the Pole, should we become subjected to bondage?"[93] Advocates of this ideology leveled accusations of treason against the creators of the Constitution of the Third of May 1791, which – in their judgment – infringed upon the noble class' liberties, and hence was an act of treason against the nobility and their privileges. Moreover, members of this group came to the conclusion that in view of the blatant violation of their freedom, the principle of mutual obligations of the homeland and citizens was violated too, which was a sufficient reason to exempt them from any duty to serve the country. As one of the opponents of the Constitution of the Third of May said on the day of its proclamation: "I wish to defend the country because I am free, but if there is to be despotism I will scorn it and declare myself an enemy of Poland."[94]

So extreme an attitude could only be formed during intense political conflict. The viewpoint on which freedom was valued higher than the homeland never dominated the whole discourse. There were still voices in the seventeenth and eighteenth centuries that reminded the noble participants of public life that it was the homeland that was the only guarantor of their liberties. These voices came typically from authors of elaborate texts, many of whom discerned the urge to reform the ever-deteriorating political system of the country, such as Opaliński, Starowolski or Leszczyński.[95] For Konarski, it was a major argument in favor of the abolishment of *liberum veto*, hence his rhetorical question: "When our Commonwealth and our homeland perishes without council and without Sejms, where will this freedom be?"[96] It was paraphrased in the 1790s by Hugo Kołłątaj in a dispute with the above-mentioned defenders of freedom at any cost: "If the name of Poland perish'd, where would they raise their liberty?"[97] In this way, the classical republican vision of *amor patriae* was evoked as love for the common *Rzeczpospolita* being the only guarantor of rights and liberties.

At this time, that is, at the beginning of the 1790s, a few voices could also be heard, which significantly diverged from the traditional discourse in that they separated, or at least attempted to separate, the homeland from freedom, and patriotism from the protection of liberties. These authors approached the homeland and nation in cultural and ethnic terms rather than as political and civic concepts. "I love the Poles' name and existence in the world first of all, and then Polish liberty" declared Franciszek Salezy Jezierski, explaining that even under a despotic rule so long as it was Polish, "the nation would at least retain its name, language, and character."[98] A similar opinion was proclaimed by Stanisław Staszic, who wrote: "With the whole nation under despotism, it might recover its lost liberty under favourable political circumstances, given today's emerging enlightenment. But a nation once destroyed will never rise again."[99] Following the principle of "first nation, then freedoms," Staszic went on to assert: "An absolute monarchy would be more useful to our nation in this case than a bad republic, since the former will preserve the nation of Poles."[100] This kind of emphasis on the protection of the nation's identity transcended the vision of the homeland as the nobility's republic and additionally helped redefine patriotism, by undermining its direct connection to the liberties of noble citizens. It has to be underscored, however, that such interpretations were few and far between. Apart from the above-quoted authors, who were not fully consistent on this issue either, no one treated the homeland and freedom separately. The tragedy of the partitions was to reaffirm rather than question this connection, by depriving Poles of both at the same time. For the Kościuszko insurrectionists, not all of whom were noblemen, the struggle for freedom meant liberating the country from foreign invaders and its citizens from tyranny: "Fellow citizens!" – the insurrectionist government joyfully proclaimed – "Our homeland is being regained, and liberty along with it ..."[101]

The discussion in this chapter has so far focused on interpretations of the concept "love for the homeland." The issue to be addressed next is what a citizen's duties were, what it took to deserve the name of a patriot or a good son of the homeland. It can be asserted without any doubt that these requirements did not change significantly between the sixteenth and eighteenth centuries, being consistently steep, proportional to the responsibility incumbent upon a citizen deciding affairs on behalf of his country. They corresponded with the requirements imposed on a member of a free society in what is known as the republican vision of the state.[102] The previous chapter dealt with a number of virtues present in the nobility discourse, but they all effectively boiled down to one, as declared by a participant of the 1573 election: "love of the homeland rightly deserves priority, in glory and reverence over other virtues,"[103] seconded some decades later by Andrzej Maksymilian Fredro, for whom "the highest virtue is love for the homeland and the common good, therefore other human affairs shall be deemed of lesser value."[104] This view, modeled on ancient thinkers, gradually turned into a cliché. It should be noted that when Montesquieu explained that a virtue in democracy consists in loving the country and its laws, it was not his original idea, but a conclusion drawn from the tradition that originated in classical antiquity. This tradition was followed by the nobility too, it could therefore only be expected that the definition formulated by the author of *De l'esprit des lois* would be eagerly incorporated into their discourse. It can be found in Józef Wybicki's writing[105] in Skrzetuski's "Speeches,"[106] and it also resonates in the following statement by the priest Karpowicz: "virtue in the commonwealth, considered in civic terms, is the simplest thing; it is the pure love of the commonwealth..."[107] Not only was this virtue indispensable to all members of the *Rzeczpospolita*, it was also the source of other civic merits: "love for the homeland eradicates from citizens' hearts desires for self-serving aims, teaches one to value the common good above particular interests; it instills all civic virtues which can be in this single virtue encapsulated."[108]

Love for the homeland was a virtue that came to fruition during action. A good son of the homeland was obliged not to be "*civis segnis* and negligent,"[109] when action was required, it did not befit a citizen "to be passive."[110] From the sixteenth century on, all political speakers espoused the view that active service to the homeland was a moral and political imperative of a free citizen. An anonymous participant of the Zebrzydowski *rokosz* declared in 1606 that "service to the Commonwealth is the most certain, most glorious, and even most useful service, above all others."[111] The service included public activities, and a tradeoff between rights and obligations could be observed: free citizens of the noble *Rzeczpospolita* had a right to participate in the life of their community, but in exchange for this right, they were obliged to "serve the *Rzeczpospolita* with counsel, or with assistance, or with will and assiduousness."[112] These words would be repeated almost verbatim in the sixteenth, seventeenth and eighteenth centuries.[113] It should be seen as symptomatic how often and in how diverse circumstances labor, service or even sacrifice for the homeland were declared. Regardless of the real intentions behind such declarations, it has to be noted that the imperative to act for the homeland's cause surfaces as one of the most fundamental values in the political discourse throughout the whole existence of the Commonwealth.

Service to the country could be performed in various ways, one of the most prominent being defending the country with weapons in hand. As was mentioned before, courage and sacrificing one's life was one of the most commendable and desirable virtues of a citizen. The most deserving of respect were

> those who express their love by their courage and dependability, who scorn all things earthly, even be they highly valued, for the sake of virtue and truth, and who would not hesitate to lay down their lives for the *Rzeczpospolita*.[114]

This opinion, quoted by the author of *Krótkie rzeczy potrzebnych z strony wolności zebranie* [A Short Collection of Crucial Issues Regarding Freedom] and originally voiced by Jan Zborowski, was accepted practically unanimously by participants of political debates. The Roman saying *Dulce et decorum est pro patria mori* reverberated in Polish speeches from the sixteenth until the eighteenth centuries. Sacrificing one's life, or as a matter of fact sacrificing everything (life, health, riches), for the sake of the homeland was a recurring motif in the *Rzeczpospolita*'s political discourse. It often appeared in the form of complaints that the speaker's or writer's contemporaries are not capable of making sufficient sacrifices, in which they differ from their virtuous forebears. Since the

homeland was the sole guarantor of all goods, and especially of freedom, its defense was not only worthy of maximum sacrifice, but it was
also essentially something obvious: "[...] where there be freedom, there
is a great heart. Where there be a great heart, dangers are nothing and
death is not severe," asserted an author of a 1573 pamphlet,[115] and his
words continued to be repeated for over 200 years. Even though such
declarations were often mere platitudes, still, the observation that a citizen's obligations towards the country were one of the key elements of
the Polish vision of patriotism remains valid. It was invoked regardless
of the political stance represented by a speaker, also by the advocates of
profound reforms and modernization of the Commonwealth:

> [...] the public good is so dear to him that he would easily forgo his
> own; he cares for his life to save it for the needs of the homeland,
> he collected riches to donate them for the sake of public defense. All
> his courage and wisdom were for defeating the country's enemy by
> sword or by counsel.[116]

Presented above is a complete picture of the sacrifice for the homeland,
sketched out in 1775 by Józef Wybicki. Though he drew on Montesquieu, his statement was also directly linked to the traditional conception of patriotism. This motif tended to be naturally invoked during
wars and unrest, each time very much in the same shape. It was still
during the Kościuszko Uprising that the anonymous author of *Głosy
Polaka do współziomków* [Voices of a Pole to his Fellow Countrymen]
wrote about death on a battlefield using similar words to those found
in the 1606 text quoted above: "Glorious death, as it was in defense
of the homeland, desirable death, as it was for the sake of freedom, for
liberties, for rights [...], for everything that is dearest in the world."[117]
A key difference between the two voices is that the former's musings
were merely theoretical, despite the tense political situation at that time,
whereas the latter was referring to real deaths on a real battlefield. Both
invoked the same vision of love for the homeland, as requiring the greatest sacrifice possible.

    There is no doubt that sacrificing one's life was the highest form of
service for the country, but it was not the only one. It may not even be
the most endorsed form of service in the political discourse, except at
times of heightened threat. A free citizen should serve the homeland at
all times and in all ways, as required by circumstances. Since the beginning of the Commonwealth it had been emphasized that the duties of
a good citizen were not confined to military defense during conflicts.
In times of peace, they were of no lesser importance, and perhaps even
more challenging. In the parlance of the Commonwealth, they were
dubbed service by counsel, for which the virtue of prudence rather than
courage was required. In 1615 Wacław Kunicki put it as follows: "during

the time of peace, we shall counsel the homeland, whereas during the time of war we shall bravely fight for her fortune."[118] The postulate to defend the homeland "with counsel or with weapon in hand"[119] was repeated again and again, and it was stressed that "both fields of service are equally beautiful, honourable, and meritorious."[120]

With love for the homeland understood as the imperative to participate actively in public life, the concept of counsel covered the whole gamut of activities that did not yield any benefits for an individual (at least in theory), but which were highly beneficial for the community. On this approach, patriotism was an effort for the common good, as evidenced in this statement by an anonymous politician from the outset of the seventeenth century: "You have no greater or harder labour than work for the country."[121] This idea was reiterated in the successive centuries too, with Hugo Kołłątaj pointing out in 1789 that the republican government of the Polish-Lithuanian Commonwealth while "giving them [citizens] liberty, places upon them the yoke of labour and lasting supervision."[122] People not belonging to the noble class also had a say on that issue, such as the following opinion by Józef Pawlikowski:

> Whoever is a Pole, desires fortune for his country, each who loves her, counsels for her. When I am among those who love her dearly, I shall not bear critique for putting forth my thoughts for the sake of her fortune.[123]

Laboring on behalf of the country included participation in the Sejm and *sejmik* assemblies, pronouncing judicious rulings in courts, speaking out in public debates, conscientiously holding offices in public institutions, and also obeying the law and paying taxes.[124] Briefly put, it comprised any and all activities and decisions oriented towards the welfare of the *Rzeczpospolita*. For activities carried out in the public sphere of life, to qualify as manifestations of the virtue *amor patriae*, one fundamental condition had to be satisfied: they had to comply with the interest of the general public. Following the ancient tradition of political thought, if the free *Rzeczpospolita* was to survive, each member of the noble community ought to serve the public good.[125] As an anonymous participant of political debates carried out under the reign of John Casimir wrote, "three things are commonly needed in people residing *in nostro statu Reipublicae*, where everyone from the noble prerogative acts *ad curanda et avertanda mala publica*; namely *prudentiam, gravitatem et amorem boni publici*."[126] Another author put it succinctly in the following way: "love of the common good holds the Commonwealth."[127]

It has to be underscored that the republican *bonum publicum* was understood literally as the public good, and was distinct from *raison d'état* applied as a principle in absolute monarchies.[128] The latter notion, insofar as it appeared in the Polish discourse, was used as a kind of straw-man argument or accusation against the ruling authorities, who allegedly followed this principle. The issue of the common good and the mutual duties of an individual and community was a subject of reflection and deliberation for the humanist authors of treaties on statehood, such as Goślicki, Wolan, Warszewicki or Górnicki.[129] However, both this term and the idea it denoted quickly caught on and became an indispensable element of public speeches. The notion of the "common good" (*dobro pospolite*) or, from the eighteenth century onwards, the "public good" (*dobro publiczne/powszechne*), was omnipresent in the speeches of noblemen, with the slogan of concern for the public good being one of the leading motifs of Polish debates on a citizen's duties to the homeland, that is, on patriotism. Sometimes caring for the public good was even identified with patriotism: an anonymous author complaining about "widespread exorbitance" wrote in 1628 that "love of the common good is a virtue, called by politicians *pietas in patriam*."[130] Concern for the public good was declared and appealed for, and the lack thereof was condemned in political opponents. Speakers participating in political debates considered it vital to assert that "public good is my aim,"[131] or, as did an anonymous author from the King John Casimir era, that the reader was facing "The discourse of a free *civis*, concerned not with foreign interest, neither his own, but only the common good."[132] The popularity of this formula is evidenced by the accusations of its being abused, of carrying out activities dressed up as "*boni publici et libertatis*,"[133] or of one's adversaries "pursuing self-serving aims under the cover of service for the *Rzeczpospolita*."[134] The latter formulation gained enormous popularity, as concern for the public good was often coupled with its opposite, that is, the pursuit of self-serving aims. The preference for one's own interest over the public good was not only considered particularly reprehensible but also dangerous: "Should anyone counseling the *Rzeczpospolita* not put aside *privatos suos affectus*, he cannot be a good advisor; his counsel may harm rather than salvage the country."[135] Excessive interest in self-serving aims was seen as a source of all abuse: "The neglect of this love (of the homeland) and of the public good, very rightly and truly should be called common exorbitance, the mother to all abuse ..."[136] It has to be pointed out that the Polish political discourse abounded in remarks to the effect that citizens were not able to live to the ideal and that they did in fact pursued self-serving aims and acted "for their own, and not public benefit."[137] Such remarks, which might have been equally, or even more frequent that appeals for concern for the public good, resounded in the discourse from the first free election, until the downfall of the Commonwealth. Stanisław Poniatowski, the father of the future king, was neither the first nor the last one who begged God for "the sacred and effective endowing of our hearts so that self-serving aims, which we shamelessly and with unspeakable harm pursue, give way to public benefit."[138] Comparing Polish political texts with those written in Western Europe, and also with treatises created by Polish Renaissance humanists, it can be observed that the latter devoted more space to explicating the notion of the public good and how citizens should enact concern for it, whereas the former contained numerous complaints about citizens failing to do so. This difference is mainly due to the fact that the participants of the two-century-long debate conducted in the Commonwealth did not ponder a theoretical model but commented on the political reality. With time, however, blaming all the problems of the *Rzeczpospolita* on the pursuit of "self-serving aims" and "the oppression of the common good" became a justification of a passive stance and failure to introduce reforms of laws and institutions. It was Konarski who first insisted that "all people are naturally more inclined toward taking care of their private good than of public benefits and goods,"[139] with this statement being more of an assertion than a judgment. Konarski did not deny the need to care for the common good but did not subscribe to the view that it should provide a foundation for a community. His proposals of modifying the political parlance did not win wide recognition, with the language of the King Stanisław August era being much more significantly influenced by Rousseau, who followed the tradition linking the welfare of the state with patriotism of its citizens.[140] Rousseau's idea that any private interest always had to give way to the good of a community aligned with the Polish discourse very closely. This is not surprising, since both derived from a common ancient sources, as is confirmed by the fact that both culled examples of love for the homeland and sacrifice for the common good from Roman and, to a lesser extent, Greek history.

On the conception of patriotism that was adopted in the Polish discourse, which revolved mainly around the issue of a citizen's obligations towards his political community, be it a nation or the Commonwealth, actions undertaken for the sake of the homeland were confined to public life. Consequently, a large portion of the *Rzeczpospolita*'s inhabitants, that is, those who did not belong to the nobility, was excluded from these activities. In some speeches delivered during the turbulent times of the Four-Year Sejm, their ability to act patriotic was even questioned, especially with respect to the bourgeoisie: "he cares for good fortune only so much as his house and himself should remain intact, no matter that the whole country may turn into rubble,"[141] wrote Jacek Jezierski about a merchant. In the majority of the discourse, however, this issue was not even raised.

The set of ideas which began to be included in the model of patriotism espoused in Western thought from the eighteenth century on remained outside the horizon of the Polish nobility. The most important of these ideas is the ethos of solid work for oneself, as a foundation of the homeland's power and affluence. This issue was practically non-existent in the Polish political discourse up to mid-eighteenth century, with Samuel Chróścikowski being the first to include solid work among duties to the

homeland in his book on the "Duties of Every Citizen," stressing that
what he meant was diligence and carrying out duties specific for each
class and profession.[142] Intended for Piarist-run schools, the book was
supposed to forge the views of noble students,[143] but it did not affect the
political discourse. Greater impact was exerted by opinions voiced by
advocates of social reforms, especially those postulating improvement
in the living conditions of the peasantry, even though they mostly based
their arguments on the benefits of farming for the homeland rather than
on patriotism as such. This line of thinking can be traced in the works of
Garczyński, Leszczyński and later Wybicki, and also of the Polish physiocrats, with some of them going as far as stating that peasants are "the
most useful citizens of the country."[144] Later, thanks to texts published
in the magazine *Monitor*, and during the Four-Year Sejm thanks to authors expanding the concept of the nation, the bourgeoisie were also included. It was acknowledged that both classes "served society at large,"
and that not only public activities were essential for the common good,
but also labor in the domain of farming, trade or craftsmanship.[145] As
the *Monitor* explained, it is possible "to sacrifice talents for the public
cause" by holding public offices, producing goods or studying.[146]

Again, such conceptions remained relatively unpopular in the Polish
discourse. Despite the fact that some political thinkers recognized the
bourgeoisie as members of the nation, and then the Act on Towns (18
April 1791), and finally the Constitution of the Third of May sealed
this officially, the belief prevailed that patriotism entailed public service,
which took the highest place in the hierarchy of all activities for the sake
of the country. A good example of this approach is the *National Cate-
chism*, the author of which did avail himself of the terminology developed by Enlightenment philosophers, but still cultivated the traditional
view on a citizen's duties:

> First, to work for the fortune of the homeland, to serve her faithfully,
> supporting her with counsel and riches of all kinds, to fight against
> all foes inside and outside its borders, should such foes appear. Sec-
> ond, to sustain her laws, privileges, and prerogatives, which are the
> same for all his fellow-citizens.[147]

The vision of patriotism emerging from Polish political texts created towards the end of the eighteenth century continues to rely on the notions
of freedom, self-determination and participation in political life. The
link between the homeland and freedom still holds strong, with duties
towards the former being identified with duties towards the community
of citizens. In the *Rzeczpospolita* this conception lasted longer than in
any other European country, subsequently finding support in Montesquieu's and Rousseau's philosophy, and ultimately also in the ideas proclaimed by the French Revolution. It could thus be intimated that this

conception provided a foundation for the patriotism of the nineteenth century when the homeland and freedom were the subject of a struggle to regain them.

Notes

1 Knapik (2011, 402–415).
2 F. S. Jezierski, *Niektóre wyrazy porządkiem abecadła zebrane*, in Jezierski (1952, 235–236).
3 Quoted after Bem (1989, 151), all the citations date from the sixteenth century.
4 *Philopolites...* (1588, fol. Bv).
5 This was a common aphorism, cited already by Jan Długosz, but here in fact cited after Stanisław Poniatowski ([1744]: C2) (it appears to be a free adaptation of Quintilian, although Poniatowski describes it as a sentence taken from "a Roman senator").
6 *Obrona ojczyzny przez jednego z synów jej miłujących bratu swemu zalecona RP 1650*, in Ochmann-Staniszewska (1989, 61), in the context of limiting luxury and financial support for the homeland.
7 [Solikowski] (1596/1859, 4).
8 From Taszycki's speech, *Krótkie rzeczy potrzebnych z strony wolności a swobód polskich zebranie* (1587/1859, 50).
9 From Mikołaj Zebrzydowski's statements to the king, *Opisanie prawdziwe i porządne traktatów pod Janowcem*, in Czubek (1918, vol. 3, 149).
10 *Zdanie Polaka o wolności...* ([1790]: 26).
11 *Zdanie jednego Polaka ojczyźnie swej przychylnego o teraźniejszym jej niebezpieczeństwie* [1667], in Ochmann-Staniszewska (1991, 201).
12 [Solikowski] (1596/1859)
13 Z. *Myszkowski do M. Zebrzydowskiego* (24 November 1606), in Czubek (1918, vol. 2, 205).
14 Bogusławski (1786, 34).
15 [Szczuka?] (1709/1902, 97).
16 *Gdychżechmy przyszli...*, in Czubek (1906, 147).
17 K. Grzymułtowski?], *Projekt konfederacyi pewnej autore incerto, podrzucony senatorowi d. 2 Novembris 1662*, in Ochmann-Staniszewska (1990, 253).
18 *Modus corrigendae Reipublicae*, in Czubek (1906, 142).
19 S. Rzewuski (1789, 10).
20 S. Rzewuski ([1790a]) – this is how the hetman concluded each of the 39 points of his lecture on political ideals.
21 Foe example, for the Zebrzydowski rebellion: "as against enemies of the homeland and disturbers of the common peace and betrayers of the homeland," *Passyja pana naszego Zygmunta III*, in Czubek (1918, vol. 2, 54) (royalist, strongly anti-*rokosz*); *Żałosna mowa Rzpltej polskiej pod Koprzywnicą do zgromadzonego rycerstwa, roku 1606*, in Czubek (1918, vol. 2, 96) (a *rokosz* participant); for the Lubomirski rebellion: "being traitors of our homeland," *Skrypt pewny niewinność jm. pana Lubomirskiego ukazujący* [1665], in Ochmann-Staniszewska (1991, 41) (in defense of Lubomirski); the Constitution of the Third of May 1791 for its most vehement opponents, cf. Grześkowiak-Krwawicz (1995, 49–70).
22 [Grabowski?] (1589/1859, 9).
23 *Votum ślachcica polskiego Jana Kazanowskiego*, Czubek (1918, vol. 2, 302).

24 I have considered this issue before, and some initial conclusions from my research were published in A. Grześkowiak-Krwawicz, "Citizen, Fatherland, and Patriotism in the Political Discourse of the Polish-Lithuanian Commonwealth," in Trencsényi and Zászkaliczky (2010, 255–284).

25 *Zdanie o obieraniu nowego króla,* in Czubek (1906, 349–350); Henryk Wisner writes that at least until the mid-seventeenth century, the Lithuanian nobility used the term "homeland" (*ojczyzna*) with reference to both the Commonwealth as a whole, and more narrowly to the Grand Duchy (Wisner 2002, 52); Kiaupienė (2004, 310–318; 2009, 20–25).

26 Friedrich (2005, *passim*).

27 *Gdychżechmy przyszli...,* in Czubek (1906, 147). 154.

28 Opaliński (1995, 92); "The Commonwealth was recognized as a common homeland, but those in Lithuania did not conceal the mistrust that the Crown evoked..." Wisner (1976, 587).

29 This was pointed out by Wisner (2006, 28).

30 Cicero, *On the Laws,* II, 5; cf. Dietz (1989, 178).

31 This was pointed out by Opaliński (1995, 36); here we should make the caveat that while the "Crowners" immediately adopted, or perhaps seized, such an understanding, in Lithuania the situation was more complex and changed over time, cf. Kiaupienė (2004, 309; 2009, 21–22, 25).

32 Karpowicz (1794, 16).

33 Cf.: Choińska-Mika (2007, 16).

34 The role of the antique tradition in how *amor patriae* was understood in literature was pointed out by Koehler (2007, 33).

35 Cf. Walicki (2000, 16ff.).

36 Choińska-Mika (2007, 20); Dzięgielewski (2007, 22–23); we should add one caveat here: while we are still talking about noble discourse, that does not mean that other social groups did not develop the issue of love for the homeland; cf U. Augustyniak, "Two Patriotisms? Opinions of Townsmen and Soldiers on Duty to the Fatherland in Seventeenth-Century Poland," in Trencsényi and Zászkaliczky (2010, 461–496).

37 Meller (2004, 43–67).

38 Linde (1811, 651).

39 Kunicki (1615, fol. E 2v), here the author specifically had Turkey in mind.

40 Ł. Opaliński, *Obrona Polski przeciwko Janowi Barklayowi* [1647], in Opaliński (1959, 179).

41 Skrzetuski (1773, 302); cf. Graciotti (1991, vol. 1, 14).

42 More from the deliberations on the reasons for the rise and fall of Rome than from the *Spirit of the Laws*.

43 A. W. Rzewuski (1790, part 1, 7).

44 Puszet de Puget (1788, 59); Staszic (1787/1926, 182).

45 Trencsényi and Zászkaliczky (2010, 35).

46 [Solikowski] (1596/1859, 4).

47 Popławski (1774, 288).

48 *Iż na społecznym zjeździe...,* in Czubek (1906, 243); cf.: Kotarski (1995, 227–299); Pfeiffer (2012, 220ff.).

49 [Budny?], *Elekcyja króla krześcijańska,* in Czubek (1906, 305).

50 Goślicki (1568, fol. 17v).

51 On the old antecedents for such a stance, see Viroli (1995, 25); "Patriotism in the classical period was conceived of as a straightforward, unconditional – but also rational – identification with that fatherland which was the condition of one's liberty," Mouristen (2006, 26).

52 Ł. Górnicki, *Rozmowa Polaka z Włochem* [1616]. in Górnicki (1961, vol. 1, 350).

53 "whatever *atrox* may *Reipublicae accidere, ex aequo imminet* her sons," [J. Leszczyński], *Consideratione quibus modis ten domowy ogień uspokoić* [1665], in Ochmann-Staniszewska (1991, 50).

54 Konarski (1760–1763, vol. 1, 184).

55 Konarski (1760–1763, vol. 4, 7).

56 *Philopolites...* (1588, fol. B).

57 *Żałosna mowa Rzpltej polskiej...*, in Czubek (1918, vol. 2, 97).

58 *Lament utrapionej matki Korony Polskiej, już już konającej na syny wyrodne, złośliwe i niedbające na rodzicielkę swoję*, Starowolski ([ca. 1655]).

59 "love for the homeland, which has like a good mother conceived and raised me, feeds me, so that I shall not be a wayward son [...]," Leszczyński ([1737?]/1903, 79).

60 Receiving the most robust benefits from the universal mother, is it not meet, and not befitting the obligation of gratitude, for [the nobleman] to repay it with jeopardy to his life and with bloodshed..." Popławski (1774, 294); "the citizen owe his first gratitude, after God and his parents, to the homeland," Kamieński (1774, 9).

61 *Pismo szlachcica jednego, w którym o rozprawie znać daje do braciej*, in Czubek (1918, vol. 3, 367).

62 Karpowicz (1781, no pagination).

63 *List obywatela do sąsiada w służbie wojskowej zostającego* ([ca. 1776]: 2).

64 *Egzorbitancyja powszechna...* (1628/1858, 8).

65 J. Chądzyński, *Dyskurs kapłana jednego polskiego [...], w którym pokazuje za co Bóg Koronę Polską karze i jako dalszego karania ujść mamy* [1657], in Ochmann-Staniszewska (1989, 186).

66 Leszczyński ([1737?]/1903, 111).

67 Garczyński (1753, 221, 241–243).

68 *O skutkach z poniżenia stanu szlacheckiego*, in *Materiały do dziejów Sejmu Czteroletniego* (1959, vol. 2, 482); more broadly see Grześkowiak-Krwawicz (2000a, chapter "*Wolni mówią do wolnych*").

69 *Poparcie „Uwag nad życiem Jana Zamoyskiego"* ([1788]: 118).

70 Herburt (1570, fol. A 4v).

71 J. Zamoyski, *Mowa na sejmie 1605*, in Czubek (1918, vol. 2, 92).

72 Opaliński (1983, 797).

73 Opaliński (1983, 800ff.).

74 Sucheni-Grabowska (1994, *passim*).

75 Which does not mean that the author was a republican; he strongly stressed the obligation to obey overlordship, and also the fact that it is in the interests of the state for the king to strive to ensure the love of subjects, but he did not deliberate this in terms of love for the homeland.

76 J. Zamoyski, *Mowa na sejmie 1605*, in Czubek (1918, vol. 2, 95). Edward Opaliński writes about the "patriotic-political education" that the ruler received from the noble society, Opaliński (1983, 798; 1995, 93).

77 Grześkowiak-Krwawicz (1999, 166–168).

78 J. S. Herburt, *Strzała, którą korona Polska, śmiertelna już matka strażą obtoczona z więzienia swego do dziatek swych stanu rycerskiego wypuściła*, in Czubek (1918, vol. 2, 167).

79 *Pismo szlachcica jednego...*, in Czubek (1918, vol. 3, 367); on page 362 the author declares: "We were prepar'd to die for the homeland and dear freedoms" (in a clash against royal troops at Guzów).

80 Formulations about love of the king and homeland lasted all the way until the eighteenth century, not only in panegyrics and statements addressed to the rulers, they also appeared in statements made during the course of political disputes. A telling example is the assurance given by an advocate

of Marshal Lubomirski that the Lubomirski house is a model of *fidelitas circa patriam et principem – Skrypt pewny niewinność jm. pana Lubomirskiego ukazujący* [1665], in Ochmann-Staniszewska (1991, 39); in the eighteenth century the author of *Eclipsis poloniae* lamented "faith broken with respect to king and homeland," [Szczuka?] (1709/1902, 109).

81 *Przyczyny dla których konwokacyja złożona być nie może*, in Czubek (1918, vol. 3, 395).

82 P. Ostrowski, J. Wolski, letter to sejmiks, in Czubek (1918, vol. 3, 396).

83 "Having only the good of this kind homeland and freedoms as goals...," *Zdanie szlachcica polskiego cudzych interesów...* ([1697]: fol. 303).

84 *Pismo szlachcica jednego...*, in Czubek (1918, vol. 3, 358).

85 "To do one's duty to the homeland in repairing and augmenting its freedom," *Krótkie rzeczy potrzebnych z strony wolności a swobód polskich zebranie* (1587/1859, 5) (from Taszycki's speech); similarly *Philopolites...* (1588, fol. I 3v), for whom glory was due to he who "expends his blood and life for freedom, for the native laws, for the whole of the preservation of the *Rzeczpospolita*.

86 Viroli (1995, 19); "The primary duty of a good patriot was to put himself in the service of the fatherland and to fight for liberty," Van Gelderen (1996, 120); in England, during the time of the Glorious Revolution and later, "'patriot' was tied to a particular set of political principles: the defense of liberty and the rights of Englishmen against tyranny, the laws and constitution of England against the king and court," Dietz (1989, 183).

87 Viroli (1995, 82).

88 Cf. Dzięgielewski (2007, 30).

89 It was precisely during the confederation that a slow change occurred in the discourse, evidently under the influence of external factors – the image of violated liberty and faith from the beginning of the confederation was, by the end, increasingly supplemented with (though not yet replaced by) a vision of a suffering homeland; cf. Grześkowiak-Krwawicz (2010, 251).

90 Viroli (1995, 33).

91 An anonymous opponent to the succession of the throne felt that it would be better for the country to collapse than for it to lose its freedom: "It is a terrible thing to prolong life so that the later days of yoke and disgrace should ruing the glory of the earlier ones," *Bezstronne zastanowienie się nad proponowaną ustawą następstwa tronu w Polszcze* ([1789]: 10); Wojciech Turski, in turn, argued that foreign subjugation was better than domestic despotism, Turski (1790a: 5).

92 S. Rzewuski (1789, 30).

93 *O polepszeniu sposobu elekcyi królów polskich...* ([1788]: 3).

94 Jan Suchorzewski, speech 3 May 1791, cited after: Michalski (1985, 48).

95 Leszczyński ([1737?]/1903, 6); "through our insufficient forces in wars, unable to avoid certain *cladem*, we face the inevitable loss not only of the homeland, but of our freedoms and liberties," Leszczyński ([1737?]/1903, 74).

96 Konarski (1760-1763, vol. 2, 152).

97 H. Kołłątaj, *Ostatnia przestroga dla Polski*, in Kądziela (1991, 121).

98 F. S. Jezierski, *Niektóre wyrazy porządkiem abecadła zebrane*, in Jezierski (1952, 215); cf. Walicki (2000, 51ff.).

99 Staszic (1790/1926, 210); cf. Kostkiewiczowa (2002, 86–89).

100 Staszic (1790/1926, 209 and 4); Staszic (1787/1926, 52, 204ff.).

101 Rada Zastępcza Tymczasowa 30.04.1794, in Askenazy and Dzwonkowski (1918, 83); on the concept of patriotism during the Kościuszko Uprising cf. Walicki (2000, 113–115 *passim*); Kostkiewiczowa (2010, 146–149).

102 Opaliński (2002, 160ff.); Vetterli and Bryner (1996, 20); Viroli (1995, 27).
103 [Budny?], *Elekcyja króla krześcijańska*, in Czubek (1906, 316).
104 Fredro (1660/2014, 472).
105 Wybicki (1775/1984, 50).
106 Skrzetuski (1773, 35).
107 Karpowicz (1786, no pagination).
108 Skrzetuski (1773, 35), after Montesquieu.
109 Iż na społecznym zjeździe..., in Czubek (1906, 239).
110 "And so it is not fitting for the citizen to be inactive? It is not permitted for him to distance himself from interests, so that he lived for himself alone," *Katechizm narodowy* (1791, 9).
111 *Pismo szlachcica jednego...*, in Czubek (1918, vol. 3, 368).
112 *Philopolites...* (1588, fol. Bv).
113 "In time of peace I shall honorably consult about the homeland, and in time of war I shall seek to ensure its fortune" Kunicki (1615, fol. K 3v); "Citizens, equal in dignity, serve the *Rzeczpospolita* with their virtue, fidelity and love, and faithfully ensure what has been entrusted to them, not as servants, but precisely as citizens," A. M. Fredro, *O potędze narodu (Punctum primum de potentia populi)* [1668], in Ogonowski (1979, 348); "[the citizen] may not distance himself from interests [...] correctness imposes on him an obligation to work and labor for the good of his homeland and contribute to it," *Katechizm narodowy* (1791, 9).
114 *Krótkie rzeczy potrzebnych z strony wolności a swobód polskich zebranie* (1587/1859, 50) (speech by Jan Zborowski).
115 *Pokazanie błędów i naprawy ich w naszej Rzplitej polskiej...*, in Czubek (1906, 163).
116 Wybicki (1775/1984, 51).
117 *Głosy Polaka do współziomnków* ([1794], *Głos I*, no pagination).
118 Kunicki (1615, fol. 3v).
119 This is how it was described by Wysocki (1740, 92), but this was a common assertion.
120 "As everywhere there is service to the homeland: with counsel or with weapon in hand," S. Konarski, *Mowa o kształtowaniu człowieka uczciwego i dobrego obywatela [De viro honesto et bono cive ab ineunte aetate formando]*, in Konarski (1955, vol. 2, 129); cf. Stasiewicz-Jasiukowa (1979, 53).
121 *Przyczyny wypowiedzenia posłuszeństwa królewicowi szwedzkiemu, anno 1607 die nativitatis Joannis Baptistae*, in Czubek (1918, vol. 3, 251).
122 H. Kołłątaj, *Listy Anonima* [1788–1789], in Kołłątaj (1954, vol. 2, 20).
123 Pawlikowski] (1789, introduction, no pagination).
124 The latter did not appear excessively often, but it did appear, e.g., Poniatowski ([1744]: fol. Cv) appeals that "whoever is a true son of the homeland" should manifest old-Polish virtue by paying the tax he proposes. Similarly, Sienicki (1764, 207).
125 Opaliński (1995, 92ff.); "Classical civil virtue, then meant the patriotic subordination of one's personal interests to the common welfare," Vetterli and Bryner (1996, 20); similarly, Pangle (1988, 67).
126 *Respons, w którym się pokazuje, że tradukcyja złośliwa i żadnej w sobie prawdy nie mająca* [1664] in Ochmann-Staniszewska (1990, 219) (a royalist).
127 *Egzorbitancyja powszechna...* (1628/1858, 9). In the author's view, every republic "stands" by means of "love for the common good, or divine honor and justice between people."

128 Cf. Viroli (1995, 43); Urszula Augustyniak noted the occurrence of the "*ratio status*" concept in a text originating from among the protestant opposition in Lithuania, but this seems to be more of the exception that proves the rule than a signal of any far-reaching change in discourse; cf. Augustyniak (2004, 43).
129 Pietrzyk-Reeves (2012, 302–315).
130 *Egzorbitancyja powszechna...* (1628/1858, 28).
131 Wielhorski (1775, 114).
132 *Dyskurs wolnego civis a nie interesów obcych albo swoich, ale tylko dobro pospolite upatrującego* [1666], in Ochmann-Staniszewska (1991, 159).
133 *Respons żwawego wiary świętej katolickiej zelanta* [...] *życzliwego i miłującego ojczyznę syna koronnego, dany na „Projekt konfederacyi pewnej incerto authore"* [1662], in Ochmann-Staniszewska (1990, 107) (a royalist).
134 *Rozmowa o rokoszu*, in Czubek (1918, vol. 2, 116).
135 *Senatora anonima deliberacyje o królu, panach, radzie i urzędnikach, sejmie i bezkrólewiu* [1569], in Ulanowski (1921, 141).
136 *Egzorbitancyja powszechna...* (1628/1858, 9).
137 *Respons albo replika na pismo jednego, który o przyjaździe królewskim pisał*, in Czubek (1906, 530).
138 Poniatowski ([1744]: fol. A 2v).
139 Konarski (1760–1763, vol. 3, 137).
140 Simon (2001, 340); Viroli (1995, 93–94); Michalski (1977, 69, 76).
141 J. Jezierski, *Wszyscy błądzą, rozmowa pana z rolnikiem, obaj z błędu wychodzą*, [1790], in *Materiały do dziejów Sejmu Czteroletniego* (1955, vol. 1, 300).
142 Chróścikowski (1761, 66ff.) (he mentions the soldier, public official, and craftsman); the short chapter devoted to duties with respect to the homeland is an interesting combination of a traditional view (in Cicero's approach) and newer concepts of patriotism; cf. Stasiewicz-Jasiukowa (1979, 54).
143 It stood considerable chances of doing so, as it was reprinted several times (1761, 1766, 1768).
144 Skrzetuski (1773, 67).
145 F. S. Jezierski, *Niektóre wyrazy...*, in Jezierski (1952, 244); cf. Grześkowiak-Krwawicz (2000a, chapter "*Wolni mówią do wolnych*").
146 Kostkiewiczowa (2010, 128–130).
147 *Katechizm narodowy* (1791, 7); on visions of patriotism during the Four-Year Sejm, cf. Butterwick (2009, 67–76).

The Perceived Superiority
of the "Old Ways"
Dawny – Age-Old

The issue to be analyzed in this chapter is in certain respects considerably more difficult to present than those discussed in previous ones.
Such concepts as the *Rzeczpospolita*, the law, freedom and virtue – even
if they denoted certain idealized mental constructs, as opposed to actual, physical-world referents – nonetheless had fairly concrete points of
reference, defined by a clear conceptual framework. The notion behind
the adjective *dawny* (which is variously translatable as "former," "of
old," "ancient," or "age-old," and could in various configurations refer
to "the old ways," "the ancient customs," "the bye-gone system," but
also "the times of old," "yesteryear," "yore," etc.), on the other hand, is
a lot more elusive and harder to define, more amorphous, so to speak.
Its conceptual boundaries are rather blurred and the meanings and connotations of *dawny* differ widely, depending on who used the word,
when and in what context. This is partly because, being an adjective,
dawny chiefly serves to accompany and modify other concepts. Hence,
it can and was typically used in phrases that can be rendered in English
as "age-old freedom," "ancient laws," "the (good) old customs," "the
former system of government" and even "the age-old *Rzeczpospolita*."
   Despite playing such an ostensibly modest, even secondary role in
the political discourse, the concept *dawny* is nonetheless important and
goes far beyond the scope of the political discourse. What we are here
describing with the catchphrase "the old ways" is not only one of the
most important elements of the noble culture and vision of the world (by
no means only the political world) in the Polish-Lithuanian Commonwealth, but indeed it is also quite indicative of the early modern European culture as a whole. Here, I mean specifically attitudes to the past
and its heritage. Scholars of history, especially in the past few decades,
have often written about noble traditionalism and the cult of the past,
which were linked to social, political and moral conservatism, sometimes seeing them as typical characteristics of "Sarmatism."[1] However,
we must not forget that in the sixteenth century and throughout most
of the seventeenth century the whole of Europe looked more to the past
than to the future. Both the distant, half-mythical past, studied through
the accomplishments of antiquity rediscovered in the Renaissance, and

the less distant past, the history of countries, were seen as a collection of examples that should be emulated or should serve as warnings and arguments in debates on any topic, be it education, art, politics, or ethical attitudes – in short, the past was a role model, an unattainable ideal, a subject of studies as well as a myth that was invoked in very different circumstances and for very different purposes. Even in the narrow sense, limited only to the Commonwealth and only to the sociopolitical sphere, what we discuss here is an extremely broad area – after all, attitudes to the past in a sense provide a basis for the creation of the identity of every community. Hence, it must be stressed clearly that the place and role of "the old ways"/"the old times" in the political discourse are merely a fragment of a much broader phenomenon.

For some time, researchers have pointed out to the role that references to history, treated "as a repository of experience, a source of authority, and a treasure trove of knowledge,"[2] played in the noble political disputes from the sixteenth century onwards. Indeed, we should agree fully with the opinion expressed by Andrzej Lipski, who argued that "history has become an inseparable element of the culture of political life."[3] This issue remains poorly studied. Researchers have long been interested in authors' references to their own past and the classical past in literature,[4] and the vision of the history of their countries presented in treaties and historiographic writings has likewise been a subject of detailed analyses,[5] yet the role of the past in the political discourse has so far attracted less interest. Indeed, even if this topic was addressed, it was done in the context of references to history, with researchers focusing on such issues as the level of knowledge of history among those who expressed their opinions about political matters and on the question of which facts and figures (whether real or legendary) were invoked, how they were interpreted, how history was used in political disputes and so on.[6] In this chapter, I have decided to focus on something slightly different. As I wrote above, I mean to examine "the old ways" and "the times of old" as a certain idea present in the political discourse as well as a political value that was invoked there. It must be said clearly that it is impossible to separate these issues completely, and it is particularly true that it is impossible to understand the idea of "the old ways" and "the times of old" in isolation from attitudes to the past, also because the word "old" refers both to something that currently exists yet has a long tradition and to something that people remember once existed before, in the past. We could say that the word *dawny* encapsulates both tradition and the past. Although the past is present and important in these considerations, what I have decided to treat as a point of departure for this chapter is not the vision of history, but "the old ways" and "the times of old," attitudes towards them, their place in the discourse, their role in constructing the picture of the political world, also as an argument in disputes. As yet, this question has not attracted much interest from historians, who have not been very fond of this concept, linking it almost automatically to noble conservatism and blind attachment to tradition.[7] However, this notion appears to be an interesting and important element of the political discourse that is worth analyzing more carefully *sine ira et studio*. Once studied more closely, it will facilitate our understanding of not only the political discourse but also certain attitudes on the part of participants in political life in the Polish-Lithuanian Commonwealth.

We should start from the somewhat banal statement that "the old ways," as a value, were held in high regard in discourse, not only in the period of the political crisis and stagnation of the Saxon era. From the sixteenth to eighteenth centuries, references to "the old ways" carried clearly positive connotations in an overwhelming majority of statements, and in essence, the adjective *dawny*, when applied to any institution, law, custom or stance, automatically meant its acceptance, often even admiration for it. In short, it could be said that the status of being "former" or "of old" essentially meant "good." In the sixteenth and seventeenth centuries, there was a wide array of terms that were used to express this meaning, ranging from *starożytny* (ancient, related to antiquity), *starodawny* (old-time) and *staropolski* (old-Polish) to simply *stary* (old) or even *staroświecki* (old-fashioned). Although the meanings of these words differ slightly, all of them undoubtedly referred to the same concept as *dawny*. By using any of these adjectives to describe essentially any political concept, authors of statements generally intended to boost their value in the eyes of addressees. No one had any doubt that former or "old" laws and former, "old-fashioned," or even "ancient" freedom[8] meant good laws and good freedom, just as the former government was undoubtedly a good government, and old-Polish or old-time customs together with the old-Polish mind and spirit essentially meant the virtuousness of customs, something that was described as "the old-Polish simplicity, which should rightfully be called virtue."[9] Virtue was described with such adjectives as "ancient," "old-fashioned," and above all "old-Polish." As I wrote earlier in Chapter 6, devoted to virtue, this was in a sense a sign of a grudge held against contemporaries, or at the very least an appeal for a change of attitudes and better customs/morals. This is part of a broader issue, namely the role of the past in political disputes, which will be discussed later in this chapter. Here, it is worth stressing again the positive connotations carried by references to "the old ways." When made in the context of notions that were clearly positive, such as virtue, such references in a sense strengthened this characteristic. When applied to terms that were essentially neutral, however, phrases like "former" and "of old" automatically boosted their worth and made them respectable, admirable, and worthy of utmost care.

Participants in political discussions were fully aware of the role that "the old ways" played in discourse and could take advantage of this fact in political polemics. In the sixteenth, seventeenth and eighteenth centuries, they were more than eager to stress that the laws or solutions in the sphere of government that they defended were "of old." The same holds true for proposed laws and solutions, with researchers long pointing out that all proposals of reforms in the sphere of government were described as characteristic of "the times of old." A beautiful illustration of this can be found in a book by Konarski, who polemicized against "the old ways" being treated as a value in its own right yet realized that they remained an important and appreciated element of the vision of the political world of his readers and therefore did not hesitate to present the proposed majority voting as "former, old-Polish" *pluralitas*,[10] arguing that "this would be not something new but something old, restored in a reasonable and much-needed way."[11] Besides, participants in political discussions did not restrict themselves to institutions, and they used such adjectives as "former" and "old" also to describe people and their attitudes in order to stress their achievements and authority. "Having been born an old Pole, I want *antiquis moribus* to be *observantissimus*,"[12] an anonymous author declared after the abdication of King John Casimir. There is no doubt that by making two references to the concept of "the old ways," the author wanted to win the respect and trust of his compatriots. The same holds true for a statement made 120 years later by Szczęsny Potocki, who said that when attacking the Sejm's decisions, he thought and spoke "as in times of old."[13] One interesting example of such reinforcement of positive connotations through references to "the old ways" is the phrase "old Catholics," which appeared in the disputes with the Jesuits during Zebrzydowski's rebellion. It was used by opponents of the excessive influence wielded by the religious order and simultaneously defenders of religious freedoms acquired in the Confederation of Warsaw, who ascribed desired attitudes to those "old Catholics" and comparing them against Catholics who were "new."[14] In a sense, this was a variation on the motif of virtuous ancestors, but what matters here is the authors' profound belief that this notion, which carried clearly positive connotations, would boost the value of the attitudes presented by those "old Catholics." This shows that on the one hand "the old ways" were a value that held in high regard and on the other hand participants in political disputes could invoke it quite skillfully. As it turns out, "the old ways" occupy a not only significant but also permanent place in discourse. In the mid-1760s, King Stanisław August attempted to change the discourse and stop "the old ways" from being treated as a political value, which was symbolized by the famous quote from one of his speeches: "it seems that we stand before a new, or rather renewed, creation of the Polish world."[15] At that time, however, this change was definitely too radical and above all premature. The king did not manage to change the political language and made a serious propaganda mistake, thus confirming the concerns expressed by his opponents, who accused him (and the Czartoryskis who supported him) of having "thoroughly rejected the old *Rzeczpospolita*" and praying: "Dear Lord, make it so that the old-time *Rzeczpospolita*, such as it was left behind by Augustus, should be removed from its foundations."[16] When juxtaposed against the king's speech, these quotes show that what we can observe here, at least in terms of opinions on "the old ways," is a clash of two different discourses and two different systems of value, with the proviso that statements from that period, that is, the 1760s and 1770s, were clearly dominated by the traditional discourse.

Until the Four-Year Sejm, essentially no one attempted to change the political language in such a decisive way as Poniatowski did, but attempts to question the importance of this "proof by age-old status" were also made by other supporters of certain changes in the system of government in the Commonwealth. The issue was earlier addressed – albeit less loftily and more "commonsensically" – by Konarski, who stated, "One should not consider what is new or what is old, but rather what is good and useful for the homeland."[17] This ostensibly banal statement is important in that its author rejected somewhat casually "the old ways" as an evaluation criterion. In the 1770s and 1780s, the authors of serious political treatises, such as Wybicki and Popławski, referred to this issue yet in the context of defending new solutions, not criticizing "the old ways" as such. Besides, this was rather a polemic against certain views, not an attempt to change the traditional language of politics. Efforts to change the political language were not made in discussions until the Four-Year Sejm. Paradoxically, this is most clearly visible in the dispute on the choice between succession and election, in which historical arguments played an important role and were used by all participants in these discussions. However, this was exactly when statements appeared whose authors not only denied "the old ways" any value but even started to link them to phenomena that were viewed as clearly negative. Those were no longer the old-Polish virtues or "our free government's old laws,"[18] but rather "old mistakes"[19] or simply "former anarchy."[20] Similar phrases had earlier been unthinkable, as was the statement that the speeches of opponents "reek of old superstitions and blind prejudices."[21] In this sense, the description *dawny* "former/of old" was even perceived as derogatory, entailing a complete change of the meaning of long-established phrasemes. The most telling example of this is former freedom – in the writings of the most outspoken critics of the past solutions, it was depicted as "the deceptive delusion of the alleged old freedom,"[22] associated with all the things that were regarded as aberrations of the system of government in the Commonwealth.[23] This was a far-going change not only in language but also in a sense in attitudes to the political reality. All these quotes come from letters written by supporters of changes in the sphere of government and later the Constitution of the Third of May 1791. In this respect, defenders of former solutions were faithful to the traditional perception of "the old ways." Complaining that their opponents had abandoned "the way of thinking of the Poles of old,"[24] they lamented attacks against the old government, the old freedom and the old *Rzeczpospolita*.

It should be stressed that even when the unconditional acceptance of the value of "the old ways" started to be called into question, none of the participants in the political debate in that period negated it completely. As I wrote earlier, the "proof by age-old status" was invoked by all participants in disputes, and even the authors I have quoted here were not consistent in their aversion to "the old ways," referring elsewhere in their reasonings to the good character of the Poles of old and using former laws as an argument where necessary, but the difference nonetheless became increasingly conspicuous.

So far, I have attempted to illustrate how very highly "the old ways" were valued in the discourse of the Polish-Lithuanian Commonwealth. Now, I feel I should answer the quite fundamental question of why this was the case. The answer is rather complex, because references to "the old ways" fulfilled myriad functions, which partially depended on what was being described with the adjective *dawny*. For sure, this could not be attributed exclusively to the well-known conservatism of the nobles or blind attachment to the heritage of the past, although these elements could also be recognized here.

One of the major roles played by references to the past, or strictly speaking the search for the old roots of laws, solutions in the sphere of government, and even specific measures, boiled down to what could be described as their legitimization.[25] In this case, the purpose could be to legitimize very specific institutions or projects or to refer to the foundations of the system of government in the Commonwealth. Telling or even model examples of the former function included the intensive efforts to find earlier statements of this type made by the participants in Zebrzydowski's rebellion, who were apparently fully aware that their actions neither fit into the traditional forms of political activity[26] nor were legitimized by the laws of the Commonwealth. Seeking a precedent in history, they wanted to find a source of legitimacy and present themselves as being part of a certain tradition, and so to prove that they were doing "as our ancestors had done."[27] The nobility's rise against the king was commonly depicted as the heritage of ancestors in the writings from the period of the *rokosz* of 1606. In order to prevent their statements from being seen as unfounded, participants in the rebellion referred to events from the past, whether real or legendary, above all the nobility's actual rise against King Sigismund the Old in 1536, which was referred to as the rebellion of Lwów, and also the mythical rebellion of Gliniany from the reign of King Louis the Great, a legend that essentially originated in that period.[28] The purpose of those references was always the same, namely to show that "the law of rebellion is older than the king, *magistratus*, and all statutes,"[29] thereby proving the lawfulness of rebellions.

Importantly, when confederations (including those aimed against the king) in a sense became part of tradition and their legitimization was no longer needed, similar references to the past were no longer as likely to be made.[30]

This is one of the most interesting examples of "legitimization by right of age-old status," but not the first or only one. Even before the first free election, participants in political disputes attempted to prove that their actions and proposals were rooted in the times of old.[31] Such "proof by age-old status" was a very important element of political disputes, an argument that could support almost every claim and proposal. In particular, when a legal, institutional or merely procedural novelty was proposed, it was a good idea to present it as a legacy left behind by and taken up from old ancestors, not only because this would almost automatically boost its status, as I wrote earlier, but also because such references legitimized these proposals by giving them characteristics of well-established solutions, embedded in the existing system for a long time. Besides, this same argument could be used *à rebours*, with the opposed solutions being pictured as having no roots in the past, as chimeras "not founded on any old law," as Konarski wrote about the *liberum veto*, which was described by its defenders as "the old-Polish custom of '*I oppose!*'"[32] At the end of the eighteenth century, this legitimizing function was used quite skillfully by burghers, who turned "the old ways" into the main topic of their speeches when fighting for their rights. Some of their writings, for example *Prawa miast polskich* [The Rights of Polish Cities], which chiefly comprises references to former statutes and constitutions, create the impression of being historical treatises rather than political writings.[33] However, this somewhat lengthy list of the historical rights of burghers served a very specific political purpose – it was intended to substantiate the claim that burghers were not trying to usurp the rights that they were demanding, but rather these were rights that had been lawfully theirs for a long time. This was expected to lead to the conclusion that the purpose was in fact not to grant burghers new rights but to remedy the existing lawlessness. Interestingly, the townsmen remained faithful to the traditional discourse and used it very well, whereas their noble allies, especially Kołłątaj, used considerably more modern language to defend them, referring not so much (or at least not only) to former privileges as to natural laws, which were the same for everyone.[34]

In the examples cited above, references to "the old ways" were fully intentional, with statements being formulated in a way that stressed the rightfulness of actions, demands or proposals. However, what I describe here as the legitimizing function of "the old ways" also has a broader and less pragmatic aspect, which refers to issues that were more general and, to the noble participants in political discussions, fundamentally important. I mean here something that could be referred as the heritage of freedom, which involved showing that freedom was something inherited from ancestors, something rightfully owned by noble citizens. Former, old-Polish freedom was a frequent motif in political speeches from the sixteenth to the eighteenth centuries. However, the word "former" could refer both to specific laws that guaranteed noble liberties and in a sense the true history of freedom, and to the mythical freedom that the Poles had allegedly enjoyed since ancient times.[35] In a sense, the picture of old-Polish freedom was somewhat reminiscent of noble genealogies, in which the true history of noble families intertwined with heraldic legends and descriptions of their mythical origins. It also played a similar role – just as having noble ancestors was expected to highlight the fame and glory of a family and its right to bear a coat of arms, so too did the old-Polish freedom legitimize the present-day freedom by stressing its reputable and solid roots.

Such a depiction was nothing exceptional. Similar pictures of liberties were sketched out by representatives of other free nations, who attempted to equip their system of governance and their freedom with the longest possible genealogies. The Venetians argued that they derived their republic from Ancient Rome, the English referred to the Magna Carta and the times from before the Norman conquest, the Dutch to the brave Batavi, who fought against Julius Caesar's invasion, and the Swiss to William Tell and the Rütli oath.[36] It might make more sense to compare this situation not so much to noble rolls of arms as to the dynastic genealogies of ruling families. Just as rulers justified their right to rule in terms of the ancient history of their dynasties and their bloodlines, so nations that considered themselves free or aspired to freedom looked for the earliest possible examples of their liberties, in a sense also referring to the law of blood, regardless of whether this blood was spilled to defend these liberties or to gain them.[37] The blood of ancestors was invoked profusely in Polish political statements and described with almost the same words throughout the whole of the existence of the Polish-Lithuanian Commonwealth. "Freedom, which our dear forefathers won with their blood, faith, and steadiness and bequeathed unto us,"[38] was described in speech and in writing by participants in the first free election and their descendants in the period of the Four-Year Sejm. Here is one of the "bloodiest" examples of this narrative in the political commentaries from 1788–1792: "we, possessing of freedom earned by the blood of our ancestors, sustained by their blood, brought to us by their blood..."[39] Unlike in the statements made by Western defenders of freedom, this usually meant not blood spilled in direct combat but sacrifices that were made for the homeland and duly rewarded. When Jan Herburt wrote that freedom "which we have thanks to our laws, which our forebears attained not by means of gold or other deeds, but through their valiance and their blood, while fighting for their lords and homeland,"[40] he was expressing a view that would be commonly endorsed for more than the next two centuries, and just as commonly expressed. At the same time, no one usually denied that the age-old ancestors had been granted this freedom by kings, but this was less important than the fact that they deserved it, that it had long been their undeniable property, and that they had handed it down to their descendants.[41] Besides, it is worth stressing one characteristic aspect of the Polish statements, namely the depiction of the ancestors as not only those who spilled their blood for freedom but also as those who built it or, strictly speaking, built the state in which such freedom could be achieved – the Commonwealth. As Goślicki had asked with pride, "What should I say of our ancestors, who devised a commonwealth not unlike the Roman state?"[42] This topic appeared in discourse practically throughout the whole of the Polish-Lithuanian Commonwealth's existence. Konarski observed that "Our Commonwealth is shaped by the great wisdom of our ancestors."[43] The ancient traditions of the Commonwealth created by ancestors were described by Wielhorski[44] and mentioned, albeit casually, by participants in the discussions in the period of the Four-Year Sejm. However, in that period, or essentially from the mid-seventeenth century onwards, this was merely a thoughtlessly repeated platitude, a manifestation of pride in the excellent work of ancestors.[45]

Such undertones can likewise be found in the quote from Goślicki's work. In the eyes of his contemporaries, similar references were always a source of pride, and they also carried much greater importance – they were an argument in favor of a specific political concept and even a tool for creating a certain vision of the Commonwealth. In this sense, not only had the Commonwealth existed in a specific shape for a long time but also this shape was given to it not by rulers but by the predecessors of the current participants in political life. "Our ancestors, when establishing the Commonwealth..." was one of the most popular phrases starting political deliberations in the period of the first interregna or Zebrzydowski's rebellion. "About the shape and foundations of our Christian and free Commonwealth, we should know how they were established by our forebears and what order they established in it," an anonymous senator[46] lectured his readers, turning the picture of the Commonwealth as a legacy left behind by ancestors into the main topic of his treatise. After King Sigismund Augustus's death, this topic was clearly present, albeit less conspicuously, in pre-election political commentaries, whose authors constantly mentioned their ancestors and eagerly repeated that "our ancestors [...] left us *moratam et bene constitutam Rempublicam.*"[47] Here, we can hear undertones of pride in the deeds of these ancestors. However, we can also get the impression that the authors of these statements wanted to legitimize the form of the Commonwealth, which they had also helped establish, by giving it attributes characteristic of "the old ways," something that was on the one hand time-proven and on the other one owned by them as rightful heirs to the creators of the Commonwealth.

Over time, the role of such references diminished. Radical changes in the sphere of government were no longer made, so there was no need to support them with the "proof by age-old status." More importantly, no one had any doubt that the Commonwealth was owned by the noble citizens. The arguments that "our ancestors wanted to have *eum statum Reipublicae*"[48] and "such was the acumen of our ancestors in the establishment of this Commonwealth"[49] were still popular and started to be used in discussions on specific solutions in the sphere of government, even specific laws. In such disputes, however, those arguments were used to bolster the speaker/writer's own opinion with the authority of ancestors, not to stress the fact that they were the ones who created the Commonwealth. Gradually, the perspective started to change – instead of stressing that the Commonwealth was created by their ancestors, authors started to complain that this work had been squandered to a smaller or greater extent and should be restored to its former form.

This leads us to another important issue related to the role of "the old ways" and "the times of old" in the Commonwealth. In the political discourse, the Commonwealth was pictured as a legacy that was not only left behind by ancestors but also should be passed down to the next generations. In 1573, a participant in the pre-election discussions appealed to nobles, arguing that they should "love themselves, their children and offspring, and consult about this in concord and love, to pass down the whole *Rzeczpospolita,* the laws and freedoms, such as we ourselves took from our forebears…"[50] Górnicki addressed his compatriots by means of the words spoken by the "Italian" character in his work:

> But because [your ancestors] lived with dignity, they left you this *Rzeczpospolita*. And if you want to leave it behind for your descendants, you need to cherish those virtues that preserve the whole of the *Rzeczpospolita* and ensure its good fortune.[51]

In 1652, Adam Kisiel, in the face of the growing danger posed by the Cossacks, appealed to his compatriots: "And we, as we have taken the kind homeland and freedom *a maioribus nostris,* so with glory and with eternal memory *trademus posteritati nostrae, auream non latericiam Rempublicam Polonam.*"[52] In 1790, Adam Wawrzyniec Rzewuski was apparently asserting the same thing, albeit with somewhat different words: "I want my homeland to be as free and independent when I turn it over to my descendants as it was when I received it from my ancestors."[53]

I used the word "apparently," because the role played in discourse by this concern for the legacy left behind by the ancestors changed slightly over time. Essentially all of the passages quoted above, which date from the sixteenth century and the first half of the seventeenth, combine the imperative of concern for the heritage of the past with a call to action – prudent deliberations on the future of the homeland and its defense, the restoration of the ancestors' virtues, and finally (in the case of participants in rebellions) a fight for the former form of the Commonwealth. Being an heir to and simultaneously a depositary of the former *Rzeczpospolita* was linked to the imperative of action. Similar descriptions did not disappear entirely later on, but they came to be found in discourse much less frequently. They were sometimes evident in the eighteenth century, but generally in speeches by authors who stressed the need for political reform, such as Konarski, who appealed to his readers: "will you withstand it, to watch with indifferent eye and frigid heart at the demise of this free government in your hands, which your ancestors left to you?"[54] However, at the time, essentially throughout the whole of the eighteenth century, showing concern for the legacy left behind by ancestors – which was much more frequently represented as being freedom, than the Commonwealth itself – was expected to entail not taking action but actually refraining from acting.[55] From this perspective, the Poles were merely temporary beneficiaries of the Commonwealth who had no right to interfere with its foundations or structure. In periods of particularly fierce polemics, this could lead to proposals entailing the complete incapacitation of the current holders of freedoms, as is evident in the arguments voiced by an anonymous opponent of hereditary succession to the throne in the period of the Four-Year Sejm:

> because freedom is dear to us and we cannot lose it for our descendants, because we did not earn it, nor did we build it, neither do we have the power to destroy it, as that power is taken away by the sweet memory of ancestors and love for descendants.[56]

As we can see, almost the same point of departure led to completely different conclusions. This is an interesting example of how an essentially analogous political language, invoking the very same ideas and ideals, could nevertheless be used to describe vastly different attitudes to the political reality.

The perception of the Commonwealth along with its liberties and laws as a legacy left behind by ancestors not only confirmed the rights of its heirs, thus offering a sense of continuity,[57] but also stressed the durability of the state community and its system of government, not to mention the freedom of noble citizens. Another goal of references to "the old ways" involved reconfirming the durability both of specific institutions and of the whole of the Commonwealth itself. The solutions "of old" were good because they had been proven by time. One participant in the rebellion of 1606 stated this openly, suggesting the emulation of

Venetian institutions, which ensured a better order than the Commonwealth's system of government, "as is confirmed by their long and unchanged rule."[58] When invoked in this context, "the old ways" usually referred to laws and form of government. Importantly, "the old shape or form of the Commonwealth" was mentioned in speech and in writing as early as in the sixteenth century,[59] sometimes along with the argument that the Polish Crown had "already stood for a thousand years." [60] Incidentally, that was part of a broader issue, namely the overall vision of the country's history.[61] In this context, however, the conviction that the state had its roots in "the times of old" and therefore remained durable is more important here. As a different author from that period wrote about the system of government: "by which custom, and in such order, our ancestors established and grounded the *Rzeczpospolita* of this Crown of ours so well that it has persisted [...] for such a long age."[62] In 1789, an anonymous opponent of succession to the throne demanded, ignoring the actual condition of the state, that no one should touch "these foundations, which are old yet so durable that with some improvements they can securely support the current structure."[63] The fact that it existed in an unchanged form for a long time only confirmed its advantages as well as stability, offering a sense of confidence and safety.

One of the most frequently highlighted elements of the ideology of "golden liberty" was strong aversion to any novelties, combined with an attachment to somewhat mythologized "age-old laws."[64] Both attachment to those laws and the resultant fear of change were permanent elements of the political discourse. Warnings against change could be found in theoretical treatises and in statements made by participants in current discussions. Goślicki warned that "every mutation in the commonwealth, no matter how small, is a thing most perilous."[65] An anonymous senator added suspiciously that "*omnis novitas suspecta.*"[66] "Any change of laws is very harmful," an anonymous lover of the homeland stressed.[67] In the mid-seventeenth century, these views were shared by Piasecki – when describing the Commonwealth's perfect government, he wrote briefly yet resolutely that "we need no change, lest it should be harmful."[68] All these quotes (selected from among a multitude of similar statements) are presented here to show that authors often warned against hasty interference in the old laws and old form of the Commonwealth, and did so using similar words. Importantly, all these fragments date from the sixteenth and the seventeenth centuries. Stanisław Leszczyński's famous statement about the "unfortunate" Polish maxim *omnis mutatio periculosa...*, which prevented a reform of the government,[69] to some extent overshadowed the fact that it was neither typically Polish nor characteristic of eighteenth-century statements. Contrary to some opinions, both attachment to age-old solutions and fear of change were not a peculiarity of the noble discourse or merely a sign of unfounded conservatism. It appears that such opinions were influenced by an approach taken from the perspective of the eighteenth century, when they were indeed a tool used in battles against proposals of reforms in the sphere of government. However, such attitudes and their manifestations in the discourse are rooted in a much earlier period and much broader in scope.

They partially come from the Renaissance-era fears that the balance of the existing order might become upset. Order and balance were some of the fundamental ideals of the Renaissance, also in the world of politics. At that time, they were undoubtedly coupled with justified fears of chaos, rebellion and anarchy.[70] The existing order, especially if supported by old traditions, was seen as naturally better than new solutions, which could bring the danger of chaos. Such order was expected to be guarded by old laws, and this was how Goślicki explained the importance of the maxim *"legum mutatio periculosa."*[71] Similarly, the anonymous author of *Philopolites* warned "Preserving the whole of the *Rzeczpospolita* also includes not altering the rights and laws, but rather preserving them whole, because the mutation of age-old, inveterate things also turns the *Rzeczpospolita* into a mutation."[72] Górnicki voiced similar arguments and also warned against chaos caused by the enactment of too many new laws.[73] The most eloquent description of instability in the state resulting from too frequent changes was made by one participant in the first free election:

> [...] there is nothing more injurious to the *Rzeczpospolita* than laws and customs frequently altered. Because just as a tree which is frequently moved and replanted from place to place cannot take root strongly in the ground, so too the *Rzeczpospolita* cannot be firmly grounded, be it disrupted by frequent, varying changes of its laws.[74]

It is worth stressing that the words of Goślicki and the *Philopolites* did not refer – at least not exclusively – to the Polish-Lithuanian Commonwealth. They merely invoked a general rules that held true for all countries, more specifically a conviction that had its roots in Roman traditions, that the stability of a country and the safety of its citizens could only be ensured through the observance of the age-old laws, customs and government.

However, as I wrote in the introduction to this book, most of the statements centered not around some abstract country but around their authors' own *Rzeczpospolita*. Likewise, the Polish-Lithuanian Commonwealth is usually the subject of the warnings that "the foundations of the *Rzeczpospoita* should not be ruined and disturbed in any way, by the stain of which the whole construct would have to collapse and be destroy'd, thus turning freedom to captivity."[75] It is evident that the author of that statement believed that upsetting the old order of the Commonwealth carried the risk of not so much rebellions and anarchy as the lost freedom and tyranny. Again, such fears were quite common, at least among citizens of the countries that regarded themselves as free. They were rather skeptical of changes in the former laws, which guaranteed their freedom.[76] Although the Polish statements partially referred to the former privileges that directly guaranteed the liberties of the nobles, such understanding also had deeper underpinnings. They were perhaps most aptly explained by Kołłątaj, who was not a conservative defender of former laws but a leading champion of reforms in the system of government at the end of the eighteenth century:

> The *Rzeczpospolita* is embellished by old and unchanging laws, and because it is in the laws themselves that the rule of the free nation is meant to be enshrined, changing the old is tantamount in the *Rzeczpospolita* to a dangerous misdeed, like to dethrone a monarch in a monarchy.[77]

Unlike his conservative adversaries, what Kołłątaj was concerned for was not the durability of the *status quo* but the future of new laws reforming the Commonwealth's government, which in his opinion should be determined by the Sejm. However, he explained particularly adequately why the age-old laws were so important in a free country and why people feared hasty changes. If old laws provided the foundations of the Commonwealth and created a framework for its system of government, any change could upset its stability and therefore cause the whole of the system to collapse. The impact of this vision on discussions on the possibility of changing laws and the need for such changes (or usually the lack of it) was described earlier in this book. Here, I merely wish to highlight that in the context of the Commonwealth's laws and government, respect for "the old ways" which is one of the most distinctive characteristics of the political discourse, had certain theoretical underpinnings. Another thing is that although the phrases used in the political language changed very little throughout the whole of the period under study, the function of this respect for "the old ways" underwent certain changes specifically in this context. In the sixteenth century and in the early seventeenth century, such respect was not always and not merely the defense of the *status quo* but often an element of a certain vision of the state, a manifestation of a desire for stability and safety, a warning against excessive reform, not necessarily in contradiction to an active approach to politics. Over time, in particular in the eighteenth century, the role of appeals to the age-old laws and system of government was reduced to arguments against the introduction of any changes, appeals for a completely passive approach.[78]

It is worth pausing for a moment to analyze what was partially discussed earlier, namely mistrust of any novelties, which was treated as the antithesis of "the old ways." As Karwicki put it, "Novelties, although [only] sometimes dangerous, are nevertheless always suspicious to anxious liberty."[79] If "the old ways" meant stability, durability and safety, then novelty was linked to uncertainty, instability and danger to the Commonwealth. Writers repeated that "the novelty of things is wont to do more harm than good to the Commonwealth and can be the cause of rebellion and disorder"[80] or even cautioned that "the new constitutions are a stain on our freedoms and liberties and the road to tyranny."[81] This conviction was as durable as respect for "the old ways." Until the end of the eighteenth century, authors repeatedly insisted: "The goodness of new laws is uncertain, while the old experience has lasted centuries."[82] Ultimately, those statements could be summed up in the short maxim "*novitates* in the *Rzeczpospolita* are always harmful."[83] However, it appears that those fears pertained not so much to novelties as such but to the change that they entailed. Besides, warnings against change were a lot more common, and novelty as such was not so frequently found in discourse. When it did appear, it was above all an object of criticism, an accusation, an argument that discredited proposals or actions. Such mentions can usually be found in the texts written during current political disputes, where the word *nowy* (new) and *nowość* (novelty, the new ways) were often used as insults. As Zebrzydowski put it, "Those in Wiślica [supporters of the king] found this article so much to their dislike that [...] they called it *novitatem*."[84] It is therefore hardly surprising that participants in those disputes defended themselves against such accusations, even if they were creating a new Commonwealth, as did the anonymous author of a pamphlet from 1573, who asserted:

> having a *bene ordinatam rempub[licam] regni*, [...] we do not wish to create, nor will be creating a new one here: while preserving its old foundations, if something should go fall out of its old construction we wish only to place a counterweight into the old form.[85]

Attempts to defend "new ways" as such were made, albeit quite seldomly. The Renaissance-era theorists of the state did not hesitate to argue in favor of the need for new laws, especially in the sixteenth century, and statements to the effect that "new happenstances bring new laws and statutes"[86] were also found in later periods. However, such arguments were rare, and the value of novelty as such was probably noticed only by Górnicki, who cited popular opinions about the danger of changes in his works yet was prepared to accept them for the good of the state. What is more, he openly polemicized against the view that "any new thing is suspicious," arguing that every old thing was once new, listing the institutions and phenomena that were undoubtedly valued by the nobles, namely freedom, Christianity, written laws, and courts, and summed this list up with the exclamation "how many things do we have in our country that are new and yet good!"[87] Although similar statements did

rarely occur later as well,[88] Górnicki's reasonings were nevertheless not
repeated clearly until the eighteenth century, when those arguments were
voiced by such reformers as Konarski and later Wybicki and Popławski.
Konarski was the most fervent opponent of such blanket mistrust any
new solutions and argued that "to reject laws and statues that are good
and beneficial of their own right, just because they are novel, is incomprehensible."[89] It is worth mentioning that he used the same argument
as Górnicki to defend novelty, namely "all the oldest things were once
new."[90] However, the true clash of arguments, a certain quarrel of an-
cients vs. moderns, though only in the political sense, did not occur
until the period of the Four-Year Sejm. Conservative defenders of former
solutions then "dug in," expressing their aversion to all novelties in an
increasingly fiery way, whereas advocates of reforms started to suggest
that traditional solutions were so bad that their durability could only
harm the state.[91] In their statements, attempts to question the value of
"the old ways" appeared together with the comments that not so much
defended specific novelties as were apologias for the new ways. While
Stanisław Kostka Potocki declared

> I do not wish to disturb the age-old principles of our government,
> but to return to them, not to fill our country with novelties, but to
> comply with these sacred age-old laws, among which a respected
> Poland once flourished in freedom and power,[92]

Kołłątaj urged a reform of the government "which would transform
its whole nature, and which would instill a new character and new
customs."[93]

That dispute from the final decades of the Polish-Lithuanian Commonwealth partially overshadowed the fact that references to "the
age-old ways" were not always a sign of aversion to change. Here, we
should perhaps differentiate between truly conservative appeals for the
observance of the old solutions in an unchanged form and demands that
former laws, institutions, and virtues should be restored or improved.
The latter could but did not have to prove their authors' conservative
attitudes.[94] This brings us to another role that references to "the age-old
ways" played in discourse – this time, they were understood no longer
as a legacy bequeathed by ancestors but as something that existed once
yet was no longer found in the old form (hence, in English "the former
ways" starts to become a more appropriate rendition here). I realize that
this is part of the broader subject of the vision of the past found in the
political discourse of the Polish-Lithuanian Commonwealth and therefore wish to focus on only one of its aspects that could be described as
"the times of old." Although references to the times of old, and especially to illustrious and virtuous ancestors, often create the impression
of serving as a rhetorical background, platitudes seen as necessary to

mention yet devoid of any deeper meaning, the fact remains that what is hidden behind this background is a certain vision of the world, not merely the political world. The times of old were by now no longer the opposite of "the new ways" or change, but of modernity itself, and the adjective *dawny* meant no longer "age-old, and therefore good" but rather "former, and therefore better." In this sense, former laws, former virtues and former institutions did not legitimize or reconfirm the advantages of modern solutions but created an ideal picture of what had existed in some earlier, bygone days, but was now lost (albeit, we should add, not forever). The old ways understood in this way played several roles: they were an accusation leveled against contemporaries, a model example to follow, and a kind of consolation, a certain myth, a vision of a lost yet not so distant "golden age of yore." Researchers have long pointed out that one characteristic feature of that vision was the fluidity of its placement in time.[95] What we can observe here is a clash of two different interpretations of the past. On the one hand, participants in political discussions demonstrated a good knowledge of history, especially the events that confirmed their rights and liberties, and could situate it within a specific, real timeframe.[96] On the other hand, their statements referred to a rather unspecified period long ago in which their equally unspecified ancestors had lived. That vaguely defined period was sometimes identified with a specific epoch, but its boundaries were very fluid and changed over time.[97] Shaped in the sixteenth century and invoked until the end of the Commonwealth's existence, the picture of the golden times of the Jagiellonians remained particularly durable in relative terms. It was used for the last time as an argument in the battle over succession to the throne in the period of the Four-Year Sejm (*nota bene* by both sides of the dispute).[98] "The times of old" could also refer to a period nearer to the authors, such as the reign of King Władysław IV for some of the participants in the political struggle during the reign of King John Casimir[99] or the Saxon period for opponents of King Stanisław August. However, such references were usually made not in the context of a specific epoch, and phrases related to "the times of old" and the Poles from "the times of old" or simply ancestors could refer both to a distant past and to lifetimes of the fathers or grandfathers of the authors of statements or even the authors themselves.[100] After all, what lay at the heart of this reasoning was not a specific period in the past but the belief that the modern era was no match to what had existed earlier, "in that bygone, better age."[101] The clash between "then" and "now" essentially served to show that things were better "before." We could therefore describe this situation with the words of one participant of the 1606 rebellion: "a different world, a different nation, different customs."[102] The same author set the contemporary demise of morals against the reign of King Sigismund August using the following words: "just as was the *maiestas* of his reign, so too was the Senate, the chivalry, the *legum oboedientia.*"[103] In turn, a certain "Pole benevolent to the homeland" lamented, and quite rightly so, that at the end of King John Casimir's reign "Just as before our *Rzeczpospolita* was powerful and menacing to its enemies, so now is it week and scorned by them."[104] One hundred years later, Poniński wrote, describing the demise of the Poles:

> Those who were once the legislators of the country, the electors of kings, the terror of tyrants, the defenders of liberty, the conquerors of outsiders, are now puppet deputies, weak mercenary electors, lords in the service of others, an atrocity of liberty, fearful slaves to their neighbors.[105]

Authors of all such descriptions treated the comparison of the good old times and the modern demise of morals as an accusation leveled against their contemporaries. Apart from this, however, they served different purposes. For the participants in the Sandomierz rebellion, who referred very frequently to the highly idealized "times of old," this was an argument in the dispute, proof that they were demanding nothing new and merely fighting to restore age-old laws, liberties and even old customs, established, observed and practiced by their ancestors but destroyed by the king and his entourage. Similar comparisons played this role also later, especially in the period of heated disputes with the king, stretching from Lubomirski's rebellion to the Confederation of Bar. Nevertheless, such references to the past were often an element of not battles but political diagnoses, efforts to pin down the causes of ongoing woes, sometimes also a point of departure for proposed political programs, which, in the eyes of their authors, were expected to restore the former and therefore better condition of the state. The latter role was played by an accusation that Górnicki leveled against his compatriots: "you have proceeded far from the original order"[106] and Łukasz Opaliński's statement that the Poles "had abandoned the first founding of this *Rzeczpospolita*,"[107] which were followed by the authors' proposals for the system of government. That said, such references were more likely to be followed only by laments on the demise of morals in the Commonwealth.

This leads us to yet another role that the vision of the old times played in discourse: it made it possible to notice what could be described as a certain cognitive dissonance between the conviction that the system of government in place in the Commonwealth was perfect and the awareness that its actual functioning was increasingly far from perfect.[108] Such a conflict could be resolved through the transfer of this ideal in time to an unspecified period in the past, which made it possible to criticize reality without questioning the foundations of the noble community in the sphere of government and also served as a consolation, offering hope that if that ideal was once achieved, it could be achieved again or, strictly speaking, restored. "The old times" were such a vague period in the past that the "golden age" appeared to be something close, relatively easy to restore.[109] One rather late (dated 1775) yet model example of such thinking can be found in the introduction to Wielhorski's treatise. Here is how he saw Poland's situation:

> As long as our first ancestors, inspired by virtue, piously observed the domestic statutes, outsiders were never so bold as to assail their property and liberties. As long as our forefathers preserved at least the most important provisions laid down by the first legislators, their liberty and independence were secure from assaults by foreign powers.

Likewise, he had no doubt that a return to the "original laws" would restore that ideal situation from the times of his ancestors.[110] Whether what he proposed would indeed actually restore the former system was of course another matter.

It must be stressed strongly that the idealized "times of old" were set against different levels of degeneration found "today," not just in the moments of exceptional tensions or in the face of an evident political crisis in the Commonwealth. Such statements were found in discourse much earlier, starting from the beginning of the Polish-Lithuanian Commonwealth's existence or even earlier. As I wrote in the chapter devoted to virtue, we must not forget that the belief in the inevitable demise of morals derived from the ancient times was shared by all the participants in the European discussions about the state, and so was the idealization of old virtues and institutions. This held true for both participants in the noble political discussions and authors of more theoretical treatises about the state. The number of references to ancestors found in discourse starting at least from the first free election (and more probably from earlier periods) leaves no doubt that "the old Poles" were seen as a role model for their degenerate or at least less moral descendants. For the following decades or even centuries, ancestors were held up as "an ethical model"[111] and the highest authority, and the Commonwealth that they created as an unattainable ideal as a system of government. Participants in political discussions urged "maintaining the customs and deeds of those forebears of ours, the shape of the *Rzeczpospolita* which they for so many years sustained and gave to us flourishing,"[112] explained that "there is one reason for its [the *Rzeczpospolita*'s] ruin, that it has moved far from its first establishment, and so there can be no other remedy than to return to it"[113] and suggested "to return to the former arrangement of our legislators."[114] These quotes are drawn from different epochs and from the writings of authors with very different views, both those who defended the *status quo* and those who proposed measures both far from those in place at that time and far from the legacy left by their ancestors.

Improvement and the restoration of the former status, whether in the context of old customs, laws or liberties, was one of the slogans that resurfaced in political statements as a permanent element, sometimes as a deliberate maneuver intended to reassure conservative addressees, often as an argument supporting political demands with the authority of ancestors. We must also not forget that the discourse analyzed here featured a vision of degeneration and the demise of morals as a permanent characteristic and lacked the concept of progress. We could say that the description of political projects in terms different from references to the past was in a sense prevented not so much or at least not only by the conservative views held by the intended recipients (and often authors) of statements as by their political language, which lacked an appropriate conceptual apparatus.[115] That language did not prevent political programs from being formulated in the sixteenth and at least in the first half of the seventeenth century. In the eighteenth century, however, references to "the times of old" were increasingly frequently limited to ethical issues, the aforementioned futile appeals for the reinstatement of old-Polish virtues as the only remedy for all the woes, or at least equally futile laments on the demise of the Commonwealth's former power.

Perhaps those appeals met with a certain response, perhaps the former constraints of the language of demise and degeneration became insufficient at least to some of those who expressed their opinions, or perhaps writers started to look into the future more boldly and look into the past less nostalgically – the fact remains that the mid-eighteenth century witnessed the beginning of efforts to redefine references to the past, above all through the rejection of the view that "the times of old" were by definition better. The first to challenge that belief was Stanisław Leszczyński when he urged new solutions in his *Głos wolny wolność zabezpieczający* [A Free Voice Safeguarding Freedom], stating somewhat ironically:

> It is a strange thing, wherefore we have such an observant *religiose* of old customs in our country? Because if we be disgusted by *novitatibus*, as *in tanta veneratione* we hold *antiquitates*, then the contemporary world needs to be consider'd more, because the further it goes and the older it becomes, much more experience is gain'd, than was had in younger and earlier ages.[116]

Those words were a rather fundamental polemic against the principle of degeneration, one that clearly invoked the arguments of "the Moderns" in France. No one after him made such a fundamental attempt to change the vision of the world. However, the 1760s witnessed the emergence of what were initially timid voices arguing that "the times of old" were no better and ancestors were neither more virtuous nor wiser than their descendants. The authors of such comments were critical of the reality and rejected the easy consolation that "the times of old" had been better, seeing the past as the beginning of the problems that affected their contemporaries. Concerned about the condition of the Commonwealth, Césare Pyrrhys de Varille, a Frenchman serving the Sanguszko family, told the Poles: "your ancestors did not understand what true and perfect freedom was."[117] At the time, the author of an anonymous pamphlet that supported Konarski in the dispute over the *liberum veto* (indeed, perhaps Konarski himself) stated that the ancestors who had left their descendants with such a disastrous solution were not so much more virtuous than their descendants, as more stupid.[118] Over time, such statements were more frequently found, especially among advocates of governmental reform in the Commonwealth such as Wybicki and Popławski, and later among the reformers from the period of the Four-Year Sejm.[119] However, a frontal attack on the conviction that "the times of old" had been better was made by King Stanisław August. Both in his speeches and in the letters that he inspired, he argued that "to seek the causes for the demise of the vast *Rzeczpospolita* of centuries ago, one definitely has to take a trip into the past."[120] Such an approach undoubtedly remained a propaganda trick. Searching for the root causes and origins of Poland's misfortunes in the past, especially in the not so distant past, was intended to refute the allegation that the monarch had contributed to the Commonwealth's defeats. At the same time, this meant a radical change in the political language, with the phrase "as in the times of old" being no longer perceived as a model example and consolation but as a warning, not to say a nightmare: "our strength was then taken away without permission, the army was disbanded, the nation deceived."[121] This gloomy picture of "the times of old," specifically the period of the Saxon rule, would become popular in the discussions from the period of the Four-Year Sejm, especially among the reform advocates led by Kołłątaj. In the disputes from 1788–1792, we can see very clearly the emergence of a new, reversed paradigm in discourse, one that presented the current situation as good and the old situation as bad. "Oh nation, today truly free, such as you have long not been!"[122] one participant in political discussions said to his compatriots. "Who needs to be reminded of the most terrible times, the times when we were made into slaves, or semi-slaves?" Kołłataj asked,[123] and his question was rhetorical, because "Poland has become a province, and its citizens obedient slaves."[124] This was undoubtedly a reference to the real political situation, above all the expression of true feelings after liberation from the Russian diktats, the declaration of a 100,000-strong army, and the disbanding of the Permanent Council, in particular after the enactment of the Constitution of the Third of May. This was partially a propaganda gimmick, especially after 3 May 1791, one that was intended to highlight the advantages of how the old, bad situation was changed by virtue of the *Governing Act*. However, that was also when the political discourse underwent a visible change. "The times of old," even if they did not cease completely to serve as a point of departure, lost their absolutely positive connotations and were no longer seen as better than the modern times only because they were old. Interestingly, "the old ways" remained a value held in high regard, especially by people who were averse to ongoing changes, yet references to the half-mythical "times of old" were clearly less frequent than in the propaganda from the period of the Confederation of Bar, which had been only twenty years earlier. Here, I must make one important stipulation: it was not true that the entire past came to be seen as gloomy – certain epochs still served as a point of departure and an argument in disputes, but overall the age-old times and ways were no longer accepted and admired unconditionally.

Notes

1 Suchodolski (1969, 163–164); Cynarski (1974, 278); Maciejewski (1974, 14ff.); "The mythical base of the old ways ceaselessly accompanies the activity of the nobility," Falińska (1991, 127).

2 Bömelburg (2011, 216); cf. also: Opaliński (1995, 44–52); Falińska (1986, 123–126 *passim*); Rosner (1986, 270–271); Orzeł (2016).

3 Lipski (1983, 77–78).

4 See, *inter alia*, Ślęk (1978); Śnieżko (1996); Kostkiewiczowa (2002, 234–253 *passim*); Graciotti (1991, 144–147 *passim*).

5 Mainly thanks to the fundamental work by Bömelburg on the sixteenth and seventeenth centuries, although still worthy of citation is the quite old work by Ryszard Mienicki (1913); cf. also: Grabski (1976); Bartkiewicz (1979).

6 Probably the best analysis of this issue can be found in Opaliński (1995, 44–52); similarly Lipski (1983, *passim*); Niendorf (2011, 71–99), the latter also including a bibliography of earlier literature on the topic; Łukowski (2004, 161–182).

7 Łukowski (2010, 9).

8 "If then you do not wish to peddle your ANCIENT – without any exaggeration – FREEDOMS, if you still desire to be free Poles IN THE OLD WAY...," [M. Zebrzydowski], *Apologia rokoszu*, in Czubek (1918, 252); "A Method for Rescuing the Ancient Freedom" is the title of an anonymous pamphlet dating from 1733 (*Sposób ratowania wolności starożytnej*, 1733, fol. 170).

9 *Philopolites...* (1588, fol. R 3v).

10 Konarski (1760–1763, vol. 3, 313).

11 Konarski (1760–1763, vol. 3, 314).

12 *Respons na list jednego poufałego* [1668], in Ochmann-Staniszewska (1991, 303).

13 *Stanisław Potocki generał artylerii koronnej...* ([1790]: 2).

14 *Rozmowa o rokoszu*, in Czubek (1918, vol. 2, 129); *Jezuitom i inszym duchownym respons*, in Czubek (1918, vol. 3, 86).

15 Stanisław August ([1766]).

16 *Siedem psalmów, w których wolność polska czyni lamentacyją nad upadkiem swoim*, in Maciejewski (1976, 7, 16).

17 Konarski (1760–1763, vol. 3, 314).

18 Wielhorski (1775, 173).

19 "The old mistakes, that Poland is founded upon disorder," *List posła weterana do somsiada* (n.d.: 18).

20 *List odpowiedni pisany do przyjaciela względem Ustawy rządowej* (1792, 67).

21 [Kwiatkowski] (1791, 129).

22 Morski (1790, 5).

23 "Under the bombastic name of **the age-old liberties** we would have to maintain the old interregna, confederations, elections, pacifications, amnesties, the unlimited *liberum veto*, the power to disband *sejmiks*, Sejms, and if possible even tribunals..." Kołłątaj (1790, 83, emphasis mine).

24 Werpechowski (1790, 7).

25 This function of references to the past, although in sources of a different nature, was pointed out by Baczewski (2006, 51).

26 Opaliński (1995, 66); Suchodolski (1969, 7).

27 *Pokazanie niewinności rokoszan*, in Czubek (1918, vol. 3, 378).

28 Opaliński (1995, 45); Wyszomirska (2007, 74); Lipski (1983, 77); Orzeł (2016, 338).

29 *Natura albo definitio rokoszu*, in Czubek (1918, vol. 2, 413).

30 Although the Gliniany myth continued to live a life of its own, cf. Orzeł (2016, 332–387).

31 For example, the author of one of the pamphlets, after describing his proposals for how the selection of a king should be organized, summed things up as follows: "there will be a free election, *legitima*, decent, appropriate, and bequeathed to us by our dear, virtuous forebears, our simple Poles," *Iż na społecznym zjeździe...* in Czubek (1906, 239).

32 Konarski (1760–1763, vol. 2, 111); *Dyskurs o eksorbitancyjach* [1668], in Ochmann-Staniszewska (1991, 344).

33 *Prawa miast polskich do władzy prawodawczej, wykonywającej i sądowniczej*, [1789], in *Materiały do dziejów Sejmu Czteroletniego* (1959, vol. 2, 269–300); on the role of using the age-old status argument in propaganda on behalf of the burghers' cause, cf. Zienkowska (1976, 78).

34 Grześkowiak-Krwawicz (2000a: 164–165).

35 More broadly: Grześkowiak-Krwawicz (2006, part 1, chapter 1, *Historia wolności polskiej* and part VI: *Mity i rozterki wolności*, 306–314); Łukowski (2004, 161ff; 2010, 14–16).

36 Haitsma Mulier (1980, 5); Gaeta (1961, 60); Van Gelderen (1996, 100); Pallister (1971, 2, 5 *passim*); Im Hof (1991).

37 Koenigsberger (1997, 44–45); Pallister (1971, 45).

38 *Iż na społecznym zjeździe...* in Czubek (1906, 245).

39 *Myśli patriotyczno-polityczne...* ([1788], 6); cf. Łukowski (2004, 169).

40 Herburt (1570, fol. A4v).

41 Greater stress was sometimes laid on the role of rulers by authors who were advocates of strengthening the monarch's power, such as Łukasz Opaliński, who maintained that freedom had been attained not through the merits of ancestors, but rather "by the grace of kings, or by [their] inattention," *Rozmowa plebana z ziemianinem* [1641], in Opaliński (1938, 10).

42 Goślicki (1568, fol. 30).

43 Konarski (1733, 7).

44 Wielhorski (1775), a work that is essentially wholly based on that premise.

45 An interesting and thorough analysis of the function of appeals to ancestors in eighteenth-century statements can be found in Łukowski (2004, 169ff.).

46 *Senatora anonima deliberacyje o królu, panach, radzie i urzędnikach, sejmie i bezkrólewiu* [1569], in Ulanowski (1921, 113).

47 *Iż na społecznym zjeździe...* in Czubek (1906, 239).

48 *Respons wolnego szlachcica na list senatora jednego de data 20 Decembris 1665*, in Ochmann-Staniszewska (1991, 110).

49 Lubomirski ([1666], 64).
50 *Napominanie braciej stanu rycerskiego*, in Czubek (1906, 251).
51 Ł. Górnicki, *Rozmowa Polaka z Włochem o wolnościach i prawach polskich* [1616], in Górnicki (1961, 453).
52 [A. Kisiel], *Rada jednego z obywatelów, zacnego człowieka, w punktach ad considerationem Reipublicae podana* [1652], in Ochmann-Staniszewska (1989, 104).
53 A. W. Rzewuski (1790, part 1, 48).
54 Konarski (1760–1763, vol. 1, 175).
55 Łukowski (2004, 169).
56 *Sukcesyja lub elekcyja czyli zdanie wolnego Polaka niewoli znać niechcącego* (1790, 14); more broadly Grześkowiak-Krwawicz (2006, 312–313).
57 In Andrzej Lipski's opinion, this was an expression of faith "in a certain kind of intergenerational unity, significantly more alive in the sixteenth and seventeenth centuries than at present, and in the connectedness of the actions of past generations with those of contemporary ones," Lipski (1983, 85).
58 *Rokosz jaki ma być*, in Czubek (1918, vol. 3, 827).
59 [J. D. Solikowski], *Rozsądek o warszawskich sprawach na elekcyjej do koronacyjej należący*, in Czubek (1906, 580).
60 *De electione novi regis*, in Czubek (1906, 397).
61 As is considered by Bömelburg (2011).
62 *Senatora anonima deliberacyje o królu, panach, radzie i urzędnikach, sejmie i bezkrólewiu* [1569], in Ulanowski (1921, 110).
63 *Bezstronne zastanowienie się nad proponowaną ustawą następstwa tronu w Polszcze* ([1789]: 4).
64 Maciszewski (1969, 164); Tazbir (1979, 71); Cynarski (1974, 288ff.).
65 Goślicki (1568, fol. 58).
66 *Senatora anonima deliberacyje o królu, panach, radzie i urzędnikach, sejmie i bezkrólewiu* [1569], in Ulanowski (1921, 141).
67 *Philopolites...* (1588, fol. P 3v, marginalia).
68 Piasecki ([1631–1632]/1972, 264).
69 Leszczyński ([1737?]/1903, 2).
70 Kąkolewski (2007, 21, 122ff.)
71 Goślicki (1568, fol. 58).
72 *Philopolites...* (1588, fol. P 3v).
73 Ł. Górnicki, *Rozmowa Polaka z Włochem o wolnościach i prawach polskich* [1616], in Górnicki (1961, 369).
74 [S. Budny?], *Elekcyja króla krześcijańska* [1573], in Czubek (1906, 325).
75 *Iż na społecznym zjeździe...* in Czubek (1906, 245).
76 The Dutch scholar argues: "Generally, this conservatism and intense fear of change is considered highly typical of the political thought in the Dutch Republic during a large part of the eighteenth century," Worst (1992, 151).
77 H. Kołłątaj, *Listy Anonima* [1788–1789], in Kołłątaj (1954, vol. 2, 112).
78 This is excellently visible in the discussions of the Four-Year Sejm, 1788–1792.
79 S. Dunin Karwicki, *O poprawie Rzeczypospolitej*, in Karwicki (1992, 101).
80 *Philopolites...* (1588, fol. P 3v).
81 *Zdanie względem wyboru króla*, in Czubek (1906, 432).
82 Kurzeniecki ([1774], no pagination).
83 *Respons na list jednego poufałego* [1668], in Ochmann-Staniszewska (1991, 303).
84 [M. Zebrzydowski], *Apologia abo sprawota szlchacica polskiego na rokoszu pro 6 Augusti in Anno 1606*, in Czubek (1918, vol. 3, 221).
85 *Naprawa Rzeczypospolitej* [1573], in Czubek (1906, 190).

86 *Poparcie wolności* [1668], in Ochmann-Staniszewska (1991, 317) (the author was a backer of Lubomirski, promoting a whole project of protection against the king's designs).

87 Ł. Górnicki, *Droga do zupełnej wolności* [1650], in Górnicki (1961, vol. 2, 527).

88 "Not every new law is bad. Because all laws were once new," [J. Sienieński], *Responsa na obiekcyje panom duchownym przeciwko procesowi konfederacyjej* [1600–1601], in Augustyniak (2013, 144); similar views were also voiced by Stanisław Kożuchowski, see: Czapliński (1956, 521).

89 Konarski (1760–1763, vol. 3, 314).

90 Konarski (1760–1763, vol. 3, 314) (after Tacitus' *Annuals*).

91 As Ignacy Łobarzewski wrote "all the springs of administration are so ruined it would be harder to remedy them than to form then anew," [Łobarzewski] (1789b, introduction, no pagination, fol. b2); cf. Michalski (2007, vol. 2, 28–29).

92 [St. Potocki] ([1788]: no pagination).

93 [H. Kołłątaj], *Krótka rad względem napisania dobrej konstytucyi rządu* [1790], in Kądziela (1991, 154).

94 More broadly on this issue with respect to the sixteenth century and the execution of laws, cf. Grzybowski (1959, 239–245).

95 Falińska (1986, 119); Lipski (1983, 82).

96 Łukowski (2004, 167ff.).

97 The fluidity of the boundaries of the "golden age" is pointed out by Szczerbicka-Ślęk (1975, 229); Śnieżko (1996, 72).

98 Grześkowiak-Krwawicz (2000a: 258).

99 The best example here is Lubomirski, for whom the ideal times lasted until the moment when he ran into trouble, Lubomirski ([1666]: 3, 6).

100 As Fredro wrote: "remembering the Sejms from twenty-some years ago, the deputies *graves consilio uti patres* were of great solemnity and of undoubtable and unbreakable virtue [...]. Now customs are already different," A. M. Fredro, *List do poufałego przyjaciela* [1667], in Ochmann-Staniszewska (1991, 238).

101 *Rozmowa o rokoszu*, in Czubek (1918, vol. 2, 116).

102 *Rozmowa o rokoszu*, in Czubek (1918, vol. 2, 128).

103 Ibidem.

104 *Zdanie jednego Polaka ojczyźnie swej przychylnego o teraźniejszym jej niebezpieczeństwie* [1667], in Ochmann-Staniszewska (1991, 201).

105 [Poniński] (1763, 196).

106 Ł. Górnicki, *Rozmowa Polaka z Włochem o wolnościach i prawach polskich* [1616], in Górnicki (1961, 464).

107 *Rozmowa plebana z ziemianinem* [1641], in Opaliński (1938, 9).

108 This cognitive dissonance has been pointed out by researchers for a long time, cf. Hernas (1974, 7); Rosner (1986, 270).

109 I have written about this with respect to the "old liberty": Grześkowiak-Krwawicz (2006, 308).

110 Wielhorski (1775, IX).

111 "Ethics, drawing norms and criteria from the lives of forebears," Suchodolski (1969, 10).

112 [Grabowski?] (1589/1859, 18).

113 *Rozmowa plebana z ziemianinem* [1641], in Opaliński (1938, 16).

114 [Czapski] ([1787]: fol. A 8).

115 The projection into the past of solutions considered to be ideal in belletristic literature was pointed out by Ślęk (1978, 84–85); cf. also Śnieżko (1996, 80).

116 Leszczyński ([1737?]/1903, 5).
117 Pyrrhys de Varille (1764, 64).
118 [Konarski?] ([1764], no pagination).
119 As *pars pro toto* of these opinions, it is worth citing here the statement by
     Konstantyn Bogusławski on the consequences of poor education:

> From thence the disgust in people towards anything that distances them
> from those principles to which they are accustomed. From thence the
> uncomprehending and abject respect for all of antiquity, for the worst
> laws of our forebears. From thence the apprehension when they are of-
> fered new, most advantageous changes, or the best projects.
>
> Bogusławski (1786, 29ff.)

120 *List obywatela do wszystkich stanów Rzeczypospolitej Polskiej...* (1776,
     1); similarly, *Suum cuique* ([1771?], fol. A1 *passim*), both of these written
     if not by the hand of the king, then definitely at royal inspiration.
121 *Suum cuique* ([1771?], fol. A 2).
122 [Taszycki] (1790, 9).
123 Kołłątaj (1790, 46).
124 Jezierski ([1790]: 8).

9 In Conclusion, What Concepts Were Absent? Property

So far, I have been discussing the concepts and ideas comprising the political discourse of the Polish-Lithuanian Commonwealth. However, as I close the book, I would like to consider for a moment certain concepts that were excluded from this discourse. This is all the more important in that the absence of certain ideas can shape a discourse just as significantly as the presence of others.

I have already mentioned some of the terms that were lacking, for example, "sovereignty." Although the idea does appear in Polish political writings as early as the sixteenth century,[1] and it was a powerful presence as a conviction of the superiority of the nobility over the monarch since the early seventeenth century, the concept of "sovereignty" in its modern sense, as defined by Jean Bodin as a supreme, perpetual and indivisible power, did not enter the discourse of the Polish-Lithuanian Commonwealth, which remained dominated by the tripartite vision of a mixed system.[2] This would not shift until the 1770s, with the adaptation of the concept of the social contract.[3] In a way, this meant that Polish discourse and the Polish way of thinking about the state omitted the stage of identifying sovereignty with absolute power held by the monarch, such that it entered political language at a time when the concept of sovereignty of the people was already widely recognized in Europe. This was linked with another absence: that of the concept of delegation of power. While the issue was noted by authors writing during the Renaissance,[4] it did not remain a subject of reflection for long, soon disappearing from the political language entirely; it first returned in the writings of Stanisław Konarski,[5] and finally became entrenched during the Four-Year Sejm.[6]

Another conspicuous absence in the political discourse of the Polish-Lithuanian nobility was a concept of "the state" (państwo).[7] Naturally the word had been in use since at least the sixteenth century and the term never disappeared from the language or the political discourse; however, "the state" did not encompass the idea of a certain impersonal legal and political construct remaining above and beyond the individuals comprising society. This idea, clearly defined by Hobbes and expanded upon by Western theorists of the state in the seventeenth and eighteenth centuries, was in popular use by participants in political discourse in many countries in Europe until at least the end of the seventeenth century. Timid attempts to introduce such an understanding of the state in Poland can first be noted in the late eighteenth century, and they remained largely unsuccessful.

Both of these concepts are fundamental, and their absence from political language shaped the discourse as well as the way the state, society and power were perceived. Although both issues were mentioned at various places in previous chapters, they certainly deserve deeper analysis. However, here in this chapter, we will focus instead on a different concept that was long absent from the political discourse of the Polish-Lithuanian Commonwealth, one whose absence seems particularly striking against the backdrop of modern European political discourse: namely, the notion of "property." In political discourse in Europe, the concept was fundamental in the vision of the state, society, liberty and power since at least the seventeenth century.[8] The concept of property appears frequently in titles of books on modern political thought – and no wonder, since it was ever-present both in theoretical writings and actual political disputes since at least the mid-seventeenth century. In extreme cases, such as the power struggles in England, it could be said that it was one of the most important concepts in political discourse in the wake of Cromwell's revolution.[9]

This makes it all the more striking that property was largely absent from the Polish political discourse until as late as the 1770s. To preempt any skeptics, I should of course immediately concede that this was not a complete and total absence. However, it was only very rarely, if at all, that property figured in the foreground of the discourse. While the notion was occasionally mentioned, it was generally in the context of other values and almost never served as the focus of the discussion. Property owned by the nobility – their assets, estates and fortunes – was frequently brought up in political discussions as a subject of concern; as something which was protected by laws and freedoms against the designs of the monarch (although not necessarily against the coveting of a greedy neighbor). Alternatively, property may have been the subject of the monarch's plotting, in particular when taxes were concerned; finally, it was something which could and should be sacrificed for liberty and homeland, alongside one's life. However, it was not property but liberty, the *Rzeczpospolita* and laws that were the main subject of such discourse. We are given the impression that while noble participants in political discussions during the Polish-Lithuanian Commonwealth regarded property as important and valuable, they saw it as belonging to private rather than political spheres; just like their wives and children, it was their possession as citizens, and while they might sacrifice it for a greater cause, they would prefer to protect it. However, they did not seem to realize that it was actually an important element of the political universe – something which was already then widely recognized by theorists and participants in political discourse in Western Europe. Its basis, role in creating and shaping community and political significance was simply not the subject of in-depth consideration in the Polish-Lithuanian Commonwealth. This is something of a generalization, as there are certain exceptions, in particular in certain more extensive volumes, whose authors at times acknowledged its significance;[10] however, until the mid-eighteenth century, the concept of property was almost entirely absent from discourse.

One reason why this was the case is so obvious as to be almost trivial; it is explained by Jan Stanisław Jabłonowski: "the right of the nobility to allow and disallow what gets enacted at *sejmiks* is sacred and free, as it is only attainable by birth."[11] In the Polish-Lithuanian Commonwealth, class remained the foundation and guarantee of political rights and liberty until almost its very end. It was not property ownership that determined an individual's legal and civic rights but belonging to the noble class. This is something of a simplification, since not owning property could prevent a nobleman from making the most of these rights – and frequently did. However, it should be stressed here that owning property while not belonging to the noble class did not guarantee any political rights or participation in government, either. In this situation, the two roles of property, as that which gave power and that which guaranteed liberty, which were fundamental to European discourse, did not attract a great deal of interest.

It is notable that the Polish discourse did not seem to notice the relationship between liberty and property. While this relationship was almost ubiquitous, for example, in the discourse in England since the mid-seventeenth century, it was simply absent from Polish discussion.[12] It follows that the idea of property being the basis of liberty was also absent.[13] If the topic was touched upon at all – and it was never the main subject of debate on liberty – it was always presumed that the relationship had a single direction: it was liberty which guaranteed property. As clearly stated by an author writing during the Renaissance: without liberty "in vain would we claim as our property that which we deem ours."[14] Writing about the perils of absolute monarchy, in 1606 an anonymous author laid out the worst-case scenario where the monarch "is free to take everything whenever he wants from whom he wants, and decree what he wants," while the subject must "give that which he is ordered to," "and pay as much tax as he is ordered to."[15] In terms of the Polish-Lithuanian Commonwealth, commentators stressed that the monarch not only "honors lives, wives, children" but also "cannot seize property,"[16] and that he cannot interfere in the nobility's property by taxing it. Łukasz Opaliński described taxation as the "supremacy of the highest state power over citizens' property"[17]; it was only seen as acceptable when citizens played a role in this power, and therefore had the liberty to decide on how the taxes should be imposed. Attempts to disrupt this privilege, regarded as a challenge to the noble liberty, were met with genuine outrage: in 1606 Sigismund III was accused of "imposing new burdens on free citizens, counter to their rights and liberties," "assaulting people's privileges, decency, throats and property," "taking away and wasting our treasures" and "seizing belongings."[18] Regardless how they defined liberty, various participants in the two centuries of discussion on the state saw its relationship to property as running in a single direction, with the latter perceived as a benefit of liberty. While the conflation of liberty and rights was extremely common in political language of the time, the combination of liberty and property – popular in Western discourse – was entirely absent. What is more, property was often described in categories of liberty, such as this sixteenth-century author who gave suggestions on how to increase one's wealth: "without affront to noble liberty."[19] The belief that loss of property was inexorably linked with loss of liberty, while loss of liberty may not necessarily mean losing all property – typical of Dutch and English discourse – was not reflected in the *Rzeczpospolita* until its end, since it simply was not possible for it to be.

James Harrington's famous maxim "power follows property" was fundamental in English political philosophy since its publication.[20] Participants in the political discussion in Poland were not wholly unaware of the significance of property as a framework of political power, but they were a long way from Harrington's vision of the state, interpreting political systems on the basis of who owns property within it. From the sixteenth century onwards, certain statements linked property not with power *per se* but with having influence over it; one anonymous author, writing in the sixteenth century, stressed the contribution of the clergy to defending liberty: "They would say, 'it shan't be this way, king,' because their affluence gave them heart and courage."[21] Another author complained during Zebrzydowski's rebellion that problems with Sigismund III arose because he was a wealthy monarch:

> [...] when our kings were less wealthy, so that they needed us more than we needed them, as in the past, we were respected, our liberties were safeguarded, oaths remained unviolated; we always bargained with the king when he wanted something of us, and now that he no longer needs us, he lords over us.[22]

These were just casual remarks, and the aspect of combining property and power became more marked in the seventeenth and eighteenth centuries as magnates became more powerful and when reality confirmed that property – or, more precisely, property ownership – played a significant role in political life. This was reflected in discourse, for example as a vision of magnates as a counterbalance to the king and defenders of liberties. However, rather than analyzing links between property and political clout, the power of affluent families was seen as a protection against the king's absolutist tendencies. The mechanism was described using the example of ancient Rome by the anonymous author of the apocryphal *Rady pewnego konsyliarza* [Advice from a Certain Counsellor] written for Augustus II:

> as the Romans started a civil war amongst themselves, they brought themselves to ruin and killed lords and potentates through hatred. In the end, the Roman republic had no one to maintain it. And Emperor Augustus immediately stripped them of their liberties...[23]

During the Bar Confederation, Stanisław August was accused of wishing to "grind all the wealthy and prosperous to dust, one after another" so there would be no one left to defend liberty and faith.[24] Our focus here is not on analyzing the complex issue of the place assigned to magnates in the nobility's vision of the state, in particular during their domination in the seventeenth and early eighteenth centuries. This is a well-known issue, as is the fact that they willingly took on the role of the "third power" and defenders of liberty. Their power was seen as intertwining a range of factors, and property – or, more precisely, wealth – appeared alongside family eminence and holding important office. As an aside, although the significance of property/wealth remained unquestioned, it was something of a taboo subject. Perhaps the only author who addressed it directly by formulating his writings as theoretical axioms was Andrzej Maksymilian Fredro. In one chapter of his writings, entitled *Who Can Achieve the Most in the Rzeczpospolita?*, opens with an explanation of the origins of political authority: "The highest authority (*authoritas perfecta*) stems from the family's renown, from the income from their property (*in fortunarum proventu*) and from their judiciousness."[25] He went on to explain how wealth can be used for political gain: "It helps gain friends and clients [...] Moreover, it should also be sufficient for all expenses involving starting and continuing activity, and for maintaining numerous staff..."[26] However, almost no one went beyond these observations.

In any case, as has been long known, the power of magnates tended to be seen more with suspicion than admiration or even acceptance.[27] The view of an anonymous author writing in 1697 that "liberty and *aequalitas* are hurt far more by the renowned and affluent *civibus* than by its own kings..."[28] was widely accepted. This statement made by an unknown participant in pre-election discussions is significant in that it seems to reveal another reason why property was seen as problematic – related not so much to its actual functioning in society, but to a certain aspect of it as was perceived in the discourse. It was about the confrontation of equality and property. Although equality among the nobility never meant equal access to property,[29] at least in theory it was intended to be a kind of equality in spite of material differences.[30] Participants in political discussions were fully aware that the reality differed considerably from this theory. Kasper Siemek wrote simply:

> the beginnings of inequality lie in riches, long acting as a temptation for evil deeds and brash conceit. The rich dare anything and commit many evil deeds when they draw those poorer than them to their side and strive to put their aspirations for evil.[31]

He was echoed by numerous participants in political debates, who lamented violations of equality in terms of both equal subjugation to the law, and equal involvement in decision-making about the state.[32] Their complaints concerned less wealth *per se* than "power," although there could be no doubt that at the root of power lay vast fortunes. In spite of this knowledge and the complaints, no one drew a direct link between property and power,[33] and apart from Fredro's rather banal commentary no one attempted to analyze its role in politics. The idea of equality, present both in the ideology of the nobility and in the political discourse, prevented this truth from being accepted, and even hampered it from being articulated. It could be said that by hoping to defend the ideal, or perhaps even maintain the fiction of equality, it was preferable to simply remain silent on the subject. It may sound like an exaggeration, but in a sense, rashly adding the issue of property into political discourse could have undermined the existing vision of the state and society. This indeed came true in the late eighteenth century, as discussed below.

Until now, we have been examining external reasons for the absence of the concept of property in the *Rzeczpospolita's* political discourse, but reasons can also be found in the discourse itself. As we have frequently stressed, it was shaped during the sixteenth century in reference to classical traditions, filtered somewhat by Christian thinking. In this tradition, property – understood as material goods – was seen with ambivalence, while wealth was regarded with outright suspicion. Greek and Roman philosophies (in particular Stoicism), as well as Christian theology, stressed the virtues of moderation and the supremacy of spiritual over material goods and of integrity over wealth. This was mainly framed in a broad philosophical and moral context, although it also shaped the philosophy of statehood. According to Andrzej Wolan, Plato taught us "that it is not possessing wealth that makes these people happy and blessed, but rather using it justly."[34] Kasper Siemek explained the difference "between the great and the powerful": "we speak about the great because of their virtues, and about the powerful because of their wealth,"[35] leaving no doubts as to whom he held in higher esteem. The excerpts quoted above originate from political treatises with major theoretical ambitions, in particular Wolan's writing; however, they are an accurate reflection of the place of property in discourse. Although it was not specifically about the nobility's property and more about general considerations about the state, if property was mentioned at all it was paired or juxtaposed with concepts that concealed other values, considered by the author as more important. This could be virtue, as invoked by Siemek (and, *de facto*, by Wolan), or common good or liberty.

In the case of the latter, this was something of a logical conclusion stemming from belief in it being a guarantee of property. As without liberty riches "are worth nothing,"[36] liberty was seen as more valuable by definition. The truth found in Aesop's maxim "*non bene pro toto libertas venditur auro*"[37] was repeated throughout Europe from the sixteenth to the eighteenth centuries. It appears that Orzechowski also alluded to these words in his acclaimed text juxtaposing the wealth of European countries with Poland's liberties;[38] a text which was later quoted directly by authors such as Jan Herbut and Stanisław Witkowski[39] or abridged as in *Zwierciadło królewskie* [The King's Mirror]: "While other nations have copper, gold, silver in abundance, the Polish nation taketh pure liberty as its greatest treasure..."[40] The high value placed on liberty was discussed in an earlier chapter; here it is important that in this context property – material goods – was seen as less valuable, as "inferior goods." "Poverty in liberty should be held up above all delights of the wealthy, which might smell of servitude," Andrzej Wolan wrote,[41] clearly following antique masters, and another Renaissance humanist went on to say: "Though liberty may be poor, 'tis a delight above all riches."[42] These quotes date back from the sixteenth century, but this resolute placement of liberty above property remained in place until the eighteenth century. It is no wonder, then, that property was given significantly less attention. To clarify, let us remember that we are still talking about discourse; about the place of property in descriptions of the political world rather than the actual attitude of the nobility to property ownership.

In fact, in discourse it turned out to be not only less important, but suspicious. In part, this attitude was inherited from the classical masters (in the antique and Christian traditions) and their distrust of wealth and luxury as being contradictory to virtue and a threat to the state. It was tied even more closely with a political vision placing the public over the private good. Excessive self-interest, including in personal fortune, was by definition seen as dangerous because it could lead to indifference to the good of society or, even worse, taking advantage of it for personal gain. Krzysztof Warszewicki wrote: "all profit is ignoble, and all the more so when it is drawn from the Commonwealth."[43] The anonymous "lover of the homeland" stated directly: "those who, when taking upon themselves matters of the *Rzeczpospolita*, suffer themselves to be overcome by greed for money, either abandon the *Rzeczpospolita* or bring it into peril."[44] "Private greed" was in principle contradictory to concern for the common good. Szymon Starowolski wrote with clear reproach of his contemporaries: "[our ancestors] multiplied the common good and were beware of private greed."[45] This did not mean that ignoring personal property was accepted or encouraged; after all, its depletion meant depletion of the wealth of the *Rzeczpospolita*.[46] However, striving to amass personal wealth was seen as reprehensible, given that it led to greed – an insatiability contradictory with the common good and civic virtue. It was not until the Piarist priest Konarski noted in the eighteenth century something that had been discovered by at least some Western theorists two centuries previously:[47]

> We wish for wealth for our homeland, but some says that riches would lead to its downfall, as it did to Rome and Sparta's. Yet what do all Kingdoms and Republics strive for if not to make themselves as wealthy as possible? A wealthy state, what even is it? Only people are wealthy. A poor state, what even is it? Just that all the people in it are poor. Because a Republic has nothing if individuals have nothing. It is individuals who must be wealthy first, for to make the Republic wealthy, since poverty of individuals goes hand in hand with poverty of the public. [...] this means the more particular they are about multiplying their wealth, the more they multiply the state's property, since all contribute proportionally to their Republic.[48]

In Polish discourse, this was verging on the revolutionary. Until Konarski's speech, none of the participants in political discussions had thought to frame concern for one's own property as concern for the homeland. However, while Konarski's views may have been revolutionary, they did not cause any kind of breakthrough. There were voices as early as the Four-Year Sejm recalling the traditional juxtaposition of wealth and concern for the homeland, although they were more likely to belong to defenders of the old order. The famous defense of royal elections penned by Seweryn Rzewuski is a quintessence of such views or catchphrases. He wrote about advocates of succession:

> they quake for their houses and harvests, and would rather submit their necks to the yoke of monarchy voluntarily than have the courage to defend liberty, and during an interregnum put everything to an uncertain fate, everything that luxury combined with delight have stashed and hoarded in their homes.[49]

This text was demagogy in its purest sense, but it is hard to deny that the author was recalling former traditions of thinking and speaking about property, where the point of pride was not amassing wealth but rather losing it for the good of the *Rzeczpospolita* or liberty. A participant in the first free election wrote: "those who amass wealth at this time when good, true sons of the homeland are fighting for the *Rzeczpospolita*, shedding their own feathers, are self-serving."[50]

This benchmark of a citizen who, rather than worrying about his own property, was prepared to sacrifice it for his homeland or for liberty, dominated the discourse for a long time. Dating back to ancient Roman traditions, it was a permanent fixture of Polish discourse. Speakers frequently recalled Manius Curius Dentatus: "May that I become poor as ye see me for the kind homeland; I wish not for gold, but for it not to be injured in any way."[51] Wishing to highlight their own or their political allies' virtues, participants in political debates were quick to point out any blood they had shed and any material losses incurred for the homeland. Jerzy Lubomirski wrote about his father: "whatsoever he had of health and fortune, he saw none as his own but devoted them to the good of the homeland..."[52] Authors presented specific examples of sacrifice of property for the common good: one of Mikołaj Zebrzydowski's defenders stated that if the Kraków voivode "ever lost anything of the fortune bequeathed unto him by his parents, it was not on trivialities [...] but lost it by serving his Lords and the *Rzeczpospolita* at all times."[53] Even more frequently, authors described sacrifices made generally by "noble houses" or forebears, who "for the glory and protection of their Lords and for a good, safe homeland found it easy to give up not just levies but their entire fortunes, to spill blood and die savagely."[54] This also brought up the topic of those who "gave up their *patrimonia* and other property and regretted none of it [...] having lost them for their beloved homeland"[55] – that is, the nobility who had fallen on hard times by serving their homeland. A poor but virtuous citizen is a common theme appearing in political statements until as late as the Four-Year Sejm. A typical statement might be: "The fortune my ancestors bequeathed to me is only liberty, the knowledge to respect it, hatred for tyrants, love for my homeland."[56]

However, by the late 1780s, the place of property in discourse had undergone a major shift. First and foremost, it was no longer presented simply as wealth, excess or fortune held by the nobility, but as property itself: an important element of the political world no longer confined to the background. Adding property to the political discourse of the Polish-Lithuanian Commonwealth was one of the most significant signs of its revival and modernization, even if those were both late and insufficient. The first commentator who founded his deliberations about the *Rzeczpospolita* on the economy, even if he did not go as far as to conduct theoretical analyses on the role of property in the state, was Stefan Garczyński. Historians of the era had long been aware of the "singularity" of his diagnosis.[57] This was partly due to the clearly "theological" nature of his statements.[58] However, we should not ignore the shift in the political language, resulting from the author's belief that anyone who ignores economic concerns – who is not an "economist"[59] – is precluded from being a "statist." Garczyński strived to be just such an "economist," and he adapted his language to the subject of analysis, that is the material foundations of a state's power. He introduced certain new terms, such as *ludność* meaning the people, population; he also introduced changes to how older terms were perceived or even understood. For example, in his vocabulary wealth was given a strong positive meaning; he even had good things to say about luxury as a factor stimulating the economy, albeit – as he added with disappointment – not in Poland.[60] He took issue with his compatriots not for lacking virtue but for their incompetence at managing the economy. He made it very clear what he thought when he wrote:

> [...] senators and *et equestri ordine* all wish *consilio totam Rempublicam* to bring *ad bonum statum*, while their own heritage remains in a *pessimo* state. They look upon it every day, do nothing to bring it *ad honestatem*, yet they want *consilio suo Rempublicam*, which *constat ex pluribus societatibus repare*.[61]

This approach also became a starting point for his proposed improvements to the situation faced by the peasants and burghers. The important point here is not the reforms he proposed but the noticeable shift in language, taking account into the material factors of how the state should function. Garczyński talked about matters of the state differently than his predecessors – and, it should be added, his successors. He was a highly individual writer and he tended to focus on other issues than many of his contemporaries. What connected him to his successors and a few of his predecessors is the fact that he frequently linked issues of material possessions with noting that the nobility were not the only members of the *Rzeczpospolita's* population. In earlier years, similar links were made in Leszczyński's *Głos wolny wolność zabezpieczający* [Free Voice Safeguarding Freedom], and later in a series of writings by authors in the 1770s, in particular Wybicki's *Listy Patriotyczne* [Patriotic Letters].[62]

However, the similarities were superficial, especially in terms of the political language used. Neither Garczyński nor Leszczyński had analyzed property *per se*, and they barely even used the term at all.[63] A radical shift was not to come until the 1770s and 1780s. In statements by authors such as Wybicki and Popławski, and later Stroynowski, Ładowski and Bogusławski, property became a full-fledged component of political discourse. This list mainly consists of authors of theoretical volumes or even textbooks, since they were the first to introduce the term into discourse. In their case, it also included adopting other terms found in writings by Western authors, such as "natural laws," "human rights" and the "social contract."

The latter attracted a great deal of attention from authors of political treatises who, like their Western masters, set the goal of the social contract to be the secure exercise of ownership and a clear separation of what belongs to whom. Wybicki wrote that the aim of people coming together as a society was "the security of property, reputation, life," and the goal of the state to defend property.[64] Wincenty Skrzetuski believed that the "political community," as he defined it, was created "so that the property, life and liberty of all citizens would be protected and safe-guarded."[65] This view was echoed by Remigiusz Ładowski, who stated that "people living in a well-ordered society create bonds and contracts to protect the greatest right to property."[66] Hieronim Stroynowski ex-pressed a similar vision of the "common contract,"[67] as did Stanisław Staszic, who wrote: "community provides each citizen with property and liberty."[68] Polish adopters of the theory paid more attention to its role in securing liberty than their Western counterparts; however, what is notable here is that regardless of the form of the social contract they adopted, it always included property. In any case, it was perceived not as a result of the contract, but as a natural human right, an "innate right of ownership."[69] Wybicki wrote: "the right to ownership is rooted in nature. Together they took their beginning and their respect."[70] The society and government which arise as a result of the contract are only meant to guarantee property. Stroynowski explained:

> [...] what every individual has naturally [...], in a civil society it all of course remains intact: so human liberty and property in its en-tirety and surety is protected and affirmed by the new civic state.[71]

For all authors presented here property was now an integral element of political discourse. In their view, without it, it would have been im-possible to talk about the state or society, or to describe their goals and functioning. Perhaps the best illustration of this approach is the follow-ing statement by Wybicki, aimed at a potential critic of his calculations of Poland's population: "you might count all that live in Poland and bear surnames, yet I would only list those residents who have their own property [...] Your count would be moral, mine political."[72] For at least some authors (Wybicki, Popławski, Stroynowski and to some extent Bo-gusławski), adding property to discourse was linked to the fact that they were no longer considering just the nobility but the entire society. Even if their specific suggestions for changing the situation of the unprivileged classes were quite moderate, if not to say illusory,[73] the fact remains that they were operating in a completely different political language. They introduced the previously unknown catchphrase "liberty and property" (*wolność i własność*) into Polish discourse; it appears in writings by Stroynowski and Ładowski, and later Staszic and Kołłątaj. It is quite another thing that none of them went as far as English writers to notice the dependence of liberty on property, since they traditionally regarded the former as a guarantee of the latter. Popławski wrote that "there can be no property without liberty."[74] Adam Wawrzyniec Rzewuski was an exception, describing "the right to property, the most sacred amongst people, the only reason for society and aim without which you have no liberty nor security but violation and injustice."[75] The incredibly high value he placed on property[76] is made all the more interesting in that despite the clear influence of Rousseau, he was still using traditional discourse and recalling a traditional vision of a society of the nobility.

The change of discourse described here was hardly common in the 1770s or even later, and it would be difficult to expect to come across references to the social contract or to the theory of natural laws in ongoing political discussions.[77] However, echoes of these changes do resound in them – for instance, in writings by one anonymous author, who hoped to teach young people "what kind of public institutions should be built in a free state to ensure that each and every citizen has full certainty and liberty in terms of their property, protecting them against domestic and foreign infringement."[78] This statement simply referred to protecting the property of the nobility, but it cannot be denied that the language used by the author to demand this was now different.

Property and concepts of broadly understood material foundations of the functioning of the state were attracting growing attention. The late 1780s and early 1790s saw the publication of several serious treatises on the economy.[79] During the Four-Year Sejm, these issues were appearing with increasing frequency in publications on subjects under discussion in the Chamber or the lobbies. To an extent, they concerned the situation faced by unprivileged classes, as was the case in the 1770s. The issue was less about property than it was about the role of peasants and burghers in creating income and building prosperity of the state.[80] Noted earlier, for example by Garczyński, it was now being formulated in more modern categories of labor as the source of national wealth. Crucially, it was becoming an important argument in discussions on social issues, in particular concerning the rights of city residents. An anonymous participant of the Four-Year Sejm discussion wrote: "each inhabitant, not through superficial virtue but the proportion of benefit his labor brings to the nation, ought to earn respect and protection of legislative power."[81] Additionally, as in previous years, the issue of property appeared in statements by those postulating to improve the situation faced by peasants.[82]

The period between 1788 and 1792 also saw the publication of in-depth analyses of the concept of property and its role in society and the state and introduced these concepts into actual political discourse. Staszic and Kołłątaj were deeply engaged in ongoing discussions, and they both regarded property as a basis of life in society. Staszic studied it from a more economic angle; he went as far as to write a great apologia for property as that which would endow the *Rzeczpospolita* with wealth and therefore power.[83] He dedicated a lot of space to its role in mobilizing members of the community: "property and its security are the reason for all continuing labor,"[84] "a person who is an owner does not eat, does not sleep, but works night and day" – in order to pay taxes, we should add.[85] In his writings, this served as an argument to award peasants with at least an illusion of property. However, it would be unfair to limit the significance of his words to issues affecting peasants only. His

specific, almost interventionist goals were always accompanied by theoretical foundations. Staszic proposed a precise definition of property:
"true property means complete power and freedom to use and create
not just one's property, but also all benefits that come with it."[86] What
is more, property was an integral component of all his considerations of
the state, including the economic and social aspects and the theoretical
foundations,[87] as well as contemplations concerning the system. It could
be said that it by then was an important and, frankly, obvious element
of discourse.

The case is similar in Kołłątaj's texts, although he was able to assim-
ilate the issue of property even more closely in specific political proposals. It does not mean that he gave up on theoretical considerations of the
genesis of property[88] or that he ignored the social aspects of invoking
it.[89] His major achievement was noticing the significance of property as
the foundation of a well-functioning free state. He wrote: "All the conditions of free governance come down only to this – for man to be the truly
free owner of his own person and property," then continuing: "stressing
the inheritance of land as the foundations of a free and just government,
finding a dual nature of land ownership: rural and urban inheritance."[90]
Rather than being general statements, they referred specifically to the
Rzeczpospolita and led to concrete and very radical conclusions. The
most important was the belief that citizenship did not originate from belonging to a particular class, but was instead tied to property ownership.
The first to formulate this concept so clearly was Staszic:

> It is the first rule of legislative power to ensure that the law gov-
> erning property is set by all those whose lives and fortunes will be
> ruled by such law [...]. Where no individual holds greater power
> and personal liberty than the law allows, and all owners without
> exception are involved in enacting laws [...] we call such community
> a commonwealth.[91]

Kołłątaj was no less decisive, albeit he was less concerned with theoretical considerations and his statements referred directly to the realities
of the *Rzeczpospolita*. He postulated that "a foundation of a free and
just government" should be "inheritance of land,"[92] because, as he explained elsewhere, "land owners, or inheritors, of whose particular heritage the lands of the *Rzeczpospolita* is comprised, have the greatest need
for government and this government should belong to none other than
to them [...]."[93] In certain aspects, this made his ideas similar to those
the Torries in England, in particular when he stated that only "land-
owners" could be true protectors of the homeland, because only they
would be willing to risk losing everything.[94] However, unlike them and
many Polish opponents of granting the townsmen political rights, he saw
"rural and urban inheritance" on equal footing.[95] Both were to serve
as a foundation of participation in public life and by extension make the

"power follows property" principle a reality, which was in no way an expression of an influence of English ideas but simply reflected a more modern vision of the state.

Based on the principle of ownership, a census-based vision of citizenship would help expand political rights to burghers, but it also led to proposals of stripping those rights from impoverished nobles who did not own landed property. This was postulated by Kołłątaj, who suggested that individuals who do not own property cannot make decisions on matters concerning the community, and not just because nothing tied them to their homeland where they owned nothing, but also because they were not free to make judgement since their wellbeing – and essentially their entire livelihood – depended on others.[96] These discussions about the rights of non-landowners ("the unpossessed" as they were then called) are all the more interesting in that they exhibited a very distinctive clash of political views and political languages – no longer couched in protracted theoretical disquisitions but rather prominently evident in a very concrete political dispute. Supporters of limiting political rights of non-landowners used a notably more modern language, in which property was the foundation of political rights. In turn, their defenders recalled traditional concepts and values of the nobility's virtue and equality. Seweryn Rzewuski's text from 1790 once again referred to impoverished supporters of their homeland; he was also incensed that basing civic rights on property ownership would mean that "to be born a citizen would be an empty feeling and every citizen would feel uncertain every day, would they still be a citizen to-morrow,"[97] while his antagonists would refuse citizenship to "those who, by having nothing, can contribute nothing to their homeland."[98]

It would be an exaggeration to say that the concept of property became a foundation of the discourse of the Four-Year Sejm, but it certainly carved out a place for itself. Concept of property and its protection and security, and the alignment of liberty with property, were increasingly present in political statements of the time. Including this concept in the discourse was an indicator and a highly significant factor of change. Although specific ideas for improving the situation of unprivileged classes and political reforms proposed at the time were rarely radical and often simply timid, the language used to discuss them was wholly different than that used just a decade or so earlier. Furthermore, this language gave at least certain authors tools to sketch visions of the state and society that were vastly different than the traditional ones.

Notes

1 On the earlier antecedents, cf. Backvis (1975, 49).
2 As Wachlowski wrote with respect to the fifteenth and sixteenth centuries: "the literature dealing with this specific issue – although it sometimes realizes

all too clearly the existence of certain attributes of this concept [sovereignty] – did not bring about a concrete redefinition during this period [...]" Wachlowski (1927, 223).

3 Grześkowiak-Krwawicz (2000b: 120ff.).

4 Grzybowski (1959, chapters 1 and 2).

5 Grześkowiak-Krwawicz (2016, 17).

6 Grześkowiak-Krwawicz (2006, 121).

7 It is worth pointing out here that Polish *państwo* derives from a completely different source than English "state," namely from the words *pan* "lord" and *panować* "to reign."

8 Ellen Meiksins Wood's book *Liberty and Property: A Social History of Western Political Thought from Renaissance to Enlightenment* published in 2012, is an important volume dedicated to the subject, and indeed it was not the first.

9 Dickinson (1979); Gunn (1983); Horwitz (1992, 265–297); Nenner (1992, 88–121).

10 For instance, Łukasz Opaliński in his highly theoretical Latin treatise, Opaliński (1668).

11 [Jabłonowski] (1730, 37).

12 A simple search for "Liberty and Property" in the British Library catalog turns up dozens of writings from the second half of the seventeenth and from the eighteenth century with this phrase in the title.

13 On the English and Dutch view of the issue, and property moving to the fore as a guarantee of liberty, cf. the articles in the collective volume Wotton (1994).

14 *Krótkie rzeczy potrzebnych z strony wolności a swobód polskich zebranie* (1587/1859, 13).

15 *Libera respublica quae sit?*, in Czubek (1918, vol. 2, 409–411).

16 Ł. Górnicki, *Rozmowa Polaka z Włochem o wolnościach i prawach polskich* [1616], in Górnicki (1961, 345).

17 Opaliński (1669, 224).

18 [Pękosławski], *Rytwiański 1607*, in Czubek (1918, vol. 2, 160).

19 Grabowski (1595/1858, 107).

20 Ottow (1993, 277–306). On earlier, French antecedents of this concept, cf. Meiksins Wood (2012, 167ff.); cf. also Scott (2004, 116 *passim*).

21 *Senatora anonima deliberacyje o królu, panach, radzie i urzędnikach, sejmie i bezkrólewiu*, in Ulanowski (1921, 140).

22 *Rewersał listu szlachcica jednego do drugiego pisany, w którym się obmawia, że nie przybył na sejmik w Opatowie pro 16 martii 1606 złożony*, in Czubek (1918, vol. 2, 242).

23 *Rada Augustowi Wtóremu* ([1697]: 253); cf.: Olszewski (1961, 55ff.)

24 *Siedem psalmów w których wolność polska czyni lamentacyją nad upadkiem swoim*, in Maciejewski (1976, 13).

25 Fredro (1660/2014, 525).

26 Fredro (1660/2014, 525, 527).

27 Cf. *inter alia* Tazbir (1979, 70); Maciszewski (1969, 162); Opaliński (1995, 8).

28 *Egzamen wolności polskiej* (1697, 414, 413) (cf. Handelsman 1911, 10–11).

29 From time to time, mentions were made of the advantages of greater property equality, although these were not really appeals for it to be brought about: "Hence, in free states, there were always warnings that this should not be private power, because it was rightfully muzzled by harsh laws and statutes," Opaliński wrote, mentioning the equal division of land in Sparta and the Venetian laws protecting mediocrity, but with respect to

the *Rzeczpospolita* he spoke more about the wicked actions of the wealthy than about their property; Ł. Opalinski, *Rozmowa plebana z ziemianinem* [1641], in Opaliński (1938, 22).

30 Ekes (2001, 35–37).
31 K. Siemek, *Lakończyk czyli rozmowa o tajemnicach należytego urządzenia państwa* (Lacon seu de reipublicae recte constituendae) [1625] trans. by L. Joachimowicz in Ogonowski (1979, vol. 1, 173); cf. Czapliński (1966, 94).
32 More broadly: Grześkowiak-Krwawicz (2006, 165–185).
33 The approach that was nearest to the Western one, albeit probably unconsciously, was that of an anonymous author in 1762 who, criticizing the influence of the magnates, and above all their being of the poorer nobility, stated that in Poland "freedom is not granted by law, but borne out of the power of wealth and out of gluttony," *Opisanie krótkie...* (2011, 23, with phrasing repeated on 24); cf. Wyszomirska (2010, 235ff.).
34 Wolan (1572/1606/2010, 87).
35 K. Siemek, *Lakończyk czyli rozmowa o tajemnicach należytego urządzenia państwa* (Lacon seu de reipublicae recte constituendae) [1625] trans. by L. Joachimowicz, in Ogonowski (1979, 174).
36 *Philopolites...* (1588, fol. E4v).
37 *Philopolites...* (1588, fol. E4v).
38 S. Orzechowski, *Mowa do szlachty polskiej* (*Oratio ad equites Polonos*) [1551], trans. J. Starnawski in Orzechowski (1972, 99).
39 Herburt (1570, fol. A4) (actually a quotation from Orzechowski); Witkowski (1609, foreword, no pagination) (who is also *de facto* quoting).
40 [Kossobudzki]/Januszowski [1606], in Ulanowski (1921, 262).
41 Wolan (1572/1606/2010, 79) cited the classical anecdote about Diogenes, who preferred to lick salt in Athens than to live in luxury as a servant of the ruler; this same story is quoted by the anonymous *Philopolites...* (1588, fol. FF.).
42 *Philopolites...* (1588, fol. FF.).
43 Warszewicki (1598/2010, 179 in Latin, 338 in Polish), in the context of payments made for services to the king, at the expense of the Commonwealth.
44 *Philopolites...* (1588, fol. I 2v).
45 Starowolski (1650, 16), here concerning the payment of taxes.
46 *Rozmowa senatora koronnego z ślachcicem*, in Czubek (1906, 540); Warszewicki (1598/2010, 145 in Latin, 291 in Polish).
47 Meiksins Wood (2012, 138 *passim*).
48 Konarski (1760–1763, vol. 1, 134ff.).
49 S. Rzewuski (1789, 10).
50 *Rozmowa o rokoszu*, in Czubek (1918, vol. 2, 117).
51 *Votum albo ostatnia decyzyja rokoszowych peroracyi pod Sendomirzem szlachcica polskiego*, in Czubek (1918, vol. 3, 64).
52 Lubomirski ([1666], 5).
53 *Na pisma potwarzające ludzie cnotliwe pod tytułem „Otóż tobie rokosz" wydane na ohydę rycerstwa na rokoszu będącego, prawdziwa i krótka odpowiedź*, in Czubek (1918, vol. 2, 50).
54 [Grabowski?] (1589/1859, 18).
55 *Votum albo ostatnia decyzja...*, in Czubek (1918, vol. 3, 63); the author himself, besides, was clearly counting on some compensation from the king.
56 *Odezwa szlachcica do sejmu* (1790, fol. A2v).
57 Konopczyński (1966, 143).
58 Łukowski (2010, 58–60).
59 Garczyński (1753, 18).

60 Garczyński (1753, 114, 122ff.)
61 Garczyński (1753, 71).
62 Leszczyński ([1737?]/1903, chapter "Plebei"); Wybicki ([1777–1778]/1955); also J. Michalski, „*Wolność*" *i* „*własność*" *chłopska w polskiej myśli reformatorskiej XVIII wieku*, in Michalski (2007, vol. 2. 130–205).
63 This was already noted by Michalski (2007, vol. 2, 131).
64 Wybicki (1775/1984, 60); Wybicki ([1777–1778]/1955, 57 *passim*).
65 Skrzetuski (1773, 347).
66 [Ładowski] (1780, 64ff.)
67 Stroynowski (1785, 100).
68 Staszic (1926, 155).
69 Bogusławski (1786, 76).
70 Wybicki ([1777–1778]/1955, 18).
71 Stroynowski (1785, 74); similarly, Popławski (1774, 53): "This right taken from nature, which everyone has to their own person, labor and assets, cannot be revoked by any other right of another person."
72 Wybicki ([1777–1778]/1955, 68).
73 As was pointed out in Michalski (2007, vol. 2. 130–205).
74 It is a different issue that, perhaps following Mirabeau, he saw both as contingent upon security: "this property and liberty [could not exist] without certainty," Popławski (1774, 183).
75 A. W. Rzewuski (1790, part 1, 82).
76 He went on to write: "since when a person's right to property is taken away from him, he ceases to be a person, to become a beast, so to destroy this right is the same as to destroy society" A. W. Rzewuski (1790, part 1, 90).
77 Although sometimes such references were made, cf. Grześkowiak-Krwawicz (2000b: 122–124 *passim*).
78 *Kopia pierwszego listu z Warszawy do podkomorzego* (1776, no pagination).
79 See *inter alia* Nax (1790); Dziekoński (1790); cf. also Rosicka (1984), unfortunately a very poor analysis.
80 Cf. Grześkowiak-Krwawicz (2000a, 166ff.).
81 *Uwagi ogólne nad stanem rolniczym i miejskim* [1789], in *Materiały do dziejów Sejmu Czteroletniego* (1955, vol. 1; 116).
82 Michalski (2007, vol. 2. 171ff.).
83 Staszic (1790/1926, 116–193).
84 Staszic (1790/1926, 168).
85 Staszic (1790/1926, 117); He had written about this earlier: "people will labor harder when they become capable of buying their own property," Staszic (1787/1926, 192).
86 In his view, there was no such property under absolutism, Staszic (1787/1926, 118).
87 This is more visible in Staszic (1787/1926), where it appears for instance in deliberations on the social contract, Staszic (1787/1926, 49, 155).
88 H. Kołłątaj, *Listy Anonima* [1788–1789], in Kołłątaj (1954, vol. 1, 290; vol. 2, 301–303).
89 H. Kołłątaj, *Do prześwietnej Deputacyi dla ułożenia konstytucyi rządu polskiego od Sejmu wyznaczonej* [1789], in Kołłątaj (1954, vol. 2, 166).
90 H. Kołłątaj, *Listy Anonima* [1788–1789], in Kołłątaj (1954, vol. 2, 146, 151).
91 Staszic (1787/1926, 49).
92 H. Kołłątaj, *Listy Anonima* [1788–1789], in Kołłątaj (1954, vol. 2, 146).
93 H. Kołłątaj, *Prawo polityczne narodu polskiego* [1790], in Kołłątaj (1954, vol. 2, 219).

94 H. Kołłątaj, *Listy Anonima* [1788–1789], in Kołłątaj (1954, vol. 1, 292).
95 H. Kołłątaj, *Listy Anonima* [1788–1789], in Kołłątaj (1954, vol. 2, 151).
96 H. Kołłątaj, *Listy Anonima* [1788–1789], in Kołłątaj (1954, vol. 1, 296ff.); *Prawo polityczne narodu polskiego* [1790], in Kołłątaj (1954, vol. 2, 222); to a certain extent Kołłątaj fit in here with the traditional conviction that participation in public life should be for people who are independent financially. It is a different issue that in public statements, at least in the eighteenth century, the narrative of equality was dominant, combined with the discourse of virtue.
97 S. Rzewuski ([1790b], 7).
98 [I. Potocki?] ([1790], 5).

Bibliography

Primary Sources

Some of the primary sources are cited under two dates: first the original date (of publication or manuscript), followed by the date of the edited version (published in the nineteenth or twentieth centuries). This convention is followed to ensure that the reader remains well-oriented with respect to the original timeframe of the works cited, while also enabling the page number for critical editions to be cited.

Askenazy, Szymon, and Włodzimierz, Dzwonkowski. (eds) 1918. *Akty Powstania Kościuszki*, vol. 1. Kraków.

Augustyniak, Urszula. (ed.) 2013. *Państwo świeckie czy księże? Spór o rolę duchowieństwa katolickiego w Rzeczypospolitej w czasach Zygmunta III Wazy. Wybór tekstów*. Warsaw.

Bezstronne zastanowienie się nad proponowaną ustawą następstwa tronu w Polszcze. [1789]. n.p.

[Bieliński, Franciszek]. 1775. *Sposób edukacyi w XV listach opisany*. [Warsaw].

[Boczyłowicz Jakub]. 1699. *Orator politicus albo wymowny polityk różne traktujący materyje*. Toruń.

Bogusławski, Konstantyn. 1786. *O doskonałym prawodawctwie*. Warsaw.

Bystrzonowski Wojciech. 1730. *Polak sensat w liście, w komplemencie polityk, humanista w dyskursie, w mowach statysta na przykład dany szkolnej młodzi*. Lublin.

Chmielowski, Benedykt. 1745. *Nowe Ateny albo akademia wszelkiej sciencyi pełna*. n.p.

Chróścikowski, Samuel. 1761. *Powinności każdego człowieka w rozmowie, mianej od Kawalerów uczących się in Collegio Nobilium S.P. R.P. 1761, krótko zebrane*. Warsaw.

Cicero. *De re publica*. Translated by Clinton W. Keyes (1928) http://www.attalus.org/translate/republic2.html

Czapski, Franciszek. [ca. 1787] *Uwagi treść samą zawierające w sobie, przez co nachylamy się do upadku i jakimi sposobami temu złemu najprędzej zapobiegać trzeba*. n.p.

Czartoryski, Adam Kazimierz. 1774. *Katechizm Kadecki*. Warsaw.

Czubek, Jan (ed.). 1906. *Pisma polityczne z czasów pierwszego bezkrólewia*. Kraków.

—— (ed.). 1918. *Pisma polityczne z czasów rokoszu Zebrzydowskiego 1606–1608*. vols. 2–3. Kraków.

[Dembowski, Sebastian Antoni]. 1733/1904. *Wolność polska rozmową Polaka z Francuzem roztrząśniona*. Edited by T. Wierzbowski. Biblioteka zapomnianych poetów i prozaików polskich XVI–XVIII w., folio 21. Warsaw.

[Dmochowski, F. K.] 1787. *O cnotach towarzyskich i występkach im przeciwnych*. Warsaw (translation from French)

Do obywatelów mających się zebrać na następujące sejmiki. [1792]. n.p.

Dzieduszycki, Jerzy. 1707/1906. *Traktat o elekcyi królów polskich, spisany die 19 Augusti 1707*, published from manuscript by T. Wierzbowski. In *Biblioteka zapomnianych poetów i prozaików polskich XVI–XVIII w.*, folio 23. Warsaw 1906.

Dziekoński, Bartłomiej. 1790. *Zasady o rolnictwie, rękodziełach i handlu*. Supraśl.

Egzamen wolności polskiej. 1697. Czartoryski Library, manuscript 191.

Egzorbitancyja powszechna która Rzeczpospolitą królestwa polskiego niszczy, zgubą grożąc. 1628/1858. Edited by K. J. Turowski. Kraków.

Fredro, Andrzej Maksymilian. 1660/2014. *Scriptorum seu togae et belli notationum fragmenta. Fragmenty pism, czyli uwagi o wojnie i pokoju*. Translated by J. Chmielewska, and B. Bednarek. Introduction and notes by M. Tracz-Tryniecki. Warsaw.

———. 1668/2015. *Militarium, seu axiomatum belli ad harmoniam togae accommodatorum libri duo (Kwestia wojskowa, czyli o prawidłach wojny i pokoju dwie księgi)*. Translated by J. Chmielewska, and B. Bednarek. Introduction and notes by M. Tracz-Tryniecki. Warsaw.

Frycz Modrzewski, Andrzej. 1577/2003. *O poprawie Rzeczypospolitej księgi czwore*. Translated by C. Bazylik, edited by M. Korolko. Piotrków Trybunalski.

Garczyński, Stefan. 1753. *Anatomia Rzeczypospolitej Polskiej*. Wrocław.

Gierowski, J. (ed.) 1955. *Rzeczpospolita w dobie upadku 1700–1740. Wybór źródeł*. Wrocław.

Głos obywatela dobrze swej ojczyźnie życzącego. 1788. n.p.

Głosy Polaka do współziomnków. [1794]. [Kraków].

Goślicki, Wawrzyniec. 1568. *De optimo senatore libri duo*. Venice.

Górnicki, Łukasz. 1961. *Pisma*. Edited by R. Pollak. Warsaw.

[Grabowski, Piotr?]. 1598/1859. *Zwierciadło Rzeczypospolitej Polskiej na początku roku 1598 wystawione*. Edited by K. J. Turowski. Kraków.

Grabowski, Piotr. 1595/1858. *Zdanie syna koronnego o piąciu rzeczach Rzeczypospolitej Polskiej należących (1595)*. Edited by K. J. Turowski. Kraków.

Groicki, Bartłomiej. 1559/1953. *Porządek sądów i spraw miejskich prawa magdeburskiego*. Kraków. (1953 reprint Warsaw).

Grześkowiak-Krwawicz, Anna. (ed.). 1992a. *Za czy przeciw Ustawie rządowej. Walka publicystyczna o Konstytucję 3 Maja*. Warsaw.

Herburt, Jan. 1570. *Statuta y przywileje koronne z Łacińskiego ięzyka na Polskie przełożone nowym porządkiem zebrane y spisane*. Kraków.

Historyja polityczna państw starożytnych, od pewnego towarzystwa napisana. 1771–1772. Includes introduction by Karol Wyrwicz. Warsaw.

[Jabłonowski, Jan Stanisław]. 1730. *Skrupuł bez skrupułu w Polsce, albo oświecenie grzechów narodowi naszemu zwyczajnych, a za grzechy nie mianych*. Lwów.

Januszowski, Jan. 1600. *Statuta, prawa i konstytucyje koronne*. Kraków.

———. 1602/1920. *Wywód y obmowa z strony Statutów koronnych od siebie dla Correctury praw sporządzonych spisanych y wydanych.* 1602Kraków. In *Dwie broszury prawne z r. 1602 i 1608.* Edited by B. Ulanowski. 1920. Kraków.

Januszowski, Jan. 1613/2009. *Wzór Rzeczypospolitej rządnej do ciała człowieczego przystosowany, krótko spisany.* Kraków 1613. In '*Wzór Rzeczypospolitej rządnej' Jana Januszowskiego.* Edited by J. Kiliańczyk-Zięba, *Politeja,* 2009. vol. 12/2, 523–526.

[Jezierski, Franciszek Salezy]. 1790. *O bezkrólewiach w Polszcze i o wybieraniu królów* [...]. Warsaw.

Jezierski, Franciszek Salezy. 1952. *Wybór pism.* Edited by Z. Skwarczyński. Warsaw.

Jezierski, Jacek. [1790] *Zdanie swoje o panowaniu dożywotnim i sukcesjonalnym rozwadze publiczności oddaje,* [Warsaw].

Kądziela, Łukasz. (ed.) 1991. *Kołłątaj i inni. Z publicystyki doby Sejmu Czteroletniego.* Warsaw.

Kaliszewski, Celestyn. 1760. *Rozmowa o pierwszym edukacyi celu.* In *Rozmowy w ciekawych i potrzebnych filozoficznych i politycznych materiach* [...], vol. 1. Warsaw.

Kamieński, Adolf. 1774. *Edukacyja obywatelska.* Warsaw.

Karnkowski, Stanisław. 1574. *Ad Henricum Valesium Poloniarum Regem* [...]. *Panegirycus.* Kraków.

[Karnkowski, Stanisław]. 1596. *Eksorbitancyje i naprawa koła poselskiego.* Poznań.

Karpiński, Hilarion. 1766. *Leksykon geograficzny dla gruntownego pojęcia gazet i historii, z różnych autorów zebrany.* Wilno.

Karpowicz, Michał. 1781. *Kazanie o miłości ojczyzny.* n.p.

———. 1786. *Kazanie o zgodzie i jedności obywatelów.* Wilno.

———. 1794. *Kazanie na żałobnym obchodzie pamiątki tych obywateli, którzy w dniu powstania narodu w Wilnie i w następnym gonieniu nieprzyjaciół życie swe mężnie za wolność i ojczyznę położyli, w kościele S. Jana miane w Wilnie dnia 20 maja 1794, a z rozkazu Rady Najwyższej Litewskiej do druku podane.* Wilno.

Karwicki, Stanisław Dunin. 1992. *Dzieła polityczne z początku XVIII wieku.* Translated and edited by A. Przyboś, and K. Przyboś. Kraków.

Katechizm narodowy. 1791. Warsaw.

Kluczycki, Franciszek. (ed.) 1880–1881. *Pisma do wieku i spraw Jana Sobieskiego,* vol. 1, cz. 1–2. Kraków.

Kochowski, Wacław. 1683. *Annalium Poloniae ab obitu Vladislai IV,* Climacter Primus, Cracoviae 1683, liber 5

Kołłątaj, Hugo. 1790. *Uwagi nad pismem które wyszło z drukarni Dufourowskiej pt. Seweryna Rzewuskiego* [...] *o sukcesyi tronu w Polszcze rzecz krótka.* Warsaw.

———. 1954. *Listy Anonima i Prawo polityczne,* vols. 1–2. Edited by B. Leśnodorski, and H. Wereszycka. Warsaw.

Konarski, Stanisław. 1733. *Rozmowa pewnego ziemianina z sąsiadem o teraźniejszych okolicznościach.* n.p.

[Konarski, Stanisław]. 1757. *Rozmowa na czym dobro i szczęście Rzeczypospolitej zaległo.* Warsaw.

Konarski, Stanisław. 1760–1763. *O skutecznym rad sposobie.* vols. 1–4. Warsaw.

[Konarski, Stanisław?]. [1764]. *Projekt do pogodzenia "Myśli" przeciwnych pokazujący jako zgodzić razem cum pluralitate taki prawdziwie wolny głos jaki jest opisany konstytucyją Anni 1609.* n.p.

———. 1921. *Wybór pism politycznych.* Edited by W. Konopczyński, BN I, 35. Kraków.

———. 1955. *Pisma wybrane*, vol. 2. Edited by J. Nowak-Dłużewski. Warsaw.

Konopczyński, Władysław. (ed.). 1949. *Reforma elekcji czy naprawa Rzeczypospolitej.* Kraków.

———. (ed.). 1928. *Konfederacja barska.* Kraków. 2nd edition, 1991. Warsaw.

Korolko, Mirosław. 1974. *Klejnot swobodnego sumienia. Polemika wokół Konfederacji Warszawskiej w latach 1573–1658.* Warsaw.

[Kossobudzki, Mikołaj]. 1606/1921. *Zwierciadło królewskie z wielu miejsc ludzi wielkich zebrane i na polskie przełożone* (Kraków 1606). Translated by J. Januszowski. In Ulanowski. 1921.

Krótkie rzeczy potrzebnych z strony wolności a swobód polskich zebranie, przez tego, który wszego dobrego życzy ojczyźnie swojej roku 1587, 12 februarii, 1587/1859. Edited by K. J. Turowski. Kraków.

Krótkie uwagi nad pismem JP. Wojciecha Turskiego O królach. Warsaw 1790.

Kunicki, Wacław. 1615. *Obraz szlachcica polskiego.* Kraków.

Kurzeniecki, Ignacy. [1774]. *Refleksyje nad projektem Consilii Permanentis.* n.p., no pagination.

[Kwiatkowski, Kajetan]. 1791. *Próbka pióra bezstronnego obywatela nad stanem teraźniejszym i przyszłym Polski.* Warsaw.

[Leszczyński, Stanisław]. [1733]/2007. *Przestroga braterska w teraźniejszym podczas interregnum Ojczyzny naszej zamieszaniu stanom Rzeczypospolitej od szlachcica i ziemianina polskiego podana* [n.p.]. In *Censura Reflexionum Amici ad Amicum…Pismo polityczne w obronie króla Stanisława Leszczyńskiego z 1733 roku.* Edited by R. Niedziela. Kraków.

Leszczyński, Stanisław. [1737?]/1903. *Głos wolny wolność ubezpieczający.* Edited by S. Rembowski. Warsaw.

Linde, Samuel Bogumił. 1811. *Słownik języka polskiego.* vol. 2, pt. 2. Warsaw, oai:kpbc.umk.pl:13062, accessed 12.12.2015.

List do przyjaciela na sejmiki. [1790]. n.p.

List obywatela do sąsiada w służbie wojskowej zostającego. [ca. 1776]. n.p.

List obywatela do wszystkich stanów Rzeczypospolitej Polskiej i W. Ks. Litewskiego. Roku 1776 dnia 10 maja. 1776. n.p.

List odpowiedni pisany do przyjaciela względem Ustawy rządowej. 1792. n.p.

List posła weterana do sąsiada. 1790. n.p., n.d.

Lubomirski, Jerzy Sebastian. [1666]. *Jawnej niewinności manifest, Bogu, światu i ojczyźnie przez… podany…Roku Pańskiego 1666.* n.p.

Lubomirski, Stanisław Herakliusz. 1699/1916. *O znikomości rady.* Edited by A. Marylski. Warsaw.

[Ładowski, Remigiusz]. 1780. *Krótkie zebranie trzech praw początkowych, to jest prawa natury, politycznego i narodów z różnych autorów wyjęte.* Lwów.

[Łobarzewski, Ignacy]. 1789a. *Testament polityczny zostawiony synowi ojczyzny* […]. Warsaw.

————. 1789b. *Zaszczyt wolności polskiej angielskiej wyrównywający*, [Warsaw].

Łubieński, Wacław. 1740. *Świat we wszystkich swoich częściach okryślony*. Wrocław 1740.

Maciejewski, Janusz. (ed.) 1976. *Literatura barska*, BN I, 108. Wrocław.

Majchrowicz, Szymon. 1764. *Trwałość szczęśliwa królestw, albo ich smutny upadek wolnym narodom przed oczy stawiona na oszacowanie nieoszacowanej szczęśliwości swojej*, parts 1–4. Lwów.

Materiały do dziejów Sejmu Czteroletniego, vols. 1–5. Edited by J. Michalski, E. Rostworowski, J. Woliński. Wrocław 1955–1964.

Mikucki, Antoni. 1776. *Krótkie zebranie geografii naturalnej, politycznej i historycznej*. Wilno.

Montesquieu, Charles de Secondat. 1949–1951. *Oeuvres completes*, ed. R. Caillois, vol. 1–2. Paris.

Morski, Tadeusz. 1790. *Uwagi nad pismem Seweryna Rzewuskiego...o sukcesyi tronu w Polszcze*, [Warsaw].

Myśl względem poprawy formy rządu, 1790 [actually 1789]. Warsaw.

Myśli patriotyczno-polityczne do Stanów Rzeczypospolitej Polskiej na sejm 1788 roku zgromadzonych. [1788]. [Warsaw]

Myśli obywatela patrioty nie partyzanta 1776 anno. n.d. n.p. Czartoryski Library manuscript 2619.

[Nax, Jan Ferdynand]. 1789. *Uwagi nad Uwagami* [...]. Warsaw.

Nax, Jan Ferdynand. 1790. *Wykład początkowych prawideł ekonomiki politycznej*. Warsaw.

O polepszeniu sposobu elekcyi królów polskich myśli obywatela województwa podlaskiego ziemi bilskiej. [1788]. n.p.

Ochmann-Staniszewska, Stefania. (ed.) 1989. *Pisma polityczne z czasów panowania Jana Kazimierza Wazy 1648–1668. Publicystyka, eksorbitancje, projekty, memoriały* – vol. 1: *1648–1660*. Wrocław–Warsaw–Kraków.

————. (ed.) 1990. *Pisma polityczne z czasów panowania Jana Kazimierza Wazy 1648–1668. Publicystyka, eksorbitancje, projekty, memoriały* – vol. 2: *1661–1664*. Warsaw.

————. (ed.) 1991. *Pisma polityczne z czasów panowania Jana Kazimierza Wazy 1648–1668. Publicystyka, eksorbitancje, projekty, memoriały* – vol. 3: *1665–1668*. Wrocław–Warsaw–Kraków.

Odezwa szlachcica do sejmu. 1790. n.p.

Ogonowski, Z. (ed.) 1979. *Filozofia i myśl społeczna XVII wieku*. Warsaw.

Ohryzko, J. (ed.) 1859. *Volumina legum*, vol. 1, Petersburg.

[Olizar, Leonard Wołczkiewicz]. [1790]. *Co uważać ma Rzeczpospolita Polska w prawodawstwie tak przed dopuszczeniem jako i po dopuszczeniu składu rządu angielskiego*. [Studenica].

Olizarowski, Aaron. 1651. *De politica hominum societate libri tres*. Gedani.

Opaliński, Łukasz. 1668. *De officiis libri tres*. Amsterdam.

————. 1938. *Pisma polskie*. Edited by L. Kamykowski. Warsaw 1938.

————. 1959. *Wybór pism*. Edited by S. Grzeszczuk. Wrocław.

Opisanie krótkie niektórych interesów wewnętrznych Najjaśniejszej Rzeczypospolitej Polskiej w roku 1762. 1762/2011. Edited by M. Wyszomirska, and A. Perłakowski. Kraków.

244   *Bibliography*

Orzechowski, Stanisław. 1972. *Wybór pism*. Edited by J. Starnawski, BN I, 210. Wrocław.

——. [1565]/1984. *Policyja Królestwa Polskiego na kształt Arystotelesowych Polityk wypisana i na świat dla dobra pospolitego trzema knihami wydana*. Edited by J. Starnawski, Przemyśl.

[Pawlikowski, Józef]. 1789. *Myśli polityczne dla Polski*. Kraków.

[Pęski, Walenty]. 1727. *Domina Palatii regina libertas*. In *Różne mowy publiczne, sejmikowe i sejmowe*. Edited by J. Dębiński. [Częstochowa].

Philopolites, to jest miłośnik ojczyzny, albo powinności dobrego obywatela, ojczyźnie dobrze chcącego i onę miłującego, krótki traktat. 1588. Kraków.

Piasecki, Paweł. [1631–1632]/1972. *Responsum de absoluto dominio*. Edited by W. Czapliński. In *Miscellanea staropolskie*, vol. 4. Edited by R. Pollak. Wrocław.

[Plater, Kazimierz Konstanty]. [1790]. *Kosmopolita do narodu polskiego*. n.p.

Poniatowski, Stanisław. [1744]. *List ziemianina do pewnego przyjaciela z inszego województwa*. n.p.

[Poniński, Jan Nepomucen]. 1763. *Projekt uszczęśliwienia ojczyzny*, Czartoryski Library, manuscript 2619.

Poparcie "Uwag nad życiem Jana Zamoyskiego." [1788]. [Warsaw].

Popławski, Antoni. 1774. *Zbiór niektórych materyi politycznych*. Warsaw.

[Potocki, Ignacy?]. [1790]. *Odpowiedź J. W. Sewerynowi Rzewuskiemu... na Uwagi nad prawem, które by szlachcice bez posesyi activitatem na sejmikach odbierało*. n.p.

[Potocki, Stanisław Kostka]. [1788]. *Myśli o ogólnej poprawie rządu krajowego*. n.p.

Potocki, Szczęsny. [1790]. *Odezwa obywatela i posła do narodu przed sejmikami... 16 novembris nastąpić mającymi*. n.p.

Przyłuski, Jakub. 1551. *Leges seu statuta ac privilegia Regni Poloniae*. Kraków.

Puszet de Puget, Józef. 1788. *O uszczęśliwieniu narodów*, vol. 1. Warsaw.

Pyrrhys de Varille, Césare. 1764. *Listy o bezkrólewiach polskich*. Warsaw.

Racyje przywodzące Confederacyją do wypowiedzenia posłuszeństwa Królowi JM. 1703. Biblioteka Naukowa PAU i PAN w Krakowie, manuscript 1060.

Rada Augustowi Wtóremu w roku 1697 przez pewnego konsyliarza zaraz po koronacyi dana jak ma sobie postąpić w zamieszaniu Rzeczypospolitej i jakim by sposobem mógł zostać dziedzicznym panem Korony Polskiej i Wielkiego Księstwa Litewskiego. [1697]. Czartoryski Library. Manuscript 190.

Rada patriotyczna dla teraźniejszego stanu Polski od dobrze życzącego krajowi swemu publico podana. [1775]. Warsaw.

Radawiecki, Andrzej. 1625. *Prawy szlachcic*. Kraków.

[Radzewski, Franciszek] alias Franciszek Poklatecki, n.d. *Kwestyje politycznie obojętne*. [1743]. n.p.

Refleksyje do następującej elekcyi. 1696. Czartoryski Library, manuscript 190.

Respons Rzeczypospolitej Polskiej na uniwersał i manifest książęcia Imci Franciszka Ludwika de Borbon de Conti. [1697]. n.p.

Rotundus, Augustyn. 1564/2009. *Rozmowa Polaka z Litwinem*. In *Stanisława Orzechowskiego i Augustyna Rotundusa debata o Rzeczypospolitej*. Edited by K. Koehler. 2009. Kraków.

Rousseau, Jean Jacques. 1966a. *Considerations sur le gouvernement de Pologne*, ed. J. Fabre. In J. J. Rousseau, *Oeuvres complètes*, vol. 3, ed. B. Gagnebin, and M. Raymond. Paris.

———. 1966b. *Du contrat social*, ed. R. Derathé. In J. J. Rousseau, *Oeuvres complètes*, vol. 3, ed. B. Gagnebin, and M. Raymond. Paris.

Rzewuski, Adam Wawrzyniec. 1790. *O formie rządu republicanckiego myśli*, vol. 1–2. Warsaw.

Rzewuski, Seweryn. 1789. *O sukcesyi tronu w Polszcze rzecz krótka*. Amsterdam [Warsaw?].

———. [1790a]. *Punkta do formy rządu*. n.p.

———. [1790b]. *Nad prawem, które by szlachcie bez posesyi activitatem na sejmikach odbierało uwagi*. n.p.

[Rzewuski, Wacław]. 1756. *Myśli w teraźniejszych okolicznościach Rzeczypospolitej*. Poczajów.

———. [1764a]. *Myśli o mądrych uwagach naganiających niezawodny sposób utrzymania sejmów i liberi veto R.P. 1764*. n.p.

———. 1764b. *Myśli o niezawodnym utrzymaniu sejmów i liberii veto*. n.p.

Sarnicki, Stanisław. 1594. *Statuta i Metrika przywileiow, koronnych językiem polskim spisane*. Kraków.

Siemek, Kasper. 1632. *Civis bonus*. Kraków.

Sienicki, Szczepan. 1764. *Sposób nowoobmyślony konkludowania obrad publicznych dla utwierdzenia praw kardynalnych wolności liberis sentiendi et iuris vetandi*. vol. 1–3. Łowicz.

Skarga, Piotr. 1597/1999. *Kazania sejmowe i wzywanie do pokuopisaty*. Edited by M. Korolko. Warsaw.

Skibiński, Mieczysław. 1913. *Europa a Polska w dobie wojny o sukcesję austriacką*. vol. 2: *Źródła*. Kraków.

Skotnicki, Bogoria Piotr. 1576. *Politicae vitae recte instituendi, secundum quam vivere unumquenq[ue] et conversari deceat, via et ratio*. Kraków.

Skrzetuski, Wincenty. 1773. *Mowy o główniejszych materyjach politycznych*. Warsaw.

———. 1782–1784. *Prawo polityczne narodu polskiego*. vol. 1–2. Warsaw.

[Solikowski, Jan Dymitr]. 1596/1859. *Votum szlachcica polskiego ojczyznę wiernie miłującego o założeniu skarbu rzeczypospolitej i o obronie krajów ruskich, napisane od autora roku 1589, a teraz między ludzie podane (1596)*. Edited by K. J. Turowski. Kraków 1859.

Sposób ratowania wolności starożytnej. 1733. Biblioteka Kórnicka PAN. manuscript 434.

Stanisław, August. [1766]. *Mowa JKMci na sejmie 1766 dnia 11 octobris miana*. n.p.

Stanisław Potocki generał artylerii koronnej, poseł bracławski do Benedykta Hulewicza posła wołyńskiego, dnia 22 czerwca 1790 roku z Wiednia. [1790]. n.p.

Starowolski, Szymon. 1650. *Reformacyja obyczajów polskich*. Kraków.

———. 1648/1858. *Prawy rycerz*. Edited by K. J. Turowski. Kraków.

———. [ca.1655]. *Lament utrapionej matki Korony Polskiej, już już konającej na syny wyrodne, złośliwe i niedbające na rodzicielkę swoję*. Kraków.

———. 1990. *Wybór pism*. Edited by I. Lewandowski. Wrocław.

Staszic, Stanisław. 1787/ 1926. *Uwagi nad życiem Jana Zamoyskiego*. Edited by S. Czarnowski, Biblioteka Narodowa I, 90. Kraków.

———. 1790/1926. *Przestrogi dla Polski*. Edited by S. Czarnowski. Kraków.

Stroynowski, Hieronim. 1785. *Nauka prawa przyrodzonego, politycznego, ekonomiki politycznej i prawa narodów*. Wilno.

Sukcesyja lub elekcyja czyli zdanie wolnego Polaka niewoli znać niechcącego. 1790. n.p.

Suski, Jędrzej. 1621/1893. *Deklaracyja statutów koronnych o rozdawaniu dygnitarstw kościelnych i beneficyi ruskich* (Kraków 1621). In *Trzy broszury prawne z r. 1607 i 1612.* Edited by B. Ulanowski. Kraków 1893.

Suum cuique. [1771?] n.p.

[Szczuka, Stanisław?]. 1709/1902. *Zaćmienie Polski światu powszechnemu wykazane przez Szczerotę Prawdzickiego.* Edited and translated by F. Kluczycki. Kraków.

[Taszycki, Gabriel]. 1790. *Projekt bezkrólewia wiecznego przez pewnego.* n.p.

Third Lithuanian Statute. 1610. *Statut Wielkiego Księstwa Litewskiego od najjaśniejszego Hospodara Króla J.M. Zygmunta III na koronacyjej w Krakowie roku 1588 wydany.* Vilnius.

Thomas Aquinas. *Summa Theologica. Trasl. by Fathers of the English Dominican Province:* URL: http://www.documentacatholicaomnia. eu/03d/1225-1274,_Thomas_Aquinas, _Summa_Theologiae_%5B1%5D, _EN.pdf Accessed: 22. 01. 2020

Treść pism różnych względem formy rządu i sukcesyi tronu polskiego. 1791. Sandomierz.

Trojanowski, Feliks. [1780]. *Uwagi na niektóre punkta nowo utworzonego prawa i dowody, że mimo wolą J.W. Zamoyskiego musieli być umieszczone.* n.p.

Turski, Wojciech. 1790a. *Myśli o królach, o sukcesyi, o przeszłym i przyszłym rządzie.* Warsaw.

———. 1790b. *Odpowiedź na dzieło ks. Hugona Kołłątaja referendarza W.X.Lit. Uwagi nad pismem etc.* Warsaw.

Ulanowski, B. (ed.). 1921. *Sześć broszur politycznych z XVI i początku XVII stulecia.* Kraków.

Uwagi nad pismem z druku wyszłym pod tytułem Usprawiedliwienie się JW. Dłuskiego, [1791]. n.p.

Uwagi względem Konstytucyi dnia 3 maja zapadłej. 1791. "Pamiętnik Historyczno-Polityczny" June 1791.

Waga, Teodor. 1767. *Krótkie zebranie historyi i geografii polskiej.* Supraśl.

Warszewicki, Krzysztof. 1598/2010. *De optimo statu libertatis (O najlepszym stanie wolności).* In *Krzysztofa Warszewickiego i Anonima uwagi o wolności szlacheckiej.* Edited by K. Koehler, 2010. Kraków.

Werpechowski, Szymon (ps.). 1790. *Odpowiedź na list Imci Pana Bartłomieja Werpechowskiego.* n.p.

Wielhorski, Michał. 1775. *O przywróceniu dawnego rządu według pierwiastkowych Rzeczypospolitej ustaw.* n.p.

Wieruszewski, Kazimierz. 1733. *Fama polska stany publiczne, młódź szkolną informująca,* 2nd edition. Wilno.

Witkowski, Stanisław. 1609. *Złota wolność Koronna sejmom i zjazdom na potomne czasy służąca.* Kraków.

Wolan, Andrzej. [1572/1606/2010]. *De libertate politica seu civili. O wolności Rzeczypospolitej albo ślacheckiej.* First Latin version published 1572, first Polish version published 1606, Critical version published 2010. Edited by M. Eder, and R. Mazurkiewicz. Warsaw.

Wolność polska dla ewakuacyi wojsk egzotycznych, życzy się brać ad arma defensionis. 1733. Biblioteka Kórnicka PAN, manuscript 434.

Wybicki, Józef. [1777–1778]/1955. *Listy patriotyczne*. Edited by K. Opałek, BN I, 155. Wrocław.

———. 1775/1984. *Myśli polityczne o wolności cywilnej*. Edited by Z. Nowak. Gdańsk.

Wyrwicz, Karol. 1771–1772. Introduction to *Historyja polityczna państw starożytnych, od pewnego towarzystwa napisana*. 1771–1772. Warsaw.

———, 1773. *Geografia powszechna czasów teraźniejszych*. 2nd edition. Warsaw.

Wysocki, Samuel. 1740. *Orator Polonus*. Warsaw.

Zalaszowski, Mikołaj. 1702. *Ius Regni Poloniae*. vol. 2. Poznań.

Zamoyski, Andrzej. [1764]/1954. *Mowa na sejmie convocationis dnia 16 maja 1764 roku w Warszawie miana*. In *Historia Polski 1764–1795. Wybór tekstów*. Edited by J. Michalski. Warsaw.

Zawisza z Kroczowa, Jakub. 1613/1899. *Wskrócenie prawnego procesu koronnego* (1613). Edited by A. Winiarz. Kraków.

Zdanie Polaka o wolności, czyli myśli w teraźniejszych okolicznościach do Najjaśniejszych Stanów przez pewnego obywatela w-wdztwa sandomierskiego podane, [1790]. n.p.

Zdanie szlachcica polskiego cudzych interesów wiadomego o Książęciu IMci de Baden, Stanom Rzeczypospolitej podane. [1697]. Czartoryski Library, manuscript 190.

Secondary Sources

Andrzejuk, Izabella. 2007. *Filozofia przyjaźni w Komentarzu Tomasza z Akwinu do Etyki Nikomachejskiej Arystotelesa*. Warsaw. URL: http://katedra. uksw.edu.pl/publikacje/izabella_andrzejuk/filo_przyjazni_ksiazka.pdf [accessed: 22.10.2016].

Augustyniak, Urszula. 1981. *Informacja i propaganda w Polsce za Zygmunta III*. Warsaw.

———. 1989. *Koncepcje narodu i społeczeństwa w literaturze plebejskiej od końca XVI do końca XVII wieku*. Warsaw.

———. 1999. *Wazowie i "królowie rodacy."* Warsaw.

———. 2004. "Polska i łacińska terminologia ustrojowa w publicystyce politycznej epoki Wazów." In Axer 2004b, 33–56.

———. 2007. "Granice wolności obywatela Rzeczypospolitej w XVI–XVII w. Jednostka wobec władzy, prawa i społeczeństwa." In *Wolność i jej granice. Polskie dylematy*. Edited by J. Kloczkowski, 13–36. Kraków.

———. 2010. Two Patriotisms? Opinions of Townsmen and Soldiers on Duty to the Fatherland in Seventeenth-Century Poland. In Trencsényi and Zászkaliczky 2010, 461–496.

———. 2015. "Szlachecki program reformy państwa po rokoszu sandomierskim." *Przegląd Historyczny*, vol. 106, no. 1, 1–30.

Axer, Jerzy. 1995. "'Latinitas' jako składnik polskiej tożsamości kulturowej." In *Tradycje antyczne w kulturze europejskiej – perspektywa polska*. Edited by J. Axer, 71–82. Warsaw.

———. 2004a. "Łacina jako drugi język narodu szlacheckiego Rzeczpospolitej." In Axer 2004b, 151–156.

———. (ed.) 2004b. *Łacina jako język elit*. Warsaw.

——. 2010. "Kultura polska z punktu widzenia mechanizmów recepcji tradycji antycznej. Prolegomena do syntezy." In *Humanistyczne modele kultury nowożytnej wobec dziedzictwa starożytnego.* Edited by M. Prejs, 15–82. Warsaw.

Axerowa, Anna. 2004. "Próba klasyfikacji wtrętów łacińskojęzycznych w staropolskich tekstach dwujęzycznych." In Axer 2004b, 157–160.

Backvis, Claude. 1975. *Szkice o kulturze staropolskiej.* Warsaw.

Baczewski, Sławomir. 2006. "Mit początku i władza szlachty. Dyskurs genealogiczno-historyczny w XVII-wiecznych kazaniach pogrzebowych." *Wschodni Rocznik Humanistyczny,* vol. 3, 37–55.

——. 2009. *Szlachectwo. Studium z dziejów idei w piśmiennictwie polskim. Druga połowa XVI wieku–XVII wiek.* Lublin.

Baczko, Bronisław. 2009. *Rousseau: samotność i wspólnota,* 2nd edition. Gdańsk.

Ball, Terence, 1998. "Conceptual History and the History of Political Thought." In Hampsher-Monk, Tilmans, and Van Vree 1998, 75–86.

Ball, Terence, James, Farr, and Russel, L. Hanson. (eds). 1989. *Political Innovation and Conceptual Change.* Cambridge.

Bałuk-Ulewiczowa, Teresa. 2000. "A Brief Essay on Translation (to those who do not believe in the art of archaism in translation)." In Kochanowski, Jan. *Kto mi dał Skrzydła/Who Hath Bewinged Me.* Translated by Teresa Bałuk-Ulewiczowa. Kraków.

——. 2009. "Z dziejów zwierciadła władcy." In *O senatorze doskonałym. Studia.* Edited by A. Stępkowski, 35–82. Warsaw.

Bardach, Juliusz. 1999. *Statuty litewskie a prawo rzymskie.* Warsaw.

Baron, Hans. 1955. *The Crisis of the Early Italian Renaissance: Civic Humanism and Republican Liberty in an Age of Classicism and Tyranny.* Princeton–Oxford.

Bartkiewicz, Kazimierz. 1979. *Obraz dziejów ojczystych w świadomości historycznej w Polsce doby oświecenia.* Poznań.

Baturo, Eugeniusz. 1958 "Idea mieszanej formy państwa [mieszanego rządu] w staropolskiej literaturze od XV do XVIII w." *Sprawozdania TNT,* r. 12, z. 1

Bem, Ewa. 1989. "Termin 'ojczyzna' w literaturze XVI i XVII wieku," *Odrodzenie i Reformacja w Polsce,* vol. 34, 131–156.

Bem-Wiśniewska, Ewa. 1998. *Funkcjonowanie nazwy Polska w języku czasów nowożytnych.* Warsaw.

——. 2007. "Wizja Rzeczpospolitej w epoce staropolskiej. Od historii języka do historii kultury." In *Rzeczpospolita w XVI–XVIII wieku. Państwo czy wspólnota?.* Edited by B. Dybaś, P. Hanczewski, and T. Kempa, 11–42. Toruń.

Biskupski, Mieczysław B., and Pula James S. 1990. *Polish Democratic Thought.* New York.

Blythe, James M. 1992. *Ideal Government and the Mixed Constitution in the Middle Ages.* Princeton.

Bömelburg, Hans-Jürgen. 2011. *Polska myśl historyczna a humanistyczna historia narodowa (1500–1700).* Kraków.

Boulton, James T. 1967. *Arbitrary Power: An Eighteenth-Century Obsession.* Nottingham.

Bouwsma, William J. 1995. "Liberty in the Renaissance and Reformation." In *The Origins of Modern Freedom in the West*. Edited by R. W. Davis, 203–234. Stanford.

Brugger, Bill. 1999. *Republican Theory in Political Thought: Virtuous or Virtual?* Basingstoke.

Brunner, Otto, Werner Conze, and Reinhardt Koselleck. (eds.) 1972–1997. *Geschichtliche Grundbegriffe. Historisches Lexicon zur politisch-sozialen Sprache in Deutschland*, vols. 1–8. Stuttgart.

Brzeziński, Szymon. 2008. "Tyran i tyrania w staropolskim języku politycznym (XVI–XVII wiek)." In *Społeczeństwo staropolskie*, new series, vol. 1: *Społeczeństwo i polityka*, 287–389. Warsaw.

Butterwick, Richard. 2005. "Political Discourses of the Polish Revolution, 1788–1792." *English Historical Review*, vol. 120, 695–731.

———. 2009. "Spory o patriotyzm w dobie Sejmu czteroletniego. Przykłady z retoryki świeckich i duchownych." In Nowak and Zięba, 2009, 67–76.

———. 2012. *Polska rewolucja a Kościół katolicki 1788–1792*. Kraków.

Butterwick-Pawlikowski, Richard. 2017a. "Chrześcijanin i obywatel w dyskursie politycznym drugiej połowy XVIII wieku." In *Wartości polityczne Rzeczypospolitej Obojga Narodów. Struktury aksjologiczne i granice cywilizacyjne*. Edited by A. Grześkowiak-Krwawicz in collaboration with J. Axer, 175–195. Warsaw.

———. 2017b. "Koncepcja narodu w polskim dyskursie końca XVIII wieku. Rozważania nad Konstytucją 3 maja." In *O ziemię naszą, nie waszą. Ideowe aspekty procesów "narodowotwórczych" w Europie Środkowej i Wschodniej*. Edited by Ł. Adamski, 135–151. Warsaw.

Céard, Jean, 1972. "« République » et « républicain » en France au XVIe siècle." In *L'Esprit républicain. Colloque d'Orléans 4 et 5 septembre 1970*. Edited by J. Viard, 97–105. Paris.

Chanteur, Janine. 1991. "La loi naturelle et la souveraineté chez Jean Bodin." In *Théologie et droit dans la science politique de l'état moderne*. Actes de la table ronde de Rome (12–14 novembre 1987), 283–294. Rome.

Choińska-Mika, Jolanta. 2007. "'Jako miłujący tej ojczyzny synowie' – kilka uwag o staropolskim patriotyzmie." In Kloczkowski 2007, 11–19.

Dzięgielewski, Jan. 2007. "Od staropolskiego 'miłośnika ojczyzny' do 'sarmackiego patrioty.'" In Kloczkowski 2007, 21–32.

Condren, Conal. 1994. *The Language of Politics in Seventeenth-Century England*. New York.

Conti, Vittorio. 2002. "The Mechanisation of Virtue: Republican Rituals in Italian Political Thought in the Sixteenth and Seventeenth Centuries." In Van Gelderen and Skinner 2002, 73–83.

Cynarski, Stanisław. 1974. "Sarmatyzm – ideologia i styl życia." In *Polska XVII wieku. Państwo – społeczeństwo – kultura*. Edited by J. Tazbir, 269–295. Warsaw.

Czapliński, Władysław. 1956. "Stanisław Kożuchowski nieznany pisarz polityczny połowy XVII wieku." *Przegląd Historyczny*, vol. 47, 515–530.

———. 1966. *O Polsce siedemnastowiecznej. Problemy i sprawy*. Warsaw.

Czarniecka, Anna. 2009. *Nikt nie słucha mnie za życia... Jan III Sobieski w walce z opozycyjną propagandą (1684–1696)*. Warsaw.

Dagger, Richard. 1989. "Rights." In Ball, Farr and Hanson 1989, 293–308.

Dawidziak-Kładoczna, Małgorzata. 2012. *Językowe aspekty kultury politycznej Sejmu Wielkiego.* Częstochowa.

Derrida, Jacques. 1985. *Des Tours de Babel.* Translated by Joseph F. Graham. In *Difference in Translation.* Edited by Joseph F. Graham. Ithaca.

Dickinson, Harry T. 1979. *Liberty and Property: Political Ideology in Eighteenth-Century Britain.* Methuen.

Dietz, Mary. 1989. "Patriotism." In Ball, Farr and Hanson 1989, 177–194.

Dzelzainis, Martin. 2002. "Anti-monarchism in English Republicanism." In Van Gelderen and Skinner 2002, 27–41.

Eco, Umberto. 2001. *Experiences in Translation.* Translated by Alastair McEwen. Buffalo, Toronto.

Ekes, Janusz. 2001. *Trójpodział władzy i zgoda wszystkich. Naczelne zasady "ustroju mieszanego" w staropolskiej myśli politycznej.* Siedlce.

Estreicher, Stanisław. 1931. *Kultura prawnicza w Polsce XVI wieku.* 1931. Kraków.

Falińska, Maria. 1986. *Przeszłość a teraźniejszość.* Warsaw.

———. 1991. "Mit polityczny w świadomości społecznej szlachty w XVI–XVIII w." *Kultura i Społeczeństwo,* vol. 35, no. 2, 123–140.

Fink, Zera, 1945. *The Classical Republicanism: An Essay in the Recovery of a Pattern of Thought in 17th-century England.* Urbana.

Freylichówna, Judyta. 1938. *Ideał wychowawczy szlachty polskiej w XVI i początkach XVII wieku.* Warsaw.

Friedrich, Karin. 2005. *Inne Prusy. Prusy Królewskie i Polska między wolnością a wolnościami (1569–1772).* Translated by G. Waluga. Poznań.

Friedrich, Karin. 2007. "Polish-Lithuanian Political Thought, 1450–1700." In *History of European Political Thought, 1450–1700.* Edited by H. Lloyd, G. Burgess, and S. Hodson, 212–231. New Haven.

Frost, Robert. 1990. "'Liberty without Licence?': The Failure of Polish Democratic Thought in the Seventeenth Century." In *Polish Democratic Thought from the Renaissance to the Great Emigration: Essays and Documents.* Edited by M. B. Biskupski, and J. S. Pula, 29–54. New York.

Fumurescu, Alin. 2013. *Compromise: A Political and Philosophical History.* Cambridge.

Gaeta, Franco. 1961. "Alcune considerazioni sul mito di Venezia," *Bibliothèque d'humanisme et renaissance,* vol. 23, 58–75.

Gardiner, Patrick. 1984. "Rousseau on Liberty." In *Conceptions of Liberty in Political Philosophy.* Edited by Z. Pelczyński, and J. Gray. London.

Godek, Slawomir. 2004. *Elementy prawa rzymskiego w III Statucie litewskim (1588).* Warsaw.

———. 2013. "Prawo rzymskie w Polsce przedrozbiorowej w świetle aktualnych badań." *Zeszyty Prawnicze,* vol. 13, no. 3, 39–64.

Goldsmith, Maurice M. 1994. "Liberty, Virtue and the Rule of Law, 1689–1770." In Wotton 1994, 197–232.

Górska, Magdalena. 2005. *Polonia – Respublica – Patria. Personifikacja Polski w sztuce XVI–XVIII wieku.* Wrocław.

Grabski, Andrzej Feliks. 1976. *Myśl historyczna polskiego oświecenia.* Warsaw.

Graciotti, Sante. 1991. *Od renesansu do oświecenia.* Warsaw.

Grodziski, Stanisław. 1963. *Obywatelstwo w szlacheckiej Rzeczypospolitej.* Kraków.

————. 2004. *Z dziejów staropolskiej kultury prawnej.* Kraków.

Gromelski, Tomasz W. 2008. "The Commonwealth and Monarchia Mixta in Polish and English Political Thought in the Later Sixteenth Century." In *Britain and Poland-Lithuania Contact and Comparison from the Middle Ages to 1795.* Edited by R. Unger with the assistance of J. Basista, 165–182. Leiden–Boston.

————. 2013. "Liberty and Liberties in Early Modern Poland-Lithuania." In *Freedom and the Construction of Europe.* Vol. 1: *Religious Freedom and Civil Liberty.* Edited by Q. Skinner, and M. Van Gelderen, 215–234. Cambridge.

Grześkowiak-Krwawicz, Anna. 1992b. "Klasyfikacja form rządów w literaturze politycznej czasów stanisławowskich." In *Studia z dziejów polskiej myśli politycznej, vol.* 4: *Od reformy państwa szlacheckiego do myśli o nowoczesnym państwie.* Edited by J. Staszewski, 47–61. Toruń.

————. 1994–1995. "Z dziejów terminologii politycznej czasów stanisławowskich." *Teki Historyczne.* Vol. 21, 84–94. London.

————. 1994. "Rara avis czy wolni wśród wolnych? Obraz krajów wolnych w polskiej literaturze politycznej XVIII wieku." In *Trudne stulecia. Studia z dziejów XVII i XVIII wieku ofiarowane profesorowi Jerzemu Michalskiemu w siedemdziesiątą rocznicę urodzin.* Edited by Ł. Kądziela, W. Kriegseisen, and Z. Zielińska, 167–183. Warsaw.

————. 1995. Zdrada 3 Maja? Ustawa Rządowa w opiniach malkontentów. In *Bo insza jest rzecz zdradzić. Insza dać się złudzić. Problem zdrady w Polsce przełomu XVIII i XIX w..* Edited by Anna Grześkowiak-Krwawicz. Warsaw. 49–70.

————. 1999. U początków czarnej i białej legendy Stanisława Augusta, *Wiek Oświecenia*, 15. 165–183.

————. 2000a. *O formę rządu czy o rząd dusz? Publicystyka polityczna Sejmu Czteroletniego.* Warsaw.

————. 2000b. "O recepcji idei umowy społecznej w czasach stanisławowskich." *Czasopismo Prawno-Historyczne*, vol. 52, no. 1–2, 109–126.

————. 2002. "Anti-monarchism in Polish Republicanism in the Seventeenth and Eighteeenth Centuries." In Van Gelderen and Skinner 2002, 147–166.

————. 2003. "Czy król potrzebny jest w republice? Polscy pisarze polityczni wieku XVIII o miejscu i roli monarchy w Rzeczypospolitej. Zarys problematyki." In *Dwór a kraj między centrum a peryferiami władzy.* Edited by R. Skowron, 467–485. Kraków.

————. 2004. Veto – wolność – władza w polskiej myśli politycznej wieku XVIII, *Kwartalnik Historyczny*, vol. 111, no. 3, 141–160.

————. 2006. *Regina libertas. Wolność w polskiej myśli politycznej XVIII wieku*, Gdańsk.

————. 2007. "'Admirabilis ordo' Polacy wobec mitu Wenecji XVI–XVIII w." In *Literatura – historia – dziedzictwo. Prace ofiarowane Teresie Kostkiewiczowej.* Edited by T. Chachulski, and A. Grześkowiak-Krwawicz, 67–77. Warsaw.

————. 2010. "'Przyszłam do Polski z Lechem...' Konfederaci barscy a polska tradycja wolności." In *Konfederacja Barska, jej konteksty i tradycje.* Edited by A. Buchmann, and A. Danilczyk, 237–254. Warsaw.

————. 2012a. *Queen Liberty: The concept of freedom in the Polish-Lithuanian Commonwealth.* Translated by Daniel J. Sax. Leiden, Boston.

———. 2012b. "Rzeczpospolita — pojęcie i idea w dyskursie politycznym Rzeczypospolitej Obojga Narodów. Rekonesans." *Odrodzenie i Reformacja w Polsce*, vol. 56, 5–35.

———. 2013. "Moja, twoja, nasza… Wolność i zaimki w polskiej myśli politycznej XVIII w." *Horyzonty Polityki*, vol. 4, no. 7, 89–108.

———. 2014. "Obraz Sparty w myśli politycznej Rzeczypospolitej Obojga Narodów." In *Sparta w kulturze polskiej, cz. 1: Model recepcji, spojrzenie europejskie, konteksty greckie*. Edited by M. Borowska, M. Kalinowska, J. Speina, and K. Tomaszuk, 25–44. Warsaw.

———. 2015. "Spór o Ustawę Rządową jako zderzenie dwóch dyskursów politycznych?." *Wiek Oświecenia*, vol. 31, 195–211.

———. 2016. "'Nowe wino w starych butelkach.' O języku politycznym Stanisława Konarskiego." *Wiek Oświecenia*, vol. 32, 11–28.

Grzybowski, Konstanty. 1956. "Systematyka prawa w Polsce odrodzenia, jej rola i podłoże klasowe." *Odrodzenie w Polsce*, vol. 2, 175–212.

———. 1959. *Teoria reprezentacji w Polsce epoki Odrodzenia*. Warsaw.

Guilhaumou, Jacques. 1989. *La langue politique et la Révolution française. De l'événement à la raison linguistique*. Paris.

———. 1998. *L'avènement des porte-parole de la république (1789–1792). Essai de synthèse sur les languages de la Révolution française*. Paris.

———. 2006. *Discours et événement. L'histoire langagière des concepts*. Besançon.

Guilhaumou, Jacques, and Régine Robin (eds). 1974. *Langage et Idéologie. Le discours comme objet de l'histoire*. Paris.

Gunn, John A. W. 1983. *Beyond Liberty and Property. The Process of Self-Recognition in Eighteenth-Century Political Thought*. Kingston–Montreal.

Haitsma Mulier, Eco. 1980. *The Myth of Venice and Dutch Republican Thought in the Seventeenth Century*. Assen.

Hampsher-Monk, Iain, Karin Tilmans, and Frank Van Vree. (eds.) 1998. *History of Concepts: Comparative Perspectives*. Amsterdam.

Handelsman, Marceli. 1911. "Zamach stanu Augusta II." *Studia historyczne*. Warsaw.

Hankins, James. (ed.) 2000. *Renaissance Civic Humanism: Reappraisals and Reflections*. Cambridge.

Herman, Stefan. 1985. *Żywa postać Rzeczypospolitej. Studium z literatury staropolskiej XVI i pierwszej połowy XVII wieku*. Zielona Góra.

Hernas, Czesław. 1974. "Złota wolność (notatki do interpretacji)." *Teksty*, vol. 4, 1–11.

Honohan, Iseult. 2002. *Civic Republicanism*. London–New York.

Horwitz, Henry. 1992. Liberty, Law, and Property, 1689–1776. In Jones 1992, 265–297.

Hörnquist, Mikael. 2000. "The Two Myths of Civic Humanism." In Hankins 2000, 105–142.

Im Hof, Ulrich 1991. *Mythos Schweiz: Identität – Nation – Geschichte 1291–1991*. Zurich.

Janicki, Marek A. 2004. "Wolność i równość w języku prawno-politycznym oraz ideologii szlachty polskiej (od XIV do początków XVII wieku)." In Axer 2004b, 73–107.

Janowska, Aleksandra, Pastuchowa, Magdalena, and Pawelec, Radosław. (eds.) 2011. *Humanizm w języku polskim. Wartości humanistyczne w polskiej leksyce i refleksji o języku.* Warsaw.

Janowski, Maciej. 2009. "Rozpacz oświeconych? Przemiana polskiego języka politycznego, a reakcje na upadek Rzeczypospolitej." *Wiek Oświecenia*, vol. 25, 29–60.

Jarra, Eugeniusz. 1931a. *Aaron Aleksander Olizarowski jako filozof prawa.* In *Księga pamiątkowa celem uczczenia 350-letniej rocznicy założenia USB w Wilnie*, 33–72. Warsaw.

———. 1931b. *Wawrzyniec Goślicki jako filozof prawa.* Warsaw.

———. 1933. "Le Bodinisme en Pologne au XVIIe siècle." *Archives de Philosophie du Droit et de Sociologie juridique*, vol. 1–2, 120–132.

———. 1945. "Andrew Wolan, Sixteenth Century Polish Calvinist Writer and Philosopher of Law." in *Studies in Polish and Comparative Law*, 124–155. London.

———. 1968. *Historia polskiej filozofii politycznej 966–1795.* London.

Jones, Francis R., and Allan Turner. 2004. "Archaisation, Modernisation and Reference in the Translation of Older Texts." *Across Languages and Cultures*, vol. 5, no. 2, 159–185.

Jones, James Rees (ed.) 1992. *Liberty Secured? Britain Before and After 1688.* Stanford.

Junker, Detlef. 1996. "Preface." In *The Meaning of Historical Terms and Concepts: New Studies on Begriffsgeschichte.* Edited by Hartmut Lehmann and Melvin Richter. 5–6. Washington, D.C..

Kąkolewski, Igor. 2007. *Melancholia władzy. Problemy tyranii w europejskiej kulturze XVI stulecia.* Warsaw.

Kelley, Donald R. 1991. "Law." In *The Cambridge History of Political Thought 1450–1700.* Edited by J. H. Burns with the assistance of M. Goldie, 66–94. Cambridge.

Kiaupienė, Jurate, 2004. "Naród polityczny Wielkiego Księstwa Litewskiego w XVI wieku: pojęcie ojczyzny." In Axer 2004b, 295–318.

———. 2009. "'My Litwa' – formuła patriotyzmu narodu politycznego Wielkiego Księstwa Litewskiego w XVI wieku." In Nowak and Zięba, 2009, 20–25.

Kloczkowski, Jacek. (ed.) 2007. *Patriotyzm Polaków: Studia z historii idei.* Kraków.

Knapik, Kinga. 2011. "Semantyczny rozwój leksemów 'patria', 'patriotyzm' i bliskoznaczników 'obywatelstwo', 'ojczyzna.'" In Janowska, Pastuchowa and Pawelec 2011, 402–415.

Knychalska, Agnieszka. 2005. "Senat w koncepcjach politycznych publicystów epoki saskiej." In *Czasy nowożytne. Studia poświęcone pamięci profesora Władysława Eugeniusza Czaplińskiego w 100 rocznicę urodzin.* Edited by K. Matwijowski, 251–260. Wrocław.

Kochan Anna. 2010a. "Człowiek – obywatel – prawo. Kwestie prawne a myśl i praktyka humanistyczna w procesach budowania polskiego społeczeństwa i narodu (do przełomu oświeceniowo-romantycznego)." In *Humanizm polski i wspólnoty: Naród – społeczeństwo – państwo – Europa.* Edited by M. Cieński, 55–83. Warsaw.

———. 2010b. "Prawo natury i prawo naturalne w dziełach autorów staropolskich." In *Człowiek wobec natury. Humanizm wobec nauk przyrodniczych*. Edited by J. Sokolski, 35–54. Warsaw.

Koehler, Krzysztof. 2007. "Patriotyzm w okresie kontrreformacji." In Kloczkowski 2007, 32–59.

Koenigsberger, Helmut G. 1997. "Republicanism, Monarchism and Liberty." In *Royal and Republican Sovereignty in Early Modern Europe. Essays in Memory of Ragunild Hatton*. Edited by R. Oresko, G. C. Gibbs and H. M. Scott, 43–74. Cambridge.

Konopczyński, Władysław. 1930. "Narodziny nowoczesnej idei niepodległości w Polsce (1733–1775)." In *Pamiętnik V Zjazdu Historyków Polskich*, vol. 1, 462–475. Lwów.

———. 1966. *Polscy pisarze polityczni XVIII w. (do Sejmu Czteroletniego)*. Warsaw.

———. 2012. *Polscy pisarze polityczni XVIII wieku*. Kraków.

Koranyi, Karol, 1967. *La costituzione di Venezia nel pensiero politica della Polonia (Eta del Rinascimento)*. In *Italia, Venezia e Polonia tra umanesimo e rinascimento*. Edited by M. Brahmer, 206–214. Wrocław.

Korolec, Jerzy B. 2006. *Wolność, cnota, praxis*. Edited by M. Olszewski. Warsaw.

Koselleck Reinhart. 1998. "Social History and 'Begriffsgeschichte.'" In Hampsher-Monk, Tilmans, and Van Vree 1998, 23–35.

Kostkiewiczowa, Teresa. 2002. *Polski wiek świateł – obszary swoistości*. Wrocław.

———. 2010. *Z oddali i z bliska. Studia o wieku oświecenia*. Warsaw.

Kot, Stanisław. 1911. *Wpływ starożytności antycznej na teorie polityczne Andrzeja Frycza z Modrzewa*, Rozprawy AU. Wydział Historyczno-Filozoficzny, series II, vol. 29.

———. 1919. *Rzeczpospolita Polska w literaturze politycznej Zachodu*. Kraków.

Kotarski, Edmund. 1995. *Sarmaci i morze. Marynistyczne początki w literaturze polskiej XVI–XVII wieku*. Warsaw.

Lasocińska, Estera. 2002. "O pojęciu wielkiego umysłu i cnocie wielkomyślności. Stoicyzm i jego związki z etyką Arystotelesa w literaturze polskiej XVII wieku." *Barok*, vol. 9, no. 1–2, 97–115.

———. 2010. "Recepcja etyki starożytnej w literaturze renesansu, baroku i wczesnego oświecenia." In *Etos humanistyczny*. Edited by P. Urbański, 21–50. Warsaw.

Leduc-Fayette, Denise. 1974. *Rousseau et le mythe de l' «antiquité»*. Paris.

Legomska, Julia. 2010. *Państwo, naród, ojczyzna w dawnej polszczyźnie. Leksykalno-semantyczny opis pojęć*. Katowice.

Leśnodorski, Bogusław. 1967. "Idee polityczne J. J. Rousseau w Polsce." In *Wiek XIX. Prace ofiarowane Stefanowi Kieniewiczowi*. Warsaw.

Lipski, Andrzej. 1983. "Tradycja państwa jako czynnik integracji narodowej w XVI i pierwszej połowie XVII wieku." *Odrodzenie i Reformacja*, vol. 28, 75–91.

Lis, Rafał. 2015. *W poszukiwaniu prawdziwej Rzeczypospolitej. Główne nurty myśli politycznej Sejmu Czteroletniego*. Kraków.

Litwin, Henryk. 1993. "Narody Pierwszej Rzeczypospolitej." In *Tradycje polityczne dawnej Polski*. Edited by A. Sucheni-Grabowska, and A. Dybkowska, 168–218. Warsaw.

————. 1994. "W poszukiwaniu rodowodu demokracji szlacheckiej. Polska myśl polityczna w piśmiennictwie XV i początków XVI wieku." In Sucheni-Grabowska and Żaryn 1994, 13–53.

Lizisowa, Maria T. 2006. "Modelowanie treści pojęć prawo – własność – władza w języku prawnym Korony i Wielkiego Księstwa Litewskiego." In *Litwa w epoce Wazów*. Edited by W. Kriegseisen, and A. Rachuba, 97–112. Warsaw.

Łukowski, Jerzy. 1994. "Od Konarskiego do Kołłątaja – czyli od realizmu do utopii." In *Trudne stulecia. Studia z dziejów XVII i XVIII wieku ofiarowane profesorowi Jerzemu Michalskiemu w siedemdziesiątą rocznicę urodzin*. Edited by Ł. Kądziela, W. Kriegseisen, and Z. Zielińska, 184–194. Warsaw.

————. 2004. "The Szlachta and Their Ancestors in the Eighteenth Century." *Kwartalnik Historyczny*, vol. 111, no. 3, 161–182.

————. 2010. *Disorderly Liberty: The Political Culture of the Polish-Lithuanian Commonwealth in the Eighteenth Century*. London.

————. 2014. "Stanisław Konarski – polski Machiavelli?" In *W cieniu wojen i rozbiorów. Studia z dziejów Rzeczypospolitej XVIII i początków XIX wieku*. Edited by U. Kosińska, D. Dukwicz, and A. Danilczyk, 181–196. Warsaw.

Maciejewski, Janusz. 1974. "Sarmatyzm jako formacja kulturowa." *Teksty*, no. 4, 13–142.

MacIntyre, Alasdair. 2006. *Selected Essays, vol. 2. Ethics and Politics*. Cambridge.

Maciszewski, Jarema. 1969. *Szlachta polska i jej państwo*. Warsaw.

Mager, Wolfgang. 1991. "Respublica chez les juristes, théologiens et les philosophes à la fin du Moyen-âge: sur l'élaboration d'une notion-clé de la théorie politique moderne." In *Théologie et droit dans la science politique de l'état moderne*, 229–239. Rome.

Makiłła, Dariusz. 2012. "Prawo natury w szesnastowiecznej koncepcji prawa polskiego." In *Nam hoc natura aequum est... Księga jubileuszowa ku czci profesora Janusza Justyńskiego w siedemdziesięciolecie urodzin*. Edited by A. Madeja, Toruń.

Mäkinen, Virpi, and Korkman, Petter. (eds). 2006. *Transformations in Medieval and Early-Modern Rights Discourse*. Dordrecht.

Malec, Jerzy. 1986. *Polska myśl administracyjna XVIII wieku*. Kraków.

Maleszyński, Dariusz C. 1985. "Corpus politicum. Śródziemnomorskie i staropolskie konteksty topiki organicznej." *Pamiętnik Literacki*, vol. 76, no. 1, 19–46.

Matyaszewski, Paweł. 2012. "Montesquieu en Pologne. La recherche dix-huitièmiste en France et en Pologne. Bilan et perspectives." In *Ewa Rzadkowska 1913–2009 in memoriam*. Edited by I. Zatorska, 79–91. Varsovie.

————. 2018. *Monteskiusz w Polsce. Wczoraj i dziś*. Warsaw.

Meiksins Wood, Ellen. 2012. *Liberty and Property: A Social History of Western Political Thought from Renaissance to Enlightenment*. London.

Meller, Katarzyna. 2004. "Philopolites, to jest miłośnik ojczyzny – renesansowe speculum obywatela." In *Literatura i pamięć kultury*. Edited by S. Baczewski, and D. Chemperek, 43–67. Lublin.

Michalski, Jerzy. 1977. *Rousseau i sarmacki republikanizm*. Warsaw.

———. 1983. "Z problematyki republikańskiego nurtu w polskiej reformator-skiej myśli politycznej w XVIII wieku." *Kwartalnik Historyczny*, vol. 90, 327–338.

———. 1985. *Konstytucja 3 Maja*. Warsaw.

———. 1987. "'Wszystko pójdzie wyśmienicie' (O politycznym optymizmie po 3 Maja)." In *Losy Polaków w XIX–XX w. Studia ofiarowane profesorowi Stefanowi Kieniewiczowi w osiemdziesiątą rocznicę Jego urodzin*, 317–329. Warsaw.

———. 1991. "Le mouvement antiroyal sous le règne de Stanislas Auguste Poniatowski. De la contestation vers un programme positif." In *La Belgique – La Pologne et la Révolution française 1780–1830*, 13–32. Bruxelles.

———. 1998. "Publicystyka i parapublicystyka doby sejmu 1776 roku." *Kwartalnik Historyczny*, vol. 105, 21–64.

———. 2007. *Studia historyczne z XVIII i XIX wieku*, vol. 1–2. Warsaw.

Mienicki, Ryszard. 1913. "Poglądy polityczne w dziejopisarstwie polskim XVII w." parts 1–3, *Przegląd Historyczny*, vol. 16, no. 1–3, 35–66, 164–186, 257–293.

Morel, Henri. 1986. "La renaissance de Sparte." In *État et pouvoir: réception des idéologies dans le Midi, l'Antiquité et les Temps modernes, vol. 6: Actes du Colloque de Lyon 1985*, 209–219. Aix-en-Provence

———. 1996. "Le régime mixte ou l'idéologie du meilleur régime politique." In *L'influence de l'antiquité sur la pensée politique Européenne (XVI–XXème siècles)*. Aix-en-Provence.

Mouristen, Paul. 2006. "Four Models of Republican Liberty and Self-Government." In *Republicanism in Theory and Practice*. Edited by I. Honohan, and J. Jennings, 17–38. London–New York.

Mulgan, Richard. 1984. "Liberty in Ancient Greece." In *Conceptions of Liberty in Political Philosophy*. Edited by Z. Pelczyński, J. Gray, 7–25. London.

Nenner, Howard. 1992. "Liberty, Law, and Property: The Constitution in Retrospect from 1689." In Jones 1992, 88–121.

Niendorf, Mathias. 2011. *Wielkie Księstwo Litewskie. Studia nad kształtowaniem się narodu u progu epoki nowożytnej (1569–1795)*. Poznań.

Nippel, Wilfried. 1994. "Ancient and Modern Republicanism: 'Mixed Constitution' and 'Ephors'". In *The Invention of Modern Republic*. Edited by B. Fontana. Cambridge.

Nowak, Andrzej, and Zięba, Andrzej A. (eds). 2009. *Formuły patriotyzmu w Europie Wschodniej i Środkowej od nowożytności do współczesności*. Kraków.

Oake, Roger B. 1955. "Montesquieu's Analysis of Roman History." *Journal of the History of Ideas*, vol. 16, no. 1.

Ochmann, Stefania. 1990. "Rzeczpospolita jako 'monarchia mixta' – dylematy władzy i wolności." In *Kultura – polityka – dyplomacja. Studia ofiarowane profesorowi Jaremie Maciszewskiemu*. Edited by A. Bartnicki 264–278. Warsaw.

Ochmann-Staniszewska, Stefania. 1994. "Od stabilizacji do kryzysu władzy królewskiej. Państwo Wazów." In Sucheni-Grabowska and Żaryn, 1994, 211–269.

Ogonowski, Zbigniew. 1992. *Filozofia polityczna w Polsce XVII wieku i tradycje demokracji europejskiej.* Warsaw.

Olsen, Niklas. 2012. *History in the Plural. An Introduction to the Work of Reinhart Koselleck.* New York–Oxford.

Olszewski, Henryk. 1961. *Doktryny ustrojowe czasów saskich 1697–1740.* Warsaw.

———. 2002. *Sejm w dawnej Rzeczypospolitej. Ustrój i idee.* Vols. 1–2. Poznań.

Opaliński, Edward. 1983. "Postawa szlachty polskiej wobec osoby królewskiej jako instytucji w latach 1587–1648. Próba postawienia problematyki." *Kwartalnik Historyczny*, vol. 90, no. 4, 791–807.

———. 1995. *Kultura polityczna szlachty polskiej w latach 1587–1652.* Warsaw.

———. 2001. *Sejm srebrnego wieku.* Warsaw.

———. 2002. "Civic Humanism and Republican Citizenship in the Polish Renaissance." In Van Gelderen and Skinner 2002, 147–166.

Opałek, Kazimierz. 1953. *Prawo natury u polskich fizjokratów.* Warsaw.

Orzeł, Joanna. 2016. *Historia – tradycja – mit w pamięci kulturowej szlachty Rzeczypospolitej XVI–XVIII wieku.* Warsaw.

Ottow, Raimund. 1993. "'Power follows property': Zu einem Topos der britischen politischen Herrschaftssoziologie im 17./18. Jahrhundert." *European Journal of Sociology/Archives Européennes de Sociologie/Europäisches Archiv für Soziologie*, vol. 34, no. 2: *Our Scottish Ancestors*, 277–306.

Padalinski, Uladimir. 2013. "Stanowisko szlachty Wielkiego Księstwa Litewskiego wobec instytucji sejmu walnego w końcu XVI wieku." In *Kultura parlamentarna epoki staropolskiej*. Edited by A. Stroynowski, 143–156. Warsaw.

Pagden, Anthony (ed). 1987. *The Languages of Political Theory in Early-Modern Europe.* Cambridge.

Pallister, Ann. 1971. *Magna Carta: The Heritage of Liberty.* Oxford.

Palonen, Kari. 2014. *Politics and Conceptual Histories: Rhetorical and Temporal Perspectives*, London.

Pangle, Thomas. 1988. *The Spirit of Modern Republicanism: The Moral Vision of the American Founders and the Philosophy of Locke.* Chicago–London.

Pennington, Kenneth. 1993. *The Prince and the Law, 1200–1600.* Berkeley.

Pepłowski, Franciszek. 1961. *Słownictwo i frazeologia polskiej publicystyki okresu Oświecenia i Romantyzmu.* Warsaw.

Pettit, Philip. 1999. *Republicanism. A Theory of Freedom and Government*, 2nd edition. Oxford.

Pfeiffer, Bogusław. 2012. *Rex et Patria. Temat władcy, narodu i ojczyzny w literaturze i sztuce XVIII stulecia.* Warsaw.

Pietrzyk-Reeves, Dorota. 2010. "O pojęciu Rzeczpospolita (res-publica) w polskiej myśli politycznej XVI w." *Czasopismo Prawno-Historyczne*, vol. 62, no. 1, 37–63.

———. 2012. *Ład rzeczypospolitej. Polska myśl polityczna XVI wieku a klasyczna tradycja republikańska.* Kraków.

Pocock, John G. A. 1975. *The Machiavellian Moment. Florentine Political Thought and the Atlantic Republican Tradition.* Princeton.

———. 1981. "Virtues, Rights, and Manners: A Model for Historians of Political Thought." *Political Theory*, vol. 9, no. 3, 353–368.

———. 1987. "The Concept of a Language and the métier d'historien: Some Considerations on Practice." In *The Languages of Political Theory in Early-modern Europe.* Edited by A. Pagden, 19–38. Cambridge.

———. 1997. *Le moment Machiavélien. La pensée politique florentine et la tradition républicaine atlantique.* Edited by L. Borot. Paris.

———. 1998. "The Ideal of Citizenship since Classical Times." In *The Citizenship Debates.* Edited by G. Shafir, 31–41. Minneapolis–London.

———. 2009. *Political Thought and History. Essays on Theory and Method.* Cambridge.

Polska na tle Europy XVI–XVII wieku: Materiały pokonferencyjne. 2007. Warsaw.

Porazinski, Jarosław. 1993. "Ordo intermedius? Kilka uwag o politycznej roli senatu w XVII i XVIII wieku." In *Między wielką polityką a szlacheckim partykularzem. Studia z dziejów nowożytnej Polski i Europy ku czci Profesora Jacka Staszewskiego,* 217–224. Toruń.

Probulski, Andrzej. 2014. "The Rhetoric of Prudence in Stanisław Herakliusz Lubomirski's 'De vanitate Consiliorum,'" *Terminus,* vol. 16, no. 3, 305–322. source: http://www.ejournals.eu/Terminus/2014/Terminus-2014-3/art/4355/. (Accessed: 21.04.2017)

Prokhovnik, Raia. 2008. *Sovereignty. History and Theory.* Exeter.

Pryshlak, Maria. 1981. "'Forma mixta' as a Political Ideal of a Polish Magnate: Łukasz Opaliński's 'Rozmowa Plebana z ziemianinem,'" *The Polish Review,* vol. 26, no. 3, 26–42.

———. 2000. *Państwo w filozofii politycznej Łukasza Opalińskiego.* Kraków.

Radwański, Zbigniew. 1952. *Prawa kardynalne w Polsce.* Poznań

Raszewska-Żurek, Beata. 2016. *Zgoda w rozumieniu Polaków czasów staro- i średniopolskich (analiza leksykalno-semantyczna).* Warsaw.

Rawson, Elisabeth. 1969. *The Spartan Tradition in European Thought.* Oxford.

Reichardt, Rolf. 1998. "Historische Semantik zwischen lexicometrie und New Cultural History. Einführende Bemerkungen zur Standortbestimmung." In *Aufklärung und Historische Semantik: interdisziplinäre Beiträge zur westeuropäischen Kulturgeschichte,* Hrsg. R. Reichardt, 7–44. Berlin.

Reichardt, Rolf, Schmitt, Eberhard, and Lüsebrink Hans-Jürgen. (eds.) 1985–. *Handbuch politisch-socialer Grundbegriffe in Frankreich.* München.

Reid, John Phillip. 2004. *Rule of Law: The Jurisprudence of Liberty in the Seventeenth and Eighteenth Centuries.* Dekalb.

Richardson, Bill. 1998. "Deictic Features and the Translator." In Hickey, L. (ed.) *The Pragmatics of Translation,* 124–142. Clevedon.

Richter, Melvin. 1995. *The History of Political and Social Concepts: A Critical Introduction.* Oxford.

———. 1989. "Montesquieu, the Politics of Language, and the Language of Politics." *History of Political Thought,* vol. 10, no. 1. Spring, 71–88.

Richter, Michaela. 2011. "Introduction and Prefaces to the *Geschichtliche Grundbegriffe* – A Note on the Translations." *Contributions to the History of Concepts* 6(1): 1–37.

Robin, Régine. 1973. *Histoire et linguistique.* Paris.

Rosicka, Janina. 1984. *Polskie spory o własność. Narodziny nowożytnej myśli ekonomicznej na ziemiach polskich (1765–1830).* Kraków.

Rok, Bogdan. 1984. "Panegiryczne dedykacje z kalendarzy S. Duńczewskiego (Szlachecki ideał sarmaty czasów saskich)." *Śląski Kwartalnik Historyczny. Sobótka*, vol. 39, no. 2, 343–351.

Rosner, Andrzej. 1986. *Uwagi o języku politycznym w Polsce czasów saskich.* In *Polska czasów saskich.* Edited by M. Wrzosek, 263–273. Białystok.

Rostworowski, Emanuel. 1976. "Republikanizm polski i anglosaski XVIII w." *Miesięcznik Literacki*, vol. 11, no. 8, 94–103.

———. 1985. *Popioły i korzenie.* Kraków.

Sapała, Patryk. 2017. "Relacja między wolnością a prawem w pismach Stanisława Orzechowskiego." In *Wartości polityczne Rzeczypospolitej Obojga Narodów. Struktury aksjologiczne i granice cywilizacyjne.* Edited by A. Grześkowiak-Krwawicz in collaboration with J. Axer, 199–241. Warsaw.

Schleiermacher, Friedrich. 1813. "Über die verschiedenen Methoden des Übersetzens." In *Sämtliche Werke*, vol. 3, 207–245.

Schofield, Malcolm. 1999. "Cicero's definition of Res Publica." In *Cicero the Philosopher. Twelve Papers.* Editted by J. G. F. Powell, 63–84. Oxford.

Scott, Jonathan. 2004. *Commonwealth Principles: Republican Writing of the English Revolution.* Cambridge.

Shklar, Judith N. 1987. "Political Theory and the Rule of Law." In *The Rule of Law: Ideal or Ideology.* Edited by A.C. Hutchison, and P. Monahan, 1–31. Toronto.

Simon, Julia. 2001. Militarisme et vertu chez Rousseau. In *Jean-Jacques Rousseau, politique et nation.* Edited by R. Thiéry. Paris–Montmorency.

Sinko, Tadeusz. 1939. *Erudycja klasyczna Stanisława Orzechowskiego*, Rozprawy PAU, Wydział Filologiczny, vol. 65, issue 7.

Skinner, Quentin. 1978. *The Foundations of Modern Political Though*, vol. 1. Cambridge.

———. 1990a. "Machiavelli's *Discorsi* and the Pre-Humanist Origins of Republican Ideas." In *Machiavelli and Republicanism.* Edited by G. Bock, Q. Skinner, and M. Viroli, 121–141. Cambridge.

———. 1990b. "The Republican Ideal of Political Liberty." In *Machiavelli and Republicanism.* Edited by G. Bock, Q. Skinner, and M. Viroli, 293–309. Cambridge.

———. 1998. *Liberty Before Liberalism.* Cambridge.

———. 2002. Machiavelli on "Virtu" and the Maintance of Liberty. In *Visions on Politics*, CUP, vol. 2: Renaissance Virtues. 160–184. Cambridge.

———. 2008. *Hobbes and Republican Liberty.* Cambridge.

Ślęk, Ludwika. 1978. "'Przeszłych wieków sprawy' jako przedmiot poetyckiego przedstawienia w literaturze XVI w." In *Dawna świadomość historyczna w Polsce, Czechach i Słowacji.* Edited by R. Heck. Wrocław

Ślusarska, Magdalena. 1997. "Litewskie kaznodziejstwo trybunalskie czasów stanisławowskich 'o miłości ojczyzn, zgodzie i jedności obywatelów.'" In *Lietuvos valstybė XII–XVIII A.* Edited by Z. Kiaupa, A. Mickievičius, and J. Sarcevičienè, 187–214. Vilnius.

Smoleński, Władysław. 1927. *Monteskiusz w Polsce.* Warsaw.

Śnieżko, Dariusz. 1996. *Mit wieku złotego w literaturze polskiego renesansu.* Warsaw.

Spellman, W. M. 1998. *European Political Thought 1600–1700.* London.

Stasiewicz-Jasiukowa, Irena. 1979. *Człowiek i obywatel w piśmiennictwie naukowym i podręcznikach polskiego oświecenia.* Warsaw.

Stasiewicz, Krystyna. 2003. "Eques Polonus według Wacława Kunickiego." In *Między Zachodem a Wschodem. Studia ku czci Jacka Staszewskiego,* vol. 2, 555–569. Toruń.

Steiner, Georges. 1975. *After Babel.* Oxford.

Sucheni-Grabowska, Anna. 1994. "Obowiązki i prawa królów polskich w opiniach pisarzy epoki odrodzenia." In Sucheni-Grabowska and Żaryn 1994, 54–115.

Sucheni-Grabowska, Anna, and Żaryn, Małgorzata. (eds.) 1994. *Między monarchą a demokracją. Studia z dziejów Polski XV–XVIII wieku.* Warsaw.

Suchodolski, Bogdan. 1927. "Kult przeszłości wśród szlachty polskiej." *Pamiętnik Literacki,* vol. 24, no. 1, 1–13.

Sulima-Kamiński, Andrzej. 2008. "Przestrzenie obywatelskie w wieloetnicznej, wielowyznaniowej i wielokulturowej Rzeczypospolitej." In *Lex est Rex in Polonia et in Lithuania... Tradycje prawno-ustrojowe Rzeczypospolitej – doświadczenie i dziedzictwo,* 83–94. Warsaw.

Szczepankowska, Irena. 2004. *Studia nad polszczyzną epoki stanisławowskiej.* Białystok.

Szczerbicka-Ślęk Ludwika. 1975. "Mit Piastów w literaturze XVI–XVIII wieku." In *Piastowie w dziejach Polski.* Edited by R. Heck. Wrocław–Warsaw–Kraków–Gdańsk.

Szczygielski, Wojciech. 2003. "Sejm gotowy i władza typu Straży (z badań nad recepcją społeczną reformy ustroju państwa w czasach Sejmu Wielkiego)." *Przegląd Nauk Historycznych,* vol. 2, no. 1, 65–87.

———. 2008. "Z badań nad początkami obrad Sejmu Wielkiego." *Przegląd Nauk Historycznych,* vol. 7, no. 1, 21–85.

Szyjkowski, Marian. 1913. *Myśl Jana Jakóba Rousseau w Polsce XVIII w.* Kraków.

Tarnowski, Stanisław. 1886/2000. *Pisarze polityczni XVI wieku: studia do historyi literatury polskiej.* 2nd edition. Kraków.

Tazbir, Janusz, 1976. "Wzorce osobowe szlachty polskiej w XVII wieku." *Kwartalnik Historyczny,* vol. 83, no. 4, 784–797.

———. 1979. *Kultura szlachecka w Polsce. Rozkwit – upadek – relikty.* 2nd edition. Warsaw.

———. 1992. "Węgry jako symbol i przestroga w literaturze staropolskiej." *Odrodzenie i Reformacja w Polsce,* vol. 36, 147–162.

Tigerstedt, Eugène N., 1965. *The Legend of Sparta in Classical Antiquity,* Stockholm–Götteborg–Uppsala.

Touchefeu, Yves. 1999. *L'Antiquité et le christianisme dans la pensée de Jean Jacques Rousseau.* Oxford.

———. 2006. "Sparte" In *Dictionnaire de Jean-Jacques Rousseau,* sous la dir. de R. Trousson, F. S. Eigeldinger, 867–869. Paris.

Trencsenyi, Balázs. 2004. "Conceptual History and Political Languages: On the Central-European Adaptation of the Contextualist-Conceptualist Methodologies of Intellectual History." In P. Roubal and V. Veber (eds.), *Prague Perspectives (I): The History of East Central Europe and Russia,* 142–166. Prague.

Trencsényi, Balázs, and Zászkaliczky, Marton. 2010. *Whose Love of Which Country? Composite States, National Histories and Patriotic Discourses in Early Modern East Central Europe*, Leiden–Boston.

Uruszczak, Wacław. 1993. "Zasada 'lex est rex' w Polsce XVI wieku." *Śląski Kwartalnik Historyczny*. *Sobótka*, vol. 48, no. 2–3, 149–157.

Urwanowicz, Jerzy. 1994. *Ideologia a działalność polityczna szlachty w czasach Zygmunta III. Wokół wartości ustrojowych*. In Sucheni-Grabowska and Żaryn 1994, 170–190.

Van Gelderen, Martin. 1996. "Liberty, Civic Rights, and Duties in Sixteenth-Century Europe and the Rise of the Dutch Republic." In *The Individual in Political Theory and Practice*. Edited by J. Coleman, 99–122. Oxford.

———. 1998. "Epilogue." In Hampsher-Monk, Tilmans, and Van Vree 1998, 227–237.

———. 2002. "Aristotelians, Monarchomachs and Republicans: Sovereignty and Respublica Mixta in Dutch and German Political Thought." In Van Gelderen and Skinner 2002, 147–166.

Van Gelderen, Martin, and Quentin Skinner. (eds). 2002. *Republicanism: A Shared European Heritage*, vols. 1–2. Cambridge.

Velema, Wyger R. E. 2002. "That a Republic is Better than a Monarchy." In Van Gelderen and Skinner 2002, 9–25.

Venuti, Lawrence. 1995. *The Translator's Invisibility: A History of Translation*. 2nd edition, 2008. Routledge.

Vetterli, Richard, and Gary Bryner. 1996. *In Search of the Republic: Public Virtue and the Roots of American Government*, 2nd edition. London.

Vetulani, Adam. 1969. "Opory wobec prawa rzymskiego w dawnej Polsce." *Analecta Cracoviensia*, vol. 1, 372–386

Viroli, Maurizio. 1987. "The Concept of 'Ordre' and the Language of Classical Republicanism in Jean-Jacques Rousseau." In Pagden 1987, 159–178.

———. 1995. *For Love of Country: An Essay on Patriotism and Nationalism*. Oxford.

Volumina legum. 1889. Vol. 9. Kraków.

Wachlowski, Zbigniew. 1927. "Pojęcie suwerenności w literaturze politycznej polskiej XV i XVI wieku." In *Pamiętnik trzydziestolecia pracy naukowej Przemysława Dąbkowskiego*, 221–241. Lwów.

Wagner-Rundell, Benedict. 2015. *Common Wealth, Common Good: The Politics of Virtue in Early Modern Polonia-Lithuania*. Oxford.

Walicki, Andrzej. 2000. *Idea narodu w polskiej myśli oświeceniowej*. Warsaw.

Walzer, Michael. 1989. "Citizenship." In Ball, Farr and Hanson 1989, 211–219.

Węcowski, Piotr. 2013. "Ze studiów nad ideologią polityczną Kazimierza Jagiellończyka. Wątek pokoju i zgody w państwie." *Średniowiecze Polskie i Powszechne*, vol. 5, no. 9, 169–184.

Wells, Charlotte C. 1995. *Law and Citizenship in Early Modern France*, Baltimore–London.

Wilczek, Piotr. 2005. *(Mis)translation and (Mis)interpretation: Polish Literature in the Context of Cross-Cultural Communication*. Peter Lang.

Wirszubski, Chaim. 1968. *Libertas as a Political Idea at Rome During the Late Republic and Early Principate*. Cambridge.

Wisner, Henryk. 1976. Wielkie Księstwo Litewskie – Korona Polska – Rzeczpospolita, *Przegląd Historyczny*, vol. 47, no. 4, 575–591.

———. 1978. *Najjaśniejsza Rzeczpospolita. Szkice z dziejów Polski szlacheckiej XVI–XVII wieku.* Warsaw.

———. 2002. *Rzeczpospolita Wazów. Czasy Zygmunta III i Władysława IV.* Warsaw.

———. 2006. "Rzeczypospolite szlachty litewskiej (schyłek wieku XVI– pierwsza połowa XVII wieku)." *Barok*, vol. 13, no. 1, 17–28

Wołodkiewicz, Witold. 2002. Ius et lex w rzymskiej tradycji prawnej, *Ius et Lex*, vol. 1, 53–61.

Worst, I. J. H., 1992. "Constitution, History, and Natural Law: An Eighteenth-Century Political Debate in the Dutch Republic." In *The Dutch Republic in the Eighteenth Century. Decline, Enlightenment, and Revolution.* Edited by M. C. Jacob, and W. N. Mijnhardt, 147–169. Ithaca–London.

Wotton, David. (ed). 1994. *Republicanism, Liberty and Commercial Society, 1649–1776,* Stanford.

Wyrwa, Tadeusz. 1978. *La pensée politique polonaise à l'époque de l'humanisme et de la renaissance (Un apport à la connaissance de l'Europe moderne).* Paris.

Wyszomirska, Monika. 2007. "Rokosz gliniański i 'rady Kallimacha' a doktryna złotej wolności." In *Nad społeczeństwem staropolskim,* vol. 1: *Kultura – instytucje – gospodarka w XVI–XVIII stuleciu.* Edited by K. Łopatecki, and W. Walczak, 73–82. Białystok.

———. 2010. *Między obroną wolności a naprawą państwa. Rzeczpospolita jako przedmiot polemik politycznych w dobie panowania Augusta III (1734–1763).* Warsaw.

Zajączkowski, Andrzej. 1993. *Szlachta polska. Kultura i struktura,* 2nd edition. Warsaw.

Zakrzewski, Andrzej. 2013. *Wielkie Księstwo Litewskie (XVI–XVIII w.). Prawo – ustrój – społeczeństwo.* Podkowa Leśna.

Zielińska, Zofia. 1991. *"O sukcesyi tronu w Polszcze" 1787–1790.* Warsaw.

Zienkowska, Krystyna. 1976. *Sławetni i urodzeni. Ruch polityczny mieszczaństwa w dobie Sejmu czteroletniego.* Warsaw.

Zwierzykowski, Michał. 2017. "Sine iustitia in libertate żyć nie chcemy." *Prawo i sprawiedliwość w dyskursie politycznym kampanii sejmowych lat 1696–1762.* In *Wartości polityczne Rzeczypospolitej Obojga Narodów. Struktury aksjologiczne i granice cywilizacyjne.* Edited by A. Grześkowiak-Krwawicz in collaboration with J. Axer. Warsaw, 264–288.

Index

absolutism 66, 67, 76, 81, 132, 173,
174, 182, 185, 223, 237
absolute power 100, 105, 115, 221
absolutum dominium 30, 79, 106, 173
anarchy 59, 62, 79, 80, 167, 199, 207,
227, 228
Andrzejuk, Izabella 136
Aquinas, St. Thomas 54, 94, 96, 99,
119, 120, 134–136, 140, 145
Aristogeiton 67
Aristotle 8, 21, 27, 37, 42, 50, 54, 61,
67, 69, 75, 89, 94, 96–99, 103, 128,
140, 145, 148, 163, 165, 174
Askenazy, Szymon 192
Athens 30, 236
Augustus II the Strong, king of
Poland, grand duke of Lithuania,
elector of Saxony 81, 225
Augustus III, king of Poland, grand
duke of Lithuania, elector of
Saxony 155, 199
Augustyniak, Urszula 11, 12, 36, 37,
66, 68, 90, 91, 106, 112, 114, 115,
135–137, 190, 194, 219
Axer, Jerzy 12, 35
Axerowa, Anna 12

Backvis, Claude 12, 35, 38, 64, 65, 89,
112, 139, 163, 234
Baczewski, Sławomir 139,
163–166, 217
Baczko, Bronisław 90
Ball, Terence 12
Bałuk-Ulewiczowa, Teresa 18,
143, 164
Bar Confederation 81, 147, 152, 170,
180, 216, 225
Barclay, John 50, 173
Bardach, Juliusz 64
Bartkiewicz, Kazimierz 216

Baturo, E. 112
Baudouin de Courtenay, Jan 162, 168
Begriffsgeschichte 2, 3, 8, 12, 20
Bem-Wiśniewska, Ewa 11, 35, 36
Bieliński, Franciszek 87, 88, 91,
131, 137
Bion of Borysthenes 164
Biskupski, Mieczysław B. 16
Blythe, James M. 112
Bodin, Jean 3, 26, 37, 66, 67, 77, 93,
96, 105, 107, 221
Bogusławski, Konstantyn 10, 45, 56,
63, 67, 69, 84, 85, 92, 170, 189,
220, 230, 231, 237
Bömelburg, Hans-Jürgen 2, 11, 81, 90,
216, 218
Boulton, James T. 90
Bouwsma, William J. 88, 163
Brugger, Bill 64, 66, 89, 136, 163, 165
Brunner, Otto 11
Brutus (*Marcus Iunius Brutus*) 146
Bryner, Gary 165, 193
Brzeziński, Szymon 11, 66
Budny, Szymon 64, 66, 134–136, 164,
190, 193, 218
Bukaty, Franciszek 18
Butterwick-Pawlikowski, Richard 11,
166, 194
Bystrzonowski, Wojciech 80, 90, 115

Cambridge school 2, 5
Casimir III the Great, king of
Poland 61
Caesar (*Gaius Iulius Caesar*) 202
Cato (*Marcus Porcius Cato
Uticensis*) 146
Chądzyński, Jan 26, 37, 166, 177, 191
Charles I, king of England and
Scotland 3
Chmielowski, Benedykt 126, 136

Chodkiewicz, Jan Karol 146
Choińska-Mika, Jolanta 164, 190
Chróścikowski, Samuel 187, 194
Cicero (*Marcus Tulius Cicero*) 3, 21,
    22, 25, 26, 28, 31, 44, 50, 54, 55,
    59, 60, 75, 94, 96–99, 113, 119,
    134, 142, 148, 152, 163, 165, 166,
    172, 179, 190, 194
Ciesielski, Andrzej 65, 68
citizen 3, 4, 9, 14, 19, 20, 26, 27, 31,
    33, 37, 43, 44, 54–56, 62, 72, 75,
    76, 79, 81, 82, 85–87, 92, 97, 98,
    100, 119, 120, 122, 123, 126–129,
    143, 145, 152, 155–159, 161, 172,
    172–177, 188, 207, 208, 215, 222;
    community of 23–27, 35, 108, 118,
    167, 178, 188; duties of 160, 174,
    175, 180, 182–188, 191, 193; good
    141, 143, 147–149, 162, 165, 169,
    184, 229; and law 52, 54–63, 85;
    noble 7, 20, 25, 32, 52, 54, 61,
    73, 77, 83, 100, 106, 126, 130,
    143–145, 150, 153, 180, 182, 202,
    204, 205; and property 222, 223,
    231, 232; rights of 91, 179
citizenship 172, 173, 177, 233, 234
civic humanism 75, 89, 142, 147, 164
civic mirrors 143–145, 155
common good 20, 21, 26, 125, 127,
    128, 130, 141, 144, 146, 147, 149,
    154, 157, 160, 182, 183, 185–188,
    193, 227–229
Condren, Conal 11, 113
Constitution of the Third of May 45,
    46, 110, 116, 118, 133, 134, 147,
    162, 181, 188, 199, 215
Contarini, Gasparo 96
Conti, Vittorio 112
Conze, Werner 11
Coriolanus (*Gnaeus Marcius
    Coriolanus*) 175
corruption 9, 148, 152–156, 166
Cromwell, Thomas 222
Cynarski, Stanisław 216, 218
Czapliński, Władysław 11, 91, 114,
    219, 236
Czapski, Franciszek 219
Czarniecka, Anna 37, 65
Czartoryski, family 109
Czartoryski, Adam Kazimierz 164
Czechs 135
Czubek, Jan 12, 35–38, 64–69, 88–91,
    105, 112–115, 135–137, 163–168,
    189–194, 216–219, 235, 236

Dagger, Richard 64
d'Argenson, René 108
Dawidziak-Kładoczna, Małgorzata 11
Dembowski, Sebastian 59, 67, 68,
    89, 136
Demosthenes 21, 41, 42, 67
Derrida, Jacques 15, 18
Dickinson, Harry T. 68, 88, 136, 235
Dietz, Mary G. 190, 192
Diogenes 236
Długosz, Jan 189
Dłuski, Tomasz 92
Dmochowski, Franciszek Ksawery 164
Dzelzainis, Martin 90
Dzieduszycki, Jerzy Stanisław
    155, 166
Dziekoński, Bartłomiej 237
Dzięgielewski, Jan 190, 192
Dzwonkowski, Włodzimierz 192

Eco, Umberto 18
Eisenbach, Artur 12
Ekes, Janusz 37, 91, 93, 99, 103,
    112–115, 118, 125, 134–137, 236
Empedocles 134
England 30, 60, 61, 95, 96, 121,
    222, 223
Ennius (*Quintus Ennius*) 148
equality 61–63, 69, 71, 82, 83, 85, 86,
    91, 103, 104, 130, 225, 226, 234,
    235, 238
Estreicher, Stanisław 63–66, 68

factions 126
Falińska, Maria 216, 219
Filangeri, Gaetano 108
Fink, Zera 89, 113
France 12, 31, 95, 214
François Louis de Bourbon de
    Conti 38
Fredro, Andrzej Maksymilian 31,
    38, 43, 55, 76, 89, 95, 96, 98, 100,
    101, 112, 114, 120, 123, 131, 135,
    156, 157, 166, 182, 193, 219, 225,
    226, 235
Freylichówna, Judyta 163
Friedrich, Karin 50, 63, 65–67, 190
Frost, Robert 12, 106, 115
Fumurescu, Alin 136

Gaeta, Franco 217
Garczyński, Stefan 158, 177, 188,
    191, 229, 230, 232, 236
Gardiner, Patrick 168

Germany (German) 95, 131
Gierowski, Józef A. 91
Godek, Sławomir 64
Goldsmith, Maurice M. 64, 167
Gorgias 134
Goślicki, Wawrzyniec 18, 20, 40, 54,
    55, 58, 62, 68, 69, 74, 94–97, 104,
    112, 113, 124, 128, 135, 136, 143,
    148, 164, 165, 186, 190, 203, 206,
    207, 217, 218
Górnicki, Łukasz 7, 25, 48, 54, 55, 57,
    58, 62, 67–69, 79, 80, 90, 97, 105,
    114, 115, 128, 137, 140–142, 144,
    145, 149, 152, 153, 161, 163–165,
    175, 186, 190, 204, 207, 209, 210,
    212, 218, 219, 235
Górska, Magdalena 35
Grabowski, Piotr 135, 166, 189, 219,
    235, 236
Grabski, Andrzej Feliks 216
Graciotti, Sante 190, 216
Gregory of Nazianzus, St. 134
Greekphilosophy 226; republics 121;
    tradition 8, 14, 27, 187
Grodziski, Stanisław 35, 37, 64
Groicki, Bartłomiej 55, 67
Gromelski, Tomasz W. 19, 35, 88, 89,
    90, 112
Grotius, Hugo 116
Grześkowiak-Krwawicz, Anna 11, 38,
    65, 88–92, 112, 115, 116, 138, 165,
    167. 168, 189–192, 194, 217–219,
    235–237
Grzybowski, Konstanty 65, 66, 112,
    114, 219, 235
Guichardini, Francesco 96
Guilhaumou, Jacques 11
Gunn, John A. W. 91, 235

Haitsma Mulier, Eco 112, 113, 217
Handelsman, Marceli 235
Hankins, James 164
happiness 44, 47, 49, 55, 58, 61, 62,
    72, 73, 77, 80, 81, 84, 87, 110, 111,
    127, 133, 141, 148, 160, 162, 175,
    176, 177, 180, 187, 188, 199
Harrington, James 163, 224
Hartknoch, Christoph 7, 89
Helvetic States 30, 60
Herburt, Jan 66, 76, 88, 89, 191, 202,
    217, 227, 236
Herburt, Jan Szczęsny 66, 136,
    178, 191
Herman, Stefan 35

Hernas, Czesław 219
Hobbes, Thomas 71, 77, 221
Holbach, Paul 84
Holland (Netherlands) 30, 60, 61,
    95, 165
Honohan, Iseult 163
Hörnquist, Mikael 37
Horwitz, Henry 235
Hungary 121, 122, 126, 131, 135

Im Hof, Ulrich 217
Italy 126, 141

Jabłonowski, Jan Stanisław 132, 137,
    149, 155, 166, 223, 235
Jagiellon, dynasty 10, 27, 50, 52, 55,
    178, 211
Janicki, Marek A. 11, 88, 89, 91
Janowska, Aleksandra 11
Janowski, Maciej 12
Januszowski, Jan 7, 65, 68, 113, 114,
    134, 137, 236
Jarra, Eugeniusz 11, 37, 63, 66, 67,
    134, 137
Jaucourt, Louis 147, 167
Jazłowiecki, Hieronim 37, 136,
    149, 166
Jezierski, Franciszek Salezy 69, 175,
    185, 189, 192, 220
Jezierski, Jacek 187, 194
Joachimowicz, Leon 236
John II Casimir, king of Poland, grand
    duke of Lithuania 22, 23, 71, 72,
    98, 103, 150, 154, 178, 185, 186,
    198, 211, 212
Jones, Francis R., 18
Junker, Detlef 17
justice 32, 33, 41, 42, 44, 45, 55,
    61, 62, 115, 126, 140, 144, 145,
    176, 193
Justinian I the Great, Eastern Roman
    emperor 51, 64

Kaliszewski, Celestyn 69, 165
Karnkowski, Stanisław 114, 126, 136,
    140, 143, 163, 164, 166
Karpiński, Hilarion 115
Karpowicz, Michał 65, 133, 135, 176,
    182, 190, 191, 193
Karwicki, Stanisław Dunin 29, 31, 37,
    38, 49, 68, 69, 106, 107, 109, 111,
    115, 158, 208, 218
Kazanowski, Jan 189
Kądziela, Łukasz 69, 166, 192, 219

Kąkolewski, Igor 135, 164, 218
Keckermann, Barholomaeus 7, 94
Kelley, Donald R. 64, 66
Keyes, Clinton W. 113
Kiaupienè, Jurate 190
king – election 27, 47, 72, 77, 82,
    90, 111, 121, 122, 162, 199, 217,
    228; place in the state 28, 29, 111,
    178, 179; power 56, 58, 79–81, 99,
    100–103, 105, 116, 122; under law
    49–53, 60
Kisiel, Adam 204, 218
Kluczycki, Franciszek Ksawery
    17, 136
Knapik, Kinga 189
Knychalska, Agnieszka 114
Kochan, Anna 66, 67
Kochanowski Jan 119
Kochowski, Wespazjan 79, 90
Koehler, Krzysztof 190
Koenigsberger, Helmut Georg 136, 217
Kołłątaj, Hugo 23, 32, 33, 34, 36,
    38, 45, 53, 62, 63, 67, 69, 86, 87,
    91, 92, 109, 111, 116, 146, 155,
    161, 164–166, 168, 181, 185, 192,
    193, 201, 208, 210, 125, 217–220,
    231–234, 237, 238
Konarski, Stanisław 23, 31, 38, 49,
    68, 72, 75, 79, 80, 82, 83, 88–91,
    107, 109, 115, 116, 127, 133, 136,
    143, 148, 157, 158, 165, 167,
    169, 175, 181, 187, 191–194, 198,
    199, 201, 203, 205, 210, 215–221,
    228, 238
Konopczyński, Władysław 11, 88, 90,
    92, 116, 163, 236
Koranyi, Karol 38
Korkman, Petter 64
Korolec, Jerzy B. 163
Korolko, Mirosław 137
Koselleck, Reinhart 11
Kossobudzki, Mikołaj 65, 113, 114,
    165, 236
Kostkiewiczowa, Teresa 192, 194, 216
Kościuszko, Tadeusz 35, 87, 147, 163,
    172, 182, 184, 192
Kot, Stanisław 12, 37
Kotarski, Edmund 190
Kożuchowski, Stanisław 219
Kunicki, Wacław 28, 37, 141, 143,
    163, 164, 173, 184, 190, 193
Kurzeniecki, Ignacy 218
Kwiatkowski, Kajetan 166, 217

Lasocińska, Estera 163, 164
Lech 27, 37
Leduc-Fayette, Denise 67
Legomska, Julia 11
Lengnich, Gottfried 7, 89
Leszczyński, Jan 23, 36, 191
Leśnodorski, Bogusław 167
Lewis, Clive Staples 7
liberum veto 77, 82, 117, 156, 157,
    181, 201, 215
license 59, 79, 80, 142
Linde, Samuel Bogumił 190
Lippomano, Girolamo 37
Lipski, Andrzej 196, 216–219
Lis, Rafał 67
Litwin, Henryk 36, 65, 90
Livy (*Titus Livius Patavinus*) 75
Lizisowa, Maria T. 63
Louis I, king of Hungary and
    Poland 200
Lubomirski, Jerzy Sebastian 97, 98,
    102, 11–114, 118, 134, 135, 164,
    189, 192, 212
Lubomirski, Stanisław Herakliusz
    131, 137, 165
Lubomirski's rokosz 102, 104, 122,
    145, 146, 155, 170, 180, 189, 212
Lüsebrink, Hans-Jurgen 11
Lycurgus 30
Ładowski, Remigiusz 66, 230, 231, 237
Łobarzewski, Ignacy 33, 38, 58, 68,
    69, 116, 133, 137, 162, 168, 219
Łubieński, Wacław 115
Łukowski, Jerzy 116, 127, 136, 163,
    167, 216–219, 236

Mably, Gabriel Bonnot de 50, 108,
    147, 173
Machiavelli, Niccolò 57, 88, 91, 137,
    147, 148, 161, 163
Maciejewski, Janusz 65, 88, 216, 235
MacIntyre, Alasdair 163
Maciszewski, Jarema 91, 218, 235
Mager, Wolfgang 37
magnanimity 164
Majchrowicz, Szymon 145, 148,
    164, 165
Makiłła, Dariusz 67
Mäkinen, Virpi 64
Malec, Jerzy 116
Maleszyński, Dariusz C. 35, 36
Małachowski, Stanisław 45, 65,
    133, 138

Manius Curius Denatus 229
Matyaszewski, Paweł 167
Meiksins Wood, Ellen 235, 236
Meller, Katarzyna 190
Michalski, Jerzy 12, 38, 65, 72, 88,
 115, 116, 136, 137, 163, 192, 194,
 219, 237
Mienicki, Ryszard 216
Mikucki, Antoni 115
Modrzewski, AndrzejFrycz 20–22, 25,
 26, 28, 40, 49, 56, 57, 65, 67, 74, 78,
 86, 90, 94, 140, 145, 148, 152, 161
Monk, Iain Hampshir 11, 12
Montesquieu, Charles Louis de
 Secondat, baron de la Brède 33, 36,
 44, 46, 53, 59, 62, 69, 84, 87, 92,
 108–112, 116, 142, 158, 159, 162,
 167, 182, 184, 193
Morel, Henri 112, 113, 115
Morski, Tadeusz 91, 217
Moskorzowski, Hieronim 82, 91
Mouristen, Paul 68, 113, 190
Mulgan, Richard 89
Myszkowski, Zygmunt 170, 189

Nax, Jan Ferdynand 116, 127, 136,
 162, 168, 237
Nenner, Howard 68, 235
Niendorf, Mathias 216
Nihil novi constitution 99
Nippel, Wilfried 112, 114

Oake, Roger B. 167
Ochmann-Staniszewska, Stefania 12,
 36, 37, 59, 64, 65, 68, 88, 112–114,
 134, 135, 150, 164, 166, 189,
 191–194, 216–219
Ogonowski, Zbigniew 65, 89, 193, 236
Ohryzko, Jozafat 36, 134
Oleśnicki, Zbigniew 165
Olizar Wołczkiewicz, Leonard 1
Olizarowski, Aaron 37, 66, 67
Olsen, Niklas 11
Olszewski, Henryk 11, 35–37, 235
Opaliński, Edward 11, 12, 24, 35–37,
 54, 64, 65, 67, 68, 88–91, 96,
 112–114, 119, 134, 135, 137, 165,
 171, 178, 190, 191, 193, 216, 217,
 235
Opaliński, Łukasz 23, 36, 43, 50,
 55–59, 64–68, 80, 88, 90, 105, 114,
 116, 124, 136, 161, 163, 173, 181,
 190, 212, 217, 219, 223, 235, 236

Opałek, Kazimierz 64
organistic concept of the state 21, 28,
 29, 42, 97, 98
Orzechowski, Stanisław 3, 20, 21, 25,
 27, 29, 32, 35, 36, 38, 41, 53, 55,
 60, 64, 66, 67, 68, 75, 78, 89, 94,
 112, 149, 227, 236
Orzeł, Joanna 216, 217
Ostrowski, Piotr 192
Ottow, Raimund 235

Padalinski, Uladimir 36
Pallister, Ann 68, 217
Palonen, Kari 11
Pangle, Thomas 165, 193
Paruta, Paolo 96
Pastuchowa, Magdalena 11
Pausanias 49
Pawelec, Radosław 11
Pawlikowski, Józef 7, 92, 166, 168,
 185, 193
peace 33, 42–44, 72, 120, 122, 130,
 131, 135, 140, 145, 171, 176, 189
Pennington, Kenneth 66
Pepłowski, Franciszek 11
Petrycy, Sebastian from Pilzno 7, 20,
 21, 25, 27, 75, 78, 94, 140
Pettit, Philip 89, 91
Pękosławski, Prokop 37, 235
Pęski, Walenty 32, 38, 61, 67, 68, 137,
 146, 165
Pfeiffer, Bogusław 190
physiocrats 40, 44, 45, 53, 84, 86,
 162; Polish 85, 188
Piasecki, Paweł 102, 113, 114, 129,
 137, 206, 218
Piast 27, 37
Pietrzyk-Reeves, Dorota 11, 12, 35,
 38, 63, 64, 66–68, 89, 112, 114,
 135, 139, 163, 164, 194
Plater, Kazimierz Konstanty 67
Platon 42, 79, 90, 119, 128, 130, 134,
 137, 165, 175, 226
Pliny the Younger (*Caius Plinius
 Caecilius Secundus*) 65
Plutarch 119, 121, 134, 135
Pocock, John Greville Agard 11, 12,
 37, 64, 88, 163, 164
Poklatecki, Franciszek *see* Radzewski,
 Franciszek
Polybius 28, 75, 94, 96, 97, 113
Poniński, Jan Nepomucen107, 111,
 115, 166, 167, 212, 219

Popławski, Antoni 58, 69, 84, 85, 91, 92, 111, 115, 116, 174, 190, 191, 199, 210, 215, 230, 231, 237
Poraziński, Jarosław 114, 115
Potocki, Ignacy 238
Potocki, Stanisław Kostka 210, 219
Potocki, Stanisław Szczęsny 33, 162, 168, 198, 216
Probulski, Andrzej 137, 165
Prokhovnik, Raia 90
prudence 133, 144–147, 165, 184
Pryshlak, Maria 114
Pufendorf, Samuel von 107
Pula, James S. 16
Puszet de Puget, Józef 174, 190
Pyrrhys de Varille, Césare 215, 220

Quesney, François 92

Radawiecki, Andrzej 71, 75, 82, 88, 89, 91
Radwański, Zbigniew 65
Radzewski, Franciszek (alias Franciszek Poklatecki) 53, 66, 115, 155, 166
Raszewska-Żurek, Beata 134
Rawson, Elizabeth 112, 113
Reichardt, Rolf 11
Reid, John Phillip 64
Reklewski, Wojciech 113, 134, 135
Reszka, Stanisław 135
Richardson, Bill 18
Richter, Melvin 11, 12
Richter, Michaela 17
Robin, Régine 11
Rok, Bogdan 164
rokosz of Lwów 200
rokosz of Gliniany 200
rokosz of Sandomierz *see* Zebrzydowski's rokosz
Roman authors 2, 26, 75, 169; law 64, 75; republic 30, 75, 146, 152, 203, 225; philosophie 27, 33, 226; tradition 8, 14, 20, 172, 179, 187, 207, 229
Romans 30, 165, 167, 169, 183, 225
Rome 94, 95, 121, 203, 225, 228
Romulus 30
Rosicka, Janina 11, 89, 91, 216, 219
Rosner, Andrzej 11, 89, 91, 216, 219
Rostworowski, Emanuel 12, 38, 115, 166
Rotundus, Augustyn 90, 112, 119, 130, 134, 137, 152

Rousseau, Jean Jacques 3, 27, 33, 44, 45, 52, 53, 55–58, 65, 78, 83, 87, 108, 111, 115, 133, 147, 149, 157–162, 167, 168, 173, 174, 179, 187, 188, 232
Rzewuski, Adam Wawrzyniec 53, 56–58, 67, 149, 160, 161, 166–168, 174, 190, 204, 218, 231, 237
Rzewuski, Seweryn 33, 162, 168, 171, 180, 189, 192, 228, 234, 236, 238
Rzewuski, Wacław 132, 137, 167

Sallust (*Caius Sallustius Crispus*) 31, 75, 119, 134, 179
Sanguszko family 215
Sapała, Patryk 63, 89
Sapieha, Kazimierz Nestor 45, 65, 133, 138
Sapieha, Lew 51, 53, 66
Sarnicki, Stanisław 42, 64
Scaevola, Gaius Mucius 146
Schleiermacher, Friedrich 17
Schmitt, Eberhard 11
Schofield, Malcolm 37
Scott, Jonathan 113, 235
Skilurus (Scylurus), king of Scythia 121, 135
Scipio Africanus (*Publius Cornelius Scipio Africanus Maior*) 165
Seneca (*Lucius Annaeus Seneca*) 80, 120, 165
security (safety) 33, 42, 43, 60, 66, 71, 72, 102, 120, 121, 141, 175, 180, 206–209, 230
Sejm 20, 25, 28, 29, 36, 38, 77, 94, 102, 104, 109, 110, 112, 115–118, 123, 124, 181, 185, 208; Chamber of Deputies 104, 105, 110, 126, 151; Senat 100–105, 107, 110, 144, 151
sejmiks 110, 117, 118, 123, 125, 185, 217, 223
Shklar, Judith N. 67, 167
Siemek, Kasper 143, 147, 164, 165, 226, 227, 236
Sienieński, Jakub 219
Sienicki, Szczepan 55, 67, 77, 82, 88, 90, 91, 137, 157, 167, 193
Sigismund I the Old, king of Poland, grand duke of Lithuania 97, 200
Sigismund II August, king of Poland, grand duke of Lithuania 10, 58, 73, 105, 123, 203, 211

Sigismund III Vasa, king of Poland,
grand duke of Lithuania 53, 66,
178, 179, 224
Simon, Julia 194
Sinko, Tadeusz 12
Skarga, Piotr 94, 105, 119, 135, 153
Skibiński, Mieczysław 136
Skinner, Quentin 64, 88, 89, 90, 113,
163, 165, 168
Skotnicki, Piotr Bogoria 64
Skrzetuski, Wincenty 44, 58, 59, 68,
85, 107, 115, 159, 167, 173, 182,
190, 193, 194, 231, 237
Smoleński, Władysław 116, 167
social contract 108, 221, 230, 231
Solikowski, Jan Dymitr 113, 114, 135,
136, 189, 190, 218
Solon 30
sovereignty 77, 93, 105, 106, 108,
111, 221, 235; of the law 50,
52–54, 65
Sparthe 30, 78, 94, 95, 235
Spellman, W. M. 67, 68
Stadnicki, Stanisław "the Devil" 37,
136, 149, 166
Stanisław, Leszczyński king of Poland,
duke of Lorraine 23, 28, 37, 49, 65,
67, 72, 80, 81, 83, 90, 98, 107, 109,
113, 118, 134, 137, 145, 149, 158,
164–166, 176, 177, 185, 188, 191,
192, 206, 214, 218, 220, 230, 237
Stanisław August, king of Poland,
grand duke of Lithuania 9, 133,
169, 177, 178, 187, 198, 211, 215,
216, 225
Starnawski, Jerzy 38, 67, 68, 236
Starowolski, Szymon 7, 26, 37, 58,
59, 80, 90, 105, 115, 137, 150,
154, 161, 164, 168, 176, 181, 191,
227, 236
Stasiewicz, Krystyna 164
Stasiewicz-Jasiukowa Irena 193, 194
Staszic, Stanisław 7, 34, 38, 45, 53,
55–57, 67, 83, 87, 91, 108, 109,
111, 115, 116, 133, 160, 164,
167, 168, 174, 175, 181, 190, 192,
231–233, 237
Steiner, Georges 16–18
Stroynowski, Hieronim 40, 45, 53,
63, 69, 84–86, 92, 162, 168, 230,
231, 237
Stuarts, dynasty 96
Sucheni-Grabowska, Anna 42, 50,
64–66, 90, 191

Suchodolski, Bogdan163, 216,
217, 219
Suchorzewski, Jan 192
Sulima-Kamiński, Andrzej 36
Suski, Jędrzej 64
Sweden 30
Szczepankowska, Irena 11
Szczerbicka-Ślęk, Ludwika 219
Szczuka, Stanisław Antoni 132, 134,
137, 155, 170, 189
Szczygielski, Wojciech 116
Szyjkowski, Marian 167
Ślęk, Ludwika *see* Szczerbicka-Ślęk,
Ludwika
Ślusarska, Magdalena 137
Śnieżko, Dariusz 216, 219

Tacitus (*Publius Cornelius Tacitus*) 57,
68, 219
Tarnowski, Stanisław 11
Taszycki, Gabriel 220
Taszycki, Mikołaj 48, 189, 192
Tazbir, Janusz 64, 119, 121, 134, 135,
164, 218, 235
Tell, Wilhelm 202
temperance 144, 145, 164
Tigerstedt, Eugène Napoleon 113
Tilmans, Karin 11, 12
Tomaszewski, Dyzma Bończa 87,
92, 116
Touchefeu, Yves 67, 90
Trencsényi, Balázs 11, 190
Trębicki, Antoni 111, 116
Trojanowski, Feliks 62, 69
Trotz, Michał Abraham 169
Turner, Allan 18
Turski, Wojciech 53, 67, 69, 88,
168, 192

Ulanowski, Bolesław 65, 68, 135, 136,
194, 217, 218, 235, 236
Union of Lublin 6, 16, 23, 24, 29
Union of Mielnik 119
Uruszczak, Wacław 65
Urwanowicz, Jerzy 68, 88, 89, 91, 114

valor (courage) 56, 130, 144–147,
155, 164, 165, 183, 184, 224, 228
Van Gelderen, Martin 12, 68, 112,
192, 217
Van Vree, Frank 11, 12
Vasas, dynasty 178
Velema, Wyger R. E. 90
Venetians 73, 95, 202

Venice 30, 75, 95–97, 165, 206, 235
Venuti, Lawrence 17
Vetterli, Richard 165, 193
Vetulani, Adam 64
Veturia 175
Viroli, Maurizio 38, 88, 168, 190, 192 194

Wachlowski, Zbigniew 65, 115, 234, 235
Waga, Teodor 115
Wagner-Rundell, Benedict 139, 163, 166
Walicki, Andrzej 190, 192
Walzer, Michael 37
Warsaw Confederacy 113, 121, 129, 130, 198
Warszewicki, Krzysztof 20, 48, 58, 60, 67, 68, 73, 79, 80, 88, 98, 103, 113, 126, 136, 143, 152, 153, 156, 164, 166, 186, 227, 236
Wells, Charlotte C. 37
Węcowski, Piotr 134, 135
Wielhorski, Michał 3, 45, 56, 68, 76, 89, 92, 115, 116, 160, 167, 194, 203, 213, 216, 217, 219
Wieruszewski, Kazimierz 69, 82, 91
Wilczek, Piotr 18
Wirszubski, Chaim 89
Wisner, Henryk 35, 36, 65, 190
Wiśniewski, Antoni 167
Witkowski, Stanisław 227, 236
Władysław II Jagiełło, grand duke of Lithuania, king of Poland 41
Władysław IV Vasa, king of Poland, grand duke of Lithuania 211
Wolan, Andrzej 20, 21, 25, 27, 32, 38, 41, 48, 52, 54–56, 59–61, 64,

66–69, 71, 73, 74, 78, 79, 86, 88–90, 113, 120, 128, 134, 135, 137, 140, 148, 149, 152, 161, 186, 226, 227, 236
Woliński, Janusz 12
Worst, I. J. H. 88, 218
Wotton, David 37, 235
Wybicki, Józef 45, 49, 53–57, 62, 63, 65, 67–69, 73, 85, 86, 88, 89, 91, 92, 108, 109, 111, 115, 116, 141, 159, 164, 165, 167, 182, 184, 188, 193, 199, 210, 215, 230, 231, 237
Wyrwa, Tadeusz 11, 66
Wyrwicz, Karol 44, 65, 69, 84, 92, 116
Wysocki, Samuel 193
Wyszomirska, Monika 91, 217, 236

Zajączkowski, Andrzej 114
Zakrzewski, Andrzej 64, 66
Zalaszowski, Mikołaj 67
Zamoyski, Andrzej 22, 23, 35, 46, 65, 109, 110, 116, 123, 135
Zamoyski, Jan 23, 32, 82, 91, 166, 178, 191
Zawisza, Jakub from Kroczów 76, 89, 96, 112, 122, 135
Zborowski, Jan 183, 193
Zebrzydowski, Mikołaj 36, 105, 115, 170, 178, 189, 209, 216, 218, 229
Zebrzydowski's rebellion 22, 24, 30, 38, 43, 46, 48, 49, 59, 81, 94, 100, 101, 103, 104, 106, 123, 146, 150, 153, 170, 178, 180, 183, 189, 198, 200, 203, 224
Zielińska, Zofia 92
Zienkowska, Krystyna 217
Zwierzykowski, Michał 68
Żółkiewski, Stanisław 146